FLORIDA STATE
UNIVERSITY LIBRARIES

MAY 7 1997

TALLAHASSEE, FLORIDA

AN OPPOSITIONIST FOR LIFE

HISTORICAL MEMORIES

Published

*An Oppositionist for Life:
Memoirs of the Chinese Revolutionary
Zheng Chaolin*
Edited and Translated by Gregor Benton

A World Remembered: 1925 –1950
Bernard Smith

*The Prophet's Children:
Travels on the American Left*
Tim Wohlforth

AN OPPOSITIONIST FOR LIFE

MEMOIRS OF THE CHINESE REVOLUTIONARY ZHENG CHAOLIN

Edited and Translated by
Gregor Benton

HUMANITIES PRESS

Originally published as *Huiyilu* in 1986 in Beijing, China, in a restricted edition.

First English translation published 1997 by Humanities Press
International, Inc., 165 First Avenue, Atlantic Highlands, New Jersey 07716

©Zheng Chaolin, 1986, 1997

English translation © 1997 by Gregor Benton

Library of Congress Cataloging-in-Publication Data
Cheng, Ch'ao-lin, 1901–
    An oppositionist for life : memoirs of the Chinese revolutionary
Zheng Chaolin / edited and translated by Gregor Benton.
      p. cm.—(Historical memories)
    Translated from Chinese.
    Includes bibliographical references and index.
    ISBN 0–391–03966–0 (cloth).—ISBN 0–391–03967–9 (pbk.)
    1. Cheng, Ch'ao-lin, 1901–   2. Communists—China—Biography.
3. Communism—China. 4. Chung-kuo kung ch'an tang—History.
I. Benton, Gregor. II. Title. III. Series.
DS777.488.C487C44 1996
954.04′092—dc20
  [a]   95–42652
                                                                                                                        CIP

All rights reserved. No part of this publication may be reproduced
or transmitted, in any form or by any means, without written permission.

Printed in the United States of America

10 9 8 7 6 5 4 3 2 1

Contents

	List of Illustrations	vi
	Editor's Introduction	ix
	Author's 1945 Preface	xxii
1	A Consciousness Awakes	1
2	The Communist Youth Party	16
3	Twelve People	38
4	KUTV	46
5	Before and After May Thirtieth	69
6	Wuhan	105
7	Love and Politics	138
8	An Ebbing or a Flowing Tide?	172
9	My First Spell in Prison	203
10	The Left Opposition	228
11	A Self-Description at the Age of Ninety	251
12	A Brief Account of My Third Spell in Prison	258
	Postscript to the English Edition	271
	Select Biographical Reference List	275
	Notes	289
	Index	311

List of Illustrations

(Illustrations may be found after page 156.)

Figure 1	The Second Congress of the (Chinese) Communist Youth Party, Paris, February 1923
Figure 2	Leon Trotsky
Figure 3	Zheng Chaolin, Shanghai, c. 1930
Figure 4	Chen Yannian
Figure 5	Chen Qiaonian
Figure 6	Ren Bishi
Figure 7	Mu Qing
Figure 8	Cai Hesen
Figure 9	Ge Jianhao (Cai Hesen's mother)
Figure 10	Wang Ruofei
Figure 11	Liu Bojian
Figure 12	He Chang
Figure 13	Zhang Bojian
Figure 14	Deng Yanda
Figure 15	Maring (Henk Sneevliet)
Figure 16	Li Lisan
Figure 17	Luo Yinong
Figure 18	Qu Qiubai
Figure 19	Xiang Jingyu
Figure 20	Liu Jingzhen, Shanghai, the 1930s
Figure 21	Peng Shuzhi just before his and Chen Duxiu's trial in Nanjing in 1932
Figure 22	The Provincial Central Committee of the (Trotskyist) Communist League of China, Shanghai, winter 1936
Figure 23	Chen Qichang, a Trotskyist leader tortured to death by the Japanese occupiers in 1943 (Shanghai, 1936)
Figure 24	Chen Duxiu, 1937

List of Illustrations

Figure 25 Chen Duxiu sometime after his release from prison in 1937
Figure 26 Zheng Chaolin, Liu Jingzhen, and their soon-to-die son, Frei, Shanghai, c. 1942
Figure 27 Lian Zhengyan (1928–1951), a young Trotskyist shot by the Maoists in Wenzhou Prison
Figure 28 Zheng Chaolin and Liu Jingzhen in detention in Shanghai in 1979, on the eve of their freedom
Figure 29 Zheng Chaolin in 1979 outside the building in Wuhan in which the August 7 (1927) Conference was held
Figure 30 Lou Guohua, Hong Kong, 1980
Figure 31 Zheng Chaolin, Shanghai, 1984
Figure 32 Wang Fanxi, Leeds, England, 1989
Figure 33 Zheng Chaolin, Shanghai, 1989
Figure 34 Zheng Chaolin, Shanghai, 1989

Editor's Introduction

Zheng Chaolin started this book in 1944 and finished it in February 1945, but at the time, he never got around to publishing it. In 1986, after sitting on the manuscript (newly unearthed from a government vault) for several years, Chinese Communist officials finally authorized its publication minus the chapter "Love and Politics," and later they ordered a second printing. Access to these editions is restricted to privileged categories of officials and researchers. Sometime in the 1980s, that is, before it was eventually printed, a few copies of the manuscript were mimeographed for Party history workers, but I do not know in what form. This translation is probably the fullest published version of the book to date, for it includes the "Love and Politics" chapter that for reasons of prudery was cut from the 1986 Chinese edition.

The text of the original manuscript broke off rather abruptly, for two reasons. One was the death early in 1945 of Zheng's son, Frei, which broke Zheng's heart. The other was the end of the war, which brought Shanghai into a lively ferment and opened up new opportunities for Zheng's Trotskyists, who switched into a higher gear, so that Zheng's attention was soon commanded by more urgent matters. Then, in December 1952, Zheng, his comrades, and his manuscript were swept behind bars by Mao's political police. When on June 5, 1979, Zheng, his surviving friends, and his book were finally released—all of them into restricted circulation—some researchers from a Party history institute got Zheng to round out his story with a special study, completed in 1980, of Chen Duxiu's relationship to Trotskyism, which they appended to the 1986 edition.[1]

This present volume concludes with a brief autobiographical sketch in which Zheng in 1990, at the age of ninety, brings the remarkable story of his life up-to-date; and an interview, published in 1993, in which he tells the story of his imprisonment under the Chinese Communist Party (CCP) between 1952 and 1979.

* * *

What sort of a man is Zheng Chaolin? His book is, essentially, a reflection on the politics of China's revolution and on the people among whom Zheng spent his early manhood. But even a memoir announces the qualities of its author, so what manner of person does this book reveal Zheng to be? It shows him to be modest, frank, Argus-eyed, compassionate, broad-minded, humorous, playful, stubborn, inquisitive, inventive, creative, loyal, free from all vanity and pretensions, and with the memory of an elephant. Born in another age, he would have shone as an academician, a philosopher, or a poet. But instead, he was born with the twentieth century, and into eventual martyrdom. His great contribution to the Chinese Revolution—both in the official Party before 1929 and, after that, in its Trotskyist offshoot—was in the realm of theory and propaganda. He evinces little interest in practical affairs; he despises the power struggles that punctuate political life and on which others thrive. Above all, he is an "oppositionist for life"[2] to all forms of established authority. This description, originally made by Hu Shi of Zheng's mentor Chen Duxiu, fits Zheng to the letter, which is why he has spent more than one-third of his ninety-six years as a prisoner of conscience under repressive regimes of different colors.

Zheng's writing is scrupulously truthful, accurate, and stringent. He tells us what he knows, how he came to know it, and what remained unknown to him, so his testimony is a perfect source for history writers; it is also free from the self-exculpation and ideological ax grinding that distorts most political memoirs of this sort. Chinese memoirs since 1949 have all the usual drawbacks of the genre, as well as several more. They are winners' histories written in a society where "the loser is a thief." They cleave closely to the dominant political line. They are rarely designed to stand alone as records of integral, independent lives, but are meant to furnish "concrete" illustrations of the general truths of Party history that dictate their framework and their setting. To quarry the few hard truths from cultic biographies of this sort, historians must first hack through a dense layer of political shibboleths, editorial embellishment, and edifying anecdotes; even then, what remains is not necessarily the unvarnished truth. So Zheng's book is a lonely beacon that lights up a small patch on the great dark plain of China's recent past;[3] it will be seen by fair-minded observers everywhere as something rare and precious.

* * *

In his book, Zheng frequently reviews the character, motives, and behavior of his friends and enemies, but he rarely says much about himself. So it is interesting to look at what other people have said about him over the years.

Wang Fanxi, Zheng's close collaborator in the Trotskyist enterprise, was struck above all by his formidable staunchness and his total disregard, like a Buddhist monk who has attained the Way, for his own personal fate. "Even if we leave aside Cheng Ch'ao-lin's [Zheng Chaolin's] other strengths," wrote Wang in 1957, in reference to the Trotskyists' decision not to flee China in 1949, "his Peter-like spirit of martyrdom alone will ensure him a lasting place in the history of the Revolution. Our dilemma was similar in many ways to that of the early Christians under Nero—should we stay in the capital or flee to a safe place? Some approached the question mainly from the point of view of their own fate, others from the point of view of the future of the organization as a whole; but Cheng Ch'ao-lin did not wait for a voice from the heavens to ask *'Quo vadis?'*: his mind was made up from the very outset."[4]

Lou Shiyi, who knew Zheng Chaolin in the 1920s and visited him again in the 1980s, wrote a long appreciation of him in a preface to a volume of Zheng's poems,[5] most of them written while Zheng was in prison under the Communists. Lou, a veteran and orthodox member of the CCP, was for many years a senior literary editor in Beijing. So his view of Zheng is not colored by sympathy for Zheng's Trotskyist politics and is therefore all the more remarkable and reliable.

"The old man Yu Yin, Comrade Zheng Chaolin, is my teacher. He is also my old friend—one of those with whom I shared many trials and who today number very few, as few as the disappearing stars in the early morning sky. It would be presumptuous of me to add mere tittle-tattle to my teacher's book. However, as his old friend, and in order to express my delight on this occasion, I shall venture to recall some events that happened during our long friendship and that younger readers may enjoy hearing about.

"I remember that several months after the end of the May Thirtieth Movement of 1925—winter had already set in—I and a few other young people attended night school several times a week in the home of a friend on Baotong Road in Shanghai's Zhabei. We were not many, but a group of people took turns at lecturing to us. We studied current affairs and the rudiments of Marxism. Our teachers included pioneers of the revolution like Qu Qiubai, Yun Daiying, Yin Kuan, and Zhao Shiyan; they also included Comrade Zheng Chaolin. In those days, he was still a young man, with a full head of black hair and an elegant bearing. He had probably not long been back in China. He had squeezed his plump body into a neat Western-style suit; a bright watch chain protruded from his left-hand pocket and disappeared into his waistcoat buttonhole. As far as I remember, his subject was 'The Meaning for the Chinese Revolution of the May Thirtieth Movement.' He was not a very fluent speaker and he had a slight Fujian accent, but he was very kind and approachable and left a deep impression on those of us who studied under him; in my mind's eye I can still see him to this day.

"The night school was abandoned before very long; after that, I had no further occasion to meet Zheng. But fate is a strange thing, and ten or so years later, we renewed our acquaintance under remarkable circumstances—

in the Guomindang's Central Military Prison in Nanjing. His solitary cell was on the same block as mine, just eight or nine doors away, but we rarely caught a glimpse of one another. One day, I was escorted to the Education Section, where a short, thin man who was in charge talked cordially with me and allocated me to 'penal labor,' after which I was taken to a big room that had originally been part of the Education Section. It was bright and clean, with a row of ping-pong tables along the windows, each capable of accommodating six or seven people, who sat there doing literary work. I was allocated the German Military Code to translate. This threw me into confusion, for my German was quite elementary; I could remember little more than how to say the alphabet in it. How on earth was I to translate such a book? But when I lifted my head and looked around, I noticed several familiar faces. The first to greet me was Pan Zinian, who told me that I should accept the assignment, that everything would be all right. The person in charge of the Education Section was a man called Shen Bingquan. In order to make life easier for some cultural figures (I guess today you would call them 'higher intellectuals'), he had specially requested this cushy job from the Ministry of Military Administration. So we had a reason to leave our cells each day, we could get some exercise, and we got the chance to do some reading and writing. At my table were four other fellow inmates. All but one—even Pan Zinian—had only beginner's German. The exception, seated opposite Pan, was none other than Comrade Zheng Chaolin, whom I had not seen for a decade. He had aged somewhat in the meantime and had lost his hair. He was the only true translator among us. All the rest of us learned German from him. In front of each of us was a German text, a dictionary, an exercise book, and a pile of loose writing paper. We spent our time reading and writing and called it translating, but in effect, all we did was learn from our teacher. A semiliterate warder on guard in the hall used to wander around the tables to see how conscientious and diligent we were; he thought that we were working hard and was very satisfied with us. We could get up and stretch our legs at will, or take time off for a quiet chat; no one ever interfered with us. Section Director Shen often used to visit us and would sit down and talk with us about what was in the newspapers. We were not allowed to read the dailies, but we were allowed to receive large quantities of books and periodicals, so there was nothing that we did not know. Chaolin was of a different political persuasion from the rest of us, so we rarely discussed politics with him. Nevertheless, we viewed his big bald skull as a living encyclopedia. He was never averse to answering our questions. At all times, he sincerely and tirelessly helped us. He not only taught us German; he also taught two youngsters French. At the same time, he helped us all with our translations. He was extraordinarily assiduous. He read and translated nonstop. I remember that he translated Thomas Mann's

Buddenbrooks from German and D. Merezhkovsky's *Resurrection of the Gods* from Russian. We all vied to read this translation of Merezhkovsky's book, which was a fictional biography of Leonardo da Vinci. At one time, he translated from the French André Gide's *Retour de l'URSS*. Some of the people with us said that this book was anti-Soviet and told us to ignore it. But surreptitiously, I became the first reader of Zheng's Chinese translation, for which I was roundly criticized by my prison mates. I was not convinced by their strictures.

"The rest of us attended to our own research and translation. Section Director Shen helped us by posting our manuscripts to our friends in Shanghai, so they quickly appeared in print and we earned quite a lot of money. Some of us were even able to maintain our families. Chaolin, being the fastest and the most productive translator, naturally earned most. His wife, Liu Jingzhen, who had stayed behind in Shanghai, came regularly and often to visit him in prison in Nanjing and brought him large amounts of food, winter clothing, medicine, and nutriments. His own needs were few, and he often gave away the larger part to prisoners whose distress was greater and who received no assistance from outside. He did this regardless of their political views and did not even know some of the people he helped. There was one prisoner, a long-term inmate of the sick ward stricken by tuberculosis of the lymph gland, whom he met by accident only once in the clinic, while visiting the doctor. When Chaolin learned that this man was poor as well as sick, he got Jingzhen to bring a big bottle of cod-liver oil every time she came to the prison, and he passed it on to this man through one of the prison guards.

"We lived together in the same prison until 1937, when we were released after the outbreak in China of the full-scale War of Resistance against Japan. Actually, Chaolin had lost his freedom as early as 1931 and had been kept in various prisons before finally being moved to Nanjing's Military Prison, where he was an old jailbird. After our release, war beacons filled the sky all over China, and each went his own way. I heard nothing more of Chaolin after that. And so forty years passed. In the spring of 1979, I made a special trip to Shanghai to attend the memorial service for Fu Lei and his wife.[6] A friend in Shanghai told me that Chaolin had in the meantime spent another twenty years behind bars and that he had just been freed, but my friend warned me not to visit Chaolin, for he was still under strict supervision. Not until a year or so later did I discover that Chaolin had already been restored to complete liberty and that, even though he still maintained his old political position, he had been invited to become a member of Shanghai's People's Political Consultative Conference. Since I was going to Shanghai on an official mission anyway, I visited my old teacher from half a century earlier, my prison mate from forty years earlier. Being the same age as the century, he was already an old man, but even so, he was warmly hospitable, tirelessly talkative, and overflowing with high spirits. It was as if he had sustained not the slightest damage from his trials and tribulations. But on the day that he was restored to complete freedom, his wife Liu Jingzhen—who for twenty-seven years had done everything possible from the other side of prison walls to alleviate his suffering, who had defended him, and who had waited loyally for him—quietly left this world, seemingly after having completed her appointed task.[7] And of his only child, born during the war against Japan, nothing is left but a precious wide-eyed photographic image pinned to the wall of Zheng's lonely study. Zheng lives a life of great calm and great intensity. He reads, he writes, and he receives and instructs an endless flow of comrades researching special issues in the history of the Chinese Communist Party."

Another brief description of Zheng can be found in the first volume of the memoirs of the Trotskyist Peng Shuzhi. There was no love lost between Zheng and Peng, but even so, Peng draws a rather affectionate picture of Zheng in the 1920s. "Zheng Chaolin was a strapping young fellow with a broad forehead, always smiling and extremely kind-hearted. There is no denying that he was something of a pedant. He had a stammer. And politically, he was rather uninventive. But in his way, he was a linguistic genius, in the very special sense that he could learn at high speed to decipher, read, and render into decent Chinese any language whatsoever, provided that it was at the level of political discourse and provided, above all, that he was never expected to articulate a single sentence or to understand it *orally*. For example, it only took him a few months in Moscow to disentangle Russian, just as it had taken him only a few months in France to familiarize himself—also at the level of political discourse—with French. To the knowledge—political and bookish—of these two languages he soon added English, German, Italian, and Esperanto."[8]

* * *

Traditionally, Auguste Blanqui, the French revolutionary who spent thirty-three of his seventy-five years in prison (and so became known in France as *l'enfermé*), is regarded as the record holder for political imprisonment. But Zheng Chaolin had beaten Blanqui's record by one year when he stepped free in June 1979 after being locked up as a "counterrevolutionary" for twenty-seven years, in addition to the seven he had already served as a revolutionary under Chiang Kai-shek. With him were eleven other Trotskyist survivors as well as his wife Liu Jingzhen, who had voluntarily shared the last seven years of his detention. A photograph taken on the eve of Zheng and Liu's release shows them smiling serenely and beatifically.

After the death of Mao and the fall of his "Gang of Four" in 1976, tens of thousands of political prisoners were released; the freeing of Zheng and his comrades happened in that context. In May 1979, shortly before their release, Zheng had been named prisoner of the month by Amnesty International, which campaigned on his behalf, though no one knew whether he was alive or dead. Perhaps this naming jogged the memory and conscience of some official who in the 1920s had been Zheng's friend in Europe or in China, before he became a Trotskyist.

Zheng's revolutionary career had begun in the early 1920s in Paris, where he and other young Chinese students set up what was to become the European branch of the Chinese Communist Party. Among Zheng's comrades in those days were Zhou Enlai, Li Weihan (later head of the United Front Department of the Chinese Communist Party), and seventeen-year-old Deng Xiaoping. From Paris, Zheng went on to Moscow, where he was one of the first students at the new Communist University for the Toilers of the East. In 1924, he went back to China and was appointed secretary of the Party's Propaganda Department. He also translated Bukharin's *ABC of Communism*, which became the standard work for generations of Chinese revolutionaries.

The strategy imposed on the Chinese Communist Party by Moscow in the 1920s led to catastrophic defeat in 1927, after which Zheng continued to work underground for the Party. During this time, he came into contact with the views of Leon Trotsky, and he soon became Trotsky's follower.

The origins of the Chinese Trotskyist group can be found in an earlier faction that had formed in China in the mid-1920s: the so-called Moscow faction, comprising Chinese students like Zheng Chaolin sent back from Moscow to China in 1924 to staff the infant Chinese Communist Party. These students—the first of several generations of such—became important leaders of the Party back in China; they were united as one and worked in close concert as a "virtual clique," according to Zheng Chaolin.

The group's core was formed by Peng Shuzhi, Wang Ruofei, Yin Kuan, Zheng Chaolin, and Chen Qiaonian. Three of these men later became Trotskyists; Chen Qiaonian died, and Wang Ruofei became a secret Trotskyist sympathizer, though he remained in the official Communist Party. All save Peng Shuzhi had spent some time working and studying in France before going to Moscow in the early 1920s. They had joined the revolution more or less simultaneously and had gone through a long period of shared experiences at a formative time of their lives. This naturally inclined them to group together. In France they had lived a hard and taxing life, as wage slaves in capitalist industry. Zheng Chaolin in particular had learned libertarian ways of being and thinking that were alien to Chinese students like Peng Shuzhi who had gone straight from China to Russia. Zheng knew that there could not be just one idea, one leader; his experience inclined him toward skepticism, intellectual curiosity, democracy, and internationalism. In Moscow, Zheng and some of his old comrades from France suffocated under the regime of stifling orthodoxy over which Peng and others presided. Zheng's habit of questioning accepted beliefs and values inclined him to an affinity with Chen Duxiu, Chinese communism's founder as well as its most critical, freethinking, and iconoclastic leader and its most prominent Trotskyist.

While this opposition was growing up in China, Trotskyists were also becoming active among the several hundred young Communist survivors who had gone to Moscow to study after the 1927 defeat. Although these students knew next to nothing about the Soviet Union or the world Communist movement when they first arrived in Moscow, within a matter of weeks they were "more or less acquainted with the substance of the controversy" between Stalin and Trotsky.[9] What they lacked in theoretical grounding before going to Russia they made up for in direct experience of the events in China, which formed one of the main battlegrounds on which Stalin and Trotsky fought.

Even before the end of the students' first year in Moscow, the seeds of sympathy with Russia's Left Opposition had been sown in the minds of some of the new Chinese arrivals, who quickly progressed through skeptical neutrality to active support for the Opposition. Earlier, they had swallowed the official explanation that the policies followed in 1926 and 1927 were "mistakes committed by Chen Duxiu in defiance of Comintern instructions." Now the truth dawned on them: The policies ascribed to Chen Duxiu were Stalin's. Nor was Stalin's policy for China the sole issue that exercised their indignation. They had arrived in Moscow fresh from battle. They were bursting with restless, frustrated energy, moral courage, and a strong antipathy toward the high-handed ways of the Moscow leaders. By the winter of 1928, Trotskyists were everywhere among Moscow's Chinese students.

In late 1929, some two hundred of the Chinese Trotskyists in Moscow were seized by the Soviet political police. Some were imprisoned for a while, expelled from the Party after recanting, and then deported (these numbered fewer than ten). Others were sent to labor camps in Siberia or the Arctic Circle; two escaped and made it back to China sometime before 1949 to tell the tale. Some were shot. Those who made it back to China from Moscow just before this crackdown, with their beliefs intact, numbered fewer than twenty.[10]

In early 1929, the two currents of opposition—one formed in Moscow, tight and highly ideological; the other looser and vaguer in China—started out on the long and difficult journey that would eventually join them for a brief moment in Shanghai, under the leadership of Chen Duxiu, before catastrophe overtook them.

Along with most of the other Trotskyist leaders, Zheng and his wife, Liu, were arrested in May 1931 by the Guomindang in cooperation with the British police, less than three weeks after they had unified their forces in a single body. Liu was freed soon afterwards by the Magistrate of the International Settlement, but Zheng was handed over to the Chinese authorities after a formal hearing and sent to prison for fifteen years as "ringleader" of the group. After the outbreak of war with Japan and the Guomindang's adoption of "special measures for disposing of prisoners during times of war," Zheng was released in 1937, having served seven of the fifteen years. His health had worsened in prison, so he went with Liu to a small town in Anhui to get better. There, their only child was born. They called the boy Frei (German for "free") in an internationalist gesture to celebrate Zheng's regained freedom. Frei died at the age of eight, of tuberculosis.

In 1940, the couple returned to Shanghai, where Liu taught in one of two workers' schools that the Trotskyists set up under the noses of the Japanese occupiers. During the war, Zheng's main activity was writing and translating. "Most of the important articles [in the *Internationalist* during the war years] were written by Cheng Ch'ao-lin," wrote Wang Fanxi. "Cheng had long been famous as a contributor to the CCP press but it was only now that his talents as a creative theoretician began to bloom. During those darkest years he wrote his most brilliant and substantial pieces, including *Dialogue Between Three Travellers* (a theoretical treatise of revolution written in novel form), a book of memoirs (an inner history of the CCP from the early 1920s through to 1930),[11] and the *ABC of the Theory of Permanent Revolution*. But the one work to which he devoted most care and attention was his *Critical Biography of Ch'en Tu-hsiu* [Chen Duxiu], which—to judge from a reading of the manuscript—was the most brilliant history of modern Chinese thought to have been written to date. The pity of it was that apart from the *ABC*, none of his manuscripts from this period ever saw the light of day. When the Chinese Trotskyist movement was destroyed during the nation-wide round-up in December 1952, they were locked up by Mao's political police together with their author."[12]

After the war, Zheng continued to work for the Trotskyist movement in Shanghai. In 1949, just a few months before Chiang Kai-shek's rule on the Chinese mainland ended, he helped found the Internationalist Workers' Party, which never had more than a few hundred members.

At first, Zheng's old friends in the new regime that was set up in 1949 tried to talk him into joining them. Li Weihan, acting through the intermediary Shi Fuliang, sought a reconciliation, but Zheng refused to accept his offer. Finally, on the night of December 22, 1952, Zheng and two to three hundred other Trotskyists disappeared into prison. After a secret trial, Liu Jingzhen was sentenced to ten years but was released in 1957, due to illness. By then, her lameness had worsened. Her rich family was afraid to keep up relations with her, so she was homeless. Fortunately, her old neighbors helped her find a room, and friends in Hong Kong were able to send her money. During the Cultural Revolution of the late 1960s, Liu, by then half blind, was interrogated several times by Red Guards, though she was not maltreated. One of the charges against her was that in the 1930s she had smuggled messages to and from the Trotskyist leader Chen Duxiu when he was in prison under Chiang Kai-shek as a revolutionary. In 1972, when Zheng was transferred from prison to the reform-through-labor glassworks in Shanghai's Pudong, Liu was allowed to join him. In Pudong, Zheng's life eased slightly.

* * *

In prison under the Communists, Zheng wrote a number of books with political themes and hundreds of poems, but as he explains in the chapters "A Self-Description at the Age of Ninety" and "A Brief Account of My Third Spell in Prison," these writings were destroyed in the Cultural Revolution. Fortunately, he was able to reproduce a number of the poems from memory, and in 1989, Hunan People's Press published them in a slim volume. Like Mao Zedong, Zheng's character combines a belief in radical revolution with a love for poetry in the classical style. In a letter to Lou Shiyi, Zheng—whose prose style is plain and demotic even to the point of bluntness—explained why he is averse to writing poems in the modern idiom: "For prose, the literary reform of May Fourth 1919 worked. Today no one writes in classical Chinese any more. But for poetry, it failed. The first generation of literary reformers like Chen Duxiu and Lu Xun all wrote poetry in the old style. Poetry needs rules and forms. This is true of poetry (excluding free verse) in all the Western languages. I know of no new-style poetry in Chinese that is broadly read, like Lu Xun's old-style poems. So I take a very serious attitude to old-style poetry and would never stoop to writing doggerel."[13]

* * *

Did Zheng stay true to his Trotskyist beliefs after 1952? To anyone who knows even a little about the man, the question is ridiculous. That fact has not stopped Zheng's detractors from insinuating, wickedly and outrageously, that he traded his principles for his freedom in 1979 and "is now happy to render dubious services to ... die-hard Stalinists."[14] Fortunately, there is ample evidence that Zheng's convictions, and his integrity, were one hundred percent intact when he walked free in 1979, having stayed in China thirty years earlier to hold the Trotskyist flag. Even in prison he secretly celebrated his admiration for Trotsky in a poetic rebus. He wrote the poem after reading in a Chinese newspaper that at the Twenty-second Congress of the Soviet Communist Party in 1961, Khrushchev had proposed building a memorial in Moscow to the victims of Stalin's terror, and the Trotskyist Fourth International had sent a telegram to Moscow saying that when the memorial was built, Trotsky's name should be carved on it "in gold letters." "At the time, I was still in prison waiting to be dealt with," wrote Zheng in 1988. "That is to say, I could be taken out at any time and shot. I thought to myself, if there is life after death, where will my spirit go? First, it will go to Moscow to put a bouquet of flowers on that memorial."[15] The Chinese character *ding* is close in shape to the Western letter *T*, and in his prison poem Zheng used it to stand for Trotsky. The prison authorities failed to see through this thin disguise and took the poem as a piece of nonsense.

Memorial to Ding

The north wind gusts, the snowflakes dance,
vast buildings tower by the way.
Red flags on rooftops dapple white,
crowds surge like tides from subway gates.[16]
This stubborn shade, this wisp of smoke,
will face God with its granite brain:[17]
clutching fresh blooms it treads the snow,
enquiring of each passer-by,
"Where is the grand memorial?"
When last here, I was very young.
Bullet scars could still be seen
around the university.
Yet people rose above the mean
and narrow streets to dwarf the gods.
Now poverty has given way
to affluence, unlettered night
to dawning of the lettered day.
Sapling of my youth, you've grown
into a tree where people take
shade from the sun and pick fresh fruit;
those who planted it are dead,
the earth beneath is stained jade green.[18]
See, the marble comes in sight
clean and white as frozen fat.
Flowers bedeck the steps and plinth.
With spinning eyes I scan the stone
line by line for words of gold.
Framed in the blurred names' giddy ring,
whichever way I look I see
nothing but *ding*, *ding*, *ding*, and *ding*.

Nor can the publication and republication of Zheng's memoirs by the Chinese Communist authorities be taken to imply that he in any way compromised with the regime in Beijing. This fact is evident from the comment that prefaces the official Chinese edition of his book. "Zheng Chaolin is currently a member, aged eighty-two, of the People's Political Consultative Conference of the Municipality of Shanghai," the publishers wrote in August 1982. "He was an early member of the Chinese Communist Party. As he himself says, after the second half of 1927, he gradually departed from the line of the Communist International and the Chinese Communist Party and, after 1929, went over completely to Trotskyist positions; moreover, he became a main leader of the Chinese Trotskyist organization.... To this day, the author fully upholds Trotskyist positions on various important issues in the Chinese Revolution and the Russian Revolution, and still supports various of Trotsky's and of Chen Duxiu's opinions. We are now publishing this book in a limited edition, restricted to internal circulation, as reference material for leading cadres in relevant departments and for scientific workers in the field of contemporary history."

* * *

Based on traditional Chinese reckoning, Zheng Chaolin, though born in 1901, celebrated his ninetieth birthday in 1990.[19] At a birthday reception given in his honor, he reported on his life to elders of his native Zhangping in Fujian province. He told them: "Seventy-one of my ninety years were spent outside Zhangping, but I have certainly not forgotten that I am a son of Zhangping. I was born in Zhangping, I grew up in Zhangping, and I had my schooling in Zhangping. My forebears moved to Zhangping 756 years ago.... How should I report to the elders of Zhangping? What have I, who for seventy-one years have lived far from home, done in that time? And what do I still want to do? There is so much to say and so little time to say it, so I will be brief: There is nothing in my life that I feel unable to report on to the elders of Zhangping."

The publication of this translation of Zheng's book, which describes and explains the birth of Stalinism in the Chinese Communist Party, is timely, for Stalinism everywhere has either died or passed into a general crisis whose nature is best explained historically. How will Zheng greet this volume? When he heard the news that his book of poems was to be published, he wrote to a friend: "People value their old brooms, even though they're broken and of little value. When the book comes out and I have a copy in my hands, when I see that it's well published and can smell the ink, I shall pat and feel it for several minutes. And my joy at the age of ninety will be no less than the joy of a nine-year-old boy who has been given a new toy."[20]

---

*The editor would like to thank Terry Mares, Cindy Kaufman-Nixon, Linda Lotz, and Richard Owens for their expert assistance in the production of this book, and Wang Fangxi for his help with the translation and the notes.

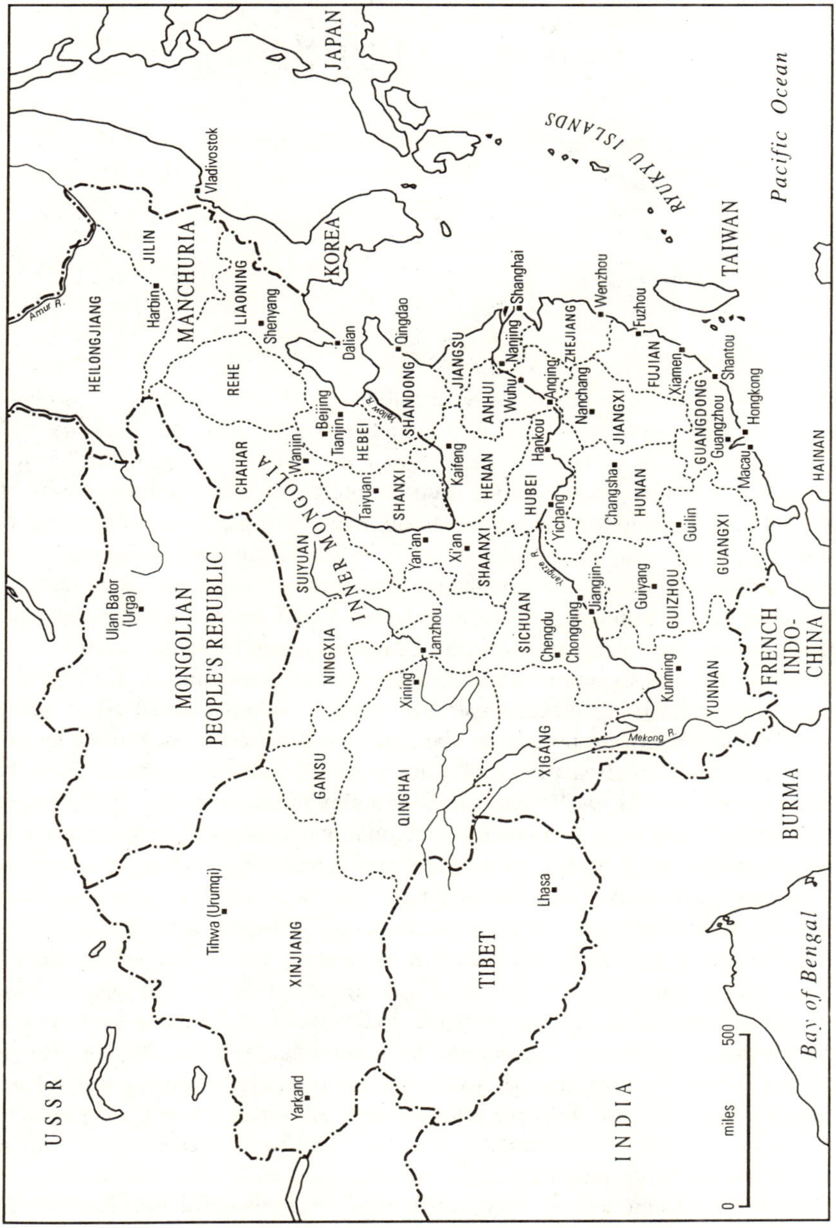

China in 1930

Author's 1945 Preface

Ten of these twelve chapters are about the 1920s, a glorious era in modern Chinese history. Few people recognize the significance of those years, but they point a way out for our country. In the 1920s, the workers became conscious of their mission; the Communist Party—the workers' political representative—was born, grew strong, and almost took state power; between 1925 and 1927, the revolution was defeated, but still the 1920s hold crucial lessons for China's coming third revolution. In sum, the 1920s were a revolutionary epoch, more so than 1911, which brought about the Republic.[21]

In the late 1860s, several studies were published in Paris on the French Revolution of 1848. These studies revived interest in the forgotten events of the 1840s. Marx noticed this interest and wrote to friends in Germany, arguing that it portended a revival of the French Revolution. Not long after, the Paris Commune was established. I hope that more books of memoirs and more studies about China in the 1920s will appear so that we can conclude—like Marx in his day—that the Chinese Revolution is about to revive.

China still has a Communist Party today, but its views on the 1920s have not been set out for all to see. Generally speaking, Communist Party leaders fear memoirs about that period, for both its positive and its negative aspects throw light on their present errors. I have not been a member of the Party for many years, but I am honored to have belonged to it in the 1920s and to have worked, struggled, and committed my own share of errors alongside many revolutionaries whose names have gone down in history. The Chinese Communist Party can also boast of its classical age. By "classical" I do not mean that we should take it as a model. On the contrary, we did many wrong things in the 1920s, and the future party of the revolution would do well to avoid our mistakes. The 1920s were classical only by comparison with what came later. The Party in the 1920s, whatever its mistakes, was a party of the workers, who had mounted the political stage and united around the Communists. In the late 1920s, workers gradually left the Party. Communists abandoned the workers' movement and turned toward the peasants and the petit bourgeois movement. Now, the Party has become the political representative of patriotism.[22]

These twelve chapters are my personal reminiscences of political life in the 1920s. The views developed in them are my personal views. Memory can err. Unfortunately, I am not in a position to check my conclusions against historical evidence. Luckily, no one is likely to take my memoirs as a history of the revolution or of the Communist Party.

I originally intended to scrap the chapter "Love and Politics" because it might be deemed too close in content to the gossip columns of the Shanghai yellow press and might attract adverse comments. My aim in writing it was to describe different sorts of love among revolutionaries of that period and to throw light on the character of certain revolutionaries; it was in no way intended to pass moral judgment. Love of any sort is permissible in a revolutionary party so long as it does not cause political damage. Most of the men and women I write about in that chapter lost their lives in the White Terror, and some survivors have abandoned the revolution for a genteel life. They will probably think that my descriptions of their youthful love affairs are slanderous. All I can do is apologize. The events described in "Love and Politics" have broader implications; otherwise I would have left them out. Readers should not forget that I, too, participated in them. Now as then, I am completely without feudal or bourgeois prejudice concerning relations between the sexes.

February 20, 1945

Postscript: Chapter 10 was completed under extremely difficult circumstances while my son, Frei, lay dying. Frei was born in the second year after my release from prison in 1937. He was conceived, he was born, and he died during the war years. His place of birth was in the countryside, where we had taken refuge from the Japanese. So he was poorly nurtured and often feverish. He finally died of tuberculosis, three weeks after I wrote the above preface. He was a clever, lovable child. His death was the greatest blow to me. Over the last six months, I have been unable to drum up sufficient enthusiasm to write the final two chapters of this book. Now I am busy with more important things, so I must let the book stand as it is.

August 29, 1945

1

A Consciousness Awakes

In the eighth year of the Chinese Republic, more easily remembered as 1919, Chinese became collectively aware, and my own small consciousness awoke.

If I had written these memoirs ten or more years ago, in the early 1930s, I would have had no need to remind readers that the May Fourth Movement broke out in 1919. But few of today's youth, for whom this book is written, know when the May Fourth Movement happened, let alone what it meant.

In 1919, I was nineteen years old. In April, the sixth class of Fujian's Ninth Provincial Middle School (in Longyan) finished its studies and was granted special leave so that we students could go home and await the final examinations in June. I returned to Zhangping and relaxed. Sometime in May, an old gentleman came to our home to chat with my father. He said that there was trouble in Beijing among the students, that they were beating people, burning houses, and boycotting lectures. After he had finished speaking, he shook his head and sighed. This old gentleman was one of just a handful of people in our town who frequently read a newspaper. My father did not read one, nor did I. Even at school, I rarely went to the reading room. It held one or two Fuzhou newspapers,[23] but as far as I know, there were none from Beijing or Shanghai, and even the Fuzhou ones were usually out-of-date. In those days, few students ever went to the reading room to look at newspapers.

There were three primary schools in Zhangping, one run by the county government, one by a clan, and one by evangelists. There were several middle school graduates in town, as well as five or six people—like me—waiting to graduate. There was a student association, but it had not met for a long time. We barely responded to the hurricane from Beijing. Other places were erupting with lecture strikes, demonstrations, and anti-Japanese consumer boycotts. The schoolmates we had left behind in Longyan wrote to tell us that they had led a demonstration of all the local primary schools and had set up a checkpoint for Japanese goods outside town on the road to Zhangzhou. They had also invaded the Chamber of Commerce, where they had banged on the table, brandished teacups, and sworn at the chairman.[24] But we students in Zhangping had barely lifted a finger. True, pupils of the New People's Primary School, run by evangelists outside the West Gate, marched into town on one occasion, and the pastor apparently gave each one a bag of sweets and made them promise never to buy Japanese products again. But that was the church school.

When I went back to take the examinations in June, the movement in Longyan had already died down. Our schoolmates told those of us who had gone home some anecdotes about what had happened. Student pickets were still active outside town, and the student association was still meeting, but it was not holding demonstrations, boycotting classes, or causing trouble. Even so, the climate had changed dramatically in those two months. Students who normally never stirred were now active; students who never spoke were now voluble. The reading room was crowded, current events were common knowledge, and, most important of all, the students now controlled their own association. Pinned to the association bulletin board were letters from people who had gone off to study in the big cities.

That was May Fourth as I experienced it. At the time, I knew nothing about May Fourth other than the anti-Japanese boycott, the attacks on traitors, the refusal to sign the treaty,[25] and things of that sort. It is unlikely that anyone else in Zhangping was any better informed. And Longyan? Had people in Longyan read the magazine *Xin qingnian* (New youth) and been carried along by the new tide? I cannot say. But even if some had, they were a rarity.

After graduating from middle school, I became unaccountably depressed. I wanted to fly, I wanted to quit the narrow cage of Zhangping, even of Fujian. While still at school, I had resolved along with several others to go to Beijing and enroll at normal school—not because I felt some "sacred calling" to become a scholar, but because I had heard that normal schools demanded no tuition fees or board expenses and even provided a small subsidy, so that one ended up paying scarcely more than I had paid at middle school. But my father could not help me, and neither he nor I could get our hands on any other source of funds. A Longyan student who had gone ahead sent me a postcard from Shanghai describing his visit to the New World Recreation Center. Once again I became agitated. But then something entirely unexpected happened.

The county education inspector in Zhangping, a man called Chen Hua, was a friend of my grandfather. My father and I were still upset because I could not go to Beijing, but Mr. Chen came up with an alternative. Mr. Chen was against me going to Beijing anyway, because he thought that the climate in the colleges there was too turbulent. But he told me that Commander Chen had issued a proclamation ordering the local magistrate, a man called Xiong, to send two students to study in France, where half their expenses would be paid out of public funds.

Commander Chen was, of course, Chen Jiongming, commander in chief of the Guangdong Army Relieving Fujian. Sometime later, Chiang Kai-shek's Nanjing government promulgated a decree giving amnesty to political offenders, and the "Communist bandits" and Chen Jiongming were on the list of those pardoned. Chen Jiongming's crime was that he had incited his subordinate Ye Ju to surround Generalissimo Sun Yat-sen's headquarters in Guangzhou and force him aboard a battleship.[26] But all these things happened several years after the events I am describing. In 1919, Chen Jiongming, far from being a traitor to the Guomindang, commanded its sole armed force. (In reality, the Guomindang did not exist then, except for a few factions around Sun Yat-sen.) When Guangdong was occupied by the Guangxi Army, the Guangdong Army (which had a revolutionary history) was unable to hold out in its native province and was forced to add the words "Relieving Fujian" to its battle standard and snatch a corner of Fujian from the Beiyang warlords.[27] It occupied the old Tingzhou-Zhangzhou-Longyan district and set up its general command at Zhangzhou.

Chen Jiongming was a new-style army man[28] who preached socialism and even anarchism. As soon as he got to Zhangzhou, he built highways in the city, opened a park, and started holding athletic events and publishing a daily newspaper. Rickshaw pullers were banned from the highway; a stone obelisk was placed in the park inscribed with the words "Freedom," "Equality," "Fraternity," and "Mutual Aid." Here, the anarchist influence of Wu Zhihui and Li Shizeng was discernible. To correspond with Wu and Li's work-study program,[29] Chen Jiongming ordered each county magistrate in the region under his jurisdiction to send two or three people to France to study. That instruction was the origin of Fujian's program of officially subsidized study abroad.

Wu and Li conceived the work-study program at the end of the First World War. During the war, France was short of labor, so 100,000 or so Chinese workers were recruited to go there. Financial assistance to Chinese students studying in France dried up, so they too started looking for jobs in French factories. The French workers, through their sacrifices, had achieved far better working conditions than those in China, and the Chinese students were happy to take advantage of this. The idea arose that Chinese students would go to France and spend half their time working in factories and the other half in school, using what they earned to subsidize their studies. Li Shizeng stayed in France to organize this program. He helped people enter the country, find work, and find a school. In a Shanghai newspaper, Wu Zhihui, already back in China, published *Cuoan kezuo tanhua* (Random talks on different subjects), part of which consisted of propaganda for the idea of work-study. *Random Talks* also appeared separately as a pamphlet, and it sold well.

According to estimates, because of the fall in the value of the French franc, you could study in France on an income of just six hundred Chinese silver dollars, even without working. So on the basis of these estimates, Chen Jiongming asked each student's family to raise three hundred dollars (a sum that my father could, in theory, just about afford) and got the county magistrate to contribute the rest.

On the eighteenth day of the seventh lunar month, another student and I boarded a boat outside Zhangping's Middle Water Gate. My father, my uncle, and one of my younger brothers came to send me off; it was the last time I ever saw them. Students from several different counties in Fujian met at Zhangzhou, where they were welcomed by Chen Jiongming at his headquarters in the former Daotai Yamen. There was a group photograph and a banquet with speeches, including one by Zhu Zhixin, but I have no memory of either event.

Altogether, more than thirty of us sailed to Hong Kong to await the boat for France. After a few days, Chen Jiongming's representative Huang Qiang invited us up to Guangzhou, where we stayed at the Zengbu Technology College, of which he was principal. He got a local woman to teach us French. We studied it for three weeks. While we were in Guangzhou, Fujianese members of the National Parliament (among them Lin Sen) held a valedictory meeting in our honor.

* * *

Finally, on November 4, we boarded a *messager maritime*, the *Paul Lecat*. This ship had started out from Shanghai and already had one to two hundred students aboard. By the time fifty or sixty more of us from Fujian and Guangdong had joined them, the fourth-class deck was full to bursting.

The thirty-three days aboard that ship sealed my fate. I experienced my personal May Fourth aboard that packet liner. Before climbing aboard, I had no idea that May Fourth meant anything other than patriotism. True, you could already buy new books and journals in Hong Kong and Guangzhou, but neither I nor my companions had bought any, and even if we had, it is unlikely that we would have read them. In Hong Kong, I bought pirated Shidetang editions of Laozi, Zhuangzi, and Liezi, as well as Commercial Press editions of *Jingshi baijia zachao* (An anthology of classics, histories, and other writings) and a small-character edition of *Laocan youji* (Travels of Laocan). In addition, I had brought from home a Guoxue Fulun edition of Gong Ding'an's *Collected Works* and a badly printed edition of *Bai xiang cipu* (*Ci* patterns). These I took with me to France. Apart from Laozi, Zhuangzi, and Liezi, to which I shall return in a moment, I lost the rest in 1927, when Tang Shengzhi's troops occupied the Communist Party's Hubei Committee headquarters in Hankou.

At sea, I had my first real contact with students from "across the river."[30] I met a new sort of student. They were not just different from the students I had known at home but also different from how I had imagined students from across the river would be, after reading *Liu dong waishi* (Informal history of Chinese students in Japan).[31] They were farsighted and intellectually lively. I learned many new things from listening to them: about many ancient and modern books I had never heard of, and that a new life awaited us in France, quite different from the one to which we were accustomed. They showed me many newly published journals, and I read a great many of their magazines, some of which had large circulations. I was astonished at this fact and at how little known were the Saturday Press publications that I usually read.

One day on the ship, I borrowed a magazine called *New Youth*. Leafing through it, I came across an article by someone called Chen Duxiu. I forget the title, but I remember the subject, Confucianism.

My Chinese-language teacher at middle school, Mr. Huang Baoshu, once had me write an essay on making Confucianism the state religion. Naturally, I supported this idea of Kang Youwei's. Mr. Huang covered my essay with circles and underlinings indicating approval, but when he met me later on the playing field, he said, "Confucius was an educationalist, his theories should not be turned into a state religion." That was the first time I realized that at least one of my old teachers opposed making a cult of Confucius. Now, reading this article by Chen Duxiu, I thought to myself, "It's that same discussion again." Only when I read further did I realize that the article was completely against Confucius. Even in ancient times, learned people had opposed Confucius. For example, Zhuangzi had opposed him. But what annoyed me was the last sentence of the article. It said: "If the way of Confucius is not blocked, the way of democracy will not flow; if the way of Confucius is not stopped, the way of democracy will not be open."[32] "If this is not blocked, that will not flow; if this is not stopped, that will not be open" was first said by Han Yu against Buddhism and Daoism in *Yuan dao* (The original way). Now, Chen Duxiu was using Han's text to attack Confucius! My first day aboard ship I started writing a diary. In it, I roundly cursed Chen Duxiu.

But on the outside, I showed no sign of all this inner dismay. None of my fellow Fujianese on board was interested in such subjects. Some had never even heard of *The Original Way*. As for the students from across the river, the more I heard them talk, the quieter I fell. Actually, I was not a good talker, and in any case, my Mandarin was not yet fluent enough to handle complicated issues. But *New Youth* and other periodicals of that sort fascinated me, and the more I reacted against them, the more I wanted to borrow and read them. Gradually, I lost interest in the classics I had previously valued. On December 7, when we stepped ashore at Marseilles, I may have looked like the same person who had boarded in Hong Kong, but inwardly I had changed. Secretly, my consciousness had flowered; from then on, I was my own master, I was in charge of my own fate. I would never again be a mere link in the chain forged for me by my father, my teacher, and former generations of my lineage.

Perhaps I should mention some of the special factors that contributed to my coming to awareness. Needless to say, it was mainly a result of the epoch we were living in; the proof is that of the thirty-odd Fujianese who went to France, after a year, all but a handful had learned to write in the vernacular,[33] could talk intelligently about the new wave of thought, and in some cases had even joined the Communist Party. But to illustrate the seriousness and the radical depth of the change from being a link in someone else's chain to becoming a new-style human being, there is no better example than my own individual case.

I was born the eldest son in an old-style landlord family, then in decline. For many generations, we had been scholars, addicted to the fragrance of the printed book. At school, I was by no means stupid. Naturally, my grandfather and my father vested their hopes in my young person. These hopes were typical of traditional landlord families in old China: to win merit by proceeding along the proper path, to go "across the river" and be an official in a place or two, and then to return home to buy land and build a house. When the imperial examinations were abolished, these hopes were, of course, dashed. My grandfather said, "You were born a few years too late, otherwise. . . ." But the education I received was still the old-style education from the days before abolition. We not only were taught the text of the Four Books[34] but also studied Zhu Xi's annotation of them,[35] together with other commentaries. Of the Five Classics, we read the *Book of Songs*, the *Book of History*, the *Book of Changes*, and the *Spring and Autumn Annals*, but not the *Book of Rites*. We also studied Lin Yunming's *Guwen xiyi* (Analysis of ancient literature). Fortunately, we did not learn how to write eight-legged essays[36] or commentaries; instead, we wrote discursive essays. In our county, there was already an official primary school (called the county primary school, following the founding of the Republic in 1911). My grandfather was an elder of the school, and my father was treasurer and manager of its property, but curiously, they allowed neither me nor my brothers to attend it. Even after three generations of students had graduated from the primary school, we and others in the same position were still enrolled in a local *sishu*, or private academy. This was obviously because it was thought that we would not be in a position to acquire the "necessary" knowledge in the primary school. But in 1914, the primary school was reorganized, and our *sishu* teacher Liu Cenzhong was appointed to teach Chinese there. In any case, by then our fathers and grandfathers had realized that the only way left of "winning merit by proceeding along the proper path" lay in the primary school, so we followed our teacher there. I went straight into the upper-third form and graduated after just six months. In 1915, I left home for the first time to go to middle school in Longyan, sixty kilometers from my native town. The Chinese teachers there were even more progressive, for they taught Yao Nai's *Guwen cilei zuan* (Selections from ancient literature) and Wang Xianqian's *Xu guwen cilei zuan* (Further selections). True, we still had to write descriptions, narratives, and essays in the old way, but we also dealt with issues of contemporary interest.

Even more important than formal education in either the old school or the new was the upbringing I received at home and in society. Consciously and unconsciously, directly and indirectly, people inculcate you with the worldview and morality requisite to their own small sphere, and so turn you into a fresh link in their chain.

Did I live up to their expectations? Generally speaking, I did. Both my grandfather and my father were satisfied with my progress. I was quiet and obedient, I was making headway, and I was always prepared to give in to their manipulation. I never refused to play any of the roles they forced on me. I thought that it was quite natural to play these roles, as natural as dressing or eating. I could see no point in resisting, and moreover, I was incapable of doing so. The only thing that dissatisfied them was my great reticence and my inability to perform in the company of guests. My mother was unhappy to see me always with a book in my hand, but I am convinced that what made me the person I am today had much to do with always having a book in my hand.

Before my tenth birthday, I was no different from other children. I liked to be naughty, I liked eating between meals, and I was particular about what clothes I wore. I was not especially keen on watching operas and listening to stories. But at eleven, I changed. One day that summer I was lying ill in bed in my uncle's house. I could not play with my cousins, and I was bored. Under the pillow I found a copy of the novel *Xue Rengui zhengdong* (Xue Rengui marches east). My uncle had been reading it. He had got as far as the fourth chapter and had rolled it up and put it under the pillow. I looked at the book and was surprised to find that I could understand it, even though it contained many characters for vernacular words like "this" or "what" that I had never come across in the classics. I had heard the story many times and had often seen it performed on the stage, so I was able to guess characters that I did not know. I could not put the volume down. I read late into the night, and by the end of the next day, I had finished all four volumes. I started pestering my uncle for more novels, and later, I started buying them myself. They were old-fashioned books of the sort that go on for dozens or even hundreds of chapters. After that, I no longer had any interest in children's play, and I became steadily more alienated from my cousins and my younger brothers.

Today there is nothing unusual about children reading novels, and even in my day, children in other parts of China read them. But in Zhangping, it was far from normal. For an eleven-year-old child to read novels—lots of novels—and never to be without a book, for him to pay not the slightest attention to the hubbub outside nor even attend an opera performance, but to stay hidden indoors with his novels, was quite unknown in my hometown. Very soon, my house became a center for books (meaning novels). Adults would come to borrow my books.

Novels opened a new world to me: an unreal world, an imaginary world. I was so entranced by it that I forgot the real world. This created, and strengthened, my weakness: taciturnity, an inability to socialize, a general isolation from others. Novels stopped me from having friends. My childhood playmates had already deserted me, and my schoolmates did not understand me, for they had read no novels, or at least not many. Most had read only the books assigned to them by their teachers. But in another way, novels made me dissatisfied with reality, with the life and thinking of our circle, and with the future that others had marked out for me. They even caused me to doubt the sacred tradition of the classics. I kept this dissatisfaction and these doubts completely to myself. However, my preference for Laozi and Zhuangzi[37] and my wish to leave for distant lands after graduation, including my wish to go to France, were probably manifestations of my inner feelings. (That was the first time I decided my own fate; previously, I had let my father decide everything on my behalf. And although he did not actually oppose my suggestion, he was not enthusiastic about it.)

I should add that I did not read only novels. Although I started with novels, I later progressed to literary sketches, essays, the pre-Qin philosophers, and the dynastic histories—in sum, the sort of books that neither my teachers nor my school friends read. In fact, I had an immediate prejudice against any book they recommended to me and read it (if at all) only as a duty. So I acquired nearly all my knowledge from self-study. I thought of school as a place to sleep, eat, and take my leisure; I seriously believed that the education I got there was useless. Thinking back, that was a one-sided view. Since the books I read were different from those that others read—in sentiment, taste, and intellectual direction—it's not surprising that although I never sought conflict and had no enemies, I was incapable of fitting into the community and had not a single friend. On the surface, I was slow and impassive, and I took things as they came, but I lived another life inside. Had I been born in another age, my imagination would gradually have been ground away by the millstones of the real world. Sooner or later, I would have compromised with the rest: I would have learned the social graces, I would have become good at receiving guests, I would have melted into my environment, I would have stopped being a bookworm and, through slow tempering, I would have learned to become competent in everyday life so that I could follow in my grandfather's and my father's footsteps and become a minor *shenshi*[38] in a minor county capital.

Luckily, May Fourth saved me. By May Fourth I do not mean the thrashing handed out to Zhang Zongxiang,[39] the lecture strike, the boycott of Japanese goods, or the patriotic movement. Instead, I mean the May Fourth that sought the help of Messrs. Science and Democracy to overthrow the Confucian family shop.[40] I heaved aside the Confucianism that weighed like a load on my shoulders; I even abandoned Laozi and Zhuangzi, those appendages of the Confucian Way. From then on, I lived only one life: What I did and what I thought were one and the same thing. I got there by serious meditation and inner struggle, not by following the times or following the crowd.

The struggle lasted more than just a day or two. Several months elapsed between my cursing Chen Duxiu in my diary and my complete acceptance of his views. Not until I had finished reading Hu Shi's *Zhongguo zhexue shi dagang* (Outline history of Chinese philosophy) were my doubts finally dispelled. After arriving in France, I felt that the French were stronger than we in many things, that Confucius was no match for Messrs. Science and Democracy, but I still believed in a "national essence," an oriental culture, a spiritual civilization, a sacred thing that the West did not possess.[41] That thing was contained in the works of the Zhou and Qin philosophers. In middle school, I had read a book that argued that Buddhism was not as good as our Laozi, Zhuangzi, Yangzi, and Mozi; Western rational philosophers such as Socrates, Plato, and Aristotle were dilettantes compared with our own thinkers. But Hu Shi taught me that the ancient Chinese masters were also philosophers, that they could be examined and researched by scientific methods, that Western philosophers had not only dealt with many of the problems thrown up by the Chinese masters but had gone even further than them. So the "national essence" lost its mystery.

We stayed in Paris for a week. On December 15, the thirty or so students from Fujian were sent from the Sino-French Education Association[42] to the Collège de Garçons in Saint-Germain-en-Laye. Saint-Germain is three-quarters of an hour from Paris by train, and an hour by tram. There is a palace there where kings used to live. Louis XIV was born there. Now, it has been turned into a museum. The palace and the town are on a hill that looks onto the Seine and the plain beyond the opposite bank. To get under the river and up the hill, the train from Paris had to shed a few coaches and add a locomotive at the rear. At the top of the hill is the terminus. The station is near the palace, and the palace park is above the tunnel. The park is rather small, but along the raised bank of the river runs a long road, straight as an arrow, through a large forest where kings used to hunt. The whole of Saint-Germain is surrounded by forest. The highway runs from the railway station through the town and out past our school; it also enters the forest at a certain point. Every spring, on weekends and on holidays, Parisians come here to walk among the trees and flowers. Three months before we arrived, the Allies signed a peace treaty with Austria in the palace.

Our dormitory was inside the school grounds. We were given a special room to live in, a refectory to eat in, and a classroom for our lessons. We studied only French. Our French teacher had been in the army and claimed to have killed many Germans. He was a perfect chauvinist. The French students were all younger than we and lived a completely separate life. There were three Serbians, two Albanians, and a Persian at the school, but they studied together with the French.

For a while, we Fujianese were held together by the fact that Chen Jiongming had sent someone with us from Zhangzhou to see us aboard the liner in Hong Kong. This man remitted our first year's publicly funded allowance directly to the Sino-French Education Association, and we asked him to remit our own money as well. Everything was arranged for us by the association; we had no choice in the matter. The association sent all of us (except one woman student) to the same school. The Saint-Germain middle school was a provisional arrangement. We were the first Chinese to go there. At first, our group was entirely Fujianese, save for one person from across the river. But a month later, thirty or forty non-Fujianese arrived, from various provinces.

The Fujianese students actively discriminated against students from across the river. If they were together in a group, they would often ridicule the outsiders. As a result, the other students turned against us and called us "barbarians." They meant not only that we were crude and rough but also that we were culturally benighted and backward. When a Hunanese student voiced an opinion of this sort, the Fujianese would gang up against him, and there would almost be a riot.

That is not to say that we Fujianese were united. We were divided into Tingzhou and Zhangzhou factions, and the Zhangzhou faction was further subdivided into an eastern and a southern party. The factional struggle had begun as early as Guangzhou and Hong Kong. There were numerous altercations on board ship during elections for the Student Association. People got up to even worse tricks in Saint-Germain. This division by provenance might appear inexplicable, but it had an objective basis. For a start, we were divided by language. Students from counties in the old Tingzhou prefecture spoke Hakka—only one or two spoke the dialect of the Zhangzhou-Quanzhou region.[43] None of the students from the old Zhangzhou prefecture spoke Hakka. The two groups were forced to communicate in Mandarin. Second, and even more important, we had received different sorts of education. The Tingzhou students had attended primary schools typical of the hinterland, not so very different from the school I had gone to. Schools of that sort stressed Chinese language and literature. The teachers were old men who had gotten their learning from stitched books. The Zhangzhou students, in contrast, had enjoyed a seaport education, a church-style education as in the treaty ports. They had learned their Chinese from young men in Western suits and leather shoes. They had probably never read *Selections from Ancient Literature*. The Tingzhou students considered the Zhangzhou students superficial; the Zhangzhou students considered the Tingzhou students backward. For example, most of the Tingzhou students had read the *Original Way*. When they saw that I had copies of Laozi and Zhuangzi in my suitcase, they knew that these thinkers were against Confucius, because Han Yu had told them so.[44] This fact meant nothing to the Zhangzhou students. When they saw my copy of Bai Xiang's *Ci Patterns*, they even insisted that it had been written by Bai Letian.[45] But neither the students from Zhangzhou nor those from Tingzhou had ever heard of Gong Ding'an.[46] The Zhangzhou students called me Academician Zheng because I had brought stitched books with me. Unlike the Tingzhou group, they despised stitched books.

I was a bystander to their struggles. I was from neither Tingzhou nor Zhangzhou but from the region under the direct jurisdiction of the provincial government—Longyan, midway between the two rival prefectures. My educational background was the same as that of the Tingzhou students, but I spoke no Hakka (though I could speak the Zhangzhou dialect). A fellow student of mine from Zhangping could speak both Hakka and the Zhangzhou dialect. He switched between the factions and caused all sorts of trouble. Once, when both groups were shaping up for a battle in the classroom, I hid in the corner and just watched. The headmaster wrote to the association about us. The Guomindang veteran Zhang Boquan, in Paris at the time, came in person to Saint-Germain to sort us out.

The students from across the river took their lessons in a separate classroom. They had brought large numbers of new publications with them, mainly journals but also some stitched volumes. Although they thought that we were barbarians, they by no means excluded us. They were like medieval missionaries spreading the word. We Fujianese gradually caught up on May Fourth. It was probably about this same time (the spring of 1920) that May Fourth penetrated Fujian, for schoolmates back home wrote us letters about the new tide.

Although writing in the vernacular and talking about new culture became the rage, the struggle between the prefectures continued. By the start of the summer holidays, the association had run out of money, so we had to start fending for ourselves. The Fujian link finally snapped; we had to seek our own way. What happened to the other Fujianese is largely a mystery to me. One joined the Communist Party in my footsteps, but after suffering some blows, he returned to the path that his father had marked out for him and devoted himself to working for the greater glory of his family.

I stayed in Saint-Germain over the summer because I was short of money. After the summer holidays, two other Fujianese and I were the only Chinese students still left, so we joined the French students instead of attending separate classes. We had studied physics, chemistry, and math in China, and we benefited little from studying French history and geography. Nor were we particularly interested in reading the French classics. When the winter holidays arrived, I was out of money.

Before the war, the Mexican silver dollars we used in China had been worth 2.5 francs each. In 1919 (the year of the Versailles peace treaty), while we were still in Hong Kong, one dollar had been worth eight or nine francs. By now, the franc had dropped in value and stood at fifteen to the dollar. While we were in Paris, an official of the association had told us, "The cost of living has gone up. In Paris you need three hundred francs a month to live. But three hundred francs is only thirty Chinese dollars; you could never live on that in Shanghai." In Saint-Germain, we had paid on average 150 francs a month for bed, board, fees, and laundry. The association had paid this amount on our behalf as a lump sum. Other expenses we had to meet from our own pockets—that is, from the money the association kept for us, which we withdrew at regular intervals.

By the end of 1920, having too little money to pay for the following term, I had no choice but to leave school. My two Fujianese friends and I left Saint-Germain and went to Melun, two hours by train to the southeast of Paris. A middle school in Melun also took Chinese students, but we did not enroll in it. Instead, we rented accommodations where we could cook for ourselves (to save money) and study. Since Melun is rather far from the capital, the cost of living there was lower. We each had our own room. I lived in the attic, where I could see through a dormer window onto a canal. I paid thirty-five francs a month in rent; my friend on the second floor paid forty. Rent was our biggest outlay; we economized on the rest. In all, we got by on a hundred francs a months. That sum paid for haircuts, baths, laundry, and postage to China. The only things it did not include were clothes, books, travel, and medicine. We skimped on food. In our case, the saying "not a taste of meat for three months" was true. We rarely ate breakfast; our other two meals consisted of bread and mashed potatoes, with an occasional plate of stir-fried cabbage as a special treat, done in pork fat rather than olive oil. I still remember that bread cost 1.3 francs a pound. After three months of this, we could stand it no longer and started adding meat to our diet once every few days. Our other expenses also increased. Our monthly budget soared by thirty percent.

Melun straddles the Seine. Once when we were walking along its banks, we met a sickly looking Chinese who told us that he was called Zeng Qi and was a member of the Young China Association. He had gone to Melun for a cure. His living conditions were far superior to ours. He became our friend. We used to visit one another and go for outings together. He lent us issues of *Shaonian Zhongguo* (Young China) and gave us copies of his *qijue*[47] to criticize; I gave him some of mine in return. At the time, he was writing a column for a newspaper in China in which he said that students on the work-study program in France could get by on one hundred francs a month—six or seven Chinese dollars. When the other students heard about this article, they cursed him as a blockhead. They did not know that we were the cause of his claim.

Li Shizeng and Wu Zhihui were no longer publishing *Xin shiji bao* (Nouveau siècle), but the Chinese printshop in Tours was still in existence and published a weekly magazine similar in format to a Shanghai tabloid. I cannot remember what it was called, but I remember that the editor was Zhou Taixuan. He was also a member of the Young China Association and a friend of Zeng Qi. Zeng Qi often wrote articles for Zhou's magazine. I think that it was Zeng Qi who wrote an article categorizing Chinese students in France into three "classes": officially sponsored students; semiofficially sponsored students and self-financing students; and work-study students. He said that the first group was bourgeois, the last group was proletarian, and the middle group was petit bourgeois. That meant that he and I were petit bourgeois.

There were statistics that showed the different sorts of students in percentages. I have forgotten the exact figures, but I remember that work-study students were in the majority and far outnumbered the other groups. There were some three thousand of them from every one of China's eighteen provinces save Gansu. The biggest groups were from Sichuan and Hunan. Most of them had been leaders of or activists in the May Fourth Movement. They were like me: They wanted to fly from their provinces and even go abroad, but also like me, they lacked wings. The cry "hard work and frugal study" was certainly no voice in the wilderness. Most of the students gathered at Shanghai to await the boat, but some waited in Beijing or Baoding. Two or three batches had preceded me to France; even more came after me. In the autumn of 1920, the flow ebbed or stopped.

The reason was that the ideal had been shattered. True, schools all over France threw open their doors to us—after all, we were worth good money—

but the factories remained closed to us. The war had been over for nearly two years. The French economy was in recession, and workers were being laid off. Why should they make room for us yellow-skins? After the work-study students had used up the money they had brought with them from China, they became real "proletarians" and were forced to seek help from the association. A tiny minority found factory jobs; the rest had to make do with a subsidy of two to three francs a day for bread and hot water. Some lived in the Education Association building. The Education Association was actually a unit of the Overseas Chinese Association. Apparently, a rich widow who sympathized with China had donated the building. On my second day in Paris, this lady made a speech at our reception. The Overseas Chinese Association was at 39, Rue de la Pointe, in Lagarenne-Colombes, twenty minutes from Paris by train, not far from the famous Beancurd Company.[48] The reason that I remember this location so clearly is that it was my mailing address for more than three years. The association was in a three-story building on its own grounds. By that time, the cellar was full of work-study students. Others lived in a tent in the garden. A rope was strung between two trees where students hung out their shirts, socks, trousers, and sheets to dry. The constant hubbub in the garden disturbed the neighbors, who petitioned the police to intervene. Once, an official of the association said to us: "The neighbors say we Chinese are not clean. Not clean? Chinese not clean? When the toilet seat gets wet, no one wants to sit on it any longer, so they squat on it instead, and break it. Then other people use the toilet standing up. It gets dirty so people start pissing in from the door. The entrance gets wet so people start pissing in the corridor." This was an exaggeration. Although the toilet was not exactly clean, it was not as dirty as this man made out, and there was no sign of shit or piss in the corridor.

The work-study students had been activists in the student movement in China; they were "student rabble, worse than soldiers." Barred from work, they were unable to continue with their studies, so they became resentful. Li Shizeng had already gone back to Beijing University to become a professor. His friend Liu Hou became the students' stand-in target. Liu Hou had to put up with all sorts of problems. When Cai Yuanpei and Wu Zhihui came to France, they held a meeting to try to sort things out.

These luminaries went to China in connection with their campaign to force France to pay back the Boxer Indemnity Fund.[49] They intended to use the fund to finance a new batch of Chinese students. The work-study students who were already in France naturally protested. They said that the aim of sending them there in the first place had been to force France to pay back the fund. Now that the aim had been achieved, they were being ditched.

There were two struggles I should mention. One was the "28 Movement" that happened on February 28, 1921, when work-study students from all over France crowded into Paris to petition the Chinese Minister Chen Lu and to make demands. The result was that they were scattered by the police. The other was the "Lyon University Movement." This Chinese university overseas had already been established by the autumn of 1921. It was housed in the Fort Sainte Irène on a small hill across the river from Lyon. Wu Zhihui had brought some students to France who were probably already living at the university. The work-study students had been abandoned. One day, the Lyon police were shocked to see a train pull into the station filled with Chinese students bound for the fortress (still under renovation, in preparation for its new role). The students marched up to the fortress, entered it, and refused to leave. The police surrounded the fortress and held the Chinese prisoners in it. A few days later, the French government ordered their repatriation to China.

I took part in neither of these movements, for I was "petit bourgeois" (to use the terminology of Zeng Qi and his friends), not "proletarian." After the Lyon movement and the deportation of some of the troublemakers, the morale of the work-study students dropped even further, but the economic depression lifted, and we yellow-skins gradually became welcome again in the factories. The mass movement had passed its peak.

As for me, I had descended from the petit bourgeoisie into the proletariat; simultaneously—was there a connection?—I stopped thinking like a mere democrat and starting thinking and even acting like a socialist.

The Communist Youth Party

Is a long period of capitalist democracy necessary to get from Chinese society, with its "feudal remnants," to socialism? This is still a controversial question. As for me personally, I got from feudal ideology to socialist ideology without a "long and stable" intervening stage of bourgeois ideology. The same is true of the collective awakening of the Chinese consciousness—at least of its main current—in the May Fourth era. Like me, it skipped the long and stable period of bourgeois democratic ideology.

I said earlier that at Saint-Germain, the students from across the river had the attitude of medieval missionaries toward us Fujianese "barbarians." Naturally, this was not true of all of them, but a few names still spring to mind. One was Xiong Xiong from Jiangxi. He had served in the army under Li Liejun and was a model officer of the early Republic. He wrote beautiful calligraphy, was a poet in the classical style, and was an avid admirer of everything new and revolutionary, but he lacked an analytical brain. Another was the Sichuanese Qin Zhigu. Qin liked to spin a yarn. He was a sincere person who spoke good English and was fond of discussing issues in the New Culture Movement. Another was Wang Songlu from Guizhou. His old-style learning was rather shallow, but he enjoyed visiting people who were inclined toward the new thinking. There were others too, but I have forgotten their names. I do not mean to give the impression that these were the only people from across the river who wanted dealings with us Fujianese. Even though my fellow Fujianese used to make fun of students from across the river behind their backs or even (in dialect) to their faces, the two sides were not averse to passing the time of day together. But the conversation rarely went beyond the weather, the Paris sights, or women. The people I mentioned had no interest in talking about such subjects. Xiong Xiong was always welcome among the Fujianese, and many Fujianese made friends with him, chiefly because he was a military officer. Qin Zhigu and Wang Songlu, in contrast, were mainly unsuccessful in their overtures to the Fujianese. Whenever they started talking about culture or ideology, the Fujianese would butt in and ask them what subject they were planning to study.

Apart from my given name, I had another name (as was often the custom in those days). This name was Zelian. Most of my fellow Fujianese knew the name, but none could guess why I had chosen it. Wang Songlu and I used to smile at each other about this. Later, Wang told me that one of his teachers, called Huang, was coming to Paris. This man also called himself Qisheng.[50] Huang Qisheng was Wang Ruofei's maternal uncle; later, I shall return to him.

One day, Wang Songlu took me into the corridor outside a classroom and introduced me to a tall thin man with a flat face and high cheekbones. He had an unhealthy flush, the color of a parboiled crab. Wang told me, "This is Mr. Yin Kuan, from Tongcheng [in Anhui]." I found it hard not to laugh, for Kuan means broad, and Yin Kuan was anything but broad. Chang (meaning tall) would have been a better name for him. Yin Kuan immediately sounded off on a long but well-organized speech about some subject or other. The three of us would often meet to hold discussions. Gradually, we arrived at the idea of setting up a research group. We decided that we three would form the nucleus and that each of us would try to recruit new members. One day, we met in the woods outside Saint-Germain and sat down among the trees to discuss the name and constitution of our group. I suggested calling it the Self-Enlightenment Society; the others immediately agreed.

Why self-enlightenment? The name requires an explanation. Although we were studying in France, the literature we read consisted mainly of periodicals posted to us from China and books published by Beijing University. In China, new thought was in its heyday. Students everywhere were challenging established authority, and their unions were even taking over the day-to-day administration of the schools. That was democracy, modeled on Europe and America, and Li Shizeng's people had settled on France as the model for China's future development. But what about the France that we saw around us? Solemnly pacing Catholic priests in black robes came to the school each day to preach to the students; the students viewed the principal and the housemaster as mice view cats; they had not the slightest notion of how to run a movement and never talked about resistance, revolution, socialism, atheism, anarchism, and the rest; the books and magazines they read never broached such subjects. Could it be that France had not yet had its May Fourth; that French students had no *New Youth*, no Chen Duxiu, no Hu Shi? Luckily, a recently arrived issue of *New Youth* carried a translation by Zhang Songnian of a "Manifesto of Independence of Spirit" signed by Romain Rolland, H. Barbusse, Bertrand Russell, and a host of others I had never heard of. Zhang Songnian had added a note explaining who these people were. He said that Barbusse had recently set up an organization in Paris called the Society of Light that published a magazine called *Clarté*.

I lost no time in going to Paris, where I somehow managed to track down the Librairie Clarté. I bought a year's subscription to the magazine and took the most recent issue home with me. It was in newspaper format, rather like *Shenbao*, and came out weekly. I took out my dictionary and began to wade my way through my purchase. It was exactly what we wanted; I conveyed the contents to like-minded friends. But the next issue did not arrive, nor the next. I wrote to the bookshop, which wrote back, inviting me to Paris. I went. The people there told me that they had been posting my subscription and that the headmaster was probably confiscating it; they advised me to use another address. It so happened that a friend of mine from Fujian who could not settle down to dormitory life had decided to rent a room outside the school. His landlord was an engineer. I went to discuss my problem with them. The landlord readily agreed to let me use his address for my subscription. He let fly a torrent of abuse at the school authorities. It turned out that he was a member of the Socialist Party. Later, the people at the Librairie Clarté wrote to me a second time, inviting me to Paris to attend a course of lectures by distinguished speakers. I knew that I would understand little of what I heard, but I went anyway. I bought four postcards at the bookshop—of Lenin, Trotsky, Lunacharsky, and Kollontai. Needless to say, I got the idea for the name Self-Enlightenment from the Society of Light. I was the first of the sixty or seventy Chinese students in Saint-Germain to subscribe to a French magazine and the first to make contact with French socialists. My fellow Fujianese considered my behavior highly eccentric and thought that there must be something wrong with me.

The Self-Enlightenment Society was a secret cabal that never developed beyond the three of us. I am not sure why we kept it secret. It was not illegal, either in France or in China. Perhaps we were afraid that people would sneer at us or pass comments. When we formed our society, the summer holidays were almost upon us. Before we could meet a second time, Wang Songlu had gone to Paris and Yin Kuan had gone to Melun. I was the only one of us left in Saint-Germain. We continued to stay in touch by letter.

During the course of our correspondence, Yin Kuan and I entered into a dispute. I forget who opened fire first. Yin Kuan contended that emotions govern reason, and I argued the opposite. Yin's position led him to approve of religious fervor. He said that people needed religion. I, on the contrary, argued that religion was a disaster for humanity. So the debate came to center on religion. Yin told me in one of his letters that he was planning to write some essays on the difference between religious rites and religious spirit. Wang Songlu mediated between us. I kept copies of my own letters, and naturally I saved Yin's. Later, when I got to know Zeng Qi in Melun, I discovered that he too was against religion. He told me that *Young China* was planning to bring out two special issues on religion, one to be edited in

China, the other in France by him. I showed him the correspondence. He wanted to publish it, but when I told Yin Kuan, Yin was against the idea. "It's too immature," he told me. I burned it, either when I left France or when I left Russia.

* * *

The work-study students were split by violent factional disputes, but the factions were based on politics, unlike the struggle between the prefectures that tore the Fujianese apart. Early on during my stay in France, I heard that there was an "eccentric" among the work-study students called Cai Hesen. He had taken his mother (who had bound feet) and his younger sister to Paris to share in his "hard work and frugal study." He never washed his face, cut his hair, changed his clothes, or paid attention to women. He was once seen with a group of people in a coffee bar. When it was time to pay the bill, he sat there without moving and let his sister pay instead. Xiang Jingyu, a student in Paris, loved him. They were already living together. Xiang Jingyu was learned, pretty, competent, and an excellent speaker. Many of the best work-study students, mainly Hunanese, were under her spell and at her command. They organized an association called the Work-Study World Society. Cai Hesen and most of his acolytes studied at Montargis Middle School.

I heard all this from others. Montargis was even smaller than Melun. It was on the Paris-Lyon-Marseilles line, an hour or so further along the track from Melun. Montargis was especially popular with Chinese students because it was run by M. Chapeau, a socialist, who was a friend of Li Shizeng and a patron of Chinese people. Later, when I went to Montargis, I met him once. A work-study student called Ouyang had died in the hospital, and M. Chapeau made a graveside speech. He was connected in some way with the rubber factory in Montargis and with the middle school, though I do not know exactly how. The work-study students used to malign him behind his back, but I don't know why.

The representatives, manifesto, and proposals of the Montargis students during the 28 Movement were quite unlike those of the rest of us. Wang Zekai was a man of rhetoric with a loud, clear voice that combined a sense of agitation and one of indignation. The Montargis manifesto said that work-study students had a right to exist and a right to study, and that the Chinese government should support us. This amounted to a frontal attack on the work-study ideal and the principle of self-reliance, for it was becoming clear that it was not possible to rely on one's own labor, to scrimp and save, and eventually to go to school and return to China after finishing. When the Montargis proposal became known, not only did the minister and the consul shake their heads, but so did the people from the Sino-French Association.

Even some of the work-study students shook their heads. The association bulletin rebutted the proposal, as did many of the duplicated news sheets put out by students in the different towns and cities. These people stuck by their anarchist ideal of hard work and frugal study. They saw labor as sacred and thought that it was shameful to live and study on the backs of others. They saw the Montargis proposal as parasitism.

This anti-Montargis group had no particular center. Its leaders were the Sichuanese Zhao Shiyan, the Hunanese Li Longzhi (who later changed his name to Li Lisan), Xiong Zhinan and Wang Ruofei from Guizhou, Wu Ming, and also perhaps Luo Han. The two sides clashed furiously in print and in speeches. The antis often changed their point of view, but the Montargis people stuck to their guns throughout. Each side tried to defame the other, for example, accusing it of being in someone else's pay.

Yin Kuan was connected to the Montargis group. Either he had a meeting with the leaders of the group during the 28 Movement or he went to Montargis at a later date and met Cai Hesen; Wang Songlu was from the same place as Xiong Zhinan, a leader of the anti-Montargis faction. I had nothing to do with this particular conflict, for my "right to exist" and my "right to study" were guaranteed by my official scholarship and money from home. But in May or June 1921, three or four months after the 28 Movement, Xiong Zhinan came to Melun to see Wang Songlu, Yin Kuan, and me. He told us that he wanted to organize a society to exchange books and magazines and was inviting Chinese students everywhere to join it. He wanted people to make lists of what they had and then to arrange by post to swap and borrow. This was the first time I had come across such an organization, but I agreed to join. Naturally, Wang Songlu joined. Yin Kuan hesitated at first, but he too agreed to go to Paris that same day. The meeting was held in Xiong Zhinan's room. He painted porcelain in a factory in Saint-Cloud, in the southwestern suburbs of Paris, where there is a beautiful palace with a hill and woods. Xiong Zhinan lived in a *pension* at the foot of the hill. It was there that I first met Zhao Shiyan, Wang Ruofei, Wu Ming, and many others. Yin Kuan kept quiet for most of the meeting, but just before the end of it, he stood up and declared that he had come just to listen, not to join. Everyone reacted with surprise, but only for a while. Afterward, I learned that the meeting had something to do with the campaign against the Montargis group, with whose members Yin was on friendly terms. But to this day, it beats me why Yin came "just to listen."

When I received the stenciled membership list, I saw many familiar names, for example, Li Longzhi and Xiong Xiong. My three books in the catalogue—Laozi, Zhuangzi, and Liezi—provoked sneers from Xiong Zhinan. Actually, others had listed the same titles, but my pirate editions of the Shidetang imprint were the best.

Several months after this meeting—I cannot remember whether it was before or after the Lyon campaign—I received a very pessimistic letter from Xiong Zhinan, asking to borrow my three books. I posted them, and he replied, thanking me. The tone of his letter was still extremely pessimistic. A short while later, I heard that he had been taken to the hospital. Apparently, he had fallen in love with a French girl and agreed to meet her on such-and-such a day in front of a railway station somewhere in Belgium to get married in the nude, but she failed to turn up. He had then come back to France, got drunk in a café at the border, and refused to pay, saying, "Why should I pay you?" It was then that he went mad.

Actually, this anecdote was something of a fairy tale. Later, I asked Zhao Shiyan about it. He said that he didn't know, but that the last time he had met Zhinan, he had thought him a bit strange in the head.

During the Lyon campaign, the two factions worked together; what brought that cooperation about, I'm not sure. Cai Hesen and his wife Xiang Jingyu, as well as Luo Xuezan, Li Longzhi, Wu Ming, and Luo Han, were all deported as a result of the campaign.

After the Lyon campaign, the remnants of the two factions, having already begun to cooperate, merged into one organization. So a new unitary chapter began in the life of the Chinese in France. Even I climbed down from my bookworm's attic to join in.

* * *

Cai Hesen's secret was Marxism. In the French course at Baoding (or Beijing), others concentrated on learning how to speak; he, however, paid sole attention to learning how to read. After just a few days of learning French, he started reading theoretical publications, with the aid of a dictionary. I do not know exactly what books he read. In those days, all sorts of socialist ideas were current in China, particularly anarchist ideas. Apparently, Cai Hesen became a Marxist even before leaving China.[51] In short, he was the first Marxist among the work-study students and among overseas Chinese of any description. You could say that he was the founder of the Communist movement that later emerged among Chinese in France. At Montargis Middle School, other students were busy planning how to save money to finance their further education and worrying about which subjects would be useful for getting into a university or a technical college. Cai Hesen, meanwhile, spent his time diving into dictionaries and reading the newly published French translation of Lenin's *State and Revolution* and similar texts. He and others close to him pointed out that the concept of hard work and frugal study was an illusion, a fraud; they decided early on what attitude to take toward the struggle of the work-study students. Although their proposals did not get majority support—and, on the contrary, provoked fierce opposition—they were very influential among Chinese circles overseas. Under the pressure of events, opponents of Cai, such as Zhao Shiyan, Li Longzhi, and Wang Ruofei, gradually came around to Cai's way of thinking and accepted his proposals—or at least his main proposal, which was Marxism.

After the Lyon campaign, the factional struggle stopped. The main leaders of the anti-Montargis group became Marxists. The Chinese Communist Party had already been founded,[52] and Zhang Songnian (who later called himself Zhang Shenfu) was its European correspondent. He and Liu Qingyang lived together in Germany as husband and wife. Zhang and Liu were not work-study students but self-financing. They had come to Europe on the same boat as work-study students, however, and had later transferred to Germany. Zhang and Liu got to know each other on the boat, and there was much salacious gossip about them. Later, they married. After the May Thirtieth Movement in 1925, they were attacked in the Beijing press, and Zhang had to write a letter to the *Chenbao* (or some similar newspaper) in self-defense.

Zhang Songnian introduced Zhao Shiyan to the Chinese Communist Party, and Zhao became its correspondent in France. Under Zhang's direction, Zhao started organizing for the Communist Youth in France. In June 1922, he set up its founding congress. I was among the eighteen delegates.

* * *

Here I must pause to explain how it was that I came down from my attic.

Chen Jiongming had already ceded to the Beiyang warlord Li Houji the part of Fujian that he had occupied and had led his Guangdong Army back to Guangdong, where he chased Lu Rongting's Guangxi Army back to Guangxi.[53] Although the northerners took back southern Fujian, they continued paying subsidies to those of us studying in France. My father collected three hundred dollars a year from the county yamen, right through the time I left Moscow and returned to Shanghai. He posted one installment to me and even added some money of his own, though it was less than the three hundred dollars he was supposed to send. Later, however, he kept the money. Some people in Zhangping blame him for that, but I forgive him. I was unlikely to starve to death without the money, and even if he had sent it, I still could not have got into a university or a technical college, for the cost of living in France had shot up in the meantime. But three hundred dollars meant a lot to a big family back in China, and it set my mind at rest to know that it was available to them.

In late 1921, I was still expecting to get my money the following year. One other student from Fujian was in the same position as I; another had put his money in the Sino-French Industrial Bank and got into difficulties when the bank went into liquidation. At that time, Lyon University had already started accepting students. Lyon University was not against accepting Chinese students in France in principle, nor was it against accepting work-study students; the only qualification one needed was the ability to pay the fees. Some fee-paying students had already passed the examinations and enrolled, among them one or two who were short of funds and had promised to pay their fees as soon as their remittances arrived. Two of the students at Lyon University who had come directly from China were from the same place as Wang Songlu; it was through them that we learned about this. Wang Songlu and we three Fujianese hoped to solve our problem in the same way, by promising to pay as soon as our money arrived. I was chosen to go to Lyon to scout things out. Armed with an introductory letter from Wang Songlu, I sought out his two contacts and learned that the students without funds were special cases, but if we moved to Lyon, we might find some way of achieving our aim. I took this information back to Melun. The general opinion was that although rents in Lyon were higher than those in Melun, other living expenses were more or less the same, so we decided to move there.

In early January 1922, we rented accommodations near the university. We got to know some students who had recently arrived from China. To us, they seemed like a new breed of student: affable, courteous, content, and fond of talking about how science and industry would save China. I felt that there was a high barrier between us and them. There was no such barrier between us and the students at Lyon who had come on work-study schemes. Outside the university, there were some work-study students who had come to take care of unfinished business in the wake of the defeat of the movement. In a coffee bar at the entrance to the university I met Liu Bojian, a pock-marked fellow from Sichuan. Being the work-study students' representative, he despised those who had enrolled at the university.

Once, a few others and I met Wu Zhihui, dean of the university, in the university courtyard and demanded that he let us enroll even though we could not yet pay our fees, but he refused. Wang Songlu said that he knew the registrar, Chu Minyi, and invited us to go along with him to meet Chu. We met Chu in his office, and Wang said nothing about enrolling. All he said was: "We have no food to eat, we want you to do something about it!" Chu replied that he could do nothing. Wang banged on the table and called Chu a rascal. Chu, too, banged on the table. Liu Hou, former secretary of the Sino-French Education Committee, tried to calm things down. Chu went into a side room, and Wang stormed out, still cursing. We three Fujianese had not uttered a word, for Wang had failed to tell us that he had come with the intention of causing a row. He was merely reflecting the anger of the great mass of work-study students.

After the defeat of the Lyon campaign, the work-study students hated university officials such as Wu Zhihui, Chu Minyi, and Zeng Zhongming. They also hated Minister Chen Lu, whom they believed to be the source of the idea to deport them. There were also conflicts between the university and the minister's office. The minister represented the Beijing government; the university had historical connections to the southern Guomindang government. Which side was the more contemptible? In my view, Wu Zhihui. The idea of work-study was his creation, and two to three thousand passionate youngsters had believed in him. They had scraped together the money to get to France, and now they had neither work nor any means of earning a livelihood. Having got back the Boxer indemnity fund, Wu was not prepared to enroll them. The decision of the French parliament to hand back the money had been made under the pressure of public opinion, which had been greatly influenced by the presence of two to three thousand work-study students in France. But no one ever intended to assassinate Wu Zhihui, whereas someone did assassinate Chen Lu.

The Sichuanese Li Heling (who later changed his name to Helin, which was written with simpler characters, thus saving himself no fewer than twenty-seven pen strokes each time he wrote it) was young, handsome, clever, and articulate; he was a first-class writer and an anarchist. He wanted to kill Chen Lu and spent several months preparing his attempt. He got someone to introduce him to Madam Zheng Yuxiu, whose secretary he became. Then he waited for his chance. Madam Zheng was a *politicante* who later became chief justice of Shanghai District Court. Many people knew her. Her Paris salon was constantly full of politicians in or out of office who were visiting France. One day, Chen Lu had dinner in her home. On his way back by car, a shot rang out behind him. It missed him and hit someone else who was newly arrived in France on a mission for the Beijing government, but the wound was superficial. Later, Li Helin said that when he saw at the banquet how lovingly Chen Lu behaved toward his daughter, it affected him, so his shot went wide. Li Helin was sent to prison for nine months and then deported to Belgium. His article on the incident was published in the Commercial Press's *Xuesheng zazhi* (Students' journal), edited by Yang Xianjiang. It's probably available somewhere in one of the big libraries. Later, I shall have more to say about Li Helin. As for Chen Lu, even though he did not die that time, a few years ago he was shot dead at a banquet in Shanghai while serving as minister of foreign affairs in the pro-Japanese puppet government.[54]

Li Helin brings to mind the Russian nihilists and the articles by Lenin and Trotsky opposing individual terror. Li's attempt to assassinate Chen Lu was a clear expression of disillusionment after the defeat of a mass movement; but there can be no doubt that even had Li's bullet found its mark, it would have made no difference.

The defeat of the Lyon campaign sped the unification of the Marxists. The arguments were no longer about work-study but about *isms*.[55]

Anarchism. Here I do not mean the anarchism that had got its hands on the Boxer funds, but the anarchism that grew up among the work-study students. After the defeat of the Lyon campaign, students in each region received a mimeographed publication called *Gongyu* (After work) brought out by Li Zhuo, Chen Yannian, and others. This was the first-ever publication by work-study students. Earlier, there had been only stenciled manifestos, open letters, and the like voicing individual or group opinions. *After Work* was warmly welcomed. As far as I remember, it did not clearly espouse anarchism, nor did it oppose Marxism. A few months later, after Chen Yannian and his brother had come over to Marxism, Li Zhuo continued to publish *After Work* and called Chen Yannian a traitor.

Nationalism. A long time after the unification of the Marxists, the nationalists also set up an organization that had almost certainly been long fomenting. It was the child of self-financing students like Zeng Qi.

As a serious political organization, the Guomindang really got going in China only after the 1924 reform.[56] The Communists supported it in its initial stages, and later, it became an important political force. But at that time, in 1922, there was no trace of the Guomindang among Chinese in France.

In late February or early March 1922, we three Fujian students who had moved to Lyon were living on just bread and water. I wrote to Qin Zhigu at the Montargis rubber factory. He wrote back saying that the factory was recruiting workers, so I packed my bags and went to Montargis. The factory, about a mile away from the town, employed a thousand-odd workers, most of them women and children; there were thirty Chinese, all of them work-study students. I worked in the tire section, where I was the sole Chinese; there were a few more Chinese in the raincoat section; and the rest were concentrated in galoshes and overshoes. After three or four months, the tire section contracted, and I was transferred to galoshes and overshoes, where I stayed until I left. In the tire section, I worked ten-hour days, as well as Saturday mornings, and was paid one franc an hour. In the footwear section, a piecework system applied, but only after you had worked yourself in. I produced ten pairs of boots a day. The others produced twenty-five or even thirty-five. They were three times as productive as I, but they earned only fifty or sixty percent more. Needless to say, the factory was happy about this. After one or two months, the foreman tried to get me to switch to piecework, but I refused. He told me one or two more times to switch, but I ignored him, and he left it at that. So I stayed on an hourly rate, and in that sense I was an anomaly. Every other Saturday was payday. Wage packets were invariably right, to the last centime.

I lived in a spacious wooden shed made available by the factory, with room in it for forty-odd beds, ten of which were empty when I arrived. All my roommates were Chinese. The shed was in a wood, five minutes' walk from the factory. Some Chinese preferred their comfort and rented accommodations (at about thirty francs a month) in town. It took them thirty or forty minutes to get to work. We shed people ate collectively. We chose two cooks and paid them by the hour, like in the factory. They had to account publicly for their expenditures. We each paid about three francs a day. We had bread and coffee for breakfast and meat at midday and in the evening. The food was much better than when I had been cooking for myself. The shed was free. After paying the cooks, I could still send 150 francs a month to my two friends who had stayed in Lyon. But I sent money for only a month or two. One of my friends got a remittance from his relatives in China and enrolled at a middle school in Orleans. The other came to Montargis to work in the rubber factory.

Most of the other Chinese in the rubber factory were from Anhui. Some had heard about me through Yin Kuan. Li Weinong from Chaoxian invited me to the middle school to meet the Montargis faction: Li Weihan, Xue Shilun, Wang Zekai, Wang Zewei, and another person called Zhang, none of whom attended classes any longer. I do not know why they were still living at the school. Very soon, they rented rooms in town, and after that, they came to work at the rubber factory. Soon Yin Kuan and Wang Ruofei came too. For some reason, the people in the shed stayed aloof from them and never even mentioned them, but they got on well with Li Weinong. They used to tease him mercilessly about his socialism and enjoyed making him lose his temper.

One Sunday, Xue Shilun came out from town and invited Li Weinong, Han Qi, and me to go to a forest south of the railway line. He told us that he was preparing to set up a Communist youth organization and asked if we would join. Li Weinong said that he would, and so did I after a moment's reflection. Han Qi took longer to make up his mind, but he too eventually agreed to join. Li Weinong's agreement was a formality: The real targets were Han Qi and I.

In 1931, in White Cloud Temple,[57] the head of the investigation team of the garrison headquarters in Shanghai asked me, "When did you join the Communist Party?"

"1922."

"Who introduced you?"

"Li Weinong."

"Where's Li Weinong now?"

"He led a strike in Qingdao. Zhang Zongchang had him shot."

* * *

We held our founding conference in Paris, in June. Montargis sent a large delegation, including Yin Kuan, Wang Ruofei, Li Weinong, Li Weihan, Xue Shilun, and me. We told other people that we were going to the annual meeting of the Work-Study World Society, even though the society had long been defunct. Zhao Shiyan fetched us from the Lyon railway station, and we went together to his home at 17, Rue Godfroy. Yuan Qingyun lived there too. The next day, we held a meeting in the Bois de Boulogne in Paris's western suburbs. As we were entering the woods, we met a pale-looking young man introduced to us as Ren Zhuoxuan. He led us to a swarthy-looking fellow called Chen Yannian. As we walked on, Ren pointed to a man in a yellow overcoat in the group in front and said that he was Zhou Enlai, representative of the German branch. It was the first time that I had heard the name. We reached a glade where a couple of dozen steel-framed chairs were waiting. We arranged them in a circle and sat down.

There were eighteen of us. Can I remember all the names? First, there was Zhao Shiyan, of course, and his fellow townsman and roommate Yuan Qingyun. Wang Linghan, a cripple, from Xichong in Sichuan. The Cantonese Xiong Rui. Ren Zhuoxuan from Sichuan. Li Weihan and Xue Shilun from Hunan. Zhou Enlai, whose family was from Zhejiang but who had been brought up in Tianjin. Chen Yannian, the son of Chen Duxiu. Pockmarked Liu Bojian, representing the Belgian branch. Wang Ruofei from Guizhou. The Sichuanese Xiao Pusheng. Yin Kuan and Li Weinong from Anhui. And I. That accounts for fifteen of us. I no longer remember who the other three were. Perhaps they were Xiong Weigeng, Li Fuchun, and Lin Wei.

Zhao Shiyan presided over the morning session and Ren Zhuoxuan over the afternoon session. I forget what we did for lunch. Of the eighteen, only Zhou Enlai spoke northern Chinese. Sometimes we had to ask him to repeat himself or even to write things down before we could understand what he was saying. For example, he had to repeat the word *yunniang* (fomentation) many times before we understood it. Another word we had difficulty with was *xuanshi* (oath). When we finally did understand what he meant, almost all of us were against it. After all, we were atheists. Who would we swear our oath to? The most violently opposed was Ren Zhuoxuan, supported by me. But Zhou Enlai explained that it was necessary and important. He gave as an example Sun Yat-sen's resignation in favor of Yuan Shikai, when Sun made Yuan swear loyalty to the Republic. Later, when Yuan proclaimed himself emperor, people were able to accuse him of going back on his oath, so he could not proceed with his plan. Zhou Enlai refused to drop his proposal. When the chairman called for a vote on it, the majority was against.

But the most heated argument was about the name of the organization. Everyone wanted to call it Communist Youth Party. Zhou Enlai was against this proposal, on the grounds that we could not use the word "party," since one country could not have two parties. Moreover, our organization would be doing youth work under the leadership of the Party, so it should be called the Communist Youth League. Again, we voted; again, Zhou lost. Later, Li Weihan went back to China and discussed our joining the Socialist Youth League with its secretary, Shi Cuntong. Only then did we stop calling ourselves the Communist Youth Party and change our name to the European Branch of the Chinese Socialist Youth League.

The next day, the conference reconvened to discuss a constitution and elect officials, but I went back to Montargis the same night, and my place at the conference was taken by someone else. I cannot remember why I left early. Perhaps it was because it was difficult to get time off from the rubber factory. As far as I remember, the first session was on a Sunday. Since I had Saturday afternoons and Sundays free, I had no need to ask for leave to go to Paris, but there would have been problems had I stayed until Monday.

Five people were elected to the leading body, the name of which I have forgotten. Zhao Shiyan became general secretary; under him were Zhang Bojian, Chen Yannian, Li Weihan, and one other, perhaps Zhou Enlai. Zhang Bojian, a Yunnanese, had not taken part in the founding conference. He was chosen on the grounds that he was the leader of a large secret association that would join the new organization en masse. He was made head of the organization bureau. Li Weihan stood in for him until Zhang returned to Paris (I have no idea where he had been in the meantime). The new leaders wanted him to hand over his membership, but he kept stalling. Finally, he was unmasked as a paper tiger: There was no association, and he represented no one but himself. He was punished by being relieved of his job, which Li Weihan took over. But being infinitely resourceful, he was soon in Moscow, where he blazed the trail for the rest of us. Whether in Moscow, Shanghai, or Guangzhou, he never became important. In 1926, he died of tuberculosis in a Guangzhou hospital.

The founding of the Communist Youth Party was a big event among Chinese in Europe. The Party grew by leaps and bounds. In the period up to 1925, when almost the entire membership went back to China after the jailing of Ren Zhuoxuan, probably three to four hundred people joined the Party or the League. But at the time of its founding, it was very small. The original eighteen delegates were not chosen on a proportional basis: Anyone who wanted to take part was welcome. It is doubtful whether we had another eighteen supporters in the whole of Europe. As far as I know, the German branch had four or five members, the Belgian branch was even smaller, and of the Montargis branch, only Wang Zekai, Wang Zewei, and Han Qi had not attended; there were others in the Creusot branch represented by Xiao Pusheng, but otherwise, probably only a few isolated individuals had not been able to attend because they lived too far away from Paris or for some other reason. Chen Yannian's younger brother, Chen Qiaonian, had not attended either. The bulk of us were members or friends of the old Montargis faction together with Zhao Shiyan and his fellow provincials and friends, Chen Yannian and a few anarchists he had brought along, and those from Germany who had nothing whatsoever to do with the work-study movement.

After setting up the organization, we started up activity in various fields. Our general headquarters was in Zhao Shiyan's boarding house. We had a mimeograph on which we produced *Shaonian* (Youth) and internal bulletins. Everyone received his or her own copy of the bulletin, which was kept absolutely secret. In one issue, we all received false names that we were told to use both in the organization and outside it, including in articles for *Youth*. This was the idea of the Montargis branch, and Han Qi had proposed it.

Han Qi was from Jiangsu (probably Haimen), but he used to tell people that he was from Anhui. When the Anhui provincial government started giving its students subsidies, he got one too, since his father, Han Qibo, a well-known revolutionary, had been killed at Anqing in the early years of the Republic and counted as an Anhui martyr. When I first went to Montargis, Qin Zhigu told me confidentially that Han "has a rather complicated brain." Among us, he was probably the only one to realize that people who engage in revolution are likely to end up losing their lives. The rest of us were not unaware that revolution demands sacrifice, but our understanding of this fact was still abstract, whereas Han Qi's father had given his life for the revolution. That's probably why he soon clashed with the organization, left it, changed his name, graduated, returned to China, and became not only an engineer but (according to what I have heard) a county magistrate under the Guomindang.

Even so, his proposal was very useful. All of us in the organization changed our names. I'm sure that many young people today have heard of Wu Hao[58] and Luo Mai,[59] false names that accompanied their owners back to China. But the rest of us kicked off our pseudonyms, like dirt on shoes, before leaving France. While preparing this chapter, I had to think for a long time before I remembered that my own pseudonym was Si Lian. I formed it by changing one syllable of my assumed name, Zelian; it had no deeper significance. Many others also chose names at random. One man chose the name S.3 by picking up two leads in the printshop where he worked. Chen Yannian wanted a name that was quick to write, so he chose Lin Mu, which means "forest" and comprises only twelve strokes. But some people took a long time over their choices. Li Weinong spent several days trying to think up a name, but to no avail; eventually, he decided to call himself Chu Fu (hoe-ax) after studying the emblem on the masthead of our paper *Youth*, even though the emblem showed not a hoe but a sickle and not an ax but a hammer. Wang Zekai called himself Luo Ti (naked); he had often represented political movements in the past and been wrongly accused of various crimes, so he wanted to show that he was above reproach. Zhang Songnian called himself R, apparently an abbreviation of the English word "realist." Zhou Enlai called himself Wu Hao (which sounds like "number five" in Chinese); people said that he chose this name because he had been the fifth person to join a secret student association in Tianjin. Later, a comrade from Fuzhou, Fang Erhao (number two Fang), also chose his name for the same reason; he had been the second person to join a secret organization, and apparently he still felt that the event was worth commemorating. Zhang Bojian was called Hong Hong (red swan). In those days, names with "red" in them were very popular, for example, Jiang Guangchi (Jiang gloriously red). In Germany, Zhang had this name transcribed into English when he went to get a Russian passport. Later, in Moscow, we used to call him Hong Hong, but the students from Russia and other countries called him Hunge-Hunge. Some people's pseudonyms were clearly related to their real names; for example, Xiong Xiong called himself Qi Guang (both names meaning "big flame"). Xiao Zizhang called himself Ai Mier, and Chen Qiaonian called himself Luo Re, since most people knew that Ai's and Chen's French names were Emile and Roger (of which their pseudonyms were Chinese transcriptions). When Xiong Rui called himself Yin Chang, Yin Kuan said: "When people see it, they're bound to think it's me." Li Weihan called himself Luo Mai, which, according to some people, stood for the first two syllables of the word "romanticism." Wang Ruofei was called Lei Yin (thunderous noise), but I do not know why.

Youth was produced in large format as a sextodecimo. It had an eye-catching cover, which showed a crossed hammer and sickle and carried the slogan "Proletarians of the world, unite!" Under the title it said in smaller letters, "Organ of the Communist Youth Party." I went to Place d'Italie to watch while the first issue was being written and printed. Wang Ruofei, Zhao Shiyan, and Zhou Enlai were sitting around the table having a discussion. Someone—I cannot remember who—said that we should add the word "newspaper" to the subheading or, rather, "Newspaper of the Organ." Zhou Enlai disagreed. He said that in German, "organ" was enough, there was no need to say "newspaper." Zhou had brought the theoretical articles with him from Germany; the articles written by the people in France were about current affairs. Zhang Songnian made a list of books to read, with titles in English, German, and French. Chen Yannian, head of the propaganda department, wrote no articles himself but was responsible for cutting the stencils. His cutting was clearer than lead type, and more beautiful. It was the first time I had ever seen a mimeographed publication that could compare with a typeset one. Apart from items such as reports on Party affairs, which Zhao Shiyan cut directly onto stencils, everything else was the work of Chen Yannian.

Originally, the work-study students had no publication of their own. Sometimes, the Tours newspaper published some of their contributions, but their literary battles were waged on wax. When someone or some group wanted to publicize a point of view, they had to go to the stationer to buy two or three stencils, a bottle of chemicals, and a few sheets of special paper. First, the article was written on the special paper with the chemicals, then it was printed on the stencil, and then the stencil was used to print on ordinary letter paper. Each stencil could print forty to fifty sheets. Then the sheets were put in envelopes and posted to schools or factories where there were Chinese working, or to individuals. Such publications were, of course, irregular, rather like the circular telegrams the warlords used to send out. After the defeat of the Lyon campaign, *After Work* had started up, and now we had *Youth*, which was a comparatively attractive publication. It helped greatly in developing our political work.

The two main fields of activity apart from internal education were among work-study students and the *Huagong*—the Chinese workers recruited during the war.[60] For some reason that I have now forgotten, the work-study movement suddenly flared up again after remaining dormant for one year. Montargis published a flurry of stencils, and Chinese in other places responded by sending delegates to Paris to organize a Work-Study Association. They elected some officials to staff the association office, among them Han Qi and Ren Zhuoxuan (there were others too, but Han and Ren ran everything). They were new to this sort of work. Li Weihan, Wang Zekai, Zhao Shiyan, and Wang Ruofei did not dare show their faces, having been responsible for the movement during its previous defeat. But behind the scenes, they controlled Han and Ren. Han Qi had ideas of his own and was not willing to be someone else's cat's-paw, so he soon clashed with Wang Ruofei and either resigned or was expelled. This was a blow to our forces in the Work-Study Association.

After the hundred thousand Chinese workers had "taken part" in the war, the majority of them were sent back to China when their contracts expired, but a few thousand or even a few tens of thousands of free laborers stayed behind in France after they had served their time. The YMCA sent people to work among them. The newly established Communist organization could hardly afford to ignore this target. Zhao Shiyan, our general secretary, worked hardest at it and made friends with large numbers of Chinese workers. In one issue of *Youth*, Zhou Enlai wrote an article about our trade union work among them.

Chen Qiaonian worked in a glass factory near Place d'Italie. Quite a few other Chinese worked there too, including some comrades, one of whom had his middle finger cut off by a machine. Zhao Shiyan and Chen Yannian were kept by the organization. Those of us who were working used to pay dues to the Party, a few francs a month—I cannot remember exactly, but not just a nominal amount. Every time I went to Paris I visited them, but I never once saw them eat. Mr. Huang Qisheng went to see his nephew Wang Ruofei; when he returned to China, he praised them as Puritans. "Chen Duxiu's two sons live such a hard life! They eat nothing but bread and sauce!" This was not Chinese soy sauce but a solid mixture that was added to water and gradually dissolved into a salty brew used for flavoring. The two Chens and Zhao Shiyan really were Puritans. The *treizième quartier* was a poor people's area.

Mr. Huang Qisheng and Mr. Xu Teli were "veteran work-study students," probably in their fifties. Xu Teli often wrote articles for a lead-type newspaper (whose name I have forgotten) and used to make propaganda for his work-study students and to spur on young people. He deeply hated Cai Hesen's Montargis movement. We used to consider Xu an enemy. I believe that he was involved in the Lyon defeat. In 1927, in Changsha, he was a leader of the Guomindang left wing.[61] At around the time of the defeat of the revolution (I cannot remember whether it was before or after), he joined the Communist Party. Later, he took part in the Long March (or went to Moscow).[62] Today he is a Communist Party veteran.

During the May Fourth Movement, Huang Qisheng led a group of students from Guizhou around China. They visited Kang Youwei, Zhang Taiyan, and other famous people. When the work-study movement started, Huang brought his students to France. Probably all the students from Guizhou were brought by him. Later, someone in China wrote an article saying that while Huang was in France, he had his students write essays "On Qin Shihuang."[63] That claim is untrue. Nevertheless, all his students eventually exceeded him, and even his nephew Wang Ruofei showed no respect for his teachings. He was not like Xu Teli, who could never stop flaunting his status as a work-study student. At the time of the Lyon campaign, Huang and Shi Ying from Hubei mediated between representatives of the work-study students and Wu Zhihui, but Wu showed Huang no respect. Before I myself went to Montargis to work, Huang had already started working there. He had a small goatee and wore a top hat and a swallow-tailed suit—not exactly appropriate for life in a factory. We urged him to live with us in the shed and eat with us, and we told him that he did not need to work in the factory. He accepted our proposal. In his free time, he used to clean up for us and tidy our things. In the evenings, he talked to us about Gong Yang's commentary on the *Spring and Autumn Annals* and about modern history. When we met to discuss household affairs, he would also proffer his opinions, with great intensity and in a loud, clear voice. He was against Marxism, but when he read in Chen Duxiu's pamphlet that Marx's landlord had once confiscated his children's toys, he was immediately on Marx's side. After returning to China, he became dean of China College in Shanghai, or some similar institution.

The Montargis branch used to hold regular meetings. Mostly, we met in the woods or in the open countryside; we rarely met indoors. To this day, I clearly recall two meetings of the branch. One was when we met to say good-bye to Li Weihan, who was going back to China. He wrote a farewell letter to the comrades in Europe and asked for our views on a draft of it. The letter was very long. I forget what it said, but I recall Li walking up and down as he spoke (in those days, we used to meet standing). He gave us his views on certain comrades. Some, he said, were able but unwilling to learn, and others were willing to learn but not able; the latter held out more hope than the former.

The other time was when we discussed the question of the Communist Party joining the Guomindang.[64] That discussion took place after the debate had already started back in China. I expressed a few doubts, whereas Yin Kuan defended the policy. He used two arguments to support his case. One was that if we joined the Guomindang, we could gradually increase our forces, like a snowball rolling down a hill. Perhaps those were not his exact words, but I still recall the simile. His second argument was based on the example of the French Communist Party. Yin said that although it was public, part of it was so secret that even Party members were unaware of its existence. These arguments were designed to rebut various opinions, the substance of which I no longer recall.

We started up a research society. Li Weinong and I got some others to join, including Qin Zhigu, but the membership stayed small. We held our meetings in the shed. All the leaders who were unpopular with the shed people used to attend. Everyone was asked to raise an issue to discuss. I was asked first. I proposed that there were three possible attitudes: help the capitalists against the proletariat, help the proletariat against the capitalists, or transcend the struggle of the two classes. I had intended to clarify my own view—that we should support the proletariat against the capitalists—but the others did not wait for that. Even before I had finished speaking, they said that there were only two possible standpoints, and no third view that transcended the others. I argued that the transcendent view did exist and that it had its supporters, for example, Romain Rolland. They immediately thought that I backed this point of view and stood up one after the other to insist that such an attitude did not exist. What they should have said is that the attitude was not correct, or that it was wrong, or that it was reactionary. They left in a huff without giving me a chance to defend myself. A few days later, they criticized me at the branch meeting and said that even noncomrades had opposed this point of view. Why, then, had I supported it? I replied that I, too, opposed it and had simply raised it for the sake of discussion, but they had not bothered to hear me out and, instead, had started arguing against me. They were still not satisfied. From then on, I became known as Romain Rolland. Admittedly, I was reading *Jean Christophe* at the time, but my aim in raising the question had been to oppose Romain Rollandism.

* * *

The revolution in European thought, from the rejection of Catholic theology to the emergence of Marxism, lasted three to four centuries, during which time Europe passed through an entire historical stage, that of bourgeois democracy. In China, we ought not to and, moreover, cannot go through such a long and complicated stage to get from Confucianism to Marxism. Chen Duxiu's development during the May Fourth Movement is clear proof of that fact. I myself, after having accepted the argument against feudalism set out in *New Youth*, had only the anticapitalist *New Youth* to read. The editions of *New Youth* I got to read in France were no longer written by Hu Shi, Qian Xuantong, Liu Fu, Lu Xun, Shen Yinmo, and Zhou Zuoren but by Li Da, Zhou Fuhai, Li Hanjun, Shi Cuntong, and, of course, Chen Duxiu.[65] But what caused my thinking to develop even further was not this Marxism of the Second International imported from Japan but the Marxism of the Third International, as propagated by the magazine *Clarté*. At first, *Clarté* was a weekly news sheet, but later it became a full-fledged fortnightly on sale at every kiosk in Paris (though I had a personal subscription). H. Barbusse was even more progressive than Romain Rolland, but he rarely wrote for *Clarté*, even though he was billed on the cover as its editor. Frequent contributors included Vaillant-Couturier (who had been to China to chair a conference against imperialism), Raimond Lefèbre (who attended the Third Congress of the Third International and drowned in the Black Sea on the way back), and Victor Serge (who later joined the Left Opposition and spent many years in Stalin's prisons). They were all Communists (at the time, Barbusse had not yet joined the Party), and they were all even more progressive than Barbusse. But in the view of Marxists in France, *Clarté* was a "confused" publication. Through *Clarté*, I got to read many Marxist writings. I also read *l'Humanité* (the organ of the French Socialist Party, later of the Communist Party) and *Communist Bulletin* (edited by supporters of the Comintern in the French Socialist Party under Vaillant-Couturier). I bought a complete set of cheap pamphlets, including the *Communist Manifesto*, *Socialism Utopian and Scientific*, and some current propaganda. On Yin Kuan's advice, I conscientiously read through the *Communist Manifesto*; Yin Kuan himself had read it at the urging of Cai Hesen or someone else in the Montargis faction.

I read *Jean Christophe* to improve my French and to widen my knowledge of French literature, but how could I have accepted Romain Rollandism when

I was under the influence of Marxism? In my view, Montesquieu, Voltaire, Rousseau, and Diderot were no better than Kang Youwei and Liang Qichao.

When I first arrived in France, Liang Qichao was in Paris collecting materials for a book called *Ou you xinjing lu* (Reflections on a tour of Europe). "Western and Oriental culture" was a fashionable theme in those days. In France (and in other countries too), many Chinese students on government scholarships wrote their dissertations on this subject. Back in China, many journals (with the exception of *New Youth*) were constantly discussing the issue. Liang Shuming published his *Dong xi wenhua jiqi zhexue* (Eastern and Western culture and philosophy), which became as popular as Hu Shi's earlier *Outline History of Chinese Philosophy*. But I could work up no interest in this subject. Reading Hu's *Outline History* resolved the issue for me. There was nothing mysterious or inexplicable about Eastern civilization. I was astonished that scholars like Liang Qichao and Liang Shuming could not see this. When I think today about this attitude, I know that it was a reaction against May Fourth, one aimed at blocking thought that was newly liberated from Confucian orthodoxy and preventing it from developing quickly in the direction of Marxism. This reaction was the product not of "feudal vestiges" but of the newly arisen bourgeoisie, which—being incapable of producing its own stable ideology, of containing liberated thought within its own ideological domain for any period of time—had no choice but to seek the help of feudal notions in order to hold back the quickening movement of ideas. Sun Yat-sen, leader of the Guomindang, had the same idea. Later, Dai Tianqiu[66] tried to include Sun Yat-sen in the pantheon of Yao, Shun, Yu, Tang, Wen, Wu, Zhou Gong, and Confucius.[67] That attempt is clear proof that Sun Yat-sen shared the same opinion as the two Liangs. This fact implies certain things about the Guomindang, but to spell them out here would lead us too far afield.

The reason China has no stable bourgeois ideology is that it has no capitalist future. Chinese capitalism developed so late that it can no longer catch up with the advanced countries, in the way that Russia and Japan caught up. The Russian proletariat has already seized state power, and the proletariats of the other advanced countries have made proletarian dictatorship the order of the day, but China is still only at the beginning of its "modernization." The rapid development of the Chinese proletariat and the aid it is receiving from its brothers and sisters throughout the world will not permit the Chinese bourgeoisie to complete the path taken by the bourgeoisies of the advanced countries. From another point of view, the violence of social development has produced a violent development of thought in China. Recently, while rereading a speech by Trotsky that I translated twenty years ago, I came across a passage that is relevant to this question: "human consciousness [is] in general frightfully conservative. When economic development proceeds slowly and systematically it tends to find it hard to break through human skulls. Subjectivists and idealists in general say that human consciousness, critical thought and so on and so forth draw history forward like a tug towing a barge behind it. This is untrue. You and I are Marxists and we know that the motive power of history consists of the productive forces which have up until now taken shape behind man's back and with which it tends to be very difficult to smash through man's conservative skull in order to produce the spark of a new political idea there and especially, let me repeat, if the development takes place slowly, organically and imperceptibly. But when the productive forces of a metropolis, of a classic land of capitalism, like Britain, encroach upon a more backward country, as with Germany in the first half of the 19th century, and with ourselves on the watershed of the 19th and the 20th centuries, and at the present time with Asia; when economic factors intrude in a revolutionary way cracking the old regime, when development takes place not gradually, not 'organically' by means of terrible shocks, and abrupt shifts in the old social layers, then critical thought finds its revolutionary expression incomparably more easily and rapidly, providing there is of course the necessary theoretical prerequisites for this."[68]

That the May Fourth Movement, as evidenced in the development of my own thinking, did not pass from feudalism to socialism through a stable bourgeois democratic stage was therefore only natural and logical. The forces that initially drove us to reject Confucianism were, after all, the same forces that drove us to reject democratism.[69] We must not forget that May Fourth happened after Russia's October Revolution.

I went through intense inner struggle to step from Confucianism to democratism, but I passed almost organically from democratism to socialism.

* * *

In November 1922, I read in *l'Humanité* that the Third International was holding its Fourth Congress in Moscow. A few days later, I went to Paris, where I saw a letter that Chen Duxiu had written to Zhao Shiyan from Moscow. The letter said that Chen was representing the Communist Party and Liu Renjing was representing the Communist Youth League at the congress. He had seen how the Soviet state was already consolidated in Russia. He urged Zhao Shiyan to go back to China. Zhang Bojian had already gone to Moscow by this time, so Chen Duxiu certainly knew about the organization in France, about Zhao Shiyan, and about Zhao's fondness for working among the Chinese laborers in France. The letter also said that there were very few comrades active back in China, and—comparing workers in China with Chinese workers in France—it added that the labor movement in China needed Zhao Shiyan more. Shortly after reading this letter, I heard from people in the Party that Chen Duxiu had already negotiated for some places at Moscow's University of the East and that he wanted the comrades in Western Europe to send people to fill them. The rumor was confirmed when I was asked if I wanted to go. Of course, I said yes. In late February or early March 1923, I collected my last wage packet at the rubber factory and moved to Paris.

Before the first group of comrades set out, the Communist Youth Party held another conference in Paris. This time it was not in the woods or in the countryside but at Billancourt, in the western suburbs of Paris, where there was a hall that could be hired for meetings. Next door was the police station. Yuan Qingyun had hired the hall, saying that he was from the Chinese Students' Association. The French police did not understand Chinese, but of course we could not sing the *Internationale*.

Even more people attended this conference than the first one, for in the previous six months we had recruited many new comrades. But my recollections of it are not very clear. All I remember is that two Chinese laborers took part: Yuan Zizhen and Wang Ziqing. I remember that some new comrades got up to speak, among them Liu Bozhuang; I also remember that the conference expelled Zhang Songnian.

I cannot recall exactly why Zhang was expelled. I already knew before the conference that he had clashed with the leadership. He had planned to control the organization by manipulating Zhou Enlai and Zhao Shiyan from behind the scenes, but Zhou and Zhao were unwilling to act as his puppets. Finally, Zhang tried to use his status as Western European correspondent of the Chinese Communist Party, but it did not help him. The conference decided to expel him. During the vote, Zhao Shiyan stepped down from the chair, unwilling to take responsibility for such a move. Almost everyone voted for the expulsion. Only Zhou Enlai and one or two northerners opposed it. Zhang's most fervent opponents were Chen Yannian and Yin Kuan, but later, Zhang Songnian blamed Zhou Enlai, saying that he had secretly stirred things up against him, and he broke off relations with Zhou.

In 1923, Zhang Songnian and his wife passed through Moscow on their way back to China. Despite the incident in Paris, the "Moscow branch"[70] still received him as a comrade. Zhao Shiyan and Chen Yannian both joined in the meeting to welcome him. After he got back to China, Zhang went to Shanghai, where he attended the Fourth Congress of the Chinese Communist Party, but without voting rights. He was the last person to speak out against entering the Guomindang. After returning to Beijing, he failed to realize his ambition. Gradually, he fell into the orbit of Zhang Shizhao and became a minor official in the Education Ministry of the Beiyang government. He received a warning from the Party's Northern District Committee, but he ignored it and was finally expelled. Today, he is a member of the Guomindang's Consultative Assembly.

3

Twelve People

On March 18, 1923, we set out from Gare du Nord in Paris, armed with passports issued by the Chinese consulate. We had said that we were going back to China via Siberia. Actually, we were going to Moscow to enroll in the University of the East. Zhou Enlai traveled with us, bound for Germany. We were to be a group of twelve: Xiong Xiong and Wang Gui were already in Berlin, and Yuan Qingyun had gone ahead to Berlin to get our Russian visas. So only nine of us set out from Paris, but Zhou Enlai made ten.

Zhao Shiyan was our leader. He had just stepped down as secretary of the Communist Youth Party and was in charge of our small group. He did most of the negotiating for us, especially when English was required, for only he spoke it. Zhao was a Sichuanese, the son of a big family. His family home was in Tianjin or Qingdao. He had learned to speak northern Chinese, but he still had a Sichuan accent. I got to know many "Sichuan rats" in France. You could tell a Sichuan rat not only by his accent and vocabulary but also by his character. What do I mean by that? I think that anyone who has made friends with a Sichuanese will know what I mean, but it is very hard to put into words. I knew that Zhao Shiyan was from Sichuan as soon as he opened his mouth, but after a while I discovered that his character was quite unlike that of other Sichuanese I had known. He was a born leader: He could reconcile differences of opinion without violating big principles, he could place a person in the right job, he was vigilant, he knew how to deal with every contingency, he was a good speaker, and he was the most obvious choice to preside over meetings and deal with the outside world. I once mentioned to him that his character was different from that of other Sichuanese. He replied that he was from such-and-such a county in Sichuan, on the Sichuan border, and that its people's attitudes and behavior were more like those of other provinces; in addition, he had grown up outside Sichuan.

At that time, he was twenty-three or twenty-four years old. On the train, he tapped the homburg he was wearing and said that he had searched nearly every hat shop in Paris before finding it. He could not wear a normal-sized hat. But although his head was big, his face and body were not. His face was positively small, tapering to a pointed chin. He looked a bit like the cartoonist Ye Qianyu's Mr. Wang. I never saw him wearing glasses; his eyes, his nose, and his cheeks were plain. You could not call him handsome, but when he gave speeches he was not unattractive. He was not in bad health, but neither was he strong. I know nothing about his life before he went to France; I have an idea he studied at a middle school in Beijing and played a prominent role in the May Fourth Movement. He was friends with Deng Zhongxia and Xu Deheng, student leaders at Beijing University.

Chen Yannian and Chen Qiaonian did not look like brothers. In 1927, Wu Zhihui, ranting against Chen Duxiu and his two sons, said: "In my view, his son Chen Yannian, another called Chen Something-or-another Nian, and the father had the ugliest faces on earth. Even if they wore long silk gowns, people would still call them thieves."[71] Wu Zhihui was talking nonsense. Chen Duxiu was not ugly. Anyone who has never seen him can consult the photo on the cover of *Shi An zizhuan* (Autobiography of Chen Duxiu), published by the Oriental Book Company. A woman comrade once said that his eyes were especially likable. Chen Qiaonian was a handsome young man, not only the best-looking of the twelve of us but, in my view, the best-looking Chinese student in the whole of Moscow. Even Li Heling (who was constantly admiring himself in the mirror) could not compare with Chen Qiaonian. Chen was strong looking, and his skin was white. His cheeks were as rosy as a pair of apples. His elder brother Chen Yannian was the complete opposite. He was in poor health; he had a fat belly, spindly legs, and a swarthy complexion, with thick eyebrows and slanting eyes; and he was nearsighted. Sometimes, when you thought that he was looking at you, it turned out that he was looking at the person next to you. He was lethargic in his movements, as if unable to brace himself. After he reached Moscow, Yuan Qingyun nicknamed him "Corruption." But he was certainly not as ugly as Wu Zhihui made out. He was by no means the ugliest of the twelve of us.

Apart from looks, these two brothers also differed in other regards. Yannian loved to talk and to tell stories about the 1911 Revolution or his family. Whenever a group of people got together, you could always hear him talking in his low voice. Qiaonian, in contrast, was forever tongue-tied. He did not speak at meetings or even at private gatherings. Only when Wang Ruofei started his horseplay did Qiaonian speak or smile. Eventually, he overcame his shyness and started speaking in public. He spoke rather well, though less so than his older brother.

The two brothers got on extremely well. They had left home together and distanced themselves not only from the bureaucratic tradition of their family but also from their father. Chen Duxiu had already become famous as a rebel against the family. For several years, people everywhere had been saying that he denounced "filial piety" as "the worst of ten thousand vices"[72] and that he had organized an "anti-father league." In 1921, Chen Jiongming asked Chen Duxiu about this. Chen replied: "My sons are qualified to set up such a league, but I'm not even qualified to be a member."[73] (See Chen Duxiu's *Autobiography*.) Although his sons never organized such a league, their attitude toward Chen Duxiu before they left for France was no less antagonistic than their father's attitude toward his grandfather. The clash between father and sons was about politics. The father was a democrat, the sons were anarchists. Later, Chen Duxiu was among the first to become a Communist; while in France, the sons too retreated from anarchism to communism, and as a result, both sides completely overcame their mutual alienation. Qiaonian went along with everything Yannian did. Yannian's conversion had a big impact on the Chinese anarchists, even in Southeast Asia and the Americas.

The two brothers were Puritans. They ate poorly, dressed poorly, and never showed the slightest interest in women. Yannian died a virgin. The first time I ever heard Yannian express dissatisfaction with his younger brother was when Qiaonian started living with Shi Jingyi in Beijing. Qiaonian was everyone's "younger brother." Yannian called him *frere*, as we did too. After we got to Moscow, we called him *Yabloko* ("apple" in Russian), on account of his rosy cheeks. (There may have been another reason, but I forget.) That year, Yannian was twenty-five, and Qiaonian was twenty-two.

Wang Ruofei's age was hardest to estimate. At first glance he seemed to be the same age as the rest of us—that is, in his mid-twenties—but if you looked carefully at his wrinkles and his stained teeth, and if you took into account his experience and behavior, he was clearly older. He was around thirty, certainly no younger than twenty-eight. He had learned a lot about political dirty tricks from his uncle Huang Qisheng and the other Guizhou politicians, but he was an able person and no less loyal to communism than youngsters fresh from school. He was short, with a squat neck, plump fingers, a slightly twisted nose, and white skin. He spoke Guizhou-style Mandarin. He was fond of drinking, like me, and liked to joke. He was boisterous and fun-loving and was the most interesting of the twelve.

The second most interesting was Yuan Qingyun. He too was boisterous and playful, but unfortunately, he was afflicted, like me, with a stammer. He was a typical "Sichuan rat," with all the strengths and weaknesses that epithet implies. He was Zhao Shiyan's friend and they had become Communists together. As far as I know, this conversion was not just based on the fact that they came from the same province but resulted from genuine political and intellectual conviction. Yuan was a tall man, lively and extremely popular. He especially liked to make friends with foreigners. Despite his stammer, he was not afraid of speaking. In Moscow, he learned Russian sooner than I did. It was he who found the meeting place for the second conference of the Communist Youth Party, next to the police station. He was the most often criticized in the Party's Moscow branch.

Yuan Qingyun's fellow provincial Wang Linghan was an even more typical Sichuan rat. He was a cripple. He joined every organization that Zhao Shiyan joined, so he ended up in the Communist Youth Party. He loved to hold the floor at meetings, but he tended to ramble. At a meeting of the Montargis branch, Yin Kuan said that at the founding conference some people had not yet grasped in what ways this new organization was different from the old ones. The example he gave was Wang Linghan.

Zhao Shiyan, Yuan Qingyun, Wang Ruofei, and the Chen brothers lived in Paris, so they were already waiting there at the time of our departure. I had met them several times during my visits to the capital and knew them well. Wang Linghan did not live in Paris, but I had met him once at the founding conference.

The three people I am about to describe were new to me, for they lived in the provinces. However, I had met them at the second conference before setting out for Moscow.

She Liya was a Hunanese, tall, broad-framed, enthusiastic, and strong. In that regard, he was a typical Hunanese, but there was no trace of the Hunanese character as represented by Cai Hesen, Li Weihan, and Wang Zekai. He rarely spoke at meetings, for he lacked systematic views of his own; he bowed to the leadership of others and loyally carried out the missions entrusted to him.

Gao Feng was also from Hunan and was also enthusiastic and strong, but unlike She Liya, he loved to discuss theoretical questions, from the origins of the universe to philosophies of life. None of the rest of us was interested in such questions, which rather disappointed him. I knew his name even before I knew him, for he had published an article or a letter in the internal bulletin proposing that we set a date for declaring war on the ruling classes and starting the insurrection.

Inseparable from Gao Feng was Chen Jiuding from Henan, the only northerner among us twelve. Gao and Chen had worked in the same factory, and because they both liked discussing worldviews and outlooks on life, they gradually became firm friends. Even their names were inseparable. We often said Gao Feng and Chen Jiuding in one breath, as if they were one name, not two. Gao Feng was a sturdy peasant type, whereas Chen Jiuding was thin, short, and pigeon-chested.

These eight (including Yuan Qingyun, who was in Berlin waiting for us), together with Zhou Enlai and me, left Paris by train for Germany. Our tickets were valid for three days, which meant that we could leave the train en route as long as we got to Berlin in time. There was a branch of the University of Labor in Charleroi in Belgium, and the comrades there had written, asking us to visit them, so we went. Liu Bojian, Xiong Weigeng, and others organized a meeting to welcome us. They showed us the university and the town, and we went out into the countryside for a photo. I forget whether we stayed in Charleroi overnight, but early the next morning we arrived in Cologne and changed the same afternoon to another train, so I know for certain that we did not stay the night in Cologne. But we did visit the famous Cologne Cathedral. Cologne is not far from the Belgian border, but when we got off the train, it was as if we were in another world. First, the language was different. In France and in Belgium, everyone spoke French, so there was no problem, but once we reached Germany, we were at a loss, for none of us spoke German. Although Zhou Enlai was resident in Berlin, he spoke German worse than we spoke French and could handle only the simplest things, such as ordering food and paying bills. One restaurant bill in Cologne came to fifty or sixty thousand marks. We were astonished. This was only the first stage of inflation in Germany—in October it got much, much worse. But when we reached Moscow, one small loaf of bread cost seven million rubles!

In Berlin, we stayed separately in several small groups. I stayed in Xiong Xiong's place, at Kantstrasse in Charlottenburg. Charlottenburg was also known as New Berlin. To get to old Berlin you had to pass through a forest, but there was an underground and also an aboveground railway. In France, I had never lived in such a splendid house. None of the work-study students, semiofficial students, or self-financing students had ever, as far as I know, lived in such beautiful accommodations. The landlady was an army officer's widow. Her daughter, who was engaged to be married, used to play the piano every day in the drawing room. To supplement their income, they rented out their best rooms to foreigners. I forget what they charged, but converted into francs, it would have rented a room fit only for a work-study student. Xiong Xiong cooked for himself. He lived very modestly, quite out of keeping with his grand surroundings. He had originally lived in France and had supplied Li Heling with the pistol Li used when he tried to assassinate Chen Lu. After the attempt, Li fled to Germany, but in his depositions to the police, he avoided implicating Xiong. The incident had a romantic, anarchistic flavor.

By the time I arrived in Berlin, Xiong Xiong had already joined the Communist Party. He recounted the events to me with an air of self-satisfaction. He had no idea that Marxism opposed individual terrorism. To tell the truth, he never learned what Marxism was about. He was childishly naive: sincere, innocent, pure, ardent, and immature. He pursued everything that was new and revolutionary and made friends with everyone who was fervent, brave, and rebellious, but he lacked judgment and was unable to distinguish between Marx and Kropotkin. He always wore hunter's clothes and long boots. A whip hung in his room. Every day, he would copy stone rubbings of the works of famous calligraphers in big and small characters, for example, Yue Fei's *Manjianghong ci*.[74] He rose early, and if it was snowing, he would go far out into the countryside before dawn to walk across the snow. He was terrible at languages and even spoke Chinese with a strong Jiangxi accent. Later, in Moscow, if you ever asked him a question during classes or discussions, he would stand up wide-eyed and wide-mouthed and finally say: "I've forgotten."

Yuan Qingyun and Wang Ruofei stayed in Wang Gui's lodgings. Wang Gui, a Hunanese, spoke fluent German and was our sole interpreter. Without him, we would have been mute. Zhao Shiyan said that he understood some German because it often sounded like English. He wanted to study German, but no one else was interested. We were simply passing through Germany. Our only reason for stopping in Berlin was to get Russian visas. There was no Soviet representative in Paris, for at that time, France had not yet recognized the USSR. Berlin was the obvious alternative. Wang Gui knew some Comintern officials through connections bequeathed by Zhang Bojian and Xiao Zizhang, who had already left Germany. The visas took many days to get, so we had plenty of time on our hands. Wang Gui and Zhou Enlai took us to the museums, the zoo, and various famous and historic sites. One day, we went to Potsdam, where there is a palace built in the manner of Versailles, but far less impressive.

Zhou Enlai also took us to a Chinese restaurant. The restaurant was not a shop on a street like most restaurants but in a private house. The waitresses were all Germans. The menu was in Chinese and German, and each dish had a number by which you ordered it. We met several Chinese students there and got the chance to read some newspapers posted out from China. Indignantly, we read the reports of Wu Peifu's massacre of striking railway workers on the Beijing-Hankou line.

Zhou Enlai took us to the Chinese restaurant for a meeting. Since Zhou's return to Berlin, Zhang Songnian and his wife had snubbed him, and they would not meet us, either. Zhou Enlai called a meeting of the German branch of the Youth League to explain his attitude about the decision to expel Zhang Songnian. The German branch was quite small. Perhaps it had some members outside Berlin, but in Berlin there was only one other person (whose name I forget) besides Zhang and his wife, Zhou Enlai, Wang Gui, and Xiong Xiong. This person arrived late at the meeting and said nothing. Zhou Enlai defended himself vigorously. Xiong Xiong and Wang Gui naturally agreed with him. The other comrade raised some simple questions and then fell silent again. Clearly, he did not agree with Zhou. After we had left

Berlin, this comrade withdrew from the Communist Youth Party.

There are two ways to Moscow from Berlin: the land route, via the Polish corridor, Lithuania, and Latvia; and the sea route, from Stettin to Petrograd, and then by train to Moscow. We chose the land route. After ten days in Berlin, we resumed our journey east. We stopped in neither Poland nor Lithuania and did not get off the train until we reached Riga in Latvia. We arrived in the morning and had to wait until the afternoon or evening for the train to Russia. It was already spring in Paris and Berlin, and the trees were green, but in Riga it was still winter. We stood on an iron bridge over a river and watched large lumps of ice drift slowly by. French and German were useless here, and we spoke no Russian, but we got by on Zhao Shiyan's English. Zhao spoke to the waiter in English while we were eating in a coffee bar, and two dancing girls who understood some English came over and asked him to dance. He blushed, and after that, we often teased him about the incident. If it had been Wang Ruofei, he would not have blushed, but he could not dance either.

When we reached the Russian border, we climbed down from the train, and our luggage was inspected—for the first time. We had crossed many frontiers in the past, but only our passports had been inspected. As soon as the inspectors learned that we were bound for the University of the East, they stopped checking. This was the first time we had seen Red Army men. They were dressed in coarse cloth overcoats and peaked caps adorned with red stars. The other passengers got back on the train, but we could not do so, for we lacked sufficient money for the ticket. At the station, we were promised free tickets for the further journey, but we would have to wait for authority to be given, which would take at least a day. We sent a telegram to the Chinese students at the University of the East and spent the night in an empty railway carriage.

The Chinese students met us at the station in Moscow. Among them was Xiao Zizhang, whom we knew from France. All the others had come to Russia straight from China. There were many of them. I remember only Ren Bishi, who had a high-pitched voice, and Wang Yifei, who had a low-pitched voice. When we left the station, Wang Yifei linked arms with me and walked with his hand twined around my waist. We had never seen anyone walk like that in France or Germany or China, but in Russia it was common to do so.

Our life of travel was at an end, and a new life was beginning. We had gone from a capitalist country to a proletarian country; we had passed from factory life to a life of study, from a life of unsystematic self-study to one of set classes and curricula. We knew that we were not about to get master's degrees or Ph.D.s, for we were to live the life of revolutionaries. Ahead lay struggle, insurrection, revolution, prison, bloodshed, sacrifice.

Twelve people! But where have they ended up, those twelve?

Yuan Qingyun joined the Northern Expedition in 1926 and died of cholera in Chenzhou in Hunan.[75]

Gao Feng was arrested at Baoding in the same year and shot by the Beiyang warlords.

Xiong Xiong escaped from the Huangpu Military Academy[76] after April 15, 1927, but was seized and shot by Li Jichen.

Chen Yannian was arrested and shot by Yang Hu in Shanghai in late April or early May of the same year.

Zhao Shiyan was seized and shot by Yang Hu not long after the death of Chen Yannian.

She Liya also died at the hands of Yang Hu at around the same time.

Chen Qiaonian was arrested in Shanghai in 1928 and shot by Xiong Shihui.

Wang Linghan disappeared while working in Wuxi in 1928. He was said to have been assassinated by local strongmen, but later, it turned out that he had given up and fled to Sichuan.

I know nothing of Chen Jiuding.

I met Wang Gui once during the Wuhan period,[77] when he was some sort of army officer, but I have heard nothing of him since.

Wang Ruofei was still in Yan'an in 1937, but today I do not know whether he is alive or dead.[78]

Finally, there is me, writing about the twelve.

In the Central Military Prison, I was under the impression that Wang Linghan, Chen Jiuding, and Wang Gui were all dead, and there were rumors that Stalin had exiled Wang Ruofei to Siberia on suspicion of being a member of the Left Opposition. Needless to say, I felt even more emotional then than I do today. I thought of us as a small company of privates with Zhao Shiyan as our captain; we had marched shoulder to shoulder into the line of fire and we had all fallen, save one or two who had been captured. But now, one prisoner has regained his freedom, and though some others are gone without a trace, there is as yet no record of their death. Only seven definitely died, but even that represents more than one in two.

KUTV

KUTV, the Communist University for the Toilers of the East, also known as Stalin University, was founded in April 1921. Its main purpose was to educate workers from backward nationalities in the Caucasian and Siberian regions of the old Russian Empire, just as the Communist University for the Toilers of the West had been set up for workers from Latvia and Lithuania. Students from parts of the East outside the old Russian Empire—for example, Chinese, Japanese, Koreans, Mongols, Indians, Persians, and Turks—were in the minority. Many of these foreign students had come to Russia to take part in the Baku Conference of the Peoples of the East or the Petrograd Conference of the Peoples of the Far East; some had even been delegates to Congresses of the Third International.

The Chinese students, like us work-study students from France, had been swept to Shanghai or Beijing by the tide of May Fourth, but they had arrived a little later than we and had therefore missed the work-study wave. They were better versed than we in the new socialist thought in China. After Chen Duxiu came out of prison, he gave up being dean of letters at Beijing University and left for Shanghai.[79] These students, or at least the most progressive among them, no longer searched out people like Li Shizeng or Wu Zhihui but looked to Chen Duxiu. Chen Duxiu was running a sort of work-study scheme in Shanghai. Many of its students formed the ranks of the Socialist Youth League. The Socialist Youth League was, of course, under the leadership of the newly formed Chinese Communist Party, but at first, it was not called the Communist Youth League, for two reasons. One was that the aim was to be a public organization; the other was that some of its members were anarchists who were prepared to cooperate under the Socialist but not the Communist banner. The students who went directly from China to Russia were members of this Socialist Youth League and had come in several waves. At that time, you still had to cross territory controlled by the White Army to get to Moscow; the journey was fraught with difficulties and dangers. One group of students was detained by armed units along the way. Since they could not speak Russian, they had no way of knowing whether their interceptors were Reds or Whites. The troops searched them thoroughly and found in the heel of someone's shoe a pass issued by representatives of the Third International. It turned out that the troops were Reds, so the prisoners instantly became honored guests. Many students were delayed for long periods along the way. One group was kept in Chita or Irkutsk for several months before it was able to travel on to Moscow. Some students never reached Moscow at all but were kept in the Far East of the Soviet Union to perform various tasks.

When we arrived in Moscow in the spring of 1923, there were thirty-odd Chinese students at KUTV. Some were from Hunan, mostly students of the School of the Common People run by Mao Zedong in Changsha; others were Zhejiangers from Hangzhou's First Normal School. There were people from other provinces too, and four Chinese laborers from Siberia, including two Red Beards.[80]

These people were the ones who remained after much sifting. How many Chinese students had been at KUTV when the university opened? I do not know, but there had certainly been at least twice as many as when we arrived. They had probably been engaged in unremitting internal struggles from the moment they left China. One obvious division was between Communists and anarchists, though there were other grounds for division as well. Differences in outlook were inextricably intertwined with personal animosities; public differences were mixed with private plots and schemes. From chaos was born order; from equality were born the leaders and the led, the givers and the receivers of commands. When we arrived in Moscow, the struggle had already been resolved. The losers had been elbowed out and had left the movement after returning home. Some of the winners had also gone home, but most had stayed. We heard only the winners' version of events, but it was clear from their tone of voice that the struggle had been intense. I never got to know the losers, but from what I saw of the winners—together with inferences from the logic of such struggles and my personal experience of them—I can permit myself a comment on the contest among the Chinese students at KUTV before my arrival in Moscow. This contest, looked at from an overall point of view, was neither entirely worthless and purely personal nor an ideological struggle between communism and anarchism. Instead, it was a struggle between two types of student. One type was sensitive, lively, intelligent, many-sided, and lofty-minded; this type loved freedom and opposed authority. But such people lack stability; they are excessively flexible and given to empty talk. The other type was stubborn, self-assured, and courageous but at the same time dull, narrow-minded, superficially informed, and a worshipper of authority who easily buckled under it. In Russia as it was then, the former group was destined to lose. It would be an exaggeration to describe what happened as a class struggle. Both groups were from broadly similar class backgrounds, though there was a herdsman and a menial among the victors. The losers were somewhat more cultured than the winners.

By the time we arrived, the main struggle was already over, but it had left scars on the minds of those thirty-odd people. In the first place, they were divided into leaders and masses. The leaders gave the orders, the masses followed. The leaders behaved not like the masses' fellow students but like their teachers. However much they feigned gentleness, there was always something unapproachable about them. In France, we had also had leaders, but they had gained their status naturally in the course of their political activity (among work-study students and Chinese laborers). We genuinely recognized them as our leaders, but we also saw them as our own sort: more capable, perhaps, but nevertheless our own sort. For example, we saw Zhao Shiyan as our squad commander—as our *elected* squad commander, not our *imposed* squad commander. We saw him even less as our brigade commander, our divisional commander, our army commander, or our commander in chief. The Moscow students' view of leaders was completely alien to us. We had expelled Zhang Songnian precisely because he had wanted us to treat him like that sort of leader. But what really surprised us was the masses, with their attitude of absolute submission. They not only submitted publicly but also dared not express their dissatisfaction in private. But deeds and words apart, I could tell from various subtle signs that they were not happy. On the contrary, deep inside they were full of rancor and contempt. All this emotion was the aftermath of the great internal struggles of the previous months and years.

These struggles had thrown up three leaders: Bu Shiqi, Luo Jiao,[81] and Peng Shuzhi, all of them from Hunan. Bu Shiqi had left for China shortly before I arrived, so I never met him. When he got back to Beijing, he became entangled in a love affair with He Mengxiong's wife, Miao Boying, which created a scandal in the Party. Later, he went to Guangzhou and left the Party to work as some sort of official for the Guomindang government.

The big chief was Luo Jiao. He was from a poor peasant family in Xiangtan, but he invariably hid his background. I remember the first time I met him: He was wearing a thick hat and had more clothes on than the rest of us. He was tall and thin, with a pale complexion and a large mouth. When he talked, you could see that the inside of his lips was red and he had large teeth. When he first saw you, he would give a loud laugh and then become serious and get down to what he had to say. He loved to tell people that he was in bad health, that he was always ill, that he often had to go to sanatoria for treatment. And it's a fact that we rarely saw him. He was secretary of the Branch of the Chinese Communist Party in Moscow and a member of the presidium of the KUTV branch of the Russian Communist Party. He represented the Chinese students to the outside world. Foreigners called him Bukharov, but we Chinese continued to call him Luo Jiao.

Second fiddle was Peng Shuzhi. Peng was short and dark. He wore leather clothes and a flat leather cap. He was hard to understand, for he spoke with a heavy Baoqing accent. He insisted on speaking whenever we met, and at great length. He was a bookworm. As a child he had worshipped Wei Moshen,[82] an illustrious son of Baoqing, and his personal ambition had been to become (like Wei) a commentator on the Confucian classics. After May Fourth, he put aside his stitched volumes and began reading magazine translations and exegeses of the essays of Dewey and Russell; later, he became a Marxist (though I do not know under what circumstances).[83] He was the most cultured of the Moscow victors. During the great struggle, he had not immediately joined the victors. At first, he had been pushed aside by them, and it was some time before he stood shoulder to shoulder with them. Luo Jiao called him "Confucius," a nickname that was supposed to represent both his culture and the contempt with which the victors viewed people of learning. We did not dare call him Confucius to his face; instead, we addressed him as Comrade Shuzhi. Foreigners called him Petrov.

Luo Jiao inhabited the lofty heights and saw little of us. Peng Shuzhi was the opposite. Although he lived in separate quarters, he often dropped in for individual chats with those of us who had come to Russia from France. He would visit each of us in turn. He gave the impression of being an old-style middle school supervisor (today called an "overseer of students' behavior").

Apart from Luo and Peng, the rest of us were "rank-and-file masses." True, there were some special people, but the great majority were absolutely submissive. Wang Yifei and Ren Bishi were in charge of the Youth League, but in everything, no matter how big or small, they had to seek permission; they had no freedom of action whatsoever. Wang Yifei, from Zhejiang, had studied at Hangzhou's First Normal School. He was short in stature and mediocre in personality. He spoke and wrote Russian rather well. He had no Russian name and was listed in the register as Wang Yifei. Ren Bishi, a Hunanese, was like a small child. He was given the Russian name Belinsky (after the famous Russian critic), but people invariably got it wrong and called him Prinsky instead. Few of the other students from Hunan and Zhejiang were remarkable in any way.

Among the special people I mentioned earlier was Li Zhongwu. Li was the pampered son of an influential family, the nephew or some such relative of Liang Qichao. He had studied with Qu Qiubai at the Russian Language School in Beijing and had come to Russia with Qu Qiubai as a journalist. Qu had gone back to China, but Li stayed on to study at KUTV. He spoke excellent Russian and adapted brilliantly to his surroundings. Later, back in

China, he acted as interpreter for General Galen. Not long after that, he resigned and went to Haining to get married, and we saw nothing more of him. In 1926, we tried to track him down, but without success.

Another was Peng Zexiang, from Yuezhou. He had come to Russia from Beijing. He always wore a closed-neck jacket. His style was in every way that of an opportunist Chinese politician. We all found it odd to have such a person in our midst. I learned later that when he first arrived in Russia, he had been a member of the Jinri (Today) faction and had written articles for it, though he had already "renounced" Today's politics. His nickname was "Fascist"; we even called him that to his face. He was able and knowledgeable. On one occasion, he started talking with me about Hu Shi's *Outline History of Chinese Philosophy*. He said that he wanted to write a history of Chinese philosophy based on an economic analysis. He could have become the leader of an opposition (i.e., to Luo Jiao and Peng Shuzhi), but he lacked mass support. Apart from this, the leaders viewed him as exceptional. Soon, after the reorganization of the Youth League, he was made "training organizer." After his appointment, he started summoning us for individual lectures. He acted more like a judge at a court martial than like a supervisor.

Of the four Chinese laborers, two adapted and two did not. Those who did not had been Red Beards. Eventually, they rose in open revolt and were sent to Vladivostok to work.

The real oppositionists were Jiang Guangchi and Bao Pu. They were the remnants of another sort of student. You could see at a glance that they were by nature incompatible with the rest. We lived at 15 Tverskaya Street, but these two lived by themselves in the convent near Pushkin Square. They were intelligent and lively, unlike both the Hunanese and the Zhejiangers. Jiang Guangchi was from Lu'an in Anhui, and Bao Pu was from Wuxi in Jiangsu. Jiang was the only poet among us, Bao the only Esperantist. They both spoke good Russian and could communicate directly with the Russians; they did not need Luo Jiao to represent them. They deliberately stayed away from meetings. When we met them, we may have exchanged a joke or two, but we never talked about anything serious. A few months later, Bao Pu returned to China. He wrote a letter from Vladivostok attacking Luo and company and even attacking communism. But the "Moscow branch" had already decided to expel him before he wrote the letter, for secretly inciting the two Red Beards to oppose the leadership. At a meeting the following year, just before he returned to China, Jiang Guangchi also came out as an oppositionist. He said that we would have to wait until we got back to China to see who the real Party loyalists were.

When Jiang got back to China, he was definitely not a good Party member. At first, he continued to work in the Party; later, however, he became a litterateur—albeit a "revolutionary" litterateur. Luo Jiao and Peng Shuzhi became important cadres of the revolution, and we students from France also provided a large number of revolutionary cadres. But almost all the students (save Luo and Peng) originally in Moscow, especially the absolute submitters, disappeared from sight, with the exception of Ren Bishi and Wang Yifei.

* * *

The twelve of us first arrived in Moscow during the spring holidays. The KUTV students were preparing to go on a trip to Petrograd. We hurried through the registration procedure so that we could join them.

In connection with registration, I should say something about our names. Either because our Chinese names were hard to remember or for some other reason, the registrar Vaks gave each of us a Russian name. According to Li Zhongwu, who interpreted for us, our new names were based on those of the twelve members of the Petrograd Soviet Executive arrested in 1905. Zhao Shiyan was Radin, Chen Yannian was Sukhanov, Chen Qiaonian was Krassin, Wang Ruofei was Nemchev, Yuan Qingyun was Yanovsky,[84] Xiong Xiong was Silverstrov, Chen Jiuding was Shiskin, and I was Marlotov. I forget what the other four were called.

On the train and in Petrograd, we gradually got to know the students who had gone to Moscow straight from China. We stayed on the second floor of the Smolny Institute. We discovered only later that this had been Trotsky's command post in the October Revolution. Petrograd was neater and cleaner than Moscow. We visited the Winter Palace, the Peter-Paul Fortress (which was empty), some factories, and a museum containing some futurist paintings. We saw a play (Molière's *Le bourgeois gentilhomme*) and went outside the city to visit Tsarskoeselo. We walked along the Nevsky Prospect almost every day. We knew little at the time about the events of the revolution, so the places we visited left no great impression on us.

When we got back to Moscow, the spring holiday was over and we began our studies. The curriculum covered economics, historical materialism, the history of class struggle, the history of the labor movement, the history of the Russian Communist Party, natural science, and Russian language. As far as I remember, that was all. Most of us had learned the Russian alphabet in France, and I had got halfway through a Russian grammar book. Even so, our teachers began teaching us from scratch. In the first lesson, we were taught the meaning of KUTV: Komunisticheski Universitet Trudiashikhsia Vostoka—or University for the Toilers of the East. Acronyms became very popular after the Russian Revolution. They were formed by taking the first letter of every word, writing them all as capitals, and separating them by full stops (though these were optional), so you could tell at a glance whether something was an acronym or not. For example, the Communist Party of the Soviet Union was known as the CPSU and the Central Executive Council of the Union of Soviet Socialist Republics was known as the CEC-USSR. (This is how the Guomindang, or Kuomintang as it was then spelled in Western languages, came to be called the KMT.) Another fashion was to join the first syllables of two or more words to form a combined word. Sometimes, if you did not know that you were dealing with one of these words, you could waste much time searching for it in a dictionary. Examples are Konsomol (the Communist Youth League) and Comintern (the Communist International). In our curriculum at KUTV, political economy was called *politekonom* and historical materialism was called *istomat*. Traditionalists shook their heads and said that this practice was destroying the integrity of the Russian language.

Overall, we benefited little from our Russian classes. Some of us thought that the pace was too slow, others that it was too fast. I got nothing from these classes. We learned to speak and understand Russian by practicing on other foreign students, and we learned to read by studying grammar books and learning new words by heart. Those like Chen Jiuding and Xiong Xiong, who were incapable of self-study, got nowhere, however attentively they listened to the teachers.

Apart from during Russian class, we had as interpreters Li Zhongwu, Wang Yifei, Ren Bishi, and Bao Pu. Occasionally, Luo Jiao helped out; even less frequently, Jiang Guangchi did so. Luo Jiao was usually busy with other things, and Jiang was often in the hospital. Peng Shuzhi and the others never interpreted for us; in fact, they needed interpreters themselves when they attended classes. The teachers would say something, and then the interpreter would repeat it in Chinese. This meant that one hour of teaching was actually half an hour. What's more, you could not always understand the translation, and it was not necessarily faithful. Our economics teacher was a girl and our *istomat* (historical materialism) teacher was an old woman. They treated us like schoolchildren and gave us only a smattering of general knowledge. There was a Jew called Something-stein who taught us the history of the international labor movement. He taught in French, and I was chosen to interpret. This man brought new materials and viewpoints into his lectures, and I had to concentrate hard to interpret them, so he left a deep impression on me. Unfortunately, he worked for the Profintern[85] and often arrived late—after a few months, he stopped coming altogether. (I once saw a photo of him with Lenin and some guests from Western Europe.) We never mixed in class with students of other nationalities. One reason was that few of us could understand Russian-language lectures. Another was that there were enough Chinese to form a class of our own; besides the twelve of us, another twenty or thirty arrived from France, and a dozen or so more came straight from China.

Needless to say, the university fed, clothed, and housed us. Haircuts, baths, and laundry were also free, and we could get tobacco too. Every month we got 1.5 new rubles in pocket money, which later went up to 3 rubles. It was hard to find anywhere to spend the pocket money. I spent mine on books. Some people bought chocolate with it; at most it stretched to two or three packets a month. Li Zhongwu and Peng Zexiang often ate in Chinese restaurants with money they had brought with them from China. The rest of us did not dare do so, for the restaurants were too expensive. I did not even know where the Chinese restaurants were.

A few days after we arrived, Chen Yannian told me that he had never lived so well in his life, meaning the food. By "life," he meant since he and his brother had left home. In Shanghai, they had worn unlined clothes even in the depth of winter, and I believe they cooked for themselves throughout their stay in France. Naturally, they ate poorly. As for the rest of us, we did not share their enthusiasm. True, the food was a little better than what work-study students ate in France, but when we first arrived, our bread was black rather than white and full of stalks. We had often heard people sing the praises of black bread, but once we got to know it, we found it barely palatable. At first, we were constipated for three or four days—in some cases, for a week. It was a month or two before our bowels settled. The veterans told us that we had nothing to complain about, that when they had first arrived there had been even more stalks in the bread, the food had been even worse, and there had never been enough of it. After our first summer in Russia, we gradually started getting white bread, and the year after that, we stopped getting black bread altogether. You could also see from the improved clothes that things were getting better in the Soviet Union. The first year, we wore thick Red Army hempen overcoats and Red Army peaked caps of all different shapes and sizes; the second year, we wore more or less uniform homespun black trousers and overcoats, though still of rough material. At first, people used old rubles on the streets, in denominations of hundreds of thousands and millions, but later, the new ruble came in and *chervonets* were used.[86]

Kitchen duty was a particular drudgery. Apart from Luo Jiao, everyone had to do it, even Peng Shuzhi. We used to take turns once every three weeks or so. You had to get to the kitchen before dawn to cut firewood, peel potatoes, fetch bread from the storeroom, and slice the bread. Three times a day you had to put on your white smock, lay the tables, dish out the soup and food, and keep a smile on your face while people shouted at you from all directions. After serving seven or eight sittings, you were allowed to eat. You could sleep for an hour or two after lunch, and you were finally released at eleven o'clock at night.

For entertainment, there were free films and sometimes free tickets for plays or operettas. In springtime, we went on outings to Sparrow Hill in the western suburbs, where Napoleon is said to have watched Moscow burn.

What did the Russian people think of us foreign students? Once Bao Pu met some ordinary citizens while he was at a hospital outside the college. According to him, ordinary people resented us. They said that the Soviet government was giving foreign students Russian people's bread and money, and that the Russians were starving as a result.

* * *

The Chinese students at KUTV formed a separate unit. True, the Japanese, Korean, Indian, Turkish, and Persian students also tended to stick together in their own national groups, but only in the same way as Cantonese or Yunnanese stick together in, say, Beijing or Shanghai. The Chinese students, however, had their own separate political organization, known as the Moscow Branch of the Chinese Communist Party. According to the statutes of the Third International, Communists living in a country other than their own must join that country's Party. So members of the Chinese Communist Party or the Socialist Youth League in Moscow who could furnish proof and references should have joined the Russian organization rather than set up branches of their own. How did the Moscow branch come into being? Was its status legal? Was it recognized by the Russian Communist Party? I cannot answer these questions, and at the time, no one asked them—no one dared ask them. We were all members of China's Socialist Youth League, but we took no part in the KUTV branch of the Russian Youth League. In foreign comrades' eyes, we were mere sympathizers. Zhao Shiyan and Xiong Xiong were members of the Chinese Communist Party, but they had no relations with the KUTV branch of the Russian Communist Party.

In foreigners' eyes, we were sympathizers, but in Chinese eyes, we were comrades. We were divided into several cells, each with four or five members. Old and new comrades, familiar and unfamiliar comrades, were cleverly mixed. Each cell met once or twice a week, and there were plenary sessions and other sorts of meetings. Each meeting lasted two, three, or four hours. The atmosphere at them was tense, excited, and ardent. What were our activities? There were none. What theoretical research did we do? We did none. Most of the time was given over to "individual criticism." The criticism was never about specific issues but about abstract psychological attitudes: You're too individualistic, you're too arrogant, you're too petit bourgeois, you have anarchist tendencies, and so on. The ones who were criticized would think up similar criticisms to hurl back against their critics. The result was that everyone ended up blushing, and seeds of hatred were sown in people's hearts. In short, everyone learned to expose motives (*zhu xin*), like Confucius in the *Spring and Autumn Annals*, and to rectify the mind (*zheng xin*), like the Song Confucianists, but the object was to upbraid others, never oneself.

The commanding and submitting among the Chinese students and this sort of personal criticism were what I found most novel after arriving in Russia. True, Russian life was new, but I had been able to imagine it in advance. Only the commanding, the submitting, and the criticizing had been beyond the power of my imagination. Whether or not the other students from France or the students direct from China thought the same way, I do not know. I suspect that, like me, they thought that this was an experience of the Russian Revolution that we ought to emulate and take back to China with us. We all learned to adapt to the environment, to recognize established authority, and to delve deep into the innermost recesses of the mind in order to criticize others' weak spots. Zhao Shiyan, Wang Ruofei, and, later, Yin Kuan, Wang Zekai, and others who had been like tigers in France no longer dared to challenge authority. They had opposed Zhang Songnian, but they did not dare oppose Luo Jiao or Peng Shuzhi. But there was at least one difference between us newcomers and the old crowd: We may have submitted, but we never did so blindly.

Zhang Bojian, now called Hunge-Hunge, was the first person to resist. He was often ill and in the hospital, so he rarely attended classes with us. He came out against Luo Jiao and wrote letters cursing him and demanding that he answer. We knew about this, but we had not read the letters and did not know what was in them. Luo Jiao refused to reply to Zhang Bojian. He said that literary wrangles were a bad habit of Chinese intellectuals that he did not intend to emulate. Xiao Zizhang also came out in opposition and was severely criticized. Zhao Shiyan and Chen Yannian had their own positions, but they knew how to push them through under the guise of compliance. I was the one who found it hardest to adapt. I was criticized more than anyone else at cell meetings. I accepted most of the criticisms, but there were two that I would never accept.

The first criticism was that I read too much, studied too much Russian, was not active enough, and did not speak often enough with other people. According to a slogan popular in the Moscow branch, we had come here not to become "academics" but for "training." Training meant meetings and criticism; academic study meant learning Russian and reading books on theory. Peng Shuzhi said: "You won't be here long. Russian is not an easy language. Fortunately, there are already people among the Chinese students who know Russian well, who know theory well, and who are experienced. It's enough to learn from them." I am convinced that had the school authorities allowed it, Peng would have proposed canceling the six hours a week we spent learning Russian. We already devoted more time and energy to meetings than to classes. What we learned in the classroom was crude and superficial, and here were people who wanted even fewer classes and more meetings. They considered it enough to read *Zhengzhi changshi* (The rudiments of politics), jointly translated by Qu Qiubai and Wang Yifei. Several copies of this manuscript had been made and distributed to us. Although I thought that this proposal was unreasonable, I did not openly oppose it. I simply carried on with my Russian and my other studies and paid no attention to the cajoling and criticizing. People gave me the nickname "Professor" in English.

The second criticism concerned my friendship with Bao Pu. When we first got to Moscow, we knew nothing of personal relations among the Chinese students. Everyone came to welcome us. We had no idea who were the leaders and the led, who were the people in power and those out of power. Chen Jiuding came from the crowd and pointed out someone called Bao Pu, who spoke Esperanto. I went up to him and said, *"Cu vi parolas Esperanton?"* (Do you speak Esperanto?) He said that he did, so we became good friends. He was the only Esperantist among the Chinese students in Moscow, and I was the only one among the Chinese students from France. Later, I found that he was more knowledgeable than other people and that he was neither unapproachable, like the leaders of the Moscow branch, nor bossy. He lived in the convent, in the same room as Jiang Guangchi and a worker comrade. Jiang was in the hospital having his eyes seen to, so I did not meet him for quite a while. It later turned out that the worker had been sent to keep an eye on the two of them. I often went there to chat for a few hours, and Bao used to take me around Moscow to see the sights. He also took me to meet some Moscow Esperantists: Polakov, Nekrassov, and a Hungarian refugee. We often went to evening parties of Esperantists or non-Esperantists.

At that time, an organization called SAT[87] (International Association of Non-Nationals) had split from the international Esperanto organization. This organization had its office in France. There were Communists in SAT, and it was sympathetic to the Soviet Union. The editor of the SAT journal had recently come back from the Soviet Union and published articles in the journal about his travels in that country. I learned a lot from those articles. I corresponded with the editor (unfortunately, I forget his name), and he set me up as a pen pal with an Esperantist worker in Paris. When I mentioned this editor to the Esperantists in Moscow, they said that they had had a visit from him just a short time earlier. They took me to see their editorial board and their printshop. Polakov wrote articles, and Nekrassov wrote poems. They set their own type and did their own printing and distribution. None of them was a Communist, but a high Communist official who was an Esperantist acted as their patron. I once heard this man give a speech in Esperanto. He had a bureaucratic manner and was not approachable like the rest of them.

Bao Pu also knew an Outer Mongolian who had relations with the Outer Mongolian government. I used to speak Esperanto with this Mongol; Bao Pu spoke Russian with him, for the Mongol's Esperanto was poor. The Mongol often looked me up at school and later asked me for news of the Beijing government. Gradually, I became estranged from him.

    It was not long before I learned about Bao Pu's position in the Moscow branch, but it made no difference to our friendship. People warned me, and at criticism meetings they obliquely criticized me. Finally, Peng Shuzhi sought me out for a private chat. He told me straight out that Bao Pu was on a dangerous political course, and he wanted me to break with him. I refused. I said that Bao was a Party member and I was only a League member. I ought to accept his leadership. If Bao was wrong, why didn't the Party put him right? Several months later, after Bao Pu had returned to China, the Moscow branch announced his expulsion. Bao Pu went back to Shanghai and wrote articles opposing communism and the Soviet Union for the *Xuedeng* (Lamp of knowledge) supplement of *Shishi xinbao* (New current affairs daily). Qu Qiubai rebutted him in the *Juewu* (Awakening) supplement of *Minguo ribao* (Republic daily), and the two men became embroiled in a long literary wrangle. In Moscow, they had been good friends. In 1925, Bao Pu went to Russia for a second time as a staff member in the Chinese consulate in Vladivostok. After that, I heard nothing more of him. On August 29, 1937, when I was being released from Nanjing's Central Military Prison, someone handed me a letter as I passed the reception desk. It was from a person called Qin Diqing of the Guomindang's Central Propaganda Bureau. It said that this man Qin had been busy trying to arrange my release. I had never heard of anyone by that name, but luckily, there was a note on the back of the letter explaining that it was Bao Pu. I tore it up at the prison gate.

    My friendship with Bao Pu delayed my promotion from League to Party. When we first arrived in Moscow, as far as I remember, only Zhao Shiyan and Xiong Xiong were in the Party. Before the start of the summer holidays, the Chen brothers, Wang Ruofei, and Yuan Qingyun were all promoted.[88] During the vacation, down in the countryside, Luo Jiao visited me one day wreathed in smiles and invited me and She Liya to go for an outing with him in the forest. I did not go. I was a bit surprised by the invitation. Later, She Liya told me that Luo Jiao had spoken to him on behalf of the Party organization. After that, She joined. I formally joined the following year, after Lenin's death. The rest joined either at the same time as I did or later.

* * *

During the summer vacation of 1923, the entire school went down to the countryside to escape the heat. It took one or two hours by train to reach our destination, and it was another couple of hours' walk from the railway station. Finally, we arrived at the KUTV estate in a small village. I forget what the village was called, but I remember a landlord's mansion at the side of a forest. In it was a big hall with four or six rooms along the two sides. Four or five hundred paces from the mansion was a two-story house with seven or eight rooms on each floor. The Chinese students lived on the first floor of this building. Apart from this, there were some typically Russian wooden cabins called *isba*. Each day, we did several hours' physical labor on the school farm—digging, weeding, ploughing, and the like. We spent most of the time planting sweet radishes. The food was more or less the same as in the city, but we started getting white bread.

During the summer vacation, the Chinese class acquired a new member called Lin Keyi, who had come straight from China. He had studied in Japan and had then taught at a private university in Beijing. Now, he had come to Russia to study Marxism. He was not in the Communist Party but was a member of the Today group. In China, apart from the Communist Party, there was a Marxist organization that published a journal called *Jinri* (Today). Its leader was the member of parliament Hu Egong. Its rank and file consisted of some people who had studied in Japan and some Beijing bureaucrats. Today adopted a left-wing position and was against the Communist Party entering the Guomindang. *Xiangdao* (Guide weekly), replying to this attack, pointed out that Hu Egong was a parliamentary hack in the pay of the Beiyang government; Hu defended himself by quoting from Lenin's newly published *Left-Wing Communism: An Infantile Disorder* on parliamentary movements. The Third International's secret envoy in China tried to patch things up and even invited Today to send a representative to Moscow to take part in the Comintern Congress. I know little about what transpired behind the scenes. Perhaps Peng Zexiang, who came to Moscow with Chen Duxiu to attend the Fourth Congress, was the Today representative. By the time we arrived, Peng had already joined the Communist Party. Later, nearly all Hu Egong's people joined the Party, but they played no role in the revolution.

Lin Keyi was the second Today representative to arrive in Moscow. The school authorities sent him down to the countryside to stay with us. We did not know before we arrived in the village that he would be coming to join us. Peng Shuzhi hurriedly called a plenary meeting to discuss how to handle this noncomrade. He said: "Lin Keyi is a university professor. He has published articles in newspapers and magazines in China, whereas we're nobodies. Maybe he will look down on us. We must apply our collective strength to conquer him." He then assigned tasks, such as who was to talk with him and what sort of things to talk about. I was one of the handful of people assigned to do this, for, like me, Lin was a Fujianese. My mission was to discuss historical materialism with him, find out what he knew about it, and probe him about the Today group. A comrade was moved from my room to empty a bed for Lin. Lin turned out to be a white-faced bookworm, a typical Fuzhou man. As a fellow Fujianese, I looked after him. My other roommates talked with him only about things like the weather, but I sometimes steered the conversation to theoretical issues. After a few conversations, I discovered that he knew nothing about historical materialism. Other people were responsible for assessing his knowledge of economics and other subjects. When the subject got around to Today, he flatly denied having anything to do with that organization.

A few weeks later, Peng Shuzhi announced that he was going to introduce Lin Keyi into the Youth League (even though he was already more than twenty-three years old). I was in the same cell as him. At the first meeting, he confessed that he had not only joined the Today group but was also on its Central Committee. After the summer vacation, he attended classes with me. He made me think of Liu Zongyuan's short masterpiece *Qianzhi lü* (The ass of Guizhou).[89]

During the summer vacation of 1924, Lin Keyi and I were supposed to return to China. He did not want to go back, and when he got the order to return, he raised many counterarguments, all to no avail. Eventually, he packed his bags and set out with the rest of us. When we reached Chita, he asked Chen Yannian, leader of the group, if he could go with Li Zhongwu on the Chinese Eastern Railway via Manzhouli. We realized what he intended to do and proposed that he go back with the rest of us via Vladivostok, but Chen granted his request. The result was that Li Zhongwu returned to China and Lin stayed in Chita. Later, he went to Vladivostok and got mixed up with Bao Pu. After he got back to China, he wrote articles in the Beijing press attacking the Soviet Union. In 1926, he represented China at the Asian Nations Conference in Japan. In 1927, he became a professor at Zhongshan University in Wuhan and wrote to *Guide Weekly* explaining this "misunderstanding." In the autumn of the same year, when Tang Shengzhi massacred the Communists,[90] for some strange reason, Lin too was taken off and shot. People said that just before he died, a Zhongshan University student who was shot at the same time as Lin ridiculed him. Lin's sole reason for going to the Soviet Union had been to acquire the status of a person who has studied abroad.

Writing about Lin Keyi leads me quite naturally to Chen Qixiu. Chen too was a Beijing University professor; he had studied in Japan and came to the Soviet Union to do research. He brought with him a letter of introduction from Li Dazhao and visited us in our dormitory at KUTV. He bowed formally in four directions and inquired, "Which of you gentlemen is Mr. Luo Jiao, which is Mr. Peng Shuzhi?" We received him. He had not come to study at KUTV, and he rented accommodations outside the university. He did independent research, but he spent much of his spare time at KUTV. Naturally enough, some of us visited him frequently at his home. I had not been assigned to the campaign to win him over, for there were quite a few Sichuanese among us. Soon afterwards, he too joined the Communist Party. Either before or after joining (I cannot remember which), the Moscow branch asked him to give some lectures, which he did on five or six occasions. His topic was the Chinese economy. Each time Peng Shuzhi got up onto the platform after Chen had finished speaking and explained in a friendly manner how he disagreed. We got nothing from Chen's lectures, but Peng Shuzhi seized the chance to show us that he was on a par with the famous professors of Beijing University. After Chen returned to China, his relations with the Party were sometimes intimate, sometimes distant. Many people know about this, so there is no need for me to discuss it further.

Toward the end of the summer vacation, students who had gone up to the capital from the countryside brought back the news that Sun Yat-sen had sent a delegation to Moscow. The leader of the delegation was a man called Jiang. The other delegates were Shen Xuanlu, Zhang Tailei, and a man called Huang. Xiong Xiong said: "It will be great if this man called Jiang turns out to be Jiang Zungui, because he owes me three hundred dollars. I can get it back from him and take you all out for a Chinese meal." A few days after we had restarted classes, we held a meeting in our dormitory to receive the four delegates. Guests and hosts sat on each side of a long table, and people for whom there was no room sat on beds. Shen Xuanlu sported a beard. He looked magnificent. We had often read his articles in *New Youth*, but by this time, he had already withdrawn from the Communist Party. Zhang Tailei was a giant of a man, and extremely handsome. He was a leader of the Chinese Socialist Youth League.[91] Huang Dengren was a secretarial type, quite undistinguished. The leader of the delegation was also unimposing and undistinguished. He was thirty-odd years old, white-skinned, dapper, and of medium build, and he spoke nonstandard Mandarin. To Xiong Xiong's disappointment (and to ours, for we had begun to look forward to our Chinese meal), he was not Jiang Zungui. Instead, he was called Chiang[92] Kai-shek, a name that few people had heard of at that time. Xiong Xiong had served as a military officer in the Guomindang, but even he had not heard of him. After the meeting, we discussed among ourselves why Sun Yat-sen had sent such a nonentity to lead the delegation. Some people suspected that the real leader of the delegation was Shen Xuanlu and that this Chiang Kai-shek was just a figurehead.

On National Day (the Double Tenth[93]), the delegation invited all the Chinese students at KUTV to a dinner. The delegation was housed in an aristocrat's mansion, which, though small, was exquisitely beautiful. We ate sumptuous food in the great hall. After the meal, there was entertainment. Shen Xuanlu did a sword dance. The sword slipped from his hand and he picked it up and continued dancing; we did not dare laugh. Peng Shuzhi then danced a Caucasian dance, and other people sang songs.[94] Chiang Kai-shek asked us into a small room at the side of the hall and lectured us on the history of the Guomindang, which he then asked us to join. He spoke on his feet, one hand resting on the back of a chair. He gave the impression of being honest but weak. We privately asked one another why Sun Yat-sen had sent such a useless person.

The Moscow branch appointed certain people to stay close to the delegates and try to win them over. Naturally, Luo Jiao and Peng Shuzhi were among those people. As a "tactic," some people—I forget who—were chosen to "enter" the Guomindang and to deal with the delegates as "Guomindang comrades." The result was that Shen Xuanlu rejoined the Party. After the Double Tenth, the only member of the delegation I saw was Zhang Tailei. I heard that the negotiations had not gone smoothly and that the man called Chiang had complained. After a few weeks, they went back to China, but Zhang Tailei stayed on in the Hotel Lux as Moscow representative of the Chinese Socialist Youth League. We often visited him in his hotel. In the spring of 1925, Luo Jiao returned to China and met Chiang Kai-shek in the Huangpu Military Academy in Guangdong. When Luo Jiao came to Shanghai, he told me, "As soon as he saw me he said, 'Are you better?' He remembered from Moscow that I had been ill."

Zhang Tailei brought with him news of the Third Congress of the Chinese Communist Party. Peng Shuzhi summoned a plenary assembly to report on it. He said that at the meeting, Li Hanjun had opposed the policy of joining the Guomindang, and that even though Li had contributed much to the Party (for example, when the journal *Gongchandang* [The Communist Party] had no money, Li paid the printing costs with fees he had received for his own articles), we should still oppose him. This was the first time I realized that there were internal struggles in the Party. But none of us in Moscow supported the opposition, for joining the Guomindang was a policy that we had already discussed and approved, and Li Hanjun had no authority as far as we were concerned.

* * *

After the summer, another group of Chinese students reached Moscow from Western Europe. There were far more of them than there had been of us: twenty or thirty in all. Almost all the people I knew had come: Yin Kuan, Li Weinong, Wang Zekai, Xue Shilun, and Yu Lüzhong. Among those who arrived was Yuan Zizhen, one of the two worker delegates at the Second

Congress. Another worker comrade among the new arrivals was Tang Ruxian. From Belgium, where they had joined the organization, came Liu Bojian and Li Heling, the famous terrorist. The rest, who were all new to me, included Ma Yufu.[95] Like us, they were "trained" by the Moscow branch, but Yin Kuan, Wang Zekai, and Xue Shilun all learned Russian and read theory. They paid no attention to the criticisms of the leaders and the rank and file. It was a shame that they arrived so late, for their Russian was not yet advanced by the time they returned to China, and they had to do all their theoretical study in French.

The people from France and Belgium had stayed in the homes of German Communists while crossing Germany on their way to Russia. The mark was devaluing uncontrollably, and the German proletariat was trying to make a revolution. Even down in the countryside, we had heard from city visitors that a revolution was going to break out in Germany. Some had heard Radek talking in Red Square about the situation in Germany, but neither *Pravda* nor *Izvestia* had published his speech. The newly arrived Chinese students said that in the German comrades' houses, they had seen people preparing first-aid materials, including bandages and medicines. We urgently read the news from Germany in the press, including news about the founding and dissolution of the Dresden workers' government and the fighting on the barricades in Hamburg. Peng Shuzhi even bought a book on the German language and studied a few chapters. After October, all our illusions about Germany were dispelled. Afterwards, we gradually learned about the internal struggle in the Russian Communist Party. The Communist Party branch at our "Stalin University" was one of the few intensely anti-"Trotskyist" branches in Moscow. At one branch meeting,[96] Kamenev spoke for the faction in power and Radek for the opposition. Each set out his own position, and there was a fierce exchange of views. As a member of Socialist Youth, I was not qualified to attend the meeting, but later, I heard Chinese students discussing the respective arguments. I have forgotten most of it, but I remember someone quoted Radek as saying, "Kamenev, who's heard of you outside Russia? But Trotsky is a household name throughout the world!"

It was true—in France I had heard next to nothing about Kamenev. Admittedly, during Lenin's second illness, *l'Humanité* had listed the duties of the three men standing in for Lenin, and Kamenev was among the troika. But apart from that, he had left no impression on me. I did not know anything about Stalin. As for Trotsky, he was as famous as Lenin and had even made a slightly greater impression on me than had Lenin, because I had read more of his writings and had been more stirred by them. I had read his *From the October Revolution to the Brest Peace Talks* (called *Avénement du bolchevisme* in French translation and *A Faithful Record of the Russian Revolution* in Chinese translation), and I had also bought *1905*, just then published in French, but I had not read it. I sensed an internationalist spirit in Trotsky's theses and pamphlets that went deeper than that of other writers. Perhaps Lenin surpassed Trotsky in his works, but I had not read them.

At that time, white cloth banners bearing Trotsky's portrait were still hanging across the streets, and although there were fewer of them than of Lenin, they were still quite plentiful. One hung in the square alongside KUTV. I never saw a portrait of Stalin, Kamenev, or Zinoviev on the street. At that time, I was reading the *History of the French Revolution*[97] and saw how Brissot, Danton, Robespierre, and Hèbert slaughtered one another. I was astonished that such a thing could happen just three or four years after the start of the revolution. The Russian Revolution had already been going on for six years, but I was convinced that it would never repeat the drama of the French Revolution, that the dispute would soon be peacefully resolved, and that as soon as Lenin recovered from his illness, all the problems would automatically disappear. How naive I was!

Lenin never recovered. I had read even before setting out from France that Lenin was on his deathbed. I said to people, we're going to Russia to attend Lenin's funeral. During the summer vacation, down in the countryside, some people had already heard rumors that Lenin would not recover; Bukharin was said to have announced in a speech that Lenin's brain had already been damaged, and that even if he did not die, he would be an idiot. On the morning of January 22, 1924, while we were breakfasting, rumors spread throughout the school that Lenin had died the day before. They were soon confirmed. The comrade in charge of the laundry, a woman in her fifties, cried and told us that she had once worked with Lenin. In the afternoon, we went out onto the streets, where a big white cloth announcing Lenin's death was hanging. The school authorities assigned students to take charge of the telephone. Only people with official permits were allowed to use it. I also took my turn at the phone. Soon, Lenin's body was brought into Moscow from the countryside and laid in state in the great hall of the National Trade Unions building. People from all the different factories, schools, and offices went to pay their respects. We formed a long line and waited for several hours before it was our turn to enter. We hurriedly filed through and out the other side. I saw Lenin's body laid out on a central bier surrounded by fresh flowers. Only his face was showing, just like on the ubiquitous portraits and on the postcard I had bought at the *Clarté* bookshop in Paris, except that the eyes were closed and the skin was bloodless. On January 27, we went to the funeral. It was bitterly cold; the temperature was more than 20 degrees (Celsius) below zero. The procession shuffled forward slowly, sometimes coming to a halt; it took almost half a day to reach Red Square. One man who looked like a peasant carelessly knocked at his frozen ear, and it dropped to the ground.

The day that Lenin was buried, Red Square was hung with huge slogans saying that now that Lenin was dead, we should unite and carry out his will. But with Lenin dead, the Russian Communist Party rushed even faster toward a split. Even if the people had been able to support the opposition, the political police (the GPU) was still in the hands of those in power. At some point, Yuan Qingyun got orders to act for the GPU among the Chinese students. The authorities still did not feel at ease. They sent Zhang Kaiyun, from Xinjiang, to KUTV to study and keep an eye on all the Chinese.

I had seen the dead Lenin with my own eyes, but I also heard the living Trotsky speak. In April 1924, KUTV held a meeting to commemorate the third anniversary of its founding, and the Party branch invited Trotsky to make a speech. He was a large, tall man with a ringing voice who dominated the platform like a fierce lion. By that time, I could almost follow a long speech in Russian. A few days later, the school journal printed the speech, which I translated into Chinese and took back to China with me. Later, it was published in issue number four of *New Youth* quarterly.

Bukharin also came to KUTV to give a speech. After the assassination of Vorovsky in Switzerland, I heard Lunacharsky speak at a demonstration in Red Square. On the second anniversary of the Soviet Constitution, I heard Zinoviev speak somewhere in the suburbs. During demonstrations on May 1 and November 7, I saw Stalin and other important leaders on the rostrum in Red Square. The veteran Japanese socialist Katayama Sen came to KUTV to talk to the Chinese students. He spoke in English, and Zhao Shiyan translated.

* * *

A few days after Lenin's death, *Pravda* published a telegram from Sun Yat-sen saying that the First Congress of the reorganized Guomindang had adjourned for three days in mourning.

From then on, we paid even more attention to events in China. As for Chinese publications, we had been receiving internal bulletins and external dailies and magazines all along. One day, Peng Shuzhi told us angrily that *New Youth*, the Party's theoretical journal, had started publishing nothing but boring and vacuous articles on philosophy and literature. Actually, the original *New Youth* had not been published for quite some time; it had become a quarterly under the editorship of Qu Qiubai and had already published its first two issues. Starting with issue number two, it had begun to publish novels and literary criticism. At the same time, the internal publication *Dangbao* (Party report) published an article titled "Should There Be a Chinese Communist Party?" This too made Peng angry. He said that the Party's very existence was now being put up for discussion. So the Moscow branch decided to contribute articles to the Party press. I proposed that *New*

Youth bring out a special Lenin issue, to commemorate the recent death of the leader of the world revolution. People supported my proposal. Articles were assigned to various individuals, and I was put in charge of sorting things out and pushing people to contribute. But no one started writing. As the deadline neared, I began to harass them, and they called me "debt collector." Even before the Lenin issue, I had contributed a few things. I had translated an article by Plekhanov on dialectics, and Yin Kuan had translated another article on the same subject; Zhao Shiyan, too, had written an article. We posted these contributions back to China. At that time, Qu Qiubai was in Guangzhou, and Chen Duxiu published the submissions from Moscow indiscriminately in the third issue of *New Youth* quarterly. Earlier, I had forged a bulletin from France for *Guide Weekly* on the basis of reports in *l'Humanité*, which I read regularly.

After the reorganization of the Guomindang, our activities in China expanded, and the Party needed personnel to take charge of them. Before the summer vacation of 1924, a group of Chinese students at KUTV got the order to return to China. Among them were Jiang Guangchi, Xiao Zizhang, Yin Kuan, Xiong Xiong, and Zhang Bojian. For the holidays, we went to another village where there was a KUTV estate closer to the railway station. There were some wooden cabins in a small forest, where we received military training.

Zhang Guotao had been arrested in Beijing; Li Dazhao fled to Moscow, and not long after that, Wang Hebo and a worker comrade called Yao also turned up. They had come to represent the Chinese Communist Party at the Fifth Congress of the Third International.

Before the end of the summer break, I received orders to return to China. Those who returned at the same time included Peng Shuzhi, Chen Yannian, Wang Zekai, Xue Shilun, Li Zhongwu, Lin Keyi, Yu Lüzhong, Cai Zhihua, Fu Daqing, and Zhou Yaoqiu. This list was decided by the Chinese delegation. My name was proposed by Peng Shuzhi. He was planning to take over the editorship of *New Youth*, and my work on the Lenin issue had demonstrated that I was not entirely useless.

All the delegates save Li Dazhao returned to China, and Peng Shuzhi traveled back with them. They went by the Chinese Eastern Railway and entered China through Manzhouli. The route they took was comparatively dangerous, but it was much quicker than the other routes. The rest of us went to Vladivostok and then took the boat to Shanghai, which was not dangerous at all.

We set out from Moscow sometime in late July and took the train direct to Chita. At Chita, we changed to a train bound for Vladivostok. We were some twenty days under way—this is the longest railway line in the world. Chen Yannian was our group leader. I looked after the funds and took charge of buying bread, sausage, and other sorts of cold food at stations along the line. Someone else took care of fetching water. The train did not stop for long at small stations, but at big stations it often stopped for two or three hours. At Irkutsk, it stopped for a whole day. We got off the train for a tour of this coldest city in the world and enjoyed a meal in a restaurant alongside Lake Baikal.

In Vladivostok, there was no boat going to Shanghai, so there was nothing to do but wait patiently. We stayed there for more than a month, in the Sailors' Club on Lenin Street down by the sea. Life was by no means lonely during our month in Vladivostok. The Sailors' Club library had a large collection of French novels, and there was a Chinese workers' May First Club on Pekinskaya Ulitsa run by Liang Botai and He Jinliang. Liang and He had originally been on their way to KUTV three years earlier to study but had stayed in the Soviet Far East to work among the Chinese community there. They were both from Zhejiang. Wu Fang, a Hunanese, had accompanied them to Russia. He was working as an inspector of Chinese laborers in the Soviet Far East and did not get to Vladivostok often. There was also Ren Zuomin, another Hunanese, who worked in Khabarovsk. Then there was a man called Wang Jun, who worked in the May First Club in Vladivostok. He was a northerner who had worked on the railways and been a delegate at a conference of the Third International. He had fled to Russia after the defeat of the Beijing-Hankou rail strike to seek refuge and to work for the movement. The club leaders wanted to keep us in Vladivostok, for they were short of officials. They had asked the Party in China to send them people, but to no effect. Just before we left, the Party in China did send someone, a man from Hubei called Zhang Jueyu, who had fled to Shanghai after the collapse of the rail strike.

There were many overseas Chinese in Vladivostok, all of them northerners. They congregated in a part of the city where there were two Beijing opera theaters, several restaurants, several bathhouses, and innumerable shops. When you entered this district, it was as if you were in China. The streets in other districts preserved a Russian character. Wang Jun, Liang Botai, and He Jinliang invited us out for a meal at one of the restaurants, for a bath at one of the bathhouses, and for an evening at the opera. We received a warm reception everywhere, and we never once had to pay. When we ate, all we needed to say was "Put it on my bill," and that was that. I asked them, "Do you pay once every four months?" They replied, "We never pay." At first, I naively imagined that since the club worked for the interests of the Chinese workers and small merchants, these people cherished its officials and were unwilling to take money from them. Later, I found out that this was not so. The Chinese feared and hated these people. The Chinese were actually opposed to the Soviet system; many were Red Beards. One of the four workers who had studied at KUTV, a man called Lü Xianji, had arrived in Vladivostok a year earlier and had been murdered just a few days after our arrival. The GPU already knew who had committed the murder but was unable to catch this person. He Jinliang asked Chen Yannian and others to go to drink tea in a Chinese restaurant frequented by the assassin and to gather information, since we were new arrivals and were not known there. I do not know what the outcome was.

In September, Zhao Shiyan and Ren Bishi also arrived from Moscow. They stayed several days in Vladivostok before going on by train to northeastern China via Yimianpo. The rest of us stayed on to await the boat, which finally arrived with twenty or thirty Chinese students on board, all bound for KUTV. Among them was Li Qiushi, a handsome young man, one of the five writers shot at Longhua in 1931.[98]

In mid-September, a British coal freighter left Vladivostok for Shanghai without passengers. We sought out the Chinese crew to see if there was any way that we could travel on this vessel. They agreed to let only three or four of us stow away, so we split into two groups for the journey back to China. Wang Zekai, Xue Shilun, and some others went ahead, while I, Chen Yannian, and the rest left several days later aboard a Russian ship. They slipped away like thieves, whereas we left legally and openly, sleeping on sofas in the ship's clubroom. On September 29, we reached Shanghai.

Xue Shilun came to the Taian Hotel to seek us out. He had already been assigned to a job, as secretary to the central presidium; Wang Zekai had already gone to work in Anyuan.[99] In his capacity as secretary, Xue Shilun informed us of our new duties. Chen Yannian was to go to Guangzhou to be district Party secretary; I was to stay in Shanghai to work in the Central Committee's Propaganda Department. The next day, we moved together with our luggage to a house on Moulmein Road.

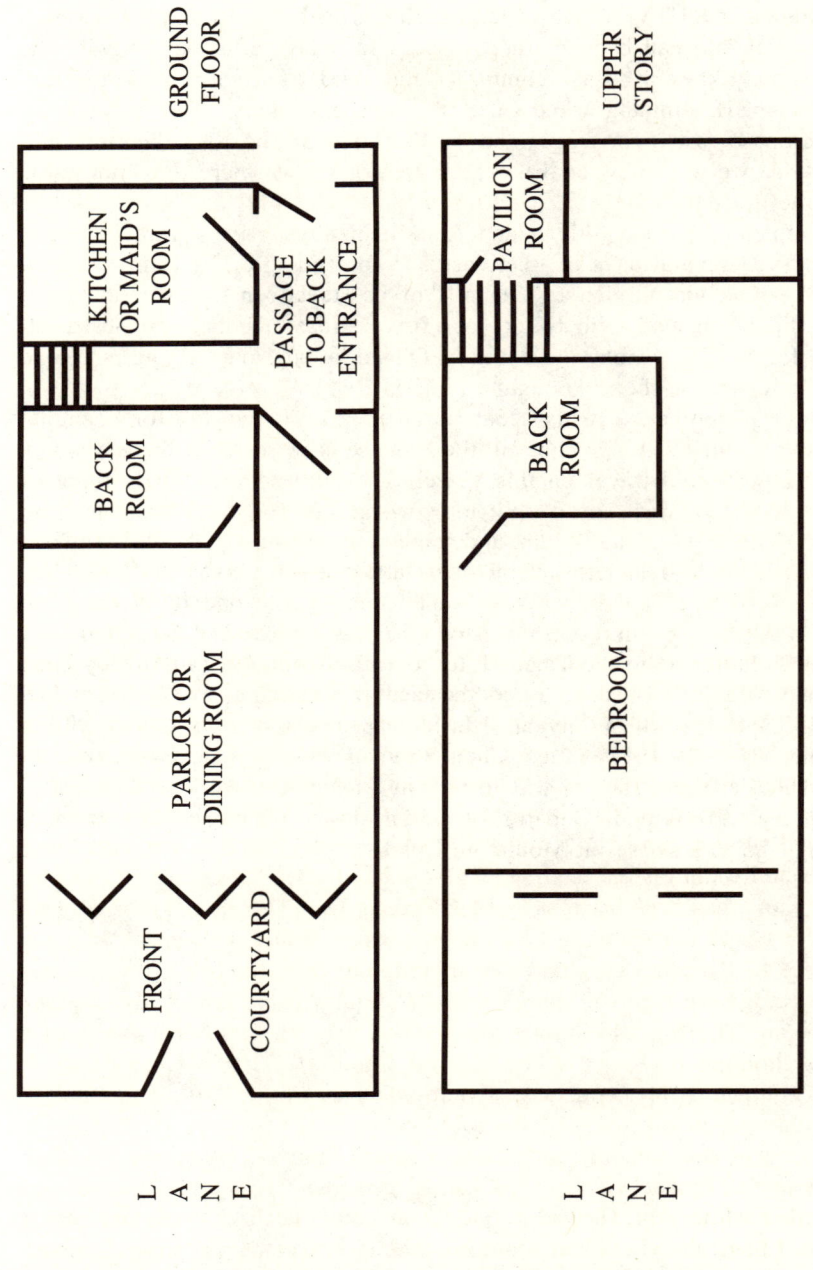

5
Before and After May Thirtieth

I arrived in Shanghai just at the time of the war between Qi Xieyuan and Lu Yongxiang.[100] There were notices posted along the roads declaring martial law in the name of the Shanghai Municipal Council. Lu Yongxiang was in a weak position, and the war was gradually getting closer to Shanghai. But within the International Settlement, things were calm. The house on Moulmein Road was double-fronted, with a wing room abutting the road and a bridging room over the alley, so that you could cross the alley from the upper wing room. Peng Shuzhi lived in this bridging room. The wing room was empty except for a large table, several untidy rows of chairs, and an empty bed, on which I spread my bedding. The rear wing room was Qu Qiubai's bedroom. His wife had died not long before. Cai Hesen and his wife, Xiang Jingyu, lived in the upstairs middle guest room. Li Longzhi[101] and his wife lived in the downstairs guest room. Zhang Tailei's mother, wife, and child occupied the downstairs wing room. Two maidservants lived in the small room off the landing.[102] One looked after Qu Qiubai; the other, Auntie Long, had been brought by Mao Zedong from Hunan and now cooked for us. We took our meals in Li Longzhi's room. While we were eating, we could see Li Yichun's bulging belly sticking out from the bed on which she was sleeping. We received guests not in the guest room but in the upstairs wing room. The big table alongside my bed was for receiving guests and also for holding meetings of the Central Committee's presidium. Besides this, it doubled as my work desk. There was no electric light in this room, so at night we lit oil lamps.

Li Longzhi shook hands with Chen Yannian, and also with me. We had already met in France. Li was from Liling in Hunan. He was tall and strong, with rather white skin. He had a loud, clear voice, flashing eyes, and heavy red lips. I have already talked about his time in France. After being deported back to China, he worked in the Anyuan collieries in Jiangxi, fomenting strikes and organizing unions and cooperatives; later, he went to Hankou,[103] and during or after the Beijing-Hankou rail strike, he was almost arrested. Now he was responsible, together with Xiang Delong,[104] for the workers' movement in Shanghai. He took Cai Zhihua, who had arrived with us, to live in a workers' club in Xiaoshadu.[105]

In the afternoon, Qu Qiubai returned from teaching at Shanghai University. I had never seen a comrade as neat as Qu. He was wearing a hat, a Western suit, and leather shoes. No one introduced us. All he saw was a newly arrived "child" proofreading *Guide Weekly* at the table for receiving visitors in the guest room. As for me, I realized that he was Qu Qiubai, the brilliant student of the Beijing Russian-language school, the publisher—together with Zheng Zhenduo and Geng Jizhi—during the May Fourth Movement of *Shuguang* (Dawn) magazine, who later became a journalist for *Chenbao* and was sent to Russia as a reporter. In Russia, he had been won to Marxism, joined the Communist Party, interpreted for Chinese students at KUTV, and written *Chi chao ji* (Red tide) and *Chidu xinshi* (An inside history of the Red capital). After returning to China, he edited *New Youth*. He was our theoretician, and now he was director of the Sociology Department at Shanghai University. It was a long time before I learned that during that period he was very unhappy. He had just been urgently summoned back to Shanghai from Guangdong, where, under the direction of Borodin, he had been engaged as a representative of the Communist Party's Central Committee in various activities of which the Central Committee disapproved.

Cai Hesen was suffering from his old ailment, asthma. He was lying on his bed, served by an old-fashioned girl wearing a white blouse and a black skirt, who entered and left by the side door of the wing room. This girl ignored the fact that there was bedding on the bed in the wing room. I already knew that she was Xiang Jingyu. The next day or the day after, a guest came, and Auntie Long sent up his name card. It was Lin Zuhan. Xiang Jingyu asked the guest to wait at the table where I was working. After a while, a tall, thin man emerged from the upstairs guest room. He was breathing asthmatically but began conversing animatedly with the new arrival. He spoke much more than the guest did. Finally, the guest took his leave. Just at that moment, Zhang Bojian arrived, probably to fetch the galley proofs, and asked Cai Hesen—for it was he—who the guest had been. Cai Hesen apparently had not had enough of talking, so the torrent continued for a while. He said, among other things, "He's a centrist." Having proofread *Guide Weekly*, I already knew that Cai divided the Guomindang into three factions: the anti-Communists were the right wing, those who approved of the proposals contained in *Guide Weekly* were the left wing, and the rest were centrists. Actually, Lin Zuhan had already joined the Communist Party (as I learned later), but Cai Hesen still did not recognize him as a true comrade.

I was rather surprised that this was Cai Hesen. In my mind's eye, Cai had been a new Wang Anshi, who talked about Marxism with tousled hair and a dirty face.[106] When I saw him that day, his face was clean, his hair was not particularly long, and he was dressed like a country *xiucai*,[107] quite the opposite of Qu Qiubai, who looked like one of the talented scribblers in the foreign settlement.

Cai Hesen was general editor of *Guide Weekly*. From an organizational point of view, he was my and Zhang Bojian's "direct superior." I was in charge of proofreading and collecting material; Zhang was in charge of printing and distribution, and before my arrival, he had also proofread. He rented a room elsewhere for himself. Although from Yunnan, he had several Sichuanese characteristics. He became my close friend. We spoke to each other without the slightest reservation about people and issues. He had arrived in Shanghai more than two months earlier than I had, and he told me everything he had learned during that period. For example, the house on Moulmein Road was a well-known center of bolshevism, and the reactionaries kept a close eye on it.

Whenever the presidium met, Chen Duxiu, Wang Hebo, and Lin Yunan came; Cai Hesen emerged through the side door of the guest room; and Peng Shuzhi emerged from the bridging room. Together they took over my working table. I automatically retreated to the room of Qu Qiubai, who was mostly away from home. Chen, Wang, and Cai formed the presidium; Lin Yunan represented the Youth League. And in what capacity did Peng Shuzhi attend? He had been sent by the Comintern and attended these meetings as a future member of the Central Committee.

Yuan Qingyun had painted a portrait of Chen Duxiu from a photograph, framed it, and hung it in our KUTV dormitory. I could now see that his portrait was a good likeness, though the real Chen looked even older than the painted one. Chen was only forty-something; but his hair had already begun to thin. He was of medium build and rather swarthy; his eyes slanted; he spoke with an Anqing accent. When he laughed, he revealed a set of neat white teeth. He did not like wearing Western clothes. When I first met him, he was wearing a traditional long gown, a mandarin jacket, and a hat. Later, when winter came, he wrapped a scarf around his neck. In the summer, he wore a long gown woven from grass linen. This was the man whom all China's revolutionary youth considered their leader and whom Confucian gentlemen everywhere heartily despised. Even then, there were already many myths and legends about him. Now I could see him with my own eyes, hear him with my own ears. The first time that I had come across his name while reading an article he had written, I had cursed him in my diary; later, I had gradually come to feel that what he said was not unreasonable, and later still, that it was eminently reasonable. Now I was carrying out revolutionary work under his direction.

* * *

In the autumn of 1924, everyone felt that China was on the brink of a revolution or a great movement; at least I felt that, and so did people I was close to. On the one hand, the government, inherited from Yuan Shikai, of the Beiyang warlords was already in decline and splitting; clearly, it would not last long. On the other hand, a new force was emerging that China had never before known: a modern proletariat. China had long known economic strikes, and by May Fourth we had begun to witness mass political strikes—the Shanghai strikes in support of the demands of the students' movement. In 1922, there was the great Hong Kong seamen's strike that finally forced British imperialism to submit. In 1923, there was the great Beijing-Hankou rail strike,[108] which ended in a massacre but did not lead to the demoralization of the working class—on the contrary, it infused the workers with new ardor. Even more important, China already had a proletarian political party. The Chinese Communist Party led not only the economic struggles of the proletariat but also the struggles of the entire country, and it took part in and developed the national and the democratic struggle. In the face of the workers' struggle and Communist activity, the whole of the petite bourgeoisie and part of the high bourgeoisie gradually lost their fear of the Beiyang warlords and dared to rise up against them and seek a way out for themselves. The awakening of the middle classes found its expression in the reorganization of the Guomindang. Before reorganization, in effect, the Guomindang did not exist. At around the time of the 1911 Revolution, this organization rapidly crumbled as a result of the defeat of the revolution[109] and betrayals by its members. There was Sun Yat-sen and a number of people close to him, and there was a vague democratic program and a faint memory of the revolution, but there was no Guomindang. It was the experience, funds, and firepower of the Soviet proletariat and the efforts of the Chinese Communist Party that fashioned a new political party, modeled on the organization of the Russian Bolsheviks, under the old and vacant signboard of the Guomindang. In January 1924, this party held its *first* all-China congress—it was only then that a Guomindang organization came into being. The Central Committee was set up in Guangzhou, and branches were set up at provincial, municipal, county, and district levels all over China. The Communists were in a small minority on the Guomindang's Central Executive Committee and Control Committee, but all major decisions were in the hands of Borodin, who was adviser to the Guomindang government. The local branches were almost exclusively under Communist control. The main exceptions were Guangzhou and Shanghai, where some so-called rightist elements could match the Communists. Apart from the Guomindang organization, a military academy funded and armed by the Soviet Union was set up at Huangpu in Guangzhou. Its main instructors were from the Soviet Union, but its head was Chiang Kai-shek. The Communist Zhou Enlai, newly returned from Europe, was also assigned to work there.

After the defeat on February 7, 1924, of the great Beijing-Hankou rail strike,[110] the Chinese Communist Party decided to take the path of "national revolution." The Chinese Communist movement was originally a product of the May Fourth Movement. After a short time, this patriotic movement—which opposed feudal Confucian ritual, reformed the Chinese language, and proposed science and democracy—turned into a Socialist or Communist movement. Chen Duxiu and Li Dazhao, professors at Beijing University, went from democratism to communism, and extreme leftists among the student leaders at Beijing University—people like Zhang Guotao, Deng Zhongxie,[111] Fan Hongjie, Gao Shangde, and Luo Zhanglong—went from the patriotic movement to the labor movement. There were no factories in Beijing, so they decided to leave the city and organize the railway workers. Changxingdian railway station became the hub from which they spread outward to railway lines throughout the north. The labor movement in the north was virgin territory. Things went less smoothly for the Communists in the south, where they met competition from remnants of the Chinese Socialist Party[112] formed in the early years of the Republic, and from Guomindang members who had become active in the labor movement before the reorganization of their party. These people had set up labor unions or workers' associations, but they had no followers. In Guangdong, there were some workers' organizations similar to the old-style guilds under the leadership of the Mechanics' Union. These bodies constituted a mass organization but resisted encroachment by the Communist Party.

At the time of its founding, the Chinese Communist Party naturally took as its banner proletarian-socialist revolution. The Guomindang did not exist; the Communist leaders and rank and file looked with contempt on its remnants, including Sun Yat-sen. They considered those in the Guomindang to be yesterday's people, whereas they saw themselves as taking giant steps toward the future. Had anyone said at the time that China first needed to go through a bourgeois-democratic revolution before carrying out proletarian-socialist revolution, and therefore the Guomindang should be revived and the Communists should join it and lead it, they would have been laughed at. In short, at the time of the Party's First Congress, no one proposed anything of the sort. Later, when such proposals finally surfaced, they came not from the Chinese Communists but from the Dutch Communist Maring,[113] who had been commissioned by the Comintern to direct the young Chinese Communist Party and by the Soviet Ministry of Foreign Affairs to liaise with China's democratic leaders. Maring proposed that the Chinese Communist Party take part in the "national revolutionary" movement and join Sun Yat-sen's

Guomindang, the revival of which Maring had urged and plotted. After its Second Congress, the Chinese Communist Party had already issued a circular telling Party and League branches to discuss joining the Guomindang. At the Third Congress,[114] Maring demanded that the Party formally resolve to adopt such a line. He met with opposition, not only from Li Hanjun but also from Zhang Guotao and even Chen Duxiu. Finally, Maring took out his order from the Comintern. More than ten years later, a historian[115] went to Holland to interview Maring about this. Maring denied that he had used the authority of the Comintern to force the Chinese Communist Party to accept this line. But at the time, Russian diplomatic interests required a government in China like Kemal's in Turkey, so Russian diplomats needed the Comintern and its Chinese section[116] to do their utmost to make such a government come about; this is an undeniable fact. No one questioned whether another position might have served the Chinese and the world revolution better, for everyone without exception believed that the interests of Soviet diplomacy and those of world revolution were identical. But in reality, it was exactly during this period that the interests of the Soviet Union and of world revolution began to part.

When I first got back to China, the Chinese Communist Party had already completed this evolution, or rather, this regression. After the February 7 defeat, the labor movement went through a temporary depression. Zhang Guotao began to show some passivity and was soon arrested and sent to prison; Li Hanjun, who was the fiercest opponent of joining the Guomindang, quit the Communist Party. The Comintern line was passed, Party opinion was unanimous, and the Party's entire work pressed on in this new direction. The Communist Party had originally set up *Guide Weekly* for the express purpose of serving the "national revolution"; now, *Guide Weekly* became the Party's official organ. I had already gone through this personal "evolution" in France, so when I returned home, I took the national revolution and joining the Guomindang for granted, even though deep inside I still had reservations about it. I had come to communism as a result of my study of the world's general development, not of China's special development.

In Shanghai, what first attracted my attention was the struggle within the Guomindang between the Communists (or Leftists) and the Rightists. This struggle took place at the Guomindang headquarters at 44 Route Vallon. Before I reached Shanghai, some Rightists had beaten up Shao Lizi there. At first, they thought that he was a Guomindang veteran, but then they discovered that he had joined the Communist Party. Of *Republic Daily*'s two chief editors, Ye Chucang was a Rightist and Shao Lizi a Leftist. They were old friends, but under the control of their respective factions, they began to fight; among the rest of the editors, Zhang Tailei and Shen Zemin were Leftists, and Chen Dezheng was a Rightist. The principal of Shanghai

University, Yu Youren, was a figurehead who sympathized with the Leftists. The dean, Deng Zhongxia (i.e., Deng Zhongxie); the director of the Sociology Department, Qu Qiubai; and Professors Shi Cuntong, Zhang Tailei, Yun Daiying, Peng Shuzhi, and Jiang Guangchi were Leftists. The director of the Department of Chinese Literature, Chen Wangdao, sympathized with the Leftists, but the director of the Department of English Literature, He Shizhen, was a Rightist. In the struggle between these various bodies, the Left invariably had the upper hand, for the Right was made up of old public figures who were disunited, lacked a central leadership, and, above all, lacked followers. They were furious but could resort only to thuggery. They had already beaten up Shao Lizi, and a fortnight or so after I arrived, they beat to death the Shanghai University student Huang Ren. That happened on Double Tenth,[117] at a commemoration held at Tianhougong in Shanghai. The chairman of the meeting was Yu Yuzhi, and Tong Lizhang was the secretary or some such—both were Rightists. A Shanghai University student raised a point from the floor, and Tong shouted, "Beat him!" A group of tattooed thugs attacked a dozen or so students. The same day, the Sichuanese Huang Ren died of his injuries. The Party presidium happened to be meeting around my table. Chen Duxiu still had not arrived. Someone came rushing in, furious, to report the incident. That man was Shi Cuntong.

The Left went on the counteroffensive. Ye Chucang was kicked off the *Republic Daily*, and He Shizhen was kicked out of Shanghai University. He Shizhen took the English Department students with him and set up Chizhi University, but he demanded that Qu Qiubai leave too.[118] Qu Qiubai did leave and was soon followed by Deng Zhongxia. Deng was replaced as dean by Han Juemin, a Communist; Zhou Yueran, a centrist, was the new director of the Department of English Literature, and Shi Cuntong was the new director of the Department of Sociology. Shanghai University students said that Shi Cuntong had secretly had a hand in Qu Qiubai's resignation because he wanted the directorship for himself. Although, by that time, I was in the Shanghai University branch of the Communist Party, I knew nothing about that charge. The Left ended up winning the struggle at the Guomindang headquarters, but I do not know the ins and outs of the victory.

A struggle also took place in the labor movement, but that struggle was not carried out in the name of the Guomindang. The Communist Party was active under its own banner in the labor movement. There had already been a Federation of Workers' Associations in Shanghai, but it was an empty shell. We had thought of taking it over, but it proved impossible, so we concentrated our activity on factories. Li Longzhi and Xiang Delong were in charge of this work: one from Hunan, one from Hubei; one in charge of west Shanghai, the other of east Shanghai. Although the strike at the Nanyang Tobacco Company failed, it increased our following. After that, our activity gradually spread and almost surpassed our capacity. The other labor movement activists[119] were no longer able to compete with us.

* * *

After the death of Huang Ren and the intensification of the struggle, for security purposes, *Guide Weekly*'s editorial department moved from Moulmein Road to South Minhouli off Hadoon Road. Zhang Bojian had found the place. The rent was high: forty dollars a month for two apartments on the first floor. The sublessors were two generations of widows who lived beneath the apartment occupied by Cai Hesen and his wife. Peng Shuzhi and I lived in another apartment, with some other tenants downstairs. Auntie Long cooked for us; Mao Zedong had returned to Hunan and left her behind to work for Xiang Jingyu. Zhang Bojian also moved to South Minhouli, but he lived in a pavilion room over the kitchen in a house two alleys further up. South Minhouli was very famous in those days. If you called a rickshaw, you only had to say Minhouli; you did not need to say which road it was on, because all the rickshaw men knew where it was. The newly published *Xing shi* (Awakening lion) weekly and its editor Zeng Qi also had their offices there; luckily, I never met him. Zhang Bojian said that the population of South Minhouli was extremely diverse. A strikingly large number of bureaucratic politicians lived there; further west, there were no lane houses, and to the east, there were none until Seymour Road. For miles around, there was nothing but Western-style mansions and empty spaces. Shanghai University was on Seymour Road, so large numbers of students lived in South Minhouli. We often used to hear them singing the *Internationale*.

Before the move, I had stopped leaving the room when the Central Committee met. After the move, it started meeting somewhere else. At first, it met in an apartment over a coal and firewood store on Weihaiwei Road, and then it moved to Guangdong Road in Zhabei. That was where the secretariat was. The secretary (who doubled as treasurer) was first Xue Shilun and then Ren Zuomin. The Party's entire expenses in those days amounted to a little over nine hundred dollars a month. I do not know if that sum included expenses incurred in Beijing and Guangzhou, but it certainly included everywhere else. Chen Duxiu, Cai Hesen, and Peng Shuzhi got forty dollars a month; Zhang Bojian, Xiang Jingyu, and I got thirty. We did our own cooking—each of us chipped in six or seven dollars a month. Although we were not overworked, we were certainly not idle. Apart from *Guide Weekly*, I also proofread *New Youth* and occasional pamphlets, for example, the proclamation and resolutions of the Fourth Congress. As for collecting material, I used to buy and save magazines such as *Yinhang zhoukan* (Bankers' weekly) and *Qianye gongbao* (Official bulletin of the old-style bankers' guild), dealing with economic issues, and annual customs reports. I bought them secondhand as well as new. Often, I bought runs covering five or six years. No one ever read or used these things. Apart from this activity, I also cut out articles from newspapers and pasted them in scrapbooks.

I also wrote articles for *Guide Weekly*. At first, I forged readers' letters under the pen name Ma Daofu. Later, I wrote articles on questions of minor importance using my real name; during the events of May Thirtieth, I started writing reports. Sometimes I wrote articles on international questions, and I also translated articles from foreign languages. Chen Duxiu was responsible for the column "Inch of Iron," but I wrote it on a few occasions. *Guide Weekly* did not publish theoretical articles, and I was not up to writing articles on political subjects. I translated quite a few articles for *New Youth*; those that I wrote myself had something of the flavor of KUTV or Shanghai University lectures. But I put considerable effort into the articles I wrote for *Zhongguo qingnian* (Chinese youth) under the name Zelian.

The moving spirit behind *Guide Weekly* was Cai Hesen, who wrote the lead articles for every issue. Chen Duxiu's articles were short and perfunctory, as if he were going through the motions rather than applying himself seriously. But Chen's "Inch of Iron" column was a brilliant literary exercise in just forty or so characters.

Peng Shuzhi achieved his aim of wresting *New Youth* from Qu Qiubai. After we moved, an issue appeared around the theme of "national revolution" (issue number four of the quarterly). Its lead article was an essay Peng had brought back from Moscow titled "Who Is the Leader of the National Revolution?" This essay later became the target of an attack by Qu Qiubai in his pamphlet *Against Peng Shuzhi-ism*, to which I shall return later. For the time being, I shall merely mention Zhang Songnian's reaction to the issue. He wrote a letter to Chen Duxiu protesting its vulgar style and mentioned, as an example, the statement on page one. This statement announced that *New Youth* was going to start publishing again as a monthly. It was written in a semiliterary style[120] and was full of clichés like *shouren aidai* (having enjoyed readers' esteem and appreciation). Zhang Songnian had been a pillar of the old *New Youth* and thought that style was important. He wanted *New Youth* to be a model of vernacular Chinese and thought that it should avoid literary terms, but if it was going to publish writing in the literary style, it should be good literary style. It is superfluous to add that the statement to which Zhang took exception was from the pen of the new editor, Peng. The first issue of the new monthly was the "Lenin issue." It consisted mostly of texts that we had brought back from Moscow. After that, Peng Shuzhi fell ill, and the next three issues were haphazardly thrown together by Qu Qiubai and me.

Apart from internal publications, I wrote articles for the *Awakening* supplement of *Republic Daily* and entered into a polemic with a journalist on the Shanghai French-language newspaper about Sun Yat-sen's passage through Shanghai. I wrote several letters in French, all of which were published.

* * *

On January 21, 1925, the first anniversary of the death of Lenin, the Chinese Communist Party held its Fourth Congress.[121]

The venue was a three-story lane house along the railroad tracks behind Guangdong Street in Zhabei, where delegates from outside Shanghai ate and slept. The dormitory was on the second floor, and the meeting was held on the first floor, which was arranged like a classroom; downstairs was the guest room. Hanging at the mouth of the stairway was a string tied to a bell that could be pulled if anything untoward happened; this would give the delegates upstairs time to put away their conference papers and take out their English textbooks or some other innocent "classroom" reading. The meeting went on for three or four days; nothing happened to disturb it.

The first-floor "classroom" was almost full, but I cannot remember exactly how many people came. I remember that the following people took part in the meeting: Chen Duxiu, Cai Hesen, and Qu Qiubai for the Central Committee; Li Weihan and Zhu Jintang representing Hunan; Chen Tanqiu representing Hubei; Yang Yin representing Guangdong; Gao Shangde representing the north; Peng Shuzhi representing Moscow; He Jinliang representing Vladivostok; Zhou Enlai representing France; Yin Kuan representing Shandong; and Zhang Tailei representing Socialist Youth. I do not remember who the Shanghai representative was. Li Qihan also took part in the meeting, but I do not recall what he represented. Zhang Guotao wrote a respectful letter to the congress but did not attend. Zhang Songnian and his wife, Shen Xuanlu and his wife, and Huang Ping attended once or twice in a nonvoting capacity. Zhang Bojian and I attended as minute takers. Zhang took minutes at only one or two sessions; I did the rest. The minutes were never sorted out and edited. Peng Shuzhi, representing the Moscow branch, concurrently headed the congress secretariat.

The Comintern representative Voitinsky attended once, and Qu Qiubai interpreted his speech. Voitinsky drafted the political resolution and other important documents; Qu Qiubai translated them into Chinese. On theoretical and political questions, the congress simply accepted Comintern instructions. None of the members of the Central Committee expressed views that differed from these instructions, nor did any of the delegates. The congress ran so smoothly that it was more like a ceremonial assembly than a political discussion, so even though I recorded eighty or ninety percent of the congress proceedings, they left no deep impression on me. But I clearly remember some minor details. For example, when Zhang Songnian got up to speak as a visitor, he spoke, among other things, about joining the Guomindang. This issue had been at the heart of the debates at the Third Congress, but now, no one save Zhang even mentioned it. We considered the argument settled; it no longer interested us. Moreover, Zhang Songnian, the person who had raised the issue, had no formal right to speak at the meeting. Even so, Qu Qiubai got up to reply to him. Qu was the best person to do so, for he was the staunchest supporter of the policy. We were familiar with his arguments even in advance of his reply, but he added an example by way of proof. To this day, I remember it: "For instance, if we want to get a seal cut, and it has words like Communist Party on it, in Shanghai, you could not take it to the seal carver, though you could in Guangzhou. That proves that the policy is beneficial to us."

I also recall the Comintern representative proposing a resolution attacking Trotsky. The other resolutions had all been drafted beforehand, mimeographed, and handed out to delegates; this was the only unscheduled resolution. The chairman (I forget who) read it out and asked if anyone wanted to oppose it. Although everyone at the meeting knew that there were differences of opinion in the CPSU, few had any idea what they were. I was a regular reader of *Correspondance internationale*,[122] which brimmed with articles against Trotskyism. Because the issues at stake in the CPSU had already become public and had spread to the Comintern, Communist Parties in the various countries were formally passing "anti-Trotskyist" resolutions to send to Moscow. Of course, the Chinese Communist Party had to be among them, even though (as I have said) few of us knew what the controversy was about. After the draft had been read, it was a long time before anyone spoke. Finally, Peng Shuzhi got up and made a speech along the lines that Trotsky was wrong on this or that point and must be opposed. The result was that the resolution was passed unanimously. I do not know how the delegates felt about this at the time. Later, when the North China Regional Committee of the Chinese Communist Party sent someone to talk with Zhang Songnian before expelling him, Zhang expressed his dissatisfaction with the Party on several points. Among other things, he said: "Trotsky was a leader of the October Revolution, and now we've turned against him!" Perhaps he was referring to the translations of articles by Zinoviev, Stalin, and others that later appeared in *New Youth* or to this resolution, but at the congress he failed to speak up for Trotsky. (It is possible that he failed to turn up on the day the resolution was adopted.)

The third thing I recall is a clash between Zhang Tailei and some other delegates. Zhang Tailei was a good-looking fellow, and some delegates inevitably lacked the urban graces. Zhang frequently made fun of these people and invented nicknames for them that were very much to the point. For example, he called Li Weihan "real powerholder." Li Weihan attracted much attention at the congress. Although there were no theoretical or political disputes, there were some disputes about minor practical matters. Every time a dispute arose, Li Weihan would at first keep silent and then come out with a few clear-cut sentences meant to decide the issue. Was this because he had good judgment and was a fluent speaker, or because he commanded a following? Zhang Tailei thought that Li Weihan's speeches were important purely because he had a following. But Li Weihan loathed his nickname.

The last thing I remember is that Yang Yin was beaten up and injured by fellow Cantonese in Shanghai. This probably had something to do with clashes between the two trade union factions in Guangzhou. Yang arrived at the Congress on the last day, his head wrapped in bandages.

On the last day, the congress elected nine people to the Central Committee, together with four alternate members. The nine were Chen Duxiu, Li Dazhao, Qu Qiubai, Cai Hesen, Zhang Guotao, Peng Shuzhi, Tan Pingshan, Li Weihan, and someone else (I forget who).[123] Of the four alternates, I recall only Wang Hebo and Zhu Jintang. The five people—Chen, Cai, Qu, Zhang, and Peng—permanently stationed in Shanghai formed the presidium. In the almost two and a half years that elapsed between the Fourth and Fifth Congresses, the Central Committee met only two or three times in plenary session. If the revolution that took place in those years had been led by the Chinese Communist Party, it would have been led, in effect, by this five-member presidium.

Chen Duxiu was a militant of the 1911 Revolution, commander in chief of the May Fourth Movement, founder of the Chinese Communist Party, and general secretary several times in succession. He was the living embodiment of China's permanent revolution; he symbolized the rapid transition from China's bourgeois revolution to its proletarian revolution. There is no denying that he had a revolutionary history, a following, and experience with revolutionary activity.

Zhang Guotao had been a student leader at Beijing University during the May Fourth Movement. He had been in the vanguard of the move from the universities to industry. He was in charge of the Secretariat of Chinese Trade Unions and had led many strikes. He had been arrested by Cao Kun and Wu Peifu[124] because of his revolutionary activity. He was a leader thrown up by the mass movement.

Cai Hesen was the first of the work-study students in France to become a Marxist. He had been a leader of the work-study movement and a harbinger of the Communist movement among Chinese students in France. The French government deported him back to China because of his involvement in the Lyon University movement. He, too, had been produced by a mass movement, though its scope and nature were different from the one that produced Zhang Guotao.

Qu Qiubai had participated in the May Fourth cultural movement. He was a Beijing journalist and was clever, learned, and popular among students. That he had now become a Communist leader was due to his history and his ability, but also to his close relations with the Comintern and the Russian comrades.

Peng Shuzhi was a newcomer. Before he got to China he was unknown in the Communist Party, not to mention outside it. He had never taken part in any mass movement. What forces did he represent in the leadership? He had been appointed by the Comintern and represented the Comintern line. He took part in Central Committee meetings even before he had been elected to it and acted as head of its Propaganda Department.

In Shanghai, I met these five men almost daily. (Zhang Guotao did not come to Shanghai until a long time after the congress.) The presidium met roughly once a week to discuss big and small questions, from organizing a national government to comrades' love entanglements. Chen Duxiu's opinion was decisive. The meetings were rarely attended by disputes, but thinking back on those days, it is now clear to me that there was unanimity only on the surface; below it lurked differences of opinion.

Under the general secretary was a secretariat that at first comprised just one person, Ren Zuomin, who served as both bookkeeper and secretary. Later, Wang Ruofei was transferred to this office and a separate secretariat was established, independent of the accounts section. Wang Ruofei had two or three office staff to attend to secret correspondence, maintain the Party archives, and work the mimeograph machine. Chen Duxiu was not only general secretary but de facto head of the organization department, for in practice, no formal organization department had been established. In late 1926 or early 1927, Zhou Enlai was assigned to take charge of organizational affairs, though he was not on the Central Committee. But Zhou was occupied with more urgent matters. The Propaganda Department had been set up before the Fourth Congress and was headed by Peng Shuzhi. Nominally, I was its secretary, but my work consisted solely of looking after *Guide Weekly*, *New Youth*, and the publication of Party pamphlets. Not until later, in Wuhan, did I learn from the wife of Pavel Mif what propaganda work was about; during my time in Shanghai, neither I nor the head of the Propaganda Department had much idea. In any case, shortly after taking up his post, Peng Shuzhi fell seriously ill and spent eight months in the hospital before returning to work. Zhang Guotao was in charge of the Workers and Peasants Department, which in reality did little more than receive comrades working in trade unions in various parts of China. The Women's Department was for a time in the handbag of Yang Zhihua, Qu Qiubai's wife, and for a time in that of Peng Shuzhi's wife, Chen Bilan.

The Youth League led an independent life. After the Party's Fourth Congress, the League also held a congress and changed its named from Socialist to Communist. Zhang Tailei was its secretary, but he was soon replaced by others, including Ren Bishi, He Chang, Liu Changqun, and Lu Dingyi. Liu Renjing edited *Chinese Youth*, the League's magazine. I was not familiar with the League's internal life, but its officials became my good friends. I often visited them in their homes to talk about films, novels, and women; we were like school friends.

After the Fourth Congress, Party activity developed rapidly. In the spring of 1924, when I formally joined the Party, it claimed more than three hundred members in China and abroad, one in ten of them in the Moscow branch. According to congress statistics, it now had more than nine hundred members. By the time of the Fifth Congress, it had claimed more than 100,000.[125] Before and after the Fourth Congress, almost all the important jobs in the Party were in the hands of comrades who had returned to China from Moscow, particularly those who had returned from France via Moscow. Peng Shuzhi was a member of the Central Committee. Zhao Shiyan was in charge of northern China, Chen Yannian of Guangdong, Yin Kuan of Shandong, and Wang Ruofei of Henan. Not long afterward, Luo Jiao took over Shanghai; Li Weihan in Hunan had also been in France. There were Moscow branch people in Hubei too, though they played no important role there. They were even in the smaller places: Wang Zekai in Anyuan, Gao Feng in Baoding, and Li Weinong in Qingdao. After these comrades had returned from abroad, the comrades in China stepped aside to make way for them. The name "Moscow branch group" or "Moscow group" was current in the Party; they were like a faction that dominated all other factions.

Actually, before we returned to China, the Party had few cadres. The main source of cadres had been Zhang Guotao's connections—that is, the comrades who had spread out from Beijing to agitate among the railway workers. Under Zhang Guotao were Luo Zhanglong, Li Zhenying, Zhang Kundi, Wu Yuming, and others. Because they had worked together in the past, these people were virtually a faction, and sometimes they actually clashed with the Moscow returnees. Those working in the labor movement in southern China could not boast the same achievements as those in the north, so they did not form a faction. Li Longzhi, Liu Shaoqi, and Lu Chen had been active together in the trade unions and the workers' clubs in Anyuan, so they had some mutual ties. Apart from these groups, there were local cells in Guangdong, Beijing, Hunan, Hubei, Shandong, and other places. They were pleased to receive the comrades from Moscow.

The machine was ready, waiting for raw materials to process. By coincidence, the materials had been prepared and were on their way.

* * *

I arrived back in China at exactly the time of the Jiangsu-Zhejiang war. Lu Yongxiang, who was in alliance with Sun Yat-sen, had been forced to go on the defensive. He had abandoned Hangzhou and retreated to Shanghai to dig in. Not long after that, he had to give up Shanghai. The Fengtian Army[126] in the north was also on the defensive. We were worried that the Zhili warlords, boosted by their string of victories, might nip the revolution in the bud. But just a few days after the end of the Shanghai war, the Zhili warlords unexpectedly fell from power. President Cao Kun was taken prisoner, and Wu Peifu fled. They had been overthrown by their own generals: Feng Yuxiang, Hu Jingyi, and Sun Yue.[127] It all happened so suddenly and unexpectedly that Cai Hesen was thrown off balance. He wrote an article for *Guide Weekly* that attacked U.S. imperialism for plotting to take over China, for he believed that the United States had been behind Feng Yuxiang's betrayal of Cao and Wu. Shao Lizi came to Party headquarters to protest. He said that Feng's coup, far from being instigated by America, was good for the revolution and that we should refrain from criticizing it. Cai Hesen said angrily, "Is Comrade Shao implying that it's possible that Chinese warlords could act without imperialists pulling the strings?" Whether Feng Yuxiang was acting independently or being stage-managed from abroad, I do not know even today, twenty years after the event. But it's a fact that not long afterward, *Guide Weekly* abandoned Cai Hesen's position. Reports from Beijing and Guangdong and information provided by the Soviet consulate or Voitinsky in Shanghai were incompatible with Cai's view. Shortly after that, Sun Yat-sen left Guangdong and went to Beijing via Shanghai and Japan. He issued slogans calling for the convention of a national assembly and the abolition of the unequal treaties.[128] In the spring of 1925, he died in Beijing. The Society to Promote a National Assembly and the movement to commemorate the death of Sun Yat-sen were launched and led by the Communist Party. These two national movements spread the Party's influence, developed its organization, and increased its membership. But it was a national movement, promoted under the banner of the Guomindang.

In the labor movement, the Communist Party showed its true face. Two years after the February 7 defeat, the labor movement revived. This time it was a movement not of transport workers but of factory workers in the big cities, starting with the Shanghai cotton mills. This was the fruit of the efforts of Li Longzhi and Xiang Delong; the two workers' clubs in east and west Shanghai played important roles in the events. The clubs drew in the factory workers; strikes took place, and workers influenced by the clubs immediately began to play a role in them; in the background, we controlled these workers. The capitalists reckoned on the basis of past experience that the strikes would cave in after two or three days, but they were wrong: The strikes went on and on, though the workers had no unions and no reserves.

Finally, the capitalists had no choice but to give in, to negotiate with the workers' representatives, to accede to their conditions, and to sign agreements. The workers' representatives did not forget to include union recognition among their conditions. The capitalists, foreign and Chinese, were surprised by all this. Where did the workers get the funds to tide them over during the strike? Where did they learn these new methods of struggle? Moreover, workers in different factories had adopted more or less similar tactics. The workers were exhilarated by their victory. They were not only happy that their demands had been met but also delighted that they had the power and the means to make the factories submit. The more progressive workers joined the Communist Party. Alongside the Society to Promote a National Assembly, there arose a labor movement in Shanghai and other cities that aided the development of the Communist Party in even greater measure. The biggest strike was in a Japanese-owned cotton mill in Xiaoshadu.

I did not directly participate in these two mass movements, but I often attended the congresses of the two organizations as an anonymous observer. On one occasion, Jiang Guangchi, Shen Zemin, and I organized a propaganda team. We got some paper flags and leaflets from the headquarters of the Society to Promote a National Assembly and addressed passersby on the road near the West Gate. A group of naughty children crowded around us asking for leaflets to wrap their sweets and peanuts in. Wang Ruofei and I, newly back in China, attended the meeting at Tanziwan in memory of Gu Zhenghong,[129] but we nearly caused a serious incident. We were both wearing Western suits. As soon as we arrived at the meeting, people began noticing us. A group of workers came over to keep an eye on us. Large numbers of people were scattered across the open ground, in the middle of which was a makeshift platform on which stood Li Longzhi. Li was dressed in a blue shirt and trousers, like the workers around the platform listening to the speeches. As Liu Hua was speaking, two of the group supervising us asked us to follow them to an empty spot beyond the edge of the crowd. They asked whether we were Japanese.

I said, "We're Shanghai University students."

A pock-marked youth said, "Then you must know the name of the man who's speaking now."

I said, "He's a student too. His name is Liu Hua."

To dispel their doubts, I added, "Look, that's Li Cheng,[130] he is also our friend."

The two men seemed to calm down. Not long after that, Li Longzhi stepped down from the platform and took us to the union office. He asked us to go back to headquarters and report on a few things for him.

Supreme commander of the strikes was Chen Duxiu. Every time an important decision was needed—for example, on whether to strike or not, what demands to raise, how to conduct negotiations, and whether to sign an agreement—the labor movement cadres made it in consultation with Chen. The usual venue for these meetings, which took place mostly at night, was a comrade's house south of Baoshan Road. One evening, Xiang Jingyu told me, the meeting did not end until very late. Chen Duxiu walked along the alley, saying, "I missed the triple prize, what a shame, all I needed were the last seven stripes, I was sure they had come, but they just would not come." He talked nonstop about this imaginary game of mahjong until the keeper of the iron gate at the end of the alley let them out; only then did he stop.

After the end of each big strike or movement, whether won or lost, the Shanghai District Committee[131] met in plenary session to assess the outcome. The meetings were convened in a primary school in the Chinese territory in the Hengbin Bridge area. They were plenary sessions in the true sense of the term—that is, all Party members had to attend—but in effect, attendance was limited by the size of the classroom. On several occasions, I took the minutes at these meetings. Chen Duxiu made the political report, the district secretary Zhuang Wengong made the work report, and Zhuang or someone else made additional reports on the movement or the strike. Sometimes, punishments or expulsions were announced. On one occasion, Qu Qiubai made a theoretical report in which he talked about the history of world communism, starting with Plato's Republic. After the end of each report, people raised questions or points of view. Once, Shao Lizi angrily stood up to denounce our discrimination against Guomindang members in the labor movement. I cannot remember how his point was dealt with. Even though we had not formally decided to bar Guomindang members from taking part in the labor movement, in reality, the labor movement in Shanghai was completely in Communist hands. I do not know whether this was because the Guomindang members did not want to join or because we did not let them join.

The district secretary Han Baihua, a man from Zhejiang and a student of the First Provincial Normal School, had studied briefly in Moscow. When *Guide Weekly* first appeared, he had been responsible for it. After the February 7 defeat, he was arrested in Shanghai and spent several months in prison before being bailed out. By this time, he had changed his name to Zhuang Wengong. He was like a primary school teacher—loyal and hardworking, but with little real ability. After the expansion of the Party as a result of the May Thirtieth Movement, he was unable to cope and was replaced.

* * *

Great movements and revolutions often catch people unawares. This generalization also holds for the Chinese Revolution of 1925 to 1927. This does not mean, however, that the revolution itself came unexpectedly—quite the contrary. We had known for a long time that a great movement was about to burst forth in China. I had said to Zhang Bojian: "Eight years after the Revolution of 1911 there was the May Fourth Movement. Quite a while has elapsed between May Fourth and now. Some sort of movement *must* be in the offing." Needless to say, my argument was based on a calculation not just of spans of time but also of various underlying factors in the situation. Yet no one imagined that the revolution would break out on May 30, 1925, and in such a form.

I know nothing of the preparations that were made for May Thirtieth. After breakfast that morning, Cai Hesen said to me: "Chaolin, if you've got nothing planned, you can go into town and watch. Today the students are going to the International Settlement to make propaganda." I immediately dressed and went out. Though Cai Hesen had not said as much, I already understood that our Central Committee had prepared this event. The All-China Students' Federation was under our control, as was the Shanghai Students' Federation. There were Communist Youth branches in a large number of schools. We controlled nearly all the Guomindang branches in the schools. We had already mobilized the students several times to go out onto the streets and make propaganda—for example, during the campaign for a national assembly, at the time of the death of Sun Yat-sen, and during the movement to aid the striking workers. But those mobilizations had been in Chinese-controlled territory. We had staged several mass rallies and demonstrations, but always outside the West Gate at the public sports grounds. We had never held a rally, a congress, or a demonstration inside the area of the International Settlement. Shanghai University students had, on one occasion, marched with banners to the area north of Suzhou Creek to take part in a commemorative meeting. The police had intervened and arrested four of them while they were passing by the Gordon Road police station. "When will we be able to hold a mass meeting at the race course?"[132] I asked Zhang Bojian.

Making public speeches in the International Settlement was certainly a novelty. When I reached Nanjing Road, nothing was afoot; I turned onto Fuzhou Road and still saw nothing. Not until I reached the intersection between Qipan Street and Jiaotong Road did I see a student dressed in Western clothes standing on a stool making a speech. An Indian policeman was arresting him and demanding that he go to the police station. I learned from passersby that the same thing had already happened many times that day on Nanjing Road. I returned to Nanjing Road and met Yu Xiusong at the Sunrise Pavilion. He said that there would be a demonstration at three o'clock that afternoon at the New Yamen.[133] The two of us walked over to the magistrate's court on North Zhejiang Road. We waited there for a long time, but nothing happened, so we crossed back slowly to Nanjing Road. But when we reached the Sincere Department Store, we saw a great crowd of people, all very agitated and all speaking of only one thing: There had just been some gunfire at the entrance to Laozha police station, and a large number of students had been shot dead. We hurried to the place mentioned—not today's entrance but the old entrance on Nanjing Road, which is now a clock and watch shop. There were no longer any crowds. There was blood on the pavement; the bodies had been carted off. Yu Xiusong and I parted company. I walked along, thinking to myself, "more material for anti-imperialist propaganda." I went to the Northern Railway Station. While passing by the small station for Wusong-bound trains, I came across a group of students telling one another about the massacre. Some of them had witnessed it with their own eyes. I discovered that after a large number of students had been arrested for making speeches on the streets and taken off to Laozha police station, other students had crowded into the entrance, demanding the release of those seized. Passersby had stopped too to watch the hubbub or join in the shouting. The crowd quickly swelled. A foreign police officer with three stripes on his sleeve gave the order to open fire. That's how the massacre began.

I later discovered that the great majority of casualties had been citizens who had stopped to watch the uproar and that only a handful of students had been killed. Among the dead students was the Communist He Bingyi of Shanghai University.

I went home and wrote an account of the massacre, based on my own observations and on the next day's press reports, for publication in the following issue of *Guide Weekly*. Later, Hua Gang copied my account in its entirety in his history of the Great Revolution.[134]

The massacre happened at just the right time to detonate an accumulation of explosives. It was not simply that a massacre could trigger revolution. History is littered with massacres of an even greater scope and brutality that triggered no revolution. The revolution made use of the Shanghai massacre of May 30, 1925.

One reason it could do so was that the Shanghai bourgeoisie nursed grievances against the International Settlement authorities. The bourgeoisie had expressed opposition and had begun to make all sorts of demands. The Chinese bourgeois, originally under the wing of foreign capital, had by this time already accumulated considerable wealth. They demanded independence, or the right to exploit on an even greater scale than before. They could not help but notice the spread of the national movement with Communist support and the victories of the strikers in the foreign factories in Shanghai. This encouraged them to raise their heads. A few days before the massacre, the Chinese press opposed the increase in the police levy and the new publishing regulations imposed by the directors' board of the municipal council of the International Settlement and demanded that Chinese be allowed to join the directors' board. At that time, a new organization called the Federation of Merchants of All Streets had been set up in opposition to and to the left of the official General Chamber of Commerce. This organization had links to Guomindang veterans and was beyond the Communist Party's control. When the massacre took place, the members of this organization were extremely angry; they also reflected the feelings of the shopworkers. They agreed to go on a business strike. The General Chamber of Commerce refused to support this proposal, but the same day, the same night, students' and workers' representatives went to its headquarters and begged on their knees, with tears in their eyes, for action. Before long, the deputy leader of the Chamber of Commerce, Fang Jiaobo, agreed to order a shutdown. The next day, business throughout Shanghai ground to a halt. The newspapers stopped publishing their "arse-end,"[135] and although shops selling daily necessities did not shut down completely, they remained outwardly closed and boarded. Foreign troops patrolled the silent streets, as if before a great enemy.

Another even more important reason that the revolution could break out was that the proletariat had just finished preparing its combat organization. It was as if the Communist Party had known that a revolution would break out between May and June. It had already completed its preparations. Even more surprising than the massacre and the shop strike, the following day, a Shanghai General Labor Union emerged to issue orders to the Shanghai workers. Every sector of workers submitted to it, carried out its commands, and reported to it. It became like a soviet in the Russian Revolution. The Shanghai workers' general command appeared as if from a conjurer's hat and enjoyed absolute authority. How did this come to be?

On May 1, 1925, the Second All-China Labor Congress had convened in Guangzhou. Even though not all the delegates were Communists, all were susceptible to Communist control. By this time, the other faction of labor movement activists—the Guomindang veterans—had been excluded; it had become clear during the workers' struggles that they lacked effective strength. When the workers at the Japanese cotton mills went on strike, these Guomindang veterans drove around in motorcars distributing leaflets in workers' areas, warning workers not to fall into the Communists' trap. The workers understood without our having to explain that these people were nothing but "running dogs." From the Labor Congress emerged the All-China General Labor Union; the congress decided that the Shanghai delegation should organize a Shanghai General Labor Union after returning home. At the end of May, the delegation had already returned from Guangzhou and was in the process of preparing such an organization. There had already been several legal and illegal mass unions produced by the spring strike wave, in many different places, all under Communist influence. The Shanghai General Labor Union was to become a federation and general command for these factory committees (for they were organized by factory rather than by industry or profession).

The original plan was to inaugurate this general command at the beginning of June, for some formal procedures had still not been completed. But as soon as the massacre happened, the procedures were dispensed with and the General Labor Union was proclaimed. Its order to go on strike was immediately obeyed. Its leader Li Lisan instantly became the leader of workers throughout Shanghai. Li Lisan was a false name, created just a few hours before it was made public; if the Xiaoshadu workers had seen this Li Lisan, they would have recognized him as Li Cheng, another false name; if the Anyuan miners had seen him, they would have recognized him as Li Longzhi, which was his real name. Naturally, the workers' strike was not as orderly as the shopkeepers', which was sudden and total. The workers' strike was ragged and irregular and spread over a considerable period of time. The merchants had decades of organization behind them, and their street federations were also of comparatively long standing, whereas the workers' General Labor Union was just a few hours old.

Similar in nature to the General Labor Union was the National Press Agency and *Rexue ribao* (Hot blood daily).[136] Just a short time before, a sum of money had been allocated for running the "national movement," and the Central Committee had decided to launch a press agency and a small-format newspaper. This agency and newspaper had been in preparation even before the massacre, and their appearance was moved up. But because there was no way of speeding up the operation of a printshop, the newspaper could not be published until just over three weeks later.

The press agency and the newspaper were run from the same office by the same people. I dropped propaganda work and joined the paper. The editorial office was alongside Xiangshan Road in Zhabei, close to the Party's district headquarters but a long way from my lodgings in Hadoon Road. The editor in chief was Qu Qiubai; apart from me, the editorial board comprised two comrades assigned by the District Committee: Shen Zemin[137] and He Weixin. Zhang Bojian looked after distribution. Why was the newspaper called *Hot Blood Daily*? Because there was already a *Gongli ribao* (Justice daily), published by the Commercial Press with an allocation of $10,000 from the Commercial Press senior management and edited by Shen Yanbing[138] and others. Although Shen was a comrade, in his position, he had no choice but to speak gray.[139] Qu Qiubai said, "What justice is there in this world? Hot blood will decide things!" *Hot Blood*'s circulation was higher than *Justice Daily*'s. The printers (not of the Party) were almost unable to keep up with the demand. Twenty days later, they were tracked down by the police, and the owner was jailed for two days. The printshop was closed, and the case was settled with a fine. We recompensed the owner for his losses. Our own printers managed with difficulty to put out one more issue, after which *Hot Blood* stopped appearing. Qu Qiubai wrote nearly all the editorials. Shen Zemin and I wrote general articles and edited reports from the District Committee and the General Labor Union. He Weixin specialized in editing news stories. Sometimes, he wrote anti-imperialist songs to the tune of popular melodies like *Eighteen Gropes* and *Mengjiang nü*.[140]

The strike movement spread out in waves, from the foreign-owned factories to the foreigners' servants and amahs. Workers at the electric company and the waterworks awaited the order to strike, but the General Labor Union let them continue to work so as not to inconvenience the general public. Even some policemen contacted the union to say that they were prepared to agitate for a police strike. The General Labor Union split into a large number of sections to deal with the rush of business; even so, it was almost overwhelmed. Li Lisan spent his time rushing between Chen Duxiu and Yu Qiaqing. The Chinese factories had not been called out, so Yu "sympathized" with the labor movement and contributed toward the strike fund; he also contributed some opinions. When Li Lisan went to Beijing on business, Yu even wrote him a letter of introduction to Li Sihao, Minister of Finance in the Beijing government. It was very much in the interests of the Chinese capitalists that the strikes in the British cotton mills and tobacco factories continue. No one was smoking Daying[141] cigarettes anymore; the British-American Tobacco Company had no choice but to change the brand name to Hongxibao[142] and to launch an advertising campaign to announce that the brand was registered in New York (though the packet still said London).

The people who were actually responsible for the General Labor Union were Liu Shaoqi and some other labor movement activists under the direct command of Zhang Guotao. He Jinliang returned from Vladivostok and was assigned to the General Labor Union; he changed his name to He Songlin. He had become very experienced in Russia; even Zhang Guotao was impressed by his ability, so he became inseparable from the Shanghai General Labor Union. A large group of Shanghai University students worked for the union. On one occasion, some thugs smashed up the union headquarters and injured some of these students; on another occasion, Li Lisan was kidnapped by thugs, dragged off to see Chang Yuqing,[143] owner of the Daguanyuan Bathhouse, and forced to call him *laotouzi* (chief). During that period, the Chinese police had not yet intervened. After September, when the Beijing government ordered the closing down of the General Labor Union and the arrest of Li Lisan, the situation changed. The union went underground; two mass demonstrations to unseal its headquarters failed.

Although the merchants and workers were unable to get results and the strikes came to a ragged end, this movement in Shanghai had an enormous influence on the rest of China. In Guangzhou, there was the June 23 Shakee Road Bridge massacre and the ensuing Hong Kong strike; in Hankou, there was a massacre and strikes. There was a sensational response in the interior of the country to these goings-on: Everyone was eager to read the newly published books and newspapers, and young people streamed into the coastal provinces, most of them in the direction of Huangpu.[144]

* * *

After *Hot Blood* ceased publishing, I withdrew from the National Press Agency too, but there was no chance of a return to the days of ease and leisure before May Thirtieth. In early June, Cai Hesen went to Beijing's Western Hills to recuperate from illness. Peng Shuzhi was in the hospital. Only Chen Duxiu and Qu Qiubai were writing articles for *Guide Weekly*. They handed in their copy and then paid no further attention to the matter, so editorial responsibility inevitably fell to me. To fill each issue, I translated articles from foreign languages or wrote about extraneous matters. When Chen and Qu were particularly busy, they wrote no articles at all, and I was responsible for the entire enterprise. Luckily, apart from this, I had no other agitprop work to distract me. But I was often busy with local work in Shanghai. I joined the reorganized District Committee. The secretary was still Zhuang Wengong; Xie Wenjin was in charge of the organization department, I was in charge of propaganda, Li Lisan was in charge of the labor movement, and Xiang Jingyu was in charge of women's work. Two worker comrades, Gu Shunzhang and Zhang Zuochen, joined the committee. Li Lisan was simply a figurehead; he rarely attended meetings. My job was rather straightforward: to write propaganda outlines, to represent the District Committee at subdistrict meetings, to lead the Commercial Press branch, and to do various other odd jobs. For example, when the order went out for Li Lisan's arrest, I escorted him to safety, booked a cabin for him on a steamship, and assigned a worker comrade to accompany him secretly to Hankou. But I did not let Li share a cabin with his wife, Yichun. When the worker comrade got back, he told me that Li Lisan had joined Yichun immediately after the ship cast off, for Yichun's cabinmate had turned out to be male, which made Li Lisan nervous.

The reorganized District Committee was still not equal to its tasks, for both Zhuang Wengong and Xie Wenjin were mediocrities. A second reorganization took place in November. Yin Kuan was transferred from Shandong, Zhuang Wengong was transferred to Zhejiang, and I stayed put. Soon after that, Yin Kuan came under attack from Shandong comrades for having fallen in love. He resigned his post on the grounds—feigned or otherwise—of illness and was replaced by Wang Yifei. I too stepped down from the District Committee, because Qu Qiubai wanted me to. He thought that propaganda work was being neglected. Only in the spring of 1926, when Luo Jiao came down to Shanghai from the north, did Shanghai local work resume its stride. Not long after that, Luo Jiao intercepted Zhao Shiyan on his way through Shanghai and kept him behind to take charge of organizational work. Yin Kuan took over local propaganda work from me. At this point, the golden age of Shanghai work started. Luo Jiao used another name after his return to China: He called himself Luo Yinong.[145]

After that, I worked exclusively for the Party journal and agitprop (save for teaching a few hours a week at Shanghai University). Before May Thirtieth, I had been a substitute lecturer. Peng Shuzhi taught "sociology," but less than a month after the start of the spring term of 1925, he fell ill and recommended me as his replacement. By "sociology" we meant the materialist conception of history, that is, the historical materialism propagated by Bukharin. I taught three classes, amounting to nine hours a week. After the summer vacation, Shanghai University moved to Qingyun Road in Zhabei. After his recovery, Peng taught the third-year classes, and I continued to teach the first and second years, no longer as a substitute. By that time, Shanghai University was almost a Communist Party school. The principal, Yu Youren,[146] did not reside in Shanghai; the deputy principal, Shao Zhonghui (Shao Lizi), was a Communist; the dean, Han Juemin, was a Communist; Shi Cuntong, the director of the Sociology Department, was a Communist; the lecturers in the Sociology Department—Li Ji, Gao Yuhan, Jiang Guangchi, Yin Kuan, Wang Yifei, Xiao Pusheng, Peng Shuzhi, and I—were Communists; Chen Wangdao, director of the Department of Chinese Literature, had been a Communist and was now working with the Communist Party, but the students believed that he was secretly plotting to destroy Communist Party influence; Zhou Yueran, director of the Department of English Literature, was nonpartisan—the students in his department tended toward anticommunism and had left the university with its ex-director, He Shizhen. Of the students, the overwhelming majority in the Sociology Department were Communists, and so were a good many in the other two departments; most of the rest were sympathizers. Shanghai University was not registered with the Beijing government's Ministry of Education. The elite universities looked down on it as a "pheasant university."[147]

It's true that the curriculum was not as it should have been, the dormitories on Qingyun Road were dilapidated, and most of the students came from provinces—especially Sichuan and Hunan—other than Jiangsu and Zhejiang.[148] In a word, Shanghai University was a miniaturized replica of the work-study movement in France. The role played by Shanghai University students in the lower ranks of revolutionary cadre was akin to that played by cadets of the Huangpu Military Academy as junior officers of the armies that carried out the Northern Expedition. What's more, a few former Shanghai University students (for example, Ouyang Jixiu) taught politics at Huangpu. The difference was that the Huangpu students gained their military expertise in the classroom, whereas the Shanghai University students got their political knowledge not in the classroom—or at least not from formal classes—but from extracurricular activities and research. Apart from Li Ji, the other Communist lecturers approached their teaching in a perfunctory and light-minded way. Li Ji translated *Students' Capital*[149] as teaching material, but the rest of us openly declared that we would not write special lectures and did little by way of preparation. If the students got anything from us, it was less from our formal appearances in the classroom than from the speeches we delivered at commemorative events, for we prepared such speeches rather more conscientiously. After a while, Peng Shuzhi even delegated third-year teaching to me. When Li Hanjun arrived, I let him take over all these classes, but he left after a couple of months, so I resumed my sociology teaching and stuck with it right up until Shanghai University was finally shut down.

Peng Shuzhi was not discharged from the hospital until just before National Day[150] in 1925. He had been there since early February. Not a single drop of the great wave of May Thirtieth sprayed his person. When he came out, the Propaganda Department had just moved to a house on Fusheng Road. Fusheng Road is a small road that runs between Range Road and Zhabei. It was close to the secretariat of the Central Committee, the Workers and Peasants Department, the District Committee, and the Shanghai General Union; it was much more convenient to live there than at Hadoon Road. The building was a three-story lane house. We met, ate, received visitors, and on occasion played mahjong on the ground floor. Peng Shuzhi occupied the whole of the first floor; the second floor was reserved for Cai Hesen and his wife, but while Cai was still in Beijing, Xiang Jingyu lived there by herself. I lived in the pavilion room. Xiang Jingyu brought in a Shanghai University female student called Yang Fulan to do secretarial work—mainly clipping and pasting newspaper reports—for two or three hours a day. Not long afterward, Yang left and Shen Yanbing or Yang Xianjiang brought in an old woman to do this work. Both Yang and the old woman were comrades. Zhang Guotao ate there, and Chen Duxiu often used to come for meetings of the presidium or for idle chats. Very soon, Cai Hesen returned. Qu Qiubai was living at Rue du Marché in the French Concession. He did not visit us often.

After the end of the great movement, our lives slipped back into a routine. Apart from when I had to get up early to give lectures, I spent my mornings in bed until ten or eleven o'clock. Before lunch, I would read the newspapers; in the afternoons, I would go to the printshop, go for a stroll, or look up old friends for a chat. I always worked at night, until two or three o'clock in the morning. I smoked, drank alcohol, went to the cinema, went to the amusement center, or played mahjong. Sometimes I went for walks, including some very long ones in the countryside around Shanghai. I rarely spent my free time on my own. I had drinking companions, opera-going companions, and fellow walking enthusiasts to accompany me on my excursions. All my friends were single men or men like Jiang Guangchi, Yin Kuan, Wang Ruofei, Yan Changyi, and Shi Qiong, whose wives or sweethearts were residing outside Shanghai. At the secretariat, I read reports from different places and learned about developments in the Party all over China; I heard from Luo Yinong, Zhao Shiyan, and Yin Kuan about the situation of the Party in Shanghai. Chatting with Qu Qiubai in his home in the French concession was quite different. He was immensely knowledgeable and witty and used to regale us with anecdotes about himself and others. He also kept us abreast of the literary journals, for apart from politics, we read nothing.

When Jiang Guangchi's novel came out, almost none of us bothered to read it. We were all deeply prejudiced against Jiang Guangchi himself, against his poems and novels, and against new literature in general. Even when we had the time to read his books, we lacked the inclination. Chen Duxiu flicked through *Shaonian piaopozhe* (Young wanderers) and said: "Even in hot weather I get goose bumps when I read this sort of stuff." Jiang gave me a copy, and I managed to struggle through it, but the next time I met him, I failed to give him the praise he was clearly seeking. He often said, "Foreign writers frequently get fan mail from their women readers, but Chinese women never write to authors." I realized that he was complaining about his own feelings of neglect. Qu Qiubai was more sympathetic to him than the rest of us and was able to converse with him about the literary world. One day after Jiang had left, Qu said, "That man really has no talent!" Jiang wrote a novel about our life in Shanghai during those years. Qu Qiubai played the main role in it, and there was even a faint shadow of me among its pages. Jiang asked Qu Qiubai what he should call the book. "Short-Trouser Party," said Qu. That was a mistranslation of the French *sans-culottes*. But in spite of his failings, Jiang pioneered the unblazed paths of revolutionary literature; the Creation Society's shift in line[151] did not happen until a year later.

Living as I did, I still had free time each month to work on a translation of *The ABC of Communism*.[152] I started work on this translation because there was downtime in our printshop. The movement had quieted down a bit, there was less call for leaflets, and the typesetters and printers were often idle. When the comrades in charge of managing the printshop asked me if I had anything to publish, I said that I could do some translating and they could print the text as I delivered it, in batches. I settled on the *ABC*, which expounds the political program of the Russian Bolshevik Party. The introduction explains what a Party program is, the second section is the *ABC*, and after that comes the Party program itself. The section on the Party program is about the same length as the *ABC*. The Russian, French, English, and German versions were all like that. I ventured to dispense with the introduction and the Party program and kept only the second explanatory section. It was translated, set, proofread, and printed bit by bit, and it was a long time before the entire text was finally published. I had never imagined that this book would have such a tremendous impact! In 1927, a Shanghai newspaper published a list of the last few years' best-sellers. At the top of the list was inevitably Sun Yat-sen's *Sanminzhuyi* (Three people's principles), but most copies of this book had been printed at official expense and distributed free. Next was the *ABC*; our central distribution department had no rules governing complimentary copies, but the book was cheap (at twenty cents), and I do not know whether reprints in other cities were distributed free or not. Third was Zhang Jingsheng's *Xing shi* (Stories of sex lives).[153]

Few people have noticed the significance of the *ABC* in the revolution of 1925 to 1927—namely, that it was the only book that told people what communism was really about. The awakening masses of the towns and villages had a great thirst for knowledge. They wanted to know where the revolution was taking them, but they could find no satisfactory answer in Guomindang propaganda, even when compiled by Communists. They could not even find one in the Communists' own publications such as *Guide Weekly*, Beijing's *Zhengzhi shenghuo* (Political life), or Guangzhou's *Renmin zhoukan* (People's weekly), for these publications simply said: "We are going to overthrow imperialism; we are going to overthrow the warlords." Was that all the Communists were after? Was that what the word "communism" meant? When the *ABC* was finally published, people at long last discovered that the Communist Party was out to abolish the system of private property, that it wanted "communal ownership," and that the revolution was the necessary product of objective developments—that it was inevitable. Thereafter, workers and peasants plunged into the daily struggle, which was against only the imperialists and the warlords, with this final goal in mind. Later, the Hunan peasants went even further than the Party leaders in promoting land revolution, and at the August 7 conference and thereafter, the Party took its "semi-Trotskyist" leap. These developments, too, were not unconnected with the appearance in Chinese of the *ABC*, which sowed seeds of revolution across the whole of China.

After the *ABC*, I translated other books, including Bukharin's *Lenin as a Marxist* and his *The Peasant Problem* and, finally, Stalin's *Problems of Leninism*. I set down two principles for myself: I would leave my name off my translations, and I would never take a fee. There were reasons for this decision.[154]

Before a year was up, we moved from Fusheng Road to a foreign-style lane house near Hengbin Bridge. Each house had a small front garden. The rooms were Western style, with bathtubs and flush toilets. The house we rented had direct access to a large bridging room attached to the house next door. Most of the other tenants were Japanese people or Western prostitutes. Peng Shuzhi had proposed this move so that the Propaganda Department could be expanded and its staff accommodated in one office. The bridging room was used for writing and equipped with four or five desks. The back part was screened off and turned into a library, with shelves to hold the economic journals I had purchased earlier and Russian books that people had brought back from Moscow. Qu Qiubai introduced Yang Muzhi, an administrative worker at Shanghai University, to help run things; the District Committee assigned the Shanghai University student Huang Wenrong to take charge of administration at a slightly higher level, and Shen Yanbing to run the Bureau of Information. Everyone save Shen lived in this house. Shen attended the office for several hours each day. I had no choice but to change my lifestyle. But by then we were already in the "insurrectionary" period.

* * *

The idea of a Shanghai "insurrection" came up at the time of Sun Chuanfang's "autumn exercises." In the autumn of 1925, Sun, the military governor of Zhejiang province, massed his troops on the pretext of holding autumn exercises and launched a surprise attack on the Fengtian Army in Jiangsu. A couple of days later, he took Shanghai almost without a fight, drove the Fengtian Army from Jiangsu, and declared himself commander in Chief of the Allied Army of Five Provinces. Zhang Guotao said: "Next time there is a war in Shanghai, we should make preparations to disarm the defeated troops, equip ourselves at their expense, and then hold talks with the victor-warlord." It had not yet occurred to him that the next time would be the war between the Northern Expedition and the Beiyang warlords.

Preparations for the insurrection were made by the Military Committee. This was a secret body—secret not only to the outside world but also to Party comrades. At that time, there were three sorts of organization in the Chinese Communist Party: the Youth League, the Party, and the Military Committee, the committee being the most rigidly disciplined and the League the least. But the committee was not established until a long time after my return to China. When I was in Moscow, the Russian Military Academy was not yet open to Chinese students. Their eventual admission was doubtless connected with the founding of the Military Academy at Huangpu. Among those studying military science in Moscow were newly arrived Chinese students like Yan Changyi, Chinese students like Nie Rongzhen who had gone to Moscow from Western Europe, and ex-KUTV students like Xiao Jingguang. Wang Yifei was transferred from KUTV to the Military Academy to be an interpreter, so he also learned some military science. A strict selection procedure governed admission to the academy. You had to be fit and strong, but even more important, you had to be from a poor family with no rich relatives or ties to high officials.

I do not know how many people studied military science, nor do I remember precisely when a Military Committee was set up under the Central Committee. I have an idea that it was at the end of 1925 or the beginning of 1926. At first, it was under Wang Yifei and Yan Changyi. The comrades on the Military Committee did not belong to ordinary branches. In principle, neither its members nor its work was known to ordinary Party members, so I did not know about the committee's activities or the military preparations for the Shanghai insurrection, though some people close to me did give me an inkling of what was going on. Yan Changyi often took me to the Military Committee's headquarters and asked me to attend his training course. A lecture on "secret correspondence" was in Russian, and since Wang Yifei and the other comrades who knew Russian could not get around to dealing with it, Yan asked me to teach it. So I also learned something about secret correspondence, but unfortunately, I have forgotten the names of many of the chemicals. During the insurrectionary period in Shanghai, the Military Committee was enlarged, and Zhou Enlai became an important figure in it. Hangzhou's insurrection in response to the Northern Expedition was the committee's work. After Gu Shunzhang returned from Hangzhou, he also joined the committee leadership to help prepare the Shanghai insurrection. But the political preparations for the insurrection were made by the District Committee.

When Luo Yinong became secretary of the District Committee, its style changed radically. Luo had guts. He acted boldly and resolutely. He put the Party's internal organization into the capable and reliable hands of Zhao Shiyan; He Jinliang easily coped with day-to-day union business, while Zhao Shiyan decided the important questions. The scope of our work grew daily, and our administration became increasingly accomplished; the Communist Party in Shanghai became a powerful force. Luo Yinong did not immerse himself in Shanghai work, unlike several of his predecessors. He participated in "diplomatic" work, which in the past had belonged to the Central Committee. For example, he liaised with important members of the Shanghai Guomindang, kept up contact with left-wing capitalists, and tried to make friendly contacts with gangsters so as to win their neutrality or support. During Chen Duxiu's "disappearance,"[155] Luo practically took over this side of Party work. For that purpose, he got himself an even more luxurious residence than ours and lived there with his wife, his mother-in-law, and his brother-in-law. He used to wear a long gown and a mandarin jacket. He had bushy eyebrows and a big mouth. He looked awe-inspiring when he did not smile, very much like a middle-class family patriarch. Zhao Shiyan lived with him, but much more simply and frugally. He Songlin, Wang Ruofei, Yin Kuan, and I were frequent guests in this house. We used to order food from nearby restaurants, drink alcohol, and play mahjong with Luo's mother-in-law.

By this time, the Northern Expedition had already made considerable progress. It had occupied Hunan and Jiangxi, and not long after that, it took Hankou. The Party in Shanghai had already put the insurrection at the top of its agenda. The Guangdong government[156] sent Niu Yongjian to Shanghai to take secret command; Du Yuesheng acted as his protector. In the course of our cooperation with Niu, we too developed relations with Du. In October or November 1926, we proposed staging an immediate insurrection and occupying Shanghai, but Niu would have none of it. We made preparations to act secretly. We had comrades on a battleship anchored off Gaochangmiao, and on land, we had already made some preparations. We hoped that if just a few people dared to act, we might sway the northern armies[157] and cause them to collapse, disintegrate, or surrender, for at the same time, Niu Yongjian was lobbying the Shanghai garrison. But when the navy fired a few salvos, there was no response on land. A few comrades of the Military Committee were locked in stalemate for a while with a police contingent in the Nantao district of Shanghai,[158] but they were defeated, and Xi Zuoyao was seized and subsequently shot at Longhua.[159] Just a few days earlier, I had played mahjong with Xi in the Military Committee headquarters. This was what was later known as the first insurrection. When the navy opened fire, Luo Yinong was visiting Niu Yongjian in his home. When Niu heard the firing, he blanched. He knew that it was our doing and blamed us for not letting him know about it in advance.

The second insurrection, in February 1927, was better prepared. Hangzhou had already fallen to the Northern Expeditionaries. We called a general strike; at the same time, our armed squads attacked police stations. That night, I was at command headquarters, helping out at the new Party school in Guanhua Alley off Route Lafayette. I watched as group after group was dispatched to its position. No one dared sleep. Everyone was waiting for good news to arrive, but none came. I went to the second floor to listen. I seemed to hear firing, but I could not be sure. The next morning, the various groups came back. Some said that the people they had been waiting for had not arrived, others that the police stations had been prepared for them, that no one had dared move, and that some people had fired a few shots and then backed off. Wang Hebo's younger brother turned up in a furious temper. He said that he had prepared weapons aboard the battleship, but no boat had arrived from Pudong to fetch them.

In March 1927, the third insurrection finally succeeded. We captured all the police stations, surrounded the garrison occupying the Oriental Library and the Northern Railway Station, captured large numbers of weapons, and set up an armed picket of two to three thousand men.

The insurrection began at midday. During the afternoon and night, the fighting intensified. We drove to Zhabei to see what was going on; dusk set in. During the night, I constantly crossed back and forth between the Propaganda Department and Hengfeng Alley in Scott Road. At that time, Chen Duxiu was living in the Propaganda Department building, and the District Committee had one of its offices in Hengfeng Alley so as to be able to pass on news from the front. We could hear firing from Zhabei throughout the night—sometimes heavy, sometimes light. On occasion, it was so heavy that it sounded like strings of firecrackers going off. People were sent out from Hengfeng Alley to take news of the battle to the Propaganda Department; sometimes Chen Duxiu sent back directives. I too passed on several notes. At around three o'clock in the morning, Chen sent a note to the people in Zhabei proposing that they withdraw to Dachang in order to avoid sacrifices. But the people at the front failed to act on the proposal. After we had stabilized our position, the northern troops were gradually overcome.

The following afternoon, I returned to Zhabei to take a second look. The northerners inside the Oriental Library had still not surrendered. The iron gate in front of the building was firmly shut. There were a dozen or so soldiers on one of the upper stories who fired whenever anyone passed by the gate. The besiegers lurked behind street corners or in the printing factory of the Commercial Press on the other side of the road. People warned me not to cross in front of the library, so I took the long way around to the back of the Commercial Press building. Inside was a command post of the insurrection, where I saw Zhao Shiyan and Zhou Enlai. Soon afterward, Gu Shunzhang arrived to report on his negotiations with the troops occupying the library. After the sealing of the General Labor Union in 1925, a warrant had been issued for Gu's arrest because of his union activities or for some other reason, so he had fled Shanghai. When the Northern Expedition reached Hangzhou, he had greeted it by organizing an insurrection in the city. Now he was one of the main organizers of the Shanghai insurrection. He wrote a note and took it personally to the iron gate in front of the library, advising the soldiers to surrender and informing them that the garrison at the Northern Railway Station had already laid down its arms. (Actually, the troops at the station were still holding out.) He brought back the troops' reply, which was that they would not surrender.

While our people were discussing what to do, some other comrades and I went on an observation tour of the Zhabei streets, which were quiet except for occasional groups of three or four people armed with rifles and revolvers. We turned into a small road to the west of the Oriental Library, where there was an insurrection post manned by several dozen armed workers; Zhao Shiyan was there too. A Commercial Press worker protested furiously that someone had taken his pistol and said that we should send people out to take revenge. It turned out that there were other units active on the Zhabei streets who did not consider themselves under the jurisdiction of the General Labor Union. They had come not to take part in the insurrection but to take away the northerners' weapons for purposes of their own. There were far fewer of them than there were of us, and they had no liaison network, but Zhao Shiyan restrained the angry workers and refused to let them cause trouble.

Just at that moment, there was a commotion in front of the Oriental Library, and shots rang out. We rushed over to see what was happening. Either the library had fallen to an attack or its occupiers had surrendered, for a large crowd of workers surrounded a knot of northern soldiers and accompanied them away from the library. By that time, the whole of Zhabei, except for the Northern Railway Station, was in the hands of insurrectionists. I wanted to go to the station to see what was happening but was ordered not to. We went back to North Sichuan Road, and while we were crossing the railroad tracks, we suddenly heard rifle fire from the direction of the Northern Railway Station. The firing got nearer and nearer. We all fled into an alley, locked the iron gate, and peered out to see what was happening. Very soon, northern troops came running down the track, some armed with rifles, others not. Some had patches of fresh blood on their gray cotton-padded greatcoats. Obviously, it was not they who had opened fire. Not long after they had run by, people outside the alley began to spread the word that the northern troops were squatting on the track and no longer moving. We went out to see for ourselves. Sure enough, just three or four hundred paces from where we had been hiding, northern troops were sitting down with their rifles on the ground to show that they had surrendered. Crowds of citizens jostled around them and took their weapons; they did not resist. By the time the General Labor Union sent someone to accept their surrender, many of the rifles had been taken away by people who had nothing to do with the insurrection.

We crossed the railroad tracks back into Zhabei and went down Baoshan Road to the Northern Railway Station, which General Xue Yue had already occupied. A handful of Hunanese troops recounted the fighting to us. In front of the station were some trenches that the northerners had started but not finished. Two headless corpses hung from the railing along the International Settlement. They were naked from the waist up, but from their leggings and trousers you could see that they were policemen, not soldiers.

There were eight or nine corpses—northerners who had been shot trying to escape into the International Settlement—hanging from the barbed wire that spread across North Henan Road. Behind the barbed wire, foreign soldiers manned machine guns.

   We went back to the headquarters on Xiangshan Road, planning to return from there to North Sichuan Road. As dusk approached, I suddenly heard rifle fire from the east. Everyone was puzzled. Soon, reports arrived to say that the firing was coming from a trainload of northerners who had arrived from Wusong; they had already left the train and were attacking in our direction. An urgent order went out to take up defensive positions, and we outsiders ran off to hide. It was not until later that I learned that these troops had fled to Wusong by train that morning. When they found that the track had been dug up, they managed some way or other to get back to Shanghai. When their train reached the area behind the Commercial Press building, they found that the track there had also been dug up, so they had no choice but to retreat to the railway station at Tiantongan Road and dig in. There were quite a few of them, and they were well armed. If they attacked Zhabei, the insurrectionists would be in no position to resist. Luckily, the troops' morale was gone. They had no idea of the real situation in Shanghai; night had already fallen, so they adopted a defensive strategy. Later, the northern soldiers at the Tiantongan Railway Station gave their weapons to the Japanese and withdrew into the International Settlement. The Central Committee of the Communist Youth League had its headquarters near the Tiantongan Railway Station. Xiao Zizhang and his Russian wife, who lived there, spent the whole night in terror.

   The next day, the situation in Zhabei had completely changed. The streets were bustling with people—not shoppers but armed workers, unarmed workers, students, and women marching up and down, demonstrating. I followed them from Baoshan Road past the Northern Railway Station toward Xinzha Bridge. The armed men were dressed in short gowns; some wore the green uniforms of postmen. After the demonstrations were over, I went to the new headquarters of the Shanghai General Labor Union, housed in the building of the Huzhou Fellow Townspeople's Association, and also to the general command post of the workers' picket in the Oriental Library. The entrances to both these places were guarded by machine guns. The people at the General Labor Union asked me to stay behind to help them; I spent the night there. We passed the whole night in fear. People brought reports saying that a group of ruffians were on their way to attack the building and disarm us. Actually, we had no weapons, in spite of the fact that the gate to our building was guarded by machine guns. We asked the people at the Oriental Library for reinforcements; for some reason, no pickets came, but a dozen or so troops of the Sappers' Battalion of the First Division eventually arrived.

Long Dadao and I welcomed the squad commander who had led these troops over to our side.

Victory in Shanghai was now assured, and Suzhou and Nanjing also fell. After Chiang Kai-shek arrived in Shanghai, Bai Chongxi took over as garrison commander. It rapidly became clear that they intended to treat us as enemies. One night, Zhou Enlai arrived at our house near Hengbin Bridge, where ever since the start of the insurrection, Chen Duxiu had stayed with us. He slept in my bed, so I slept in the office room on a bamboo bed. We had not yet retired when Zhou arrived. Chen Duxiu, other officials of the Propaganda Department, and I were all busy in the office.

Zhou Enlai said, "Three drops of water[160] has arrived. The Russian comrades told me. I was the first person to meet him. No one else knows he is here yet. He is on our side. He asked me whether comrades back in China resented the fact that he had gone abroad before the start of the Northern Expedition and returned only after its successful conclusion. I explained to him that the comrades back in China all hoped that he would quickly start to lead them. He voiced some dissatisfaction with the Russian comrades. He said that the comrades responsible for getting him back to China had treated him like a prisoner, both on the train in Siberia and on the steamship from Vladivostok to Shanghai."

Zhou Enlai proposed sending Wang Jingwei directly to Hankou and not letting him meet Chiang Kai-shek and the other Guomindang leaders in Shanghai. Chen Duxiu agreed. After that, Zhou Enlai came every day without fail, sometimes more than once. I was not present during discussions, but I do know that his proposal was not implemented. One day, he went out with Chen Duxiu. When Chen came back, he said that he had been to see Wang Jingwei. Wang told him that he had already met Chiang Kai-shek, that Wu Zhihui and others had also been present at the meeting, that Wu had loudly cursed the Communist Party, and that Chiang had kept quiet. Chen Duxiu said: Wu and Chiang are of one mind; this one plays the red-faced part, that one plays the white.[161] That night, Chen Duxiu spent a long time at his desk penning his "Wang-Chen joint manifesto." The next day, when Zhou Enlai brought the manifesto back, I noticed that Wang had endorsed it, leaving a big white space on the front. The implication was that Chen Duxiu should sign the front, but Chen signed his name beneath Wang's. When the newspapers published the manifesto, Chen Duxiu said to me: "It's a long time since the big newspapers[162] published anything by me!"

The aim of the manifesto was to scotch rumors, ensure that cooperation between the two parties continued to the end, and explain that the General Labor Union pickets had no intention of attacking the garrison headquarters at Longhua. Actually, these rumors had been deliberately started by Chiang Kai-shek to prepare the way for an attack on the pickets.

After the transfer of the First Division from Zhabei, the Second Division arrived to replace it. The divisional commander Liu Zhi was an anti-Communist. One day, when I was helping out Mao Zemin[163] in our newly opened bookshop, a soldier bought a book and then, instead of leaving, indicated that he wanted to talk with us.

Standing by the side of the counter, he said in a low voice, "Be careful, the pickets should keep their guns and ammunition by their side when they go to sleep."

"Why?" I asked.

He was unwilling to elaborate. Actually, we had known for a long time from other sources that Chiang Kai-shek was planning to attack us. A Huangpu student called Jiang Youliang was a Communist. At an officers' meeting at command headquarters, Pan Yizhi, director of the Political Department, had expressed anti-Communist opinions, and Jiang Youliang had stood up to rebut him. The order had immediately gone out for Jiang's arrest, but his fellow students secretly allowed him to escape. He had sought out Zhou Enlai and told him of Chiang Kai-shek's conspiracy. Needless to say, we got reports from other channels too. Zhou Enlai wrote a "Letter to Messrs. Chen Duxiu and Chiang Kai-shek." The letter was very long and agitated. It was not published anywhere. I was worried and told Yin Kuan so. He consoled me, saying: "Even if Chiang's attack on us succeeds, it will be only a temporary military victory; politically, he will have lost and we will have won." The organ of the District Committee that Yin edited had already secretly begun to attack Chiang Kai-shek. This newspaper was published using the typesetting and printing machines of the Commercial Press.

On the morning of April 12, I awoke in the house near Hengbin Bridge to the sound of gunfire from the direction of Zhabei. I asked the others what was happening. They told me that the firing had started at midnight. Soon after that, Zhao Shiyan's wife, Xia Zhixu, came from the District Committee with an order for me to go and work there. According to her, the shooting was being done by thugs belonging to the Green Gang; they were using pistol carbines, and there were not many of them. We prepared to rush out and disarm them. I asked her about the attitude of the garrison army. She said that it was sticking to a neutral course. By the time I arrived in Zhabei, the situation had changed dramatically. The 26th Army, under General Zhou Fengqi, had joined in the thugs' attack on the Oriental Library, the Huzhou Fellow Townspeople's Association building, and other picket centers. When I went to Baoshan Road to look for Zhou Enlai, he was just coming out of the hospital opposite the Commercial Press building. He told me that we should give out leaflets along the streets and paste up slogans opposing the new warlords; he said that there was no longer any need to worry about maintaining our collaboration with Chiang Kai-shek. I immediately got to work. I did not witness the demonstration and massacre on Baoshan Road.

Early one morning two or three days after the massacre, three people came to the house near Hengbin Bridge and awakened me. They were Chen Yannian, Li Lisan, and Nie Rongzhen. They had just arrived from Hankou. En route, they had heard about the April 12 counterrevolution and reckoned that the Propaganda Department where I lived would be comparatively safe, which was why they were there. They wanted me to take them to see Luo Yinong and Zhao Shiyan. I asked them to wait inside the house while I went off by myself to where Luo lived. Zhao was there too. I told them about the arrival of Chen, Li, and Nie and that the three were at my house waiting to see them. Luo looked at Zhao, Zhao looked at Luo; both realized what the visit was about. Luo told me to bring the three to his home, so I went back to fetch them. Only then did I discover that the Central Committee in Hankou had sacked Luo Yinong and sent Chen Yannian to replace him. Chen Yannian also brought an order from the Central Committee that concerned me. It said that all Central Committee officials still in Shanghai—Zheng Chaolin of the Propaganda Department, Luo Yan of the Peasant Department, and Yang Zhihua of the Women's Department—should proceed forthwith to Hankou. I left Luo Yinong's house and went with Li Lisan to the Three Friends' Industrial Society to buy a new quilt; even more important, I visited an optician to buy a pair of sunglasses.

On around April 22, comrade Lu Dingyi of the Central Committee of Communist Youth and I reluctantly set out for Wuhan. Chen Duxiu had already left for Hankou after issuing the Wang-Chen joint manifesto.

6

Wuhan

I met daily with Lu Dingyi, head of the Propaganda Department of the Central Committee of Communist Youth, to collect news about the insurrection, edit propaganda material, draft propaganda outlines, and formulate slogans. The Propaganda Departments of the Central Committee, of the Regional Committee of Zhejiang, Jiangsu, and Anhui, and of Communist Youth were virtually inextricable from one another in those days. Lu was a student of Communications University. He was young and bright and wrote well, but like me, he was no speaker. Sometimes I had no choice but to mount the platform and make some perfunctory speech, but Lu would not speak under any circumstances. Lu and I sailed together on a steamship belonging to the Jardine Matheson Company. All our fellow passengers thought that Lu was my younger brother, for we were both wearing Western-style clothes made of the same cloth by the same tailor.

The ship was chock-full of passengers. Two British warships escorted us and a convoy of other vessels, so the price of a ticket in steerage was temporarily raised to forty-five dollars, equivalent to more than a month's salary for Lu and me.

Many of the faces were familiar. Opposite my berth and beneath Lu's was Song Yunbin, head of the National Press Agency. I seem to recall that when he took over that job from Shao Ji'ang, it was I who showed him the way there; in any case, I was present in some capacity or other. It appeared that he no longer remembered me, so I pretended that I did not recognize him either. After several days on board, we got into a conversation about the weather or some such thing. He suddenly said, "I know you!" I replied, "I know you too!" We stopped standing on ceremony, and I drank his spirits and ate his peanuts.

Our three berths were on the starboard side to the rear. Walking over to the port side, I discovered that Big-mouth Luo[164] was also on board. He was his old happy-go-lucky self, cracking jokes with Big-shot Li[165] in the berth above. One would shout out "Big-mouth," and the other would shout back

"Big-shot." The two of them also fired random questions at a bespectacled old man in the berth alongside them. The old man was traveling with his wife and four or five sons and daughters. He said that he was going to Hankou on business and that he had originally run a fish business somewhere in Nanjing. We asked him about the price of fish and what sort of fish was best to eat. He was Wang Hebo. His brother, Wang Zhendong, was on the boat too, but never acknowledged him. Their berths were at opposite ends of the ship. Pacing the deck with Wang Zhendong, I said, "Your brother really does look like a fish-shop owner." He said, "Did you know that Yang Pusheng, vice-chairman of the Shanghai General Labor Union, is on board?"

In steerage, there were large numbers of young people in Western clothes, Chinese clothes, and students' tunic suits. If you asked them what they did, they replied, "I sell fruit," "I'm in the tea trade," I'm a general dealer," or "I peddle chinaware." Many of the passengers slept with their faces under their quilts. Very few emulated my and Lu Dingyi's habit of roaming around steerage, the cabin area, the first-class saloon, and the deck. But things changed after the first day. The ship steamed through Nanjing without stopping, and we all hid, for the troops in Pukou and Xiaguan often shot at one another across the Yangtze.[166] Once Nanjing was behind us, the sleepers woke and removed their quilts from their faces; people previously glued to their berths began promenading about the deck. A youthful "fruit seller" ran across to me and said, "Someone told me Guo Moruo is on board. Is it true?" I was astonished—a fruit seller asking about Guo Moruo. Lu Dingyi introduced me to someone who had been at the university with him, a taciturn young fellow whose false name was something-Di. (I forget his real name and also the false name he adopted in Longhua Prison in 1931.) While walking deck, I suddenly came across Pan Jiachen. I was surprised to meet him. He told me that he had just returned to Shanghai from Moscow.

I said, "Little Pan, you. . . ."

He corrected me: "People call me Old Pan now, they don't call me Little Pan anymore."

He said that he already had a girlfriend and that she was still in Moscow, a woman from Shandong called Zhuang Dongxiao.

"You're certainly lucky to be loved by such a beautiful woman," I told him.

He asked me how I knew about Zhuang Dongxiao.

"Last year in Shanghai, I met Yuan Qingyun and Ren Zhuoxuan. Yuan was pulling Ren's leg because Zhuang Dongxiao had given Ren the cold shoulder. Yuan said that Zhuang Dongxiao was the prettiest of all the women students."

On hearing the name Yuan Qingyun, Pan told me that he and Yuan had clashed on some private matter and that Yuan had forged a letter and put it in Pan's pocket and then told the GPU. Pan had spent quite a few days in jail until Voitinsky finally bailed him out.

Little Pan brought a short fellow over to meet me and introduced him as Chen Shaoyu.[167] He also introduced me to a thin man called Liu Guozhang. He said that both spoke good Russian and were able comrades.

At Wuhu, a new batch of passengers climbed aboard. After the ship had pulled up anchor, Luo Yinong and Li Lisan—Big-mouth and Big-shot—rushed over to get me and took me to a cabin full of people who had boarded at Wuhu. I recognized one of them as Wu Qi, who had worked with us in Montargis. But the person Luo and Li had come to meet was a middle-aged man with a small moustache called Zhang Shushi, a member of the Guomindang's Jiangsu Provincial Committee.[168] All the new passengers were members of the Guomindang's organization in Jiangsu. They had fled Nanjing in a small hired craft during the purge[169] and spent a week or so on the Yangtze before reaching Wuhu.

After passing through Wuhu, Datong, Anqing, and Jiujiang, these "fish-shop owners," "fruit sellers," "tea traders," and the like all began to chatter volubly. They clearly knew far more about politics than most other people in similar lines of business. But there were still a few people who uttered no sound and stayed under their quilts. Wang Zhendong said to me, "They're reactionaries; Chiang Kai-shek is sending them to Wuhan to stir up trouble." Later, I learned that people on the ship trailed them ashore in Wuhan to find out where they were staying and then reported back to the Wuhan General Labor Union, which arrested them.

While I was disembarking in Hankou, Voitinsky emerged from the first-class saloon. I nodded at him; he nodded back. Discovering that he had traveled on the same ship was the most astonishing thing of all.

* * *

On arrival in Hankou, I had nowhere to live. The Central Committee's Propaganda Department no longer existed. Its chief, Peng Shuzhi, was busy composing his reply to Qu Qiubai[170] and getting some money together in preparation for the birth of his child. Huang Wenrong had been transferred from the department to work for Chen Duxiu as his private secretary, and Yang Muzhi had been transferred to the secretariat to work as a copier.[171] *Guide Weekly*'s Hankou edition had already been appearing for some time and was being edited by someone who had returned from studying in Japan, so I had become supernumerary. In the three years since my return to China, not a single issue of *Guide Weekly* had appeared without me proofreading it. I lived for a while in the secretariat, for a while in the Chang Jiang Bookshop, and for a while in the printshop.

On my first day in Hankou, Huang Wenrong took me to "No. 61." I cannot remember the name of the road, but I do remember that the building was next door to the official residence of Tang Shengzhi. It was a three-story foreign-style house that opened directly onto the street. There was a big room on every floor, one or two medium-sized rooms, and one or two small rooms. Just inside the door were half a dozen burly northerners dressed in short gowns. They came out to interrogate us. When they saw that it was Huang Wenrong who had brought me, they let me in without further ado. Downstairs was the dining room. The other downstairs rooms belonged to these bodyguards. The big room on the first floor was laid out for meetings. The second floor was for living in: Chen Duxiu lived in the middle, Peng Shuzhi and his wife in the room to the left, Cai Hesen and his wife in the one to the right, and Huang Wenrong in another smaller room.

For a while, we exchanged social chitchat; then we were called downstairs for lunch. Chen Bilan[172] and Li Yichun[173] were not at home. We five men sat down at a table to eat. Peng Shuzhi and Cai Hesen began to argue. Peng kept on referring to "Comrade Zhongfu" and "the old gentleman."[174] "I have my own opinions," interjected Chen Duxiu, in great earnest. "Comrade Shuzhi should stop dragging me into the discussion!" After the meal, Huang Wenrong gave me a new booklet authored by Qu Qiubai. I forget its main title;[175] all I remember is its two subtitles: *Diling guoji* (Zero international) and *Fandui Peng Shuzhizhuyi* (Against Peng Shuzhi-ism).

At this point, I must return to Shanghai and recall how the split in the Chinese Communist Party came into being.

* * *

Chen Duxiu broke with Hu Shi, Qian Xuantong, Liu Fu, and the Zhou brothers,[176] his comrades in arms in the May Fourth Movement, and became a socialist. Among those who joined him in his socialist enterprise were Zhou Fohai, Li Da, Li Hanjun, and Shi Cuntong, all barely out of school; they had learned Kautsky-style Marxism from people like Kawakami Hajime and Yamakawa Hitoshi. But there were also some Guomindang veterans, including Dai Tianqiu, Shen Xuanlu, and Shao Lizi. When the Communist Party was founded, the people who had studied in Japan all joined, but the Guomindang veterans wavered. Not long after that, Chen Duxiu broke with these two groups and began to cooperate with a group of people under the leadership of Zhang Guotao who were engaged in various forms of practical activity, as well as with foreigners and Chinese sent to China by the Third International.

The development of Chen Duxiu's thinking can be gauged from the friends he made. One man who stuck by Chen Duxiu throughout the various stages of Chen's intellectual odyssey was Li Dazhao. He was Chen Duxiu's friend not only during the *New Youth* period but also during the *Jiayin*[177] period. Within the Chinese Communist Party, only he had the qualifications to vie with Chen for the leadership. But he was so modest and so sincerely submissive in his relations with Chen that he stood on Chen's side in all disputes. Apart from him, all the greater and lesser leaders of the Party were Chen's students, interpreters, or advisers—his *conseillers* or *ministres*.[178] Chen's first "minister" was Li Hanjun, from the period between the fomentation that led to the founding of the Party and the Fourth Congress of the Third International; his second was Qu Qiubai, from the Fourth Congress of the Third International to the summer of 1924; his third was Peng Shuzhi, from the Fourth Congress of the Communist Party through the unification of the Left Opposition in China.

"Chen Duxiu is no theoretician"—this judgment of Trotsky's was very much to the point. Chen was a practical politician: He was equipped with acutely sensitive antennae, and he could see both deep and far. As a theoretician, he was way behind Lenin and Trotsky, but among China's self-proclaimed "Marxist theoreticians," there was none that could approach him, nor is there any now. He enjoyed absolute authority in the Party, an authority that was established quite spontaneously. In my view, had it not been for the interference of the Third International, there would never have been great disputes and even splits in the Chinese Communist Party under his leadership. All the disputes in the Chinese Communist Party were connected in one way or another to representatives of the Comintern. I have already mentioned the case of Maring and the Third Congress. After the conclusion of that dispute, it was as if all issues had been resolved. The entire Party unanimously adopted the line of "national revolution," which meant in practice that we would first give real substance to the party of Chinese democracy (the Guomindang, which had hitherto existed in name only) and help it seize national power; then we would prepare our own revolution under its rule, overthrow it, and seize state power. This was the line of the Third International or, rather, of Russia's Commissariat of Foreign Affairs. The commissariat put the emphasis on the first stage, that is, how to transform China into an early-Kemalite Turkey or an Outer Mongolian People's Republic;[179] as for the second stage, it was supplementary and not emphasized. If China acquired a Mongolian-style government, then the second stage— what Peng Shuzhi called the Chinese proletariat's "future own revolution"— would indeed become redundant. But when the Chinese Communist Party, or at least its leader Chen Duxiu, accepted this line, it put the emphasis precisely on the second stage. If—as Lenin said of the Russian Revolution—a country cannot make socialist revolution without first going through national revolution, then we would willingly play the role of coolie and do our best to put the "braggart"[180] Sun Yat-sen onto the president's throne, but only because this would enable us to start preparing for our own revolution. Precisely because of that fact—even though we are presently carrying out national revolution and have entered the Guomindang—we should remain as a party out of power and in opposition, we should monopolize the leadership of the workers' and peasants' movement, and we should not let the Guomindang take part in that movement. In that way we can overthrow the state power of the Guomindang with the strength of China's own masses.

Clearly, under the superficial unanimity of "national revolution" lurked two different tendencies: the Comintern one and the Chinese one. The Chinese tendency was represented by the Shanghai Central Committee under Chen Duxiu. Cai Hesen was just as resolute as Chen on these issues. Peng Shuzhi brought an article back from Moscow titled "Who Leads the Chinese National Revolution?" He said that after the achievement of the national revolution, we would still need to carry out "our own" revolution, but he also said that the revolution that is "not our own" would "automatically" come under the leadership of the proletariat. This theory of the proletariat constituting the natural leadership of the national revolution was to the exact taste of the Chinese comrades and became the guiding theory in the Party during those few years. The Shanghai Regional Committee, the Hunan Regional Committee, the Northern Regional Committee, and places like Shandong and Henan all shared the same position as the Central Committee in Shanghai on this issue.

The Comintern tendency was represented by the group of advisers under Borodin. Tan Pingshan, Chen Yannian, and Zhou Enlai in Guangdong all chimed in with Borodin on this question. They had practically no comprehension of the vision of the "second-stage revolution" held by comrades in the other provinces. At the very least, they did not attach any great importance to this vision. But they lacked arguments with which to rebut it. In Shanghai, I met comrades from many other places, but I never once came across any overt or even covert expression of opposition to the Central Committee on theoretical or political questions—save for Chen Yannian. Tan Pingshan and Zhou Enlai mouthed ambiguous responses; even though they may have been dissatisfied with this or that formulation, they never once dared to voice their opinions. But Chen Yannian was different. He had not attended the Fourth Congress and had not reached Shanghai until after the assassination of Liao Zhongkai.[181] One day, we received a message from the Russian consulate saying that Chen Yannian had arrived in Shanghai a few days earlier. But we had not seen him, so we began to panic, fearing that Guomindang Rightists might have murdered him on the boat or when he landed. Then I found a small ad in *Republic Daily* saying that a man called Lin Mu wanted to know the whereabouts of Ma Daofu.[182] I was just about to go to the place indicated in the announcement to look for Lin Mu when Zhang Bojian brought Chen Yannian in. He wore his habitual comic expression that made everybody want to laugh, but his belly stuck out even further and his legs were even thinner than usual. I took him to meet his father. It is difficult to describe the emotion they expressed on meeting. This fact should put to rest the myth that Chen Duxiu had no regard for relations between father and son. I left while they were talking. That night, Chen Yannian stayed in my home. For the first time ever, I heard—from him— expressions of dissatisfaction with the Shanghai Central Committee, but he was unable to say how his disapproval had come about. I remember only that he quoted Borodin to the effect that all the articles in *Guide Weekly* were on the same theme, that they simply harped on the general idea of "Workers of the world, unite." Expressed in modern parlance, the people in Guangdong criticized the Central Committee for "not understanding political realism."

Chen Yannian praised my articles in *New Youth*. He said that he himself could not write. I had heard it all before. Chen Yannian was well-read, quick-witted in his choice of words, and a deep thinker. I liked to hear him speak, but I had never seen anything written by him. While we were bringing out *Youth* in France, he copied some articles for other people but never wrote anything himself. In Moscow, everyone practiced writing articles, and Chen Qiaonian proved capable of doing so, but Chen Yannian would never put pen to paper. So we accused him of pretending. The reason he praised my articles in *New Youth* was that he wanted me to write his reports for him. (He had brought no secretary to Shanghai.) He told me that all the reports he had sent from Guangdong had been written for him by a secretary. I got my pen. While he paced up and down my tiny room smoking and recounting the assassination of Liao Zhongkai, I wrote down his exact words, without embellishment. The result was a vivid and lucid report.

I do not know whether father and son quarreled at their reunion. When Chen Duxiu saw the reports from Guangdong in the secretariat, he often used to bang his fist on the table and explode. Once, when Chen Yannian sent a representative to talk to Chen Duxiu, I happened to be present. Pointing in my direction, Chen Duxiu said to the representative: "That is Comrade Chaolin. He[183] has written several letters requesting that Chaolin be transferred to Guangdong. Does this mean that he is deliberately trying to make the Central Committee unworkable?" Chen Duxiu often said irrational things when his temper got the better of him.

Gradually, the Comintern tendency prevailed over the Chinese tendency, or rather the Guangdong style prevailed over the Shanghai style, especially after the start of the Northern Expedition. Within the five-person presidium, Qu Qiubai belonged to the Borodin tendency. As I said earlier, when I first got back to China, Qu Qiubai was in disfavor. He had just been put under strict orders to return to Shanghai from Guangdong, for he had been engaging in activities in Guangdong under the direction of Borodin in the name of the Central Committee. People were saying that Chen Duxiu and Cai Hesen were furious with him. Qu Qiubai fundamentally disapproved of the other leaders' concept of national revolution. Qu was intelligent, spoke and wrote good Russian, had good connections among the Russian comrades, and understood the real intention of the Comintern's line of national revolution. But he obeyed instructions and returned to Shanghai, where he did what Peng Shuzhi called "high-level technical work" right up to the start of the Northern Expedition. It was only after the Northern Expedition that he revealed his oppositionist views.

The Northern Expedition inevitably became a vexing issue in the contest between the two tendencies and the two styles. *Guide Weekly* clearly opposed the expedition. Chen Duxiu's article opposing it created a sensation. The Guomindang's Central Committee in Guangzhou formally raised the issue at a meeting. At the meeting, it was decided that Zhang Jingjiang, acting chairman of the Standing Committee of the Guomindang, would write a formal letter of protest to *Guide Weekly*. When the letter arrived, Chen Duxiu published it in the "Readers' Voice" column alongside correspondence from students and shop assistants, with a short reply from "Journalist." This column was my domain, and in those days, "Journalist" was me; many comrades therefore thought that I had written the reply. Actually, the "Journalist" in this case, like the one who replied to another letter about Chen Gongbo, was Chen Duxiu. Those were the only times that happened.

Most shocked by *Guide Weekly*'s opposition to the Northern Expedition was not the Guangdong Guomindang but the Guangdong Communist Party. Chen Yannian, Tan Pingshan, and Zhou Enlai did not know what to do. They had no answer to the reproaches of the Guomindang, for they themselves did not oppose the expedition: On the contrary, they fervently supported it. The plan for a Northern Expedition had originated with Borodin. In a word, it was a proposal of the Russian government.[184]

But Chen Duxiu viewed the issue from a different angle. The Zhongshan Gunboat Incident of March 20, 1926,[185] and the Bill on Reorganization of the Party of May 15[186] were already a clear enough lesson. Political power in Guangzhou, previously dispersed among many people, now devolved uniquely on the person of Chiang Kai-shek. Borodin, "adviser to the national government," had already forfeited the power to manipulate the national government. The bait of Russian weaponry and cash was naturally still effective, for the national government could hardly do without it, but the government's need was less than it had been. Chiang Kai-shek already understood how to demonstrate his independence, especially his intention to oppose the

Communists. The Guangdong bourgeoisie and the bourgeoisie all over China trusted him; the Guomindang veterans—even the Western Hills Conference faction[187]—also trusted him. Other sources of weaponry and cash were available to him, though admittedly on a somewhat lesser scale. The struggle against Chiang Kai-shek's state power had already become a main component of the revolutionary struggle in the whole of China. "To overthrow the northern Duan Qirui we must first overthrow the southern Duan Qirui," as Gao Yuhan[188] put it in one of his speeches. After this utterance, Gao had no choice but to abandon his teaching post at Huangpu Academy and return to Shanghai.

Under these circumstances, what was the meaning of the Northern Expedition? It was an act of reconciliation with Chiang Kai-shek; it elevated Chiang's status and furnished him with even more weaponry and cash than in the past. Chiang Kai-shek was able to use the Northern Expedition to prohibit strikes and tax resistance in the rear, to restrict the activities of trade unions and peasant associations, and to keep the Communist Party under supervision; just in case the situation at the front worsened, he could still withdraw to Guangdong, and in that event he would surely want to wipe out Guangdong's Communist Party and all elements of mass power. Actually, the victory of the Northern Expedition was beyond everyone's imagination. The expedition was, of course, no novelty. Sun Yat-sen had staged a whole series of "Northern Expeditions," but they were never more than gestures; their real aim was to destroy dissident armed forces in Sun's own base in Guangdong.

Should a true revolutionary have backed the Northern Expedition, or opposed it? Even today this question is still hard to answer.

The meeting at which the Central Committee discussed the Northern Expedition happened to be held in the offices of the Propaganda Department. Chen Duxiu aired his views; Zhang Guotao said that he disagreed. The two men argued back and forth for a while. Suddenly Chen Duxiu flew into a temper, banged his fist on the table, and cursed Zhang. Zhang, being Chen's student, did not dare respond in kind. His voice gradually dropped to a whisper, and he finally fell silent. This was not the only time that Chen Duxiu resolved disputes in this way. This was one of Chen's weaknesses, for in reality, such methods cannot achieve their purpose. I cannot remember whether Qu Qiubai came out against Chen's views at this meeting. Recently, while sorting out Qu's posthumous papers,[189] I came across a passage in the author's preface to *Qu Qiubai wenji* (Qu Qiubai's collected works) saying that *Guide Weekly* had rejected an article by him on the Northern Expedition and that the manuscript was now missing. I unearthed this article from among the rest of Qu's papers. It supported the Northern Expedition.

To everyone's surprise, the Northern Expedition proceeded smoothly. Tang

Shengzhi switched sides,[190] there was next to no fighting in Hunan, and very soon, Wuhan fell to the expeditionaries. The miners' and the peasants' movements we had set up in Hunan achieved results, and measures to rope in members of the upper strata were comparatively successful. We satisfied the ambitions of these petty warlords and united with them against "Commander in Chief Chiang." The "Independent Regiment," composed at all levels exclusively of Communists, won some victories on the battlefield, swelled its ranks, and eventually grew to a division. The revolutionary tide that had temporarily ebbed after the Beijing massacre of March 18 once again began to flow. It was hard to see the drawbacks the Northern Expedition could have for us and easy to see the benefits. Clearly, the Shanghai Central Committee's disquiet was misplaced.

One day, Voitinsky came to a Central Committee meeting and afterward, in the course of chatting, raised a question: "Do you think that there might be an abrupt turn in the revolution, so that it can be achieved within a short period of time?" (I learned of this conversation indirectly.)

I was very surprised: Why should a representative of the Comintern raise such a question? In those days, though we talked and wrote frequently about "national revolution," whenever we mentioned the word "revolution" without any adjective, we were definitely referring to our own revolution,[191] which could start only after the successful conclusion of the Northern Expedition. This view of the nature of the national revolution was not unique to me. The reason Voitinsky raised this question was to show that the Shanghai Central Committee still clung to its old traditional ideas. When I talked with Peng Shuzhi about Chiang Kai-shek's coup, he said, "We'll settle accounts with him after we've captured Beijing."

Whether or not the victory of the Northern Expedition would be to the advantage of the Chinese proletariat, one thing is clear: The Central Committee's position as described above had already been superseded by that of the Comintern. Shanghai style had been replaced by Guangdong style, Chen Duxiu's standing had begun to decline, and Qu Qiubai and Zhang Guotao had gone into opposition. What's the use of working hard among society's lower strata; sharing the life of workers and peasants; risking beatings, arrest, imprisonment, and even execution if you can make revolution—and do so more effectively—wearing leather leggings[192] and a leather bandolier and carrying a leather whip?[193] Comrades from other provinces who went to Guangdong to attend meetings or for some other purpose were astounded at these Guangdong "comrades," these "revolutionaries." They were halfway to being in power. They could work for the revolution without risk to their lives, at least as far as the authorities were concerned (except for a possible coup by Chiang Kai-shek). Think for a moment of the contrast between Su Zhaozheng of the Guangdong General Labor Union and He Songlin of the

Shanghai General Labor Union. Yun Daixian, the younger brother of Yun Daiying, spent a thousand dollars on his wedding in Guangdong.

From an opposite point of view, comrades used to working in Guangdong who went to Shanghai or other places may well have thought, "Why are you so stupid?" I met many Shanghai comrades who gave me their impressions of Guangdong after coming back from there, but I met very few Guangdong comrades, so I do not know what their impressions were of Shanghai. Chen Yannian was not among those who became corrupted;[194] he stayed his old self. Tan Pingshan came to Shanghai several times; we twisted his arm to take us to Beijing opera performances and to restaurants. Chen Yannian tried to persuade me to go to Guangdong to work for the Party, but I flatly refused.

The victory of the Northern Expedition transformed people's idea of "revolution." Qu Qiubai turned Peng Shuzhi's formula for the revolution—"Start with propaganda, go on to organization, and end with insurrection"—into a laughingstock. And it seemed as if he must be right, for armed insurrection by the Guangdong masses no longer looked necessary. The insurrectionists in Hangzhou and Shanghai were no more than auxiliary units of the Northern Expedition. The Hunan peasant revolution simply provided the Northern Expeditionary armies with intelligence and guides and disarmed stragglers of the defeated northern warlord armies.

At the end of 1926, three Russian comrades came to Shanghai, where they stayed in the Soviet consulate. One young man was a representative of the Youth International; I often saw him at the headquarters of Communist Youth making propaganda against Voitinsky, but I never met the other two. Although I never attended any of the meetings with them at the consulate, I do recall that one of them, whose assumed name was "Marx," was a theoretician. Chen Duxiu, Qu Qiubai, and Peng Shuzhi often went to the consulate to discuss basic issues of the revolution with these three Russians. Chen and Peng stuck to their old positions, but Qu, together with the Russians, proposed adopting new ones. Voitinsky seemed to have the same basic ideas as Chen Duxiu. A letter arrived at around this time from Guangdong asking what attitude to take toward the Guomindang. The secretariat distributed this letter to provincial and local organizations for discussion. Shanghai approved the viewpoint of the Central Committee, and the northern region firmly supported the Central Committee and opposed Guangdong. Later, I was told that "Marx" said that although Chen Duxiu was unable to carry out the new line, it was impossible to replace him as leader, for his prestige in the Party was too high.

Not long after these discussions, Qu Qiubai, feigning illness, stopped working and receiving guests for quite a few weeks. Early, one morning, Wang Ruofei shook me awake and told me that I should go with him to Rue du Marché to visit Qu Qiubai. I was under the impression that Qu's tuberculosis had worsened and expected him to be groaning on his bed; once inside his house, however, I found him at his desk writing. I was astonished. He told us that he sometimes got bored lying down, so he would get up and sit for a while. As we went in, he concealed the article he had been working on,[195] but he retrieved a manuscript from the drawer of his desk and said that he had been busy translating Gorev's *Dialectical Materialism.* (A long time before this incident, he had asked me to propose a book for him to translate so that he could use the fee to subsidize his living costs, and I had proposed Gorev.) We talked about this and that for a while. I read some of his assemblages[196] of Gong Ding'an[197] and then left, together with Wang Ruofei. Perhaps Wang knew more than I did about what was going on, but if so, he kept it to himself. I suspected that Qu was malingering so that he could spend more time on his own work. Later, it turned out that he had been devoting his mornings to writing his polemic against Peng Shuzhi and his afternoons to translating Gorev or meeting people for discussions. Gradually, I began to hear reports that some members of Communist Youth were complaining about the Central Committee and the Shanghai District Committee. I asked Lu Dingyi about the source of these complaints. He said that he had heard them from a member of Communist Youth, who had gotten them from Qu Qiubai.

Qu went to Hankou between the second and third Shanghai insurrections, Zhang Guotao went to Wuhan with the Northern Expedition, and Cai Hesen and Tan Pingshan came back from Moscow and accompanied M. N. Roy, Tom Mann, and Doriot[198] to Hankou from Guangdong. In Hankou, these people set up the Central Committee of the Chinese Communist Party to command the revolution. They did not wait for the arrival of Chen Duxiu; on the contrary, they took advantage of his absence. Chen had stayed in Shanghai to take charge of the insurrection and got to Hankou only a few days before the massacre of April 12.

* * *

I used to make a habit of going to No. 61 for free meals or to chat with old friends I had not seen for a long time. Sometimes, I was allowed to sit in on important meetings of the Central Committee, and I also ran errands for the Party. Once, I was told to go to the nearby Siemens building to take care of some matter there. This building was Borodin's official residence. Borodin's interpreter was no longer Zhang Tailei but Li Bingxiang, an ex-student from Shanghai University and the son of an overseas Chinese. I hired a rickshaw, and one of the bodyguards, a burly northerner, not only ran along behind the rickshaw but even helped push it. I came to realize that I now belonged to the party in power, but somehow I felt uncomfortable being transported around like that. The bodyguard pushed me all the way back to No. 61, where, by coincidence, Qin Zhigu had arrived as representative of the Military Committee to inspect the bodyguards.

The first time I sat in on one of these Central Committee meetings, I noticed a difference between it and similar meetings in the past. Chen Duxiu was in the chair as usual, attended by the other Central Committee members: Cai Hesen, Qu Qiubai, Peng Shuzhi, and Zhang Guotao. Tan Pingshan, Li Lisan, and others were also present, but their air had changed radically. Chen Duxiu was no longer a leader with authority; he was simply an ordinary chairman, a person like the rest of them, and, moreover, he was in a minority on the committee. Only Peng Shuzhi supported him; the rest unanimously opposed him. There was something very odd about the extent of their "unanimity." Not until later, back in Shanghai, did Yan Changyi tell me that, by that time, Tan Pingshan, Qu Qiubai, and Zhang Guotao were holding caucuses before all important meetings to discuss the agenda. Yan lived in the house where the three men often met, but they avoided him and made sure that he was not present at their talks. In prison, I heard He Zishen describe how Tan Pingshan had opened an account at a certain restaurant where people close to him could eat and drink on credit. I remember that he was head of the newly established Ministry of Agriculture[199] at the time. Huang Wenrong told me that at one meeting, Zhang Guotao banged his fist on the table and cursed Chen Duxiu. That was his way of getting back at Chen for humiliating him in the discussion about the Northern Expedition.

The Wuhan government's most important moves were discussed and decided by the Two Parties' Joint Committee. Each party delegated a number of leaders to attend this body. I had no opportunity to listen in on any of its sessions, so it left no impression on me.

Between my arrival in Hankou and the start of the Fifth Congress, I had much idle time on my hands. I had been imperceptibly freed from my old functions in the Party, and as yet, I had acquired no new ones. Day after day, I simply strolled around enjoying myself; my only problem was that I had too little money to spend on pursuing pleasure. Not long after this, Yin Kuan arrived. He had been sent by the Party in Shanghai as a congress delegate, but like me, he lacked work. We talked to each other about our feelings and grumbled together, but in talking with others, we were both extremely circumspect, as was Wang Ruofei: When I talked to him about my discontent, he smiled and said nothing. The people we had dealings with in this period were all old acquaintances. On one occasion, Yin Kuan and I called on Shen Yanbing in the editorial office of *Republic Daily*. He was wearing leather leggings, a leather belt, and a military uniform. He invited us to a Cantonese restaurant and called in at the offices of another newspaper in the vicinity to ask Sun Fuyuan[200] to come along. Shen introduced the two of us as delegates of the Shanghai General Labor Union. Once, Wang Ruofei took me to Borodin's official residence, where a meeting was in progress. I went with Wang to Borodin's room. We took a bottle of his wine and emptied it between the two of us. I then scribbled a note in Russian saying "Thank you, Comrade Borodin" and left it sticking from the empty bottle.

In late April and early May, the Chinese Communist Party held its Fifth Congress in Wuhan. I attended as a delegate with speaking rights, but from start to finish, I never used them. The opening ceremony was held inside Wuchang's First Primary School,[201] whose headmaster, Wang Juexin, was a comrade. He stood there in a Western suit receiving guests and delegates. I had been charged with escorting the Comintern delegates across the river to Wuchang. Tom Mann was a white-haired veteran; he was so old that, as a young apprentice, he had even met Karl Marx. He did not understand French,[202] though Roy did, and so (of course) did Doriot. The ferry docked off Hanyangmen, where I called rickshaws to take us to the school. At that time, they were tearing down the city walls, so the streets were littered with bricks and the rickshaws were hard to pull. Tom Mann was fat and heavy, and his rickshaw overturned, leaving him with a grazed wrist.

The congress that day was purely ceremonial. Chen Duxiu took the chair and gave the opening address. Each of the Comintern delegates delivered a formal speech of greeting, as did Xu Qian for the Guomindang Central Committee and various delegates from the trade unions, the students' unions, the Youth League, and the Boy Scouts. Xiang Ying (i.e., Xiang Delong), leader of the Hubei General Labor Union picket, led a group of pickets into the hall to salute the gathering. Xu Qian was not the only representative of the Guomindang at the meeting—Tan Yankai and Sun Fo[203] also attended. They sat on the platform but did not speak.

The procedure for the election of the presidium was interesting. Immediately after the congress was officially opened, Luo Zhanglong, chairman of the Hubei provincial delegation, stood up and proposed a slate of names. I do not remember how many people were on the slate or who they all were, but I do remember that, apart from Chen Duxiu, they were all oppositionists (i.e., opponents of Chen Duxiu) and that none of the supporters of the line of the Shanghai Central Committee was on it. This slate was approved, and Cai Hesen was elected head of the congress secretariat.

This Communist Party congress was "secret"—that is, the press was not allowed to cover it. In those days, every newspaper in Wuhan was edited by Communists or under Communist direction. Later, one newspaper was penalized for revealing information about a Communist Youth Congress. There were two reasons for this secrecy: to avoid making the Wuhan government seem too "Red," and to forestall armed attacks by reactionaries. The Wuchang meeting was in one sense a smoke screen; the next day, there was not a delegate in sight at the school, for the venue had moved to the Huangpi County Guild Headquarters near the outskirts of Hankou. There was a gap of several days between the opening ceremony and the actual start of the congress proper.

The Huangpi guild complex was rectangular, with a big gate at one end and a three-roomed single-story building at the other. In the middle was the main hall, where the congress was held. The secretariat occupied the room to the right, which it shared with the mimeographers. The room to the left was not used for anything. Between the hall and the main gate was a rectangular courtyard traversed by a stone path with grass on both sides. The grass went right up to the outer wall. There were one or two buildings near the main gate where bodyguards lived. We took precautions against surprise attacks by reactionaries. Outside the gate, in a large open space, troops under Tang Shengzhi practiced daily with their machine guns.

The platform was adorned with portraits of Marx and Lenin, and the walls were covered by long slogans written on a red background. These slogans were the masterpiece of Cai Hesen, head of the congress secretariat. I cannot remember their entire text, but their general drift was along the lines of "Alliance of the Workers, Peasants, and Petite Bourgeoisie" and "Strive for the Noncapitalist Road." The slogans were new—we had never used them before.

The hall was filled by between two and three hundred delegates. Many were in military uniform, with leather belts and leggings. The Communist Youth delegates, many of them virtually children, passed around pieces of paper containing the latest conference jokes written in the style of a Shanghai tabloid gossip column (e.g., such-and-such a woman delegate "was staring at the handsome Li Qiushi without blinking," and some other comrade "made a pass at a young girl in the mimeography section"). Everyone viewed the congress much in the same way as one would view a religious ritual— like going to a Protestant church to hear a sermon or to a Catholic church to hear the priest officiate over mass. No one thought of it as a meeting to decide the fate of the revolution. And they were right. The real decisions were made outside the congress, which was simply a convenient place to proclaim and record them. The speakers spoke without passion, the debaters debated without fervor. Qu Qiubai's speech lacked the sharpness of his pamphlet;[204] in his rebuttal, Peng Shuzhi managed to convey the impression that his views were not so different from those of Qu. If the delegates were interested in urgent current questions, at this congress they got no answers to them.

Several dozen imperialist gunboats were anchored in the middle of the Yangtze. Would they fire on Hankou and Wuchang? The Fengtian Army had already arrived in Henan, and Chiang Kai-shek had set up his counterrevolutionary government in Nanjing. Which was more important: the Northern Expedition or an Eastern Expedition?[205] Our ex-friend Chiang Kai-shek had gone so far as to massacre workers and peasants and to shoot our comrades. What of our present friends Wang Jingwei and especially Tang Shengzhi—were they reliable? Might they not massacre us too? Everyone was asking this question, but congress speakers not only failed to answer it but even failed to raise it. All I remember is a Sichuanese comrade active around the Guangdong-Hankou Railway Station who got up on the platform and cursed "that dog's penis Xu Qian" for interfering in the railway workers' movement. I also noticed that Li Weihan delicately hinted once or twice in his speech that our relations with Tang Shengzhi were not entirely amicable. But there was no sequel or conclusion to these hints. People were clearly avoiding this important question and unwilling, in the wake of the split with the right wing of the Guomindang, to consider the future of our cooperation with its left wing.

I do not know why I harbored so many complaints in my mind. After the conference and during the pauses, I sought out old acquaintances—people I could rely on—for chats on the courtyard lawn, during which I vented some of my discontent. Later, after I had got back to Shanghai, Yin Kuan quoted my expressions of disquiet in an article he wrote for an internal Party publication. He said that early on in Hankou, I had predicted that Tang Shengzhi would split with us. Actually, I was not the only one to raise this question in private conversation or even to predict Tang's defection, nor was I the first to do so. But I did not correct Yin's statement.

During one of my conversations on the lawn, Luo Yinong intervened to say: "Have you heard? Moscow's decided to replace Chen Duxiu with someone close to the Guomindang."

"How do you know?" I asked.

"Zhuang Wengong's younger brother, Han Baicheng, said so. He is just back from Moscow. He knows all about it."

The congress proceeded very slowly. It often broke for half a day or even a day. I thought that it was very odd and went to ask Wang Ruofei about it. Wang said angrily, "They still haven't settled their negotiations behind the scenes." He meant the slate of candidates for leadership posts.

The foreigners Borodin and Roy and the Chinese Qu Qiubai, Zhang Guotao, and Tan Pingshan were the congress's puppeteers. They had a big problem on their hands: Should they keep Chen Duxiu, or should they scrap him? The tendency Chen stood for had already been defeated. He had opposed the Northern Expedition, but the Northern Expedition had proved successful; he had long refused to move the Central Committee from Shanghai to Guangdong and to cooperate even more intimately with the Guomindang, and when the Northern Expedition reached Wuhan, he was unwilling to move the Central Committee to Wuhan. Now Chen had no choice but to come, to drop his standpoint, and to submit to Borodin. But judging by past experience and his recalcitrant character, Chen was unlikely to knuckle under and become a docile agent of the "Comintern" line. He would have to go. He could be replaced by Tan Pingshan, who was close to the Guomindang; by Qu Qiubai, who had proposed an entirely new theory about the Chinese revolution; or by Zhang Guotao, who had been secretary of the Hubei Provincial Committee and was a veteran of the Chinese labor movement. But all these considerations had to be balanced against the fact that Chen Duxiu enjoyed enormous prestige both inside and outside the Party, so for the time being, it would be inappropriate to attack him too blatantly. What's more, there was a problem with the three contenders—namely, none was willing to give way to the others. So the result was a decision to keep Chen on as leader but to pinion him.

On the day of the election, the congress presidium proposed a slate of names. No one who had held an important office in the Shanghai Regional Committee or in the Northern Regional Committee was on it. No one who had been close to Chen Duxiu was on it either. Chen himself, however, was on it. The meaning of the slate was so transparent that the Comintern representative Roy had no choice but to speak against it. He spoke at great length and ended by saying: "Not even Petrov (i.e., Peng Shuzhi) or Bukhalov (i.e., Luo Yinong) are on the slate. They've carried out such important tasks in the past that they're indispensable to any new leadership, even if they have made some mistakes." After this intervention by a representative of the Comintern, the two names were finally added to the slate, and when it came to the vote, they were approved.

Before the election, Li Weihan voiced his anger to Wang Ruofei. He said that he knew what they were up to—that they were pursuing the strategy of "remove the retinue to save the emperor." But Li himself was in no position to speak out against what was happening. I was not present at this conversation, which I heard secondhand from Wang Ruofei. During his period of activity in Hunan, Li Weihan had been a practitioner of Shanghai style, not Guangdong style, and he was, of course, on the side of Chen Duxiu, but he was far away from Shanghai and, moreover, had his own base of supporters. People began to draw him over to their side, and very soon, the new Central Committee elected him and chose him as head of the Organization Department, after which he too joined in the campaign to "remove the retinue and save the emperor."

Those who are not familiar with the classical histories might not understand this expression, which was a strategy of revolt during the age of oriental despotism. People did not dare oppose the emperor but instead worked to remove his important ministers; they did not dare say that the emperor was wrong but said, instead, that his ministers were making him commit mistakes. Qu Qiubai's pamphlet against Peng Shuzhi-ism was a case in point. His real target was Chen Duxiu: Peng was just a stand-in. After the congress, the Chinese Communist Party resolved on a change of course. Chen Duxiu was still general secretary, but the line being carried out was Borodin's. Chen Duxiu's past struggle against Borodin came to an end. Guangdong style prevailed in everything, and those who represented Shanghai style were transferred from the Central Committee to other places. In a word, the Communist Party was assimilated to the Guomindang. This "assimilation" implied several different things. First, the Communist Party was no longer a closely united party but one that was rent by conspiracies and tricks, by acts of secret collusion, by mutual attacks, and by power struggles, just like the Guomindang we so despised. Second, the Communist Party adopted the Three People's Principles[206] and used Sun Yat-sen's theories to show that China had a noncapitalist future and to support peasant demands for land. Communist Party leaders quoted Sun not only in external propaganda but—for the first time ever—in internal Party education. Third, the internal Party organization gradually began to adopt Guomindang methods and even terms; for example, the Central Committee presidium came to be called the "Standing Committee." Fourth, there was hardly any difference between new Party members and the so-called Guomindang Leftists.

I got angriest of all the day that Wang Jingwei came to address the congress. Wang had not attended the inaugural session. After the congress had been meeting for several days in Hankou, word suddenly went out that Wang was going to give a speech. The original agenda was promptly dropped. Cai Hesen, head of the secretariat, rushed around taking the slogans down from the walls and putting up new ones along the lines of "The Guomindang and the Communist Party are cooperating, and victory is certain." The portraits of Marx and Lenin were relegated to either side of a portrait of Sun Yat-sen that towered above those of the two revolutionaries. The next day, Wang arrived, flanked by two powerful and grim-faced bodyguards fingering the triggers of their carbine pistols. Qu Qiubai was dressed in a brand-new Sun Yat-sen suit. He approached Wang with a broad smile on his face and escorted him into the conference hall. Compared with the left-wing leader of the Guomindang, the new leader of the Communist Party looked like a Guomindang yamen clerk. As Wang made his way up onto the platform, a great cheer went up of a sort that I had never heard before in China. Our own leader Chen Duxiu had also been greeted by a cheer the first time he appeared on the platform, but it was nothing compared with the one that greeted Wang Jingwei! What did Wang talk about in his speech? I cannot remember a thing about it.

After the new Central Committee had been formed, jobs were allocated. Peng Shuzhi was sent to Beijing to take the place of Li Dazhao. Luo Yinong was sent to Jiangxi, to be secretary of the Provincial Committee there. Wang Ruofei was sent to Shanghai. Chen Qiaonian stayed on as secretary of the Central Committee's Organization Department. Yin Kuan was sent to Guangdong to be head of the Provincial Committee's Propaganda Department. I was sent to Hubei, also to be head of the Provincial Committee's Propaganda Department.

Even to this day, I do not know who proposed me for that job. It was a fairly important post; considering how the congress had gone, the appointment was quite unexpected. As soon as I heard the news, I went to No. 61 to look for Qu Qiubai, hand in my resignation, and ask to be assigned to Shanghai. Chen Yannian, Zhao Shiyan, Wang Ruofei, and many other people in Shanghai were my old friends, and the old style was still stronger there than elsewhere. I urged Yin Kuan not to go to Guangdong but to stay in Shanghai with me. When Qu Qiubai heard my request, he instantly colored. "Everyone's trying to rock the boat," he said.

I then went to look for Chen Duxiu in the hope that he would let me go to Shanghai, but he urged me to stay in Wuhan. There was nothing to do but lug my bedding and my suitcase across the river to Wuchang. So I started my new job—or, rather, I continued to work at my old profession, but under entirely new conditions.

* * *

The Communist Party had no base in Hubei. The massacre in Hankou on February 7, 1923, had apparently delivered a severe blow to the Communist movement there. The lawyer Shi Yang was seized and shot. Liu Fen (Liu Bochui) and Xu Baihao were sent to prison and kept there for a long time. While I was in Shanghai in the secretariat of the Central Committee, I had seen reports from many places, but it had seemed to me that Hubei was the least successful. There were only a few of us activists, including Chen Tanqiu, Ren Kaiguo, Dong Yongwei (Dong Biwu), Xu Baihao, Xiang Zhongfa, and some others; we had no tradition of struggle and no important mass organizations—nothing to compare with Anyuan's role in Hunan.[207] Our activity in Hubei postdated the arrival of the Northern Expedition in that province. The Party's lower-grade officials in Hubei had been imported from Hunan, and its senior officials belonged to a group of people brought up from Guangdong by Zhang Guotao. With them, they had also brought Guangdong style.

As soon as Zhang Guotao took over as provincial secretary, he did everything within his power to boost Party membership. If not enough people were recruited through the usual method of sponsorship by existing members, then people were publicly recruited at mass meetings. How could there be a shortage of recruits if the Communist Party was the party in power? I do not know how many members the Party ended up with, but according to Zhang Guotao's report to congress, there were fifty thousand. That was exactly the same number as in Shanghai. The Shanghai figures were indubitably exaggerated, the Hubei ones even more so. Quality was, of course, more important than quantity. The Shanghai comrades had been recruited during the course of the underground struggle. True, a few of them were opportunists, but most could withstand hardship and were prepared to sacrifice their lives for the revolution. Many of the Hubei comrades later died as martyrs, but most vanished into thin air as soon as the wind changed. The Hunan comrades understandably despised the Hubei comrades. In a certain sense, the Party's activity in Hubei—particularly in the Hubei countryside—was an extension of its activity in Hunan, and initially, several counties in southern Hubei came under the direction of Changsha.[208] But whereas Hunan had developed a considerable resistance to Guangdong style, Hubei quickly succumbed to it.

After the establishment of the Central Committee in Wuhan, Zhang Guotao could not do two jobs at the same time, so he wanted to give the secretaryship of the Hubei Provincial Committee to Luo Zhanglong, his right-hand man. After the congress, Qu Qiubai wanted to give this important position to his good friend Zhang Tailei. So the two men became locked in combat, with Zhang Guotao eventually conceding. Zhang Tailei became secretary of the Hubei Provincial Committee, but Luo Zhanglong was secretary of the Hankou Municipal Committee. The workers', shop assistants', and general citizens' movement naturally came under the jurisdiction of the Municipal Committee: The only domain left for the Provincial Committee was work in the counties outside Wuhan, that is, in the peasant movement. The Municipal Committee had its headquarters in Hankou; the Provincial Committee had its in Wuchang.

Zhang Tailei was not at all happy about working with me. At the first meeting of the Provincial Committee, he proclaimed a "Standing Committee" consisting of three people: himself as the secretary, Chen Tanqiu in charge of organization, and Cai Yichen in charge of the peasant movement. This construction was contrary to regulations, but I said nothing and was even secretly glad, for it would leave me with more free time for sightseeing and observation. But the next day, when the Standing Committee came together, I was summoned to attend.

"Wasn't it decided yesterday that I wouldn't be a member?" I inquired.

"They say we can't do that," replied Zhang. He neglected to say who "they" were.

The Provincial Committee was housed in a large traditional mansion[209] halfway up the hill on Liangdao Street. As far as the outside world was concerned, this mansion was advertised as an official residence of "the adviser Borodin." It had originally belonged to a minor Hubei warlord and had been confiscated as property of a counterrevolutionary. Seven or eight bodyguards were stationed in the front section; in the building to the rear lived the members of the Provincial Committee and their staffs, for example, the secretaries of the various departments and their assistants. I lived in a room to the left of the hall together with Zhou Weizhen, chief of the Military Department. Earlier, he had headed the Provincial Committee's Organization or Propaganda Department. Zhou had worked alongside me in the factory in Montargis and had been one of the denizens of our shed. He was a Sichuanese. In Montargis, his thinking had been far removed from socialism; not until later did he become a Communist. He left France for Moscow to study military science. The new head of the secretariat was Xu Huoyun, also a Sichuanese and a student of Shanghai University; he too lived in the mansion. Zhang Tailei lived in Hushang Park in Wuchang in one of the foreign-style houses that had been allotted as living quarters for the Russian military advisers. Chen Tanqiu lived in his own house in the suburbs of Wuchang.

The offices of the various departments were housed in a foreign-style building reached through a small doorway to the left of the main hall. There many such foreign-style houses in Wuchang on the grounds of old-style mansions; the houses were either to the side of the mansions or to the rear, and they were invisible from the outside.[210]

Architecture represents culture, and this coexistence of new and old cultures within one perimeter wall intrigued me. The old-style mansion was full of heavy redwood tables and chairs—the furniture was all traditional. The new two-story foreign-style building was equipped both upstairs and downstairs with writing desks, modern chairs, and sofas. It even had modern sanitary installations, though the toilets were so unhygienic that I preferred to visit the old-fashioned latrines. I imagine that in the old days, the owner of the mansion had done everything in his power to preserve the old culture, but he had set up this artifact of new culture in the gardens of the old so that he could enjoy the comforts of modern living. At the same time, he maintained a strict dividing line between the two. In front of the foreign-style building was a space that had been turned into a rock garden.

The Propaganda Department had a new secretary and six or seven staff members. A newly purchased supply of paper, pens, and ink graced our office table. The secretary, Yun Daixian, brother of Yun Daiying, had arrived in Wuchang from Guangdong. All the staff members, apart from one from Hunan and a university student from Wuchang, had come up from Guangdong. The only female member of staff was Chen Yi, the wife of Li Qiushi; she was a tomboy, also from Guangdong.

Hankou had a Municipal Committee, and Wuchang and Hanyang both had County Committees. I could not see the point of such a big Provincial Committee. People from the County Committees approached the Organization Department and rarely visited the Propaganda Department, so the seven or eight of us were redundant. Zhang Tailei used to spend an hour or two a day with us, though he did not always show up. He spent more time in Hankou than in Wuchang, and more time attending meetings of the Central Committee than tending to Provincial Committee business. Whenever the three-man Standing Committee met, Zhang would simply make some vague report. He never informed us about events that the newspapers were not allowed to publicize, even though he knew about them.

After I went to Wuhan, I got Hong Kong foot, first on the left foot and then on the right, so I could get around only by rickshaw. Once, I could not even get down the hill to call a rickshaw, so I stayed in the office for days, and it was a long time before I could cross the river again to Hankou. Most of my old friends had left Wuhan, and those who were still there had no free time to visit me. What a paradox! When working underground, I knew about all the important events that were taking place in the world and in the Party, but now that I was occupying a rather important post in a party in power, I knew nothing, save for whatever irrelevancies were published in Wuhan's unpopular daily newspapers. Living in "the Red Capital Wuhan" was actually like living in Peach Blossom Village.[211]

Zhang Tailei must have realized that the Provincial Committee did not have enough work to occupy it, for he proposed a Delegates' Congress of Hubei Province that went on for quite a few days. Qu Qiubai came to make a report on behalf of the Central Committee. I had to draft most of the resolutions and manifestos and was also very busy taking minutes. Zhang Tailei said, "The idea of a Provincial Congress is to gather together leaders at the county level for training, so the Propaganda Department must take responsibility for the lion's share of tasks."

Apart from the Provincial Congress, the Propaganda Department held a weekly "propaganda conference." The idea for this conference came from Pavel Mif's wife, who was adviser to the Propaganda Department of the Hubei Provincial Committee. She crossed the river with an interpreter once a week to talk to me. She lectured me at great length on propaganda work, and I accepted some of her ideas. Once, Mif got Pan Jiachen to call me and Chen Qiaonian over for a discussion—I forget the subject. The propaganda conferences involved everybody working on propaganda throughout Wuhan, at whatever level. The Hankou Municipal Committee, the Wuchang and Hanyang County Committees, the Provincial Committee of Communist Youth, the All-China Students' Federation, the Hubei General Labor Union, and the Political Department of the armed forces all sent representatives. Xiang

Jingyu represented Hankou, Chen De'en represented the students, and Mei Zhonglin (Mei Dianlong's older brother) represented the labor union. The presence of Pan Hannian, the Political Department's representative, attracted quite a bit of attention, for he was wearing a military uniform. On one occasion, Gao Yihan, also uniformed, stood in for him. I made the political report, and each representative reported on his or her own work for the given week. At the end of each conference, I instructed the participants on the points to be stressed in the following week's work. It was just a lot of clichés. Bearing in mind how isolated I was from politics—like someone in Peach Blossom Village—it's no wonder that my reports and directives were so woolly.

The political situation was developing quickly, and to our disadvantage. Xia Douyin[212] proclaimed his opposition to the government and attacked Wuhan from the direction of Xindi. Wuhan was bare of troops, for the army had been sent to Henan to continue the Northern Expedition. The cadets at the Military Academy armed themselves; Zhang Guotao urged Ye Ting[213] to attack Xia with the 22nd Division, resulting in Xia's defeat. Yu Xuezhong's army, reorganized under Wu Peifu, declared its independence at Xiangyang and restored the Five-Striped Flag.[214] On the night of May 21, Xu Kexiang, a regimental commander under Tang Shengzhi, started a rebellion in Changsha. He surrounded the Hunan General Labor Union and the Peasant Association and annihilated the Communist armed forces in Changsha. Zhu Peide, governor of Jiangxi province, proclaimed his opposition to the Communist Party and tilted toward the Nanjing government.[215] The shops in Wuhan, unwilling to accept the new legal tender issued by the Hankou branches of the Bank of China and the Communications Bank, put their shutters up. Tang Shengzhi's army in Hankou was also said to be preparing to make a move. One day, Zhang Tailei told us that Deng Yanda had quit his job and left. He said, "Deng Yanda posed as even more radical and Leftist than we, but this sort of behavior is damaging."

The Communist Party's Central Committee lacked Deng Yanda's courage and preferred to preserve itself, even at the cost of humiliation. Secretary Cai Hesen ordered the pickets of the General Labor Union to hand over their arms to the troops of Tang Shengzhi.

During this crisis, the Provincial Committee moved its headquarters from Wuchang to Hankou. The Municipal Committee was abolished, and its functions were taken over by the Provincial Committee. Zhang Tailei told me: "We were wrong to neglect activity in our own region. If we had put the same energy into training Hankou worker comrades as we did into holding the Provincial Congress, we would have been many times more effective." We set up our new headquarters in a Shanghai-style lane house near the headquarters of the General Labor Union. We were cramped for space and had to let quite a few people go. Apparently, the Wuchang County Committee was also abolished. Its secretary, Ma Junshan, was transferred to the Provincial Committee to take charge of its secretariat. As things heated up, Zhang Tailei started coming every day, and we worked for longer hours than we had in the past. We dispensed with all the old formalities. We no longer wasted our energy on departmental meetings, propaganda meetings, speeches, training, and the like, but instead spent much of our time running around the various districts, making contact with the secretaries of the District Committees, and taking part in their meetings. Sometimes, we even attended branch meetings and made decisions about workers' struggles and other minutiae. Meetings were semisecret and informal, much as they had been in Shanghai, for we were preparing to go underground.

I braced my spirits, stopped complaining, and started to put my whole self into my work. Not long after we had moved to Hankou, Zhang Tailei brought Luo Yinong to see us and told us that the Central Committee had decided that Luo should be provincial secretary and that he, Zhang, should move to Guangdong. As the situation changed, the style of the Party could not help but change too, and people who had earlier been attacked at the National Congress gradually began to reappear. Chen Tanqiu, head of the Organization Department, was also transferred elsewhere and was replaced by pock-marked Liu Bojian from Sichuan, an old comrade of mine from France and Moscow, where he had become a leader. When Feng Yuxiang went to Russia after his defeat,[216] Liu had received him on behalf of the Chinese students; the two men had talked pleasantly and got on well together. When Feng returned to China with Russian weaponry, cash, and advisers, Liu was ordered to go with him. He immediately became director in chief of the Political Department of the Northwestern Army, a position almost on a par with that of Deng Yanda. By the time I met Liu in Hankou, Feng Yuxiang had already held his meeting with Chiang Kai-shek at Xuzhou[217] and had kicked Liu out. Liu brought his new wife with him to Wuhan. She was a relative of Yu Youren and also pock-marked. The head of the Propaganda Department did not change—that is, I kept my job.

After Luo Yinong assumed office, he called a "meeting of activists" in the headquarters of the old Provincial Committee in Wuchang. He had often done the same in Shanghai, where there were never any formal congresses of the Regional Committee. If anything came up, we would call a meeting of leading members of the various departments and important people in the Party or the Youth League. We used to call these "meetings of activists." They were not constitutional, and there was no established procedure for conducting them. There was no distinction between people with the right to speak and those with the right to vote, and there were no elections. The secretary of the Provincial Committee reported on whatever matters the activist comrades needed to know about and then handed down instructions and assigned people to carry them out. These meetings had played an important role in pushing things forward in Shanghai during the period leading up to and beyond the insurrections. They were closely tied to the real needs of the moment. This meeting in Wuchang was the first of its kind that I had attended since starting to work for the Provincial Committee in Hubei. Luo Yinong hinted in his report that he was dissatisfied with the way things had been done in the past in Hubei. He said that he was happy to see that we had built up a "big framework," but he added that we should work hard to "flesh it out" in order to make the organization truly Communist.

Actually, this big framework was utterly useless. A Party organization that had risen up in the wake of certain military and political forces would inevitably collapse along with those forces. On July 15, the Central Committee of the so-called left-wing Guomindang formally resolved to expel the Communists. On July 20, we prepared to launch a general strike by way of response. Before that, we had called together the secretaries of the various District Committees to discuss the matter. It seemed to us from what they said that the strike was bound to be successful. Although they were scarcely enthusiastic, no one opposed the idea or even voiced the slightest tinge of doubt about it. Early on the morning of the twentieth, Luo Yinong and I went to the wharf and toured the streets, the factories, and the workers' districts to see how things were going. But nothing at all was happening. There was no general strike; there were not even any partial strikes. Was there a single factory on strike in Hankou on that day? A single worker? I know for a fact that there was none. And even if there had been, it certainly would not have been at the behest of our Provincial Committee. Luo Yinong had no Zhao Shiyan to help him and no Party organization or members like those in Shanghai, who had matured during the struggles on the streets and in the factories. There was nothing he could do. His influence extended only to the secretaries and members of the District Committees, who were powerless to influence the Hankou workers. Under the circumstances, it is not surprising that the general strike failed.

What was surprising, and infuriating, was that local leaders of the District Committees and the unions had guaranteed that such-and-such a factory and such-and-such a group of workers would join the strike. The bankruptcy we displayed in Hankou was shameful. I'm not referring to the split between the two parties, the defeat, or the unworkability of the Comintern line but to our complete lack of any base among the Hankou workers. Luckily, there was quite some resistance to the reactionaries in the counties outside Hankou, such as those in southern Hubei along the border with Hunan. Fu Xiangyi, a comrade from Guangxi who was a member of the Provincial Committee, was sent to Xianning or Puqi to organize a peasant uprising. He succeeded, and even robbed a train to finance the rebellion. When Luo Yinong went to inspect the situation, I temporarily took over for him as provincial secretary. So the Provincial Committee had at least one achievement that it could be proud of.

I do not know the exact details of the split between the Guomindang and the Communist Party. After the Provincial Committee moved to Hankou, I had the opportunity to get close to members of the Central Committee, but I made no use of it. One reason was that I was busy with my own work and had no free time; another was that my friends had all left except for Chen Qiaonian in the Organization Department, who was busy on his own account. By then, Chen Duxiu had already moved out of No. 61 and was renting another place with Huang Wenrong. He was beginning to go underground, though he still met every day with important members of the Guomindang. He coordinated secret information from all quarters, and every night, before retiring, he dictated notes that Huang took down. These notes were copied or mimeographed and distributed to important members of the Party. One set was earmarked for the Provincial Committee, so I could read them every day. Although the information in these notes was unsystematic and often trivial, they would make first-class historical material on that period if a set could be found today. They contained a great amount of information about the views and private comments of Guomindang leaders, for we had planted secret agents around these people.

As far as I know, the split between the two parties took place in the following way: After the imperialists and Chiang Kai-shek had begun their blockade of the lower reaches of the Yangtze, the Wuhan economy collapsed. The government was carrying out an inflationary policy. Apart from the banknotes issued by the Bank of China and the Bank of Communications, the government was also issuing currency of its own—the so-called exchequer bonds. Industry and commerce were stagnating. The capitalists blamed it all on the Communist Party. They said that the Communists were stirring up the workers and the shop assistants and that the blockade by Shanghai and Nanjing was aimed at the Communists. The workers themselves had no good feelings about the Communist Party, which they saw as a second Guomindang rather than as their own party. The workers looked upon the General Labor Union as a sort of yamen that had grown up only in the wake of the Northern Expedition.

The authority of the Wuhan government rested on the army: on Zhang Fakui and Tang Shengzhi. The Communist Party's own armed forces, under Ye Ting and He Long, were a unit of Zhang Fakui's. The Guomindang leaders under Wang Jingwei relied on the assistance of Zhang, who was also friendly toward the Communists. But Tang Shengzhi's officers—all members of Hunan's rural gentry and landlord class—were anti-Communist.

Their property was under threat from the peasants; they bitterly resented the Communist Party and sympathized with Chiang Kai-shek's anti-Communist position, but they dared not start a rebellion. They feared the Communist Party's authority among the people and were also afraid that the Communists would join with Zhang Fakui to finish them off. When Xu Kexiang went ahead with his rebellion, they pretended to stand aloof, so that if Xu lost they would not be implicated. But when Xu did not lose, Tang and his troops came off the fence. It clearly would have been much easier to stage the Horse Day Incident[218] in Wuhan than in Changsha—so easy that the incident would have been entirely unnecessary there. Zhang Fakui was weaker than Tang Shengzhi in Wuhan and would never have gone to war against Tang to protect the Communists. As for the Communist armed forces under Zhang, Tang was unconcerned about them.

A directive arrived from Moscow ordering the Communists to form a workers' and peasants' army of fifty thousand people and to set up revolutionary tribunals to try the reactionary Guomindang leaders. There were also two other items in the directive. The Comintern representative Roy showed this directive to Wang Jingwei, who went into a towering rage; someone told Zhou Enlai, the leader of our Military Committee, about this incident. Borodin, Roy, and some other foreigners attended a meeting of the Central Committee, and during one of Roy's grandiose speeches, Zhou stood up and reported what he had been told, to everyone's utter amazement. Borodin requested a directive from the Comintern, which wired back, saying that Roy should be stripped of his authority. But it was too late to save the situation. The secretariat or the Organization Department of the Central Committee instructed the Party's leading members in Wuhan to go into hiding, for counterrevolution was probably imminent. Zhang Fakui's army, which was also feeling isolated, left Wuhan on the pretext of an "Eastern Expedition."[219] They went to Jiujiang and Nanchang[220] and occupied Zhu Peide's territory. Ye Ting and He Long followed Zhang to Jiangxi and staged the "August First" insurrection in Nanchang.[221] But all that happened later.

Qu Qiubai, Zhang Guotao, and Tan Pingshan all left Wuhan and went to Lushan. All the Party's top and middle-ranking leaders who had been in contact with the Guomindang left en masse for Lushan. Shen Yanbing, the editor in chief of *Republic Daily*, who later changed his name to Mao Dun, wrote a travelogue about his time in Lushan. But Chen Duxiu still remained in Hankou. Those of us on the Provincial Committee had never had anything to do with public politics, so there was no need for us to leave. In any case, our work was in Wuhan.

In Hankou, we heard reports of the August First Incident. Qu Qiubai had already returned from Wuhan, but he was the only one to do so, for all the rest had joined the Ye-He army. One or two days before August 7, Luo

Yinong told me that the Central Committee was about to hold an important meeting at which I was to represent Hubei. That was the famous August 7 Conference.

* * *

The conference was held in a Western-style hostel in Hankou's former Russian concession. We had to climb a staircase alongside a Western-style shop. In the front room, a foreigner sat reading; he paid no attention to us. This man, an American citizen and the owner of the building, later wrote a pamphlet on the Chinese Revolution. I forget what he was called. We went through into the back room, which was full of Chinese. Still more arrived later. When everyone was present, a huge and unusually fair-skinned Russian entered the room. Just as Qu Qiubai was about to introduce him, the Russian himself told us that his name was Nikola, which was later shortened to N. in some documents. Actually, he was Lominadze, shot by Stalin ten years later for "semi-Trotskyism."[222]

Apart from Peng Gongda, representing the Hunan Provincial Committee, and me, all the other people at the meeting were members of the Central Committee elected by the Fifth Congress. Chen Duxiu was the only member still in Hankou who did not attend. There were eighteen of us in all. I do not remember who they all were. The meeting was very brief and not many people spoke, so it left no deep impression on me. Qu Qiubai interpreted, so naturally he was there; Luo Yinong was there, and so were Mao Zedong and Li Zhenying. I cannot remember who the rest were.[223]

The sole aim of this meeting was to pass a lengthy resolution that Lominadze had already drafted and Qu had translated into Chinese; it was written very clearly and placed on the table. Lominadze addressed the meeting; Qu read out the resolution and invited contributions. Mao Zedong spoke, though I forget what he said. Luo Yinong also spoke, and I still recall his words. He said, "The Guomindang won't be able to stay in power," which he then translated into Russian. Lominadze reproached him, saying, "It's quite possible that the Guomindang will stabilize its rule."

Lominadze had been sent to China to take over from Roy. He brought with him the new Comintern line and told us to accept it and present it as our own resolution. Actually, many comrades knew nothing about the new Comintern line before Lominadze spoke about it and Qu read it out. When it came to the vote, I raised my hand in favor, my sole reason being that the Comintern representative had proposed it; I did not do so because I had given the matter deep thought or because I believed in my heart of hearts that it was right. In my opinion, a true revolutionary party should call things by their right names; if top leaders order lesser leaders to accept something, they should do so in the form of an order or a directive. Many copies of the August 7 Resolution (or "Letter to All Comrades") were printed, so historians will probably be able to find one. I cannot remember the exact contents of the new line,[224] but I do know that there was no proposal to quit the Guomindang. The directive to quit the Guomindang was not received until September. I still remember how Qu Qiubai and I went to the Russian consulate in Hankou in mid-September. I sat in the waiting room, and he went through the door. When he came out again, he told me, "The International has wired to say that we should withdraw from the Guomindang." Both the right-wing and the left-wing Guomindang had already expelled us, but the August 7 Resolution was still saying that under no circumstances would we abandon the Guomindang flag.

Chen Duxiu was in Hankou during the August 7 Conference, but he did not attend, even though he was a member of the Central Committee. This meeting was called precisely to oppose "his" line, but he was never once named,[225] either in speeches or in writing. No one explained why he had not been invited, and no one asked, either. I already knew privately that the International had suspended him because of his "mistakes." Not long after the meeting, he returned to Shanghai with Huang Wenrong, his personal secretary.

Sometime before the conference, Zhou Enlai invited Luo Yinong, Liu Bojian, and me to a Sichuanese restaurant (the Jiaxiu Lou?) at the corner of Tianlong Alley. He began in a guarded and roundabout way to discuss the inner-Party struggle. He criticized past mistakes and concluded by saying that we should not deal too harshly with the "two old men," by which he meant Chen Duxiu and Tan Pingshan. The latter, once earmarked by Moscow to replace Chen Duxiu as leader, was now also under attack from the International. Liu Bojian had not been in Hankou for long. He was unaware of the situation in the Party and naive to boot, so he flew into a rage when he heard Zhou say this. As for me, I just sat there, wearing a meaningful smile.

* * *

After the August 7 Conference, Qu Qiubai, in fact if not in name, occupied the position in the Party previously held by Chen Duxiu. Tan Pingshan and Zhang Guotao were both with the Communist armed forces; I don't know where Cai Hesen was.[226] Apart from Qu, the only member of the Central Committee in Hankou was Li Weihan. Later, Luo Yinong joined the Standing Committee, but neither his status nor Li's was as high as Qu's. Qu wanted to sort things out after the chaos, so I stopped doing local work and returned to the Central Committee.

Luo Yinong told me that Qu Qiubai wanted me back on the Central Committee to revive *Guide Weekly*. Luo said that he did not want to let me go, but Qu had insisted; he had no choice but to accept, so he proposed swapping me for Chen Qiaonian. This account is not necessarily reliable. I think what actually happened is that Luo, seeing that Liu Bojian lacked the competence to run the Organization Department, had asked the Central Committee for Chen Qiaonian, whereupon Qu proposed swapping Chen for me. The swap went ahead, and Liu Bojian was transferred to some other office. Li Weihan had many people under him and could easily replace Chen Qiaonian. Hua Lin took over from me as head of the Provincial Committee's Propaganda Department.

By then, *Guide Weekly* had been dormant for quite some time. After Chen Duxiu's downfall, Zhang Guotao took over everything, including *Guide Weekly*. Manuscripts edited by other people were sent to him for checking. He stuffed them in his portfolio, and it would be a week or two before he found time to look at them. So gradually, *Guide Weekly* stopped appearing, and the editorial office was disbanded. In the meantime, there had been several attempts to find someone to edit it and get it going again. One suggestion was that Shen Yanbing should be editor, but Shen was married and had children to provide for, and Zhang Guotao could not afford to pay that sort of wage. I heard from others that they had had me in mind for a long time, because I was a bachelor. After Qu Qiubai had taken real power in the Central Committee from Zhang Guotao, the plan was realized. But as soon as I got to work, it became apparent to me that as things stood, there was no hope whatsoever of reviving *Guide Weekly*. The tide of reaction was gradually flowing. Our publishing enterprise was already paralyzed. I controlled three organizations: the Chang Jiang Bookshop, the printshop, and a paper supplier. The bookshop had already closed down, and its stock had been either removed or stolen; it was in complete chaos, and I could do nothing but ignore it. The printshop and the paper business were also in a mess. Former comrades were blackmailing us by threatening to report us to the army and get us closed down as "Communist organs" if we did not agree to their demands. So I wound up the paper business and crated the printing machinery, in preparation for sending it back to Shanghai. At the same time, I dismissed the staff and workers, for I had heard that the Central Committee was to be transferred back to Shanghai. "There is no way we can revive *Guide Weekly*," I told Qu Qiubai.

Qu and his wife invited me to stay with them in a newly built Western-style hostel in the former British concession. They had four big rooms—a guest room, a dining room, and two bedrooms—on the first floor. Each bedroom had an adjoining bathroom and storage room. The kitchen had gas; in wintertime, there was steam heat. There was a similar suite of rooms on the second floor occupied by a landlord family from Hunan. In the middle of a pebbled terrace roof were two more rooms with tiled floors and glass windows on three sides, for sleeping in during the summer months. One room belonged to the first floor, the other to the second floor.

Pan Jiachen and I lived together in the guest room. Little Pan was working for the Russians as an interpreter; he also acted as a courier between Qu Qiubai and the Russians. After we had been there for a few days, Pan brought in a girl called Zhuang Dongxiao, who had just got back from Moscow. Many other women had returned along with Zhuang across the Mongolian desert into Gansu and south via Shaanxi and Henan. Feng Yuxiang had already gone over to the other side by that time, but he did not harm these women and even protected them as they crossed the region under his control. By the time they reached Hankou, it too was in the grip of reaction.

Qu and his wife slept in one bedroom, and the fifteen-year-old sister of Yang Zhihua[227] slept in the other. There was also a young man of around twenty whom Yang Zhihua said was her relative; he was called Sheng and came from a rich family but had run away to become a revolutionary. Sleeping in the same room, Sheng and the girl quickly became lovers and decided to marry without asking the consent of their parents. Yang Zhihua began to arrange for an old-style wedding to increase their protective cover. One day, the boy, who worked for the Central Committee as a secret courier, arrived home in a panic. "Everything's ruined!" he said. He said that he had been carrying five thousand dollars back from the Russians rolled up in a newspaper and had been robbed on the street. He did not dare report the robbery to Qu Qiubai but hurriedly packed his things and fled without a backward glance. When Qu and his wife got home and heard the news, they were rather suspicious. The girl was in tears, fearful that the boy would kill himself. Yang Zhihua's older brother, a petty functionary in the Ministry of Agriculture or of Labor, went out to search for him and found him on board a boat bound for Shanghai. When he came over the next day to report what he had found, Yang Zhihua told him off for not dragging the boy ashore. The girl protested the innocence of her fiancé, but later, back in Shanghai, she met him and discovered that he had opened an account at the post office. Only then was she prepared to believe that he was guilty. The boy had already forgotten his betrothal.

Luo Yinong said to me, "Qu Qiubai loves employing his relatives!" The next day, the Russians made good the missing sum.

"That money will spoil the boy's whole life," said Qu Qiubai. "A similar thing happened in one of Dostoyevsky's novels. The criminal continued to feel the prick of conscience until his dying day."

After the printshop and the paper business had been wound up, I was once again at loose ends. I frequently ate well at Qu Qiubai's place or at Luo Yinong's. Every day, I went out sight-seeing with Pan Jiachen, along the streets or along the banks of the Yangtze.

After the summer heat had passed its peak and the autumn breezes were starting to blow, the evening crowds along the river gradually thinned. When the winds came up, Wuhan assumed a desolate air. The desolation was born not just of the changing seasons. After a lively spell as the capital, Wuhan had once again reverted to its original status—a provincial city of the interior. One afternoon, in the cool air, I slowly made my way from Qu Qiubai's place to Luo Yinong's in Lanling Gardens. The Central Committee was meeting there, and Luo had invited me for a meal. As I was entering the garden, I saw two men sitting on a bench on the lawn in front of the entrance to Luo's home. At first, I paid little attention to them, but suddenly one of them called out my name. It turned out to be Li Heling. The man talking with him was Ouyang Qin of the Military Committee. Li Heling was weeping bitterly and confessing that he had made mistakes. He said that he had been overcome by a sudden fit of emotion, that he had behaved petulantly like a spoiled young master and had posted an advertisement to say that he had broken with the Party, but that he had done nothing else of a reactionary nature.

"A few days ago, someone fired a shot at me at my home," he continued. "But I do not hold it against the Party. I deserve to be punished. Luckily, the shot only grazed me, I'm all right again now. I want the Party to restore my membership. I'll go anywhere and do anything." He told me that he had bumped into Ouyang Qin on the street and invited him into the garden for a chat.

"If you write a letter, I can pass your views on," I told him.

He agreed and made a date to meet Ouyang two or three days later, at dusk, on one of the wharves along the Yangtze, to give him a report. As we were speaking, Li Weihan came walking over from the other side of the garden. When he saw that it was me standing there, he entered Luo's house without further ado. When I too went in, they asked me what had kept me so long. I told them; they flew into a panic, convinced that Li Heling was acting insincerely. Li Heling had seen Li Weihan enter the house, so he would surely guess that it was an important headquarters of the Party. (I had deliberately strolled round the garden after Li Heling had left, before going into Luo's house.) So we abandoned an excellent meal and slipped off at intervals through the back door. On the other side of the street happened to be the back door of the building where we had held the August 7 Conference. By then, the American had left Hankou, and the premises housed the Central Committee's Workers' Department or Workers' and Peasants' Department under Li Zhenying.

Ouyang Qin met Li Heling as planned. The report was unsigned, but I recognized Li Heling's handwriting. The Central Committee decided to send him to Hailufeng,[228] where he could be kept under supervision. A few days after I arrived in Shanghai, I was told at the Central Committee office that

Li and his wife were also in the city, and that they were staying at such-and-such a hotel. Not long after that, they went to Guangdong. A long time later, I cannot remember when, I heard that Li had been shot by Peng Pai. Was it for a new crime or for the old one? Or was it simply because he was unreliable and had shown that he was capable of going against the revolution? I fear that I have no answer to these questions.

On or around September 20, Qu Qiubai and I boarded the ship for Shanghai. Yang Zhihua stayed on for a few days in Hankou to arrange for the baggage and the furniture to be sent on. The two of us sailed first class. Qu Qiubai had all his meals brought directly to the cabin, which he never left throughout the voyage. As for me, I strolled around the ship, but apart from a comrade in steerage who had previously managed the Party's paper business in Hankou, I saw no one else I knew. Everyone else was just a normal passenger. Compared with the outward voyage, this Yangtze steamship had reverted to its old ways.

7
Love and Politics

Two or three months after I returned to Shanghai, an unexpected event disturbed my life: I fell in love and got married.

In this political memoir, I have been unable to abide by the principles that I originally set myself and have written a great deal about personal affairs and about issues that bear no relation to politics. I shall cut them. In this chapter, I do not intend to write about my own affairs of the heart, which I shall keep for a memoir of a different sort (should I ever write one). However, I will say a few things about other people's love affairs—love affairs that bear directly on politics.[229]

From its very inception right up to when I left France, the Communist Youth Party lacked poetic quality and could boast not a single romance. The reason was quite simple: There were no women comrades. Cai Chang, the younger sister of Cai Hesen, was still in France. I do not know if she took part in our organization, but I never saw her at either of the two congresses or on any of my frequent trips to Paris. Her lover Ouyang Ze, one of my philosopher friends, was deported from France after the Lyon University campaign. Cai Chang's mother did not like Ouyang Ze. Instead, she had set her eyes on Li Fuchun, whom she urged Cai Chang to marry while she was in France. While I was in Moscow, Ouyang Ze heard a false report that Cai Chang was also in the Soviet capital, so he sent a long diary for her to read, and it came into our hands; it was truly a tearjerker. Ouyang Ze fell ill and started spitting blood, but he could never forget his lover back in France, and many worrisome rumors reached his ears. In his diary, he recorded everything, from recollections of his life with Cai Chang to his outlook on death. I suspect that there was blood between the lines—blood from his tubercular lungs. In the spring of 1926, in Shanghai, I met Cai Chang for the first time; she had just returned from Moscow. When I mentioned the diary to her, she gave an indifferent laugh.

While I was in Moscow, there were no women comrades there. It's quite obvious from the nicknames we gave each other that we were longing for the Party back in China to send some women to join us in the Soviet Union. We used to call Ren Bishi "Girl Student" and Wang Renda "Women's Delegate"—a brilliant contrast to Li Weinong, whom we called "Peasants' Delegate." Whenever Wang Yifei introduced Chen Qiaonian to foreign comrades, he called him Kitayanka ("Chinese woman" in Russian). At KUTV, there were Korean women, Persian women, Indian women, Caucasian women, and women of many other nationalities. The only ones missing were Chinese women. We all felt very ashamed by this lack. When Bu Shiqi went back to China and arrived in Beijing, he immediately made a pass at He Mengxiong's wife, Miao Boying, which caused quite a commotion. We heard about it even in Moscow. Those returning home from Moscow seemed like sex maniacs to the comrades back in China. Luckily, the following groups to return—our groups, in 1924—turned out to be more civilized. That proved that we were no more crazy about sex than were the comrades back in China.

When we got back, it was a long time before any of us had any love affairs. It was as if we were reacting against the sacred view of love promoted by the May Fourth Movement. Jiang Guangchi was a typical example of the May Fourth attitude, for which we ridiculed him. He corresponded for many years with a girl student in Henan. Their relationship was like one in a romantic novel. He used to boast about it to other people, but no one appreciated him. We all thought that love was petit bourgeois. Unlike young people in the early period of the May Fourth Movement, most of us who had been in Russia were not against arranged marriages. Xue Shilun got leave to go home and get married, after which he stayed in Hunan to work for the Party. When He Jinliang returned to China from Vladivostok to take part in the Fourth Congress, he took advantage of the occasion to go home and get married, and he even held a traditional wedding feast. Ren Zuomin went home and brought back a wife, who turned out to be a most virtuous woman. In 1926, in Shanghai, she fell ill and died. Through carelessness, I neglected to give Ren Zuomin my condolences when I met him, which upset him a lot. Ren Bishi, our "girl student," went back to Hunan to get married and brought his "little wife" back to Shanghai with him—"little wife" not in the usual but in the literal sense,[230] for she was a tiny slip of a girl. She used to deliver documents between different offices of the Central Committee and seemed to be very capable and efficient.

The first big love affair in the Party after my return to China involved Zhang Tailei. None of the parties to it had been in Moscow. After the end of the Jiangsu-Zhejiang war, Zhang sent his mother, wife, and children back to Changzhou and stayed on by himself in Shanghai, in a house on Moulmein Road. At night, he worked in the editorial office of *Republic Daily*. At that time, the Central Committee's Propaganda Department and the editorial office of *Guide Weekly* had both moved from the Moulmein Road premises.

Qu Qiubai and Yang Zhihua, having started an affair, had gone off to live together elsewhere in a rented room. There were many empty rooms in the Moulmein Road house, so Shi Cuntong and his family moved in. His was a typical university professor's family, with a mistress of the household, children, guests who were received with polite ceremony, and mahjong parties during the New Year festivities (for Shi Cuntong was a mahjong fanatic). The house on Moulmein Road took on a new air; it was no longer a nest of Bolsheviks.

Gradually, Zhang Tailei and Shi's wife, Wang Yizhi (when Shi published articles in *Awakening,* he used to sign them "Yizhi" or "Banjie")[231], started becoming friendly and often went out together to the Great World Amusement Center or the Tianyunlou Variety Center on the roof of the Wing On Department Store. One night in the editorial office at *Republic Daily*, Shi put his head on his desk and started to cry. It was a long time before he stopped. Ye Chuchang and Shao Lizi had no idea what was going on, and Shi was not of a mind to tell them. Shortly after that, Wang Yizhi officially moved in with Zhang Tailei. At the time, Zhang was the new general secretary of Communist Youth. Lots of people attacked him, so he failed to settle into his new job. Perhaps it was the Shanghai University students who denounced him. I heard that at one time, the Central Committee wanted to send him to Outer Mongolia to represent the Chinese Communist Party. Qu Qiubai said: They want to exile him. Because Qu spoke up for him, Zhang was sent, instead, to Guangzhou to interpret for Borodin. He took Wang Yizhi with him, along with Shi Cuntong's child. This seemed to drive Shi mad, for he was a very nervous sort of person anyway. He was admitted to the hospital. Zhong Fuguang, a woman student at Shanghai University, wrote to him expressing sympathy and indignation. Gradually, Shi Cuntong became his old self again.[232]

This was the first time after arriving back in China that I had witnessed a stormy love affair. Later, in Wuhan, where I worked with Zhang Tailei, we resolved another love problem in the Organization Bureau of the Hubei Provincial Committee concerning an aide called Wei. Zhang suggested that we apply the following principle: "As long as love does not harm politics, it should be considered a personal affair and the organization should not meddle in it." I raised my head to look at him. No one else noticed the expression on my face, nor were they aware of all the implications of Zhang's comment, for they were ignorant of his romantic past.

I have already mentioned Qu Qiubai and Yang Zhihua, and here I would like to say something about their romantic history. It started before the Zhang Tailei problem but was not among the affairs that "harmed politics." Yang Zhihua was pretty, gentle, soft-hearted, clever, and able, but she was also the daughter-in-law of Shen Xuanlu. On one occasion, Shen Xuanlu wanted the Central Committee of Socialist Youth to hold a meeting in Xiaoshan,[233] because Shanghai, where the committee was based, was inconvenient for him. Wu Ming, my fellow member of the "library" in France who had been arrested and deported back to China during the Lyon University campaign, ran the Central Committee of Socialist Youth in Shanghai. Wu Ming was infatuated by Yang Zhihua's beauty and almost went out of his mind. He wrote her a number of despairing letters, but she ignored him. These letters infuriated Shen Xuanlu, who said, "there are swindlers in the Communist Party." The first time Shen Xuanlu left the Party, it was not unrelated to this problem. But Shen's son and daughter-in-law did not love each other. Shen Jianlong[234] loved a Korean girl and grew cold toward Yang Zhihua, who named her daughter Duyi[235] to demonstrate her sadness. She left home to study at Shanghai University. Qu Qiubai's wife had died of tuberculosis, shortly before this happened. Her name was Wang, and she had been a friend of Ding Ling[236] (then called Jiang Bingzhi).

No one knows how Yang Zhihua and Qu Qiubai fell in love. One morning, at around the time of the Huang Ren case, not long after Qu Qiubai and He Shizhen had both quit Shanghai University, we found three strange advertisements in *Republic Daily*. One said that "on such-and-such a day of such-and-such a month in such-and-such a year, Shen Jianlong and Yang Zhihua formally stopped being a couple"; another said that "on such-and-such a day of such-and-such a month in such-and-such a year, Qu Qiubai formally started living with Yang Zhihua"; the last one said that "on such-and-such a day of such-and-such a month in such-and-such a year, Shen Jianlong and Qu Qiubai formally became friends."[237] Zhang Danfu (alias Zhang Danweng), editor of *Jingbao* (Crystal), the best known of the Shanghai tabloids, wrote an article about the affair but gave new names to the people involved. He disguised Shen Jianlong as Shen Daohu,[238] Qu Qiubai as Qu Chunhong,[239] Yang Zhihua as Liu Shiye,[240] Shen Xuanlu as Shen Heidian,[241] Shanghai University as Lower Chang Jiang University, and the Commercial Press as the Industrial Press. For a long time after that, we called Qu Qiubai "Spring Red."

Once, when I went to Qu Qiubai and Yang Zhihua's new house, a man came in while we were talking together. They introduced him: "This is Shen Jianlong." He and Qu Qiubai were like old friends. Yang Zhihua fussed over him like a girl might fuss over her older brother who has arrived for a visit. Later, Yang Zhihua told me: "Jianlong is noble and refined, I am too vulgar for him, I am no match for him." But Shen Xuanlu was less magnanimous than his son. He maligned Qu Qiubai behind his back: "He has a narrow face, he obviously has a crafty and treacherous mind."[242] Shortly after that, Shen Xuanlu left the Communist Party for the second time. That act and his son's divorce were not unrelated. But even without this affair, he still would have left.

During this same period, student circles in Beijing were shaken by another love affair. The main female role in it was played by a friend of Ms Lu Yin, who wrote a novel about it called *Xiangya jiezhi* (Ivory ring). In Beijing's Taoranting district, there is still a bizarre tombstone where emotional people go to pay their respects after reading *Ivory Ring*. The story will last forever through the novel and the tombstone. The male role in the drama was played by our comrade Gao Shangde, alias Gao Junyu, an early member of the Communist Party and of *Guide Weekly*'s editorial board. When I first arrived in Shanghai, he happened to be there, and I met him on several occasions in the editorial department. Not long afterward, he returned to Beijing, and not long after that, he died.

We certainly did not envy these members of the May Fourth school of love, whom we called "petit-bourgeois." The women were not comrades; the love affairs were not grounded in the revolutionary cause. But we did envy the marriage between Cai Hesen and Xiang Jingyu, whom we called a "model couple." Xiang Jingyu, who was short and slight, always dressed like a woman student and had not been at all polluted by Shanghai-style frivolity. She was a sharp contrast to Yang Zhihua. She was a very active person who participated in the workers' movement, the students' movement, the women's movement, and the Guomindang movement and frequently wrote short articles for *Guide Weekly*. She detested romantics in the Party. During or after meetings, Chen Duxiu liked to make fun of relationships between men and women, but if Xiang Jingyu were present, she was quite likely to protest or to say a few serious words that would embarrass him. The other comrades were even less inclined to let themselves go in her presence. All the other women comrades, especially Yang Zhihua, feared her. Because she was fond of giving people advice and lectures, she acquired the nickname "Granny" or "Granny of the Revolution." Qu Qiubai once said, "In our Party we have Han-Confucian Marxists, like Li Ji; and Song-Confucian Marxists, like Xiang Jingyu."[243]

Immediately after my return to China, I lived in the same house as this "model couple," first on Moulmein Road, then in Minhouli, and finally on Fusheng Road. After we had been living in Minhouli for some time, Cai Hesen went to Beijing to recuperate from an illness. Xiang Jingyu stayed behind in Shanghai and threw herself into the May Thirtieth Movement. Shortly before the Mid-Autumn Festival,[244] we moved to Fusheng Road, without waiting for Cai to return. At around the same time, Peng Shuzhi returned from Baolong Hospital, after having fallen ill in February. He had missed the strike movement that preceded May Thirtieth and the spectacular movement of May Thirtieth itself; by the time he recovered, the movement was already on the retreat. On the evening of the Mid-Autumn Festival, we threw a sumptuous dinner to celebrate the festival, the move, and Peng's discharge from the hospital, and after the meal we held a soirée, which was a practice we had learned in Russia. Everyone had to give a short performance to entertain the rest. Apart from the three hosts, present were Zhang Bojian, Shen Zemin, and Shen's wife, Zhang Qinqiu. Peng Shuzhi danced a Caucasian dance, Zhang Qinqiu sang "Wretched Qiuxiang,"[245] and the rest of us gave performances too. Xiang Jingyu did not want to sing, nor did she want to put on any other act. But we refused to let her get away with it. Finally, she recited a poem by Li Houzhu:[246] "Silently and alone I climb the western tower." After the guests had left, I returned to my pavilion room to sleep, but Xiang Jingyu stayed in Peng Shuzhi's room. It was a hot night, and the doors of both my room and the front room on the same upstairs floor had been left ajar. I awakened to hear Xiang Jingyu still talking. I could not believe my ears: She was telling Peng Shuzhi that she loved him.

Presently, she went up to the second floor. Peng came to my room and said, "Something really strange has happened!" He repeated to me what I had just heard Xiang saying.

"I would never have dreamed it," he told me.

"Don't carry it any further," I told him. "It could harm the functioning of the organization."

"Don't worry, I'm not interested, and she knows that it's not right. She says that she only wanted to bare her heart to me." What he said was true.

From that day on, Xiang frequently came down from the second floor to talk with Peng Shuzhi, often for hours on end. The first few times, Peng reported to me what she had said and discussed with me "what to do about it." I could see that he was gradually beginning to waver, so I warned him even more urgently. After that, he did not discuss the situation with me. He had accepted Xiang Jingyu's love.

Cai Hesen was about to return to Shanghai from Beijing. First, he wrote to Xiang Jingyu telling her on what day and at what hour he would arrive at Shanghai's Northern Railway Station.

That day, I asked Peng Shuzhi, "Will you tell Cai Hesen?"

"Comrade Jingyu thinks it's not necessary."

Later, there was a knock at the door, and I went down from my pavilion room to open it. It was Cai Hesen, his luggage and a basketful of Tianjin pears loaded on a rickshaw. He asked me where Xiang Jingyu was. "Upstairs," I replied. He was a bit surprised that Xiang Jingyu had not come to fetch him from the station, and he thought something must have happened. The next day or the day after, the affair came out into the open. Xiang Jingyu, our "Song academician," was unable to keep up the deceit. Cai Hesen asked her what was up. At first, she said, "I'm trying to think out an article"; afterward, she told him the whole story. That day or the next, the presidium of the Central Committee met in the downstairs guest room. Chen

Duxiu, Cai Hesen, Zhang Guotao, Qu Qiubai, and Peng Shuzhi were all there, together with some nonvoting attendees (whose names I forget) from Communist Youth and the Shanghai District Committee; I also forget what the meeting was about. I was present in an unofficial capacity, as was Xiang Jingyu. At the end of the discussion, Chen Duxiu was about to proclaim the meeting closed when Cai Hesen suddenly stood up and said that there was another matter he wanted to raise for discussion.

"Comrades Jingyu and Shuzhi have fallen in love," he said.

Chen, Qu, Zhang, and the rest of them looked like the characters in the last scene of Gogol's *Government Inspector*. For a long time, no one said anything; they were too surprised.

Finally, Chen Duxiu said, "Comrade Jingyu must decide for herself."

Xiang Jingyu put her head in her hands and wailed. Not a word passed her lips.

Chen Duxiu asked, "Who do you love, Shuzhi or Hesen?"

Still Xiang Jingyu did not answer. Under the circumstances, the presidium had no choice but to decide on her behalf. The Central Committee—that is, Chen Duxiu, Qu Qiubai, and Zhang Guotao—decided to send her to Moscow with Cai Hesen. Cai had gone south from Beijing in order to go to Moscow to be the Party's permanent representative there. Xiang Jingyu raised no protest, so in this way, the matter was resolved. Chen Duxiu swore those present to strict secrecy about the affair, and he especially forbade Qu Qiubai to tell Yang Zhihua. Everyone promised to keep quiet about it, but pretty soon, it had become common knowledge. I think it highly unlikely that Yang Zhihua was the last to hear of it.

I doubt very much that the Central Committee's decision was the right one. Of course, Xiang Jingyu did not want to decide one way or the other, but it's easy to imagine that she preferred Peng Shuzhi to Cai Hesen. Even if her mind was not made up, in the course of time, her old love was definitely likely to fade and her new love to grow. If the Central Committee had decided the other way around, or if it had let the matter take its own course and had not interfered, many later wrangles could have been avoided, for the affair had serious consequences.

At the end of the meeting, Xiang Jingyu accused Cai Hesen of "selfishness."

"You knew beforehand that the Central Committee would back you up," she told him. "Otherwise you wouldn't have raised the matter."

What could Cai say? After supper, instead of going up to the second floor, he stayed downstairs and paced around the room. I, too, stayed downstairs.

"Chaolin," he told me, "it's as if my heart had been cut by a knife."

I suggested that we go and see a film. He agreed. This was something new, for in the past he had never gone to watch films or Beijing operas. We went to the Odeon Cinema, newly opened, which was showing *Love Parade*, starring Jeanette MacDonald and Maurice Chevalier. It had some beautiful scenes, bustling with noise and excitement, but Cai's heart was not in it. During the intermission, I invited him for a cup of coffee. The film started up again, but he was not interested, so I had no choice but to sacrifice my evening's entertainment and escort him back to Fusheng Road.

Several days passed. On the second floor, a person lay sighing on a bed; on the first floor lay another, similarly sighing, with Xiang Jingyu constantly climbing up and down between them. It was obvious to me that things could not go on like that, so I went to see Chen Duxiu and asked him to propose a solution. After thinking for a while, he took up his pen and wrote a short note telling Cai Hesen and Xiang Jingyu to move at once to a hotel and await the steamer for Vladivostok. I took the note home and handed it to Cai Hesen, who accepted it, but Xiang and Peng hated me bitterly. Peng even had a row with me.

The affair had numerous implications, and it influenced the later course of the inner-Party struggle. As a result of it, Cai Hesen and Peng Shuzhi became sworn enemies. At the Fifth Congress, Cai launched a ferocious attack on Peng. In the autumn of 1927, when Cai was in charge of the Party's Northern Bureau and outranked Peng, who was then secretary of the Shunzhi[247] Provincial Committee, he reported to the Party center that Peng had informed on Wang Hebo and other comrades, resulting in their arrest. The charge was so absurd that even Peng's political opponent Qu Qiubai, then in charge of the Central Committee, did not believe it.

The "model couple" finally broke up after reaching Moscow. Li Lisan and his wife, Li Yichun, accompanied them on the journey. To lessen Cai's grief, Li Lisan told his wife to console Cai en route to Moscow, but during the consolation, Cai and Li Yichun fell in love. Some say that Li Lisan did this deliberately to get rid of Li Yichun, because he was in love with her younger sister, but whatever the case, Li Lisan and Cai Hesen became deadly enemies. Not long after the Central Committee elected at the Sixth Congress in Moscow in 1928 had returned to China and started work there, an internal struggle broke out, during which Cai Hesen, then an important leader of the Party, was ousted from power by Li Lisan, who took his job. The incident had a bearing on my own work—I will come back to it in a later chapter. In Moscow, Xiang Jingyu fell in love with a Mongol. In 1927, she returned to China alone to work for the Party. In Wuhan, she had a tussle with Cai Hesen and accused Li Yichun of wronging her. She threw herself into her work and stayed on in Wuhan, even after the government there had turned reactionary. She never fell in love again to the day she died—a martyr for the revolution.

Greater still were the implications for those left behind in China. Before Cai Hesen's return from Beijing to Shanghai, a vivacious woman student arrived one day at the Propaganda Department on Fusheng Road and asked me, "Is this where Peng Shuzhi lives?" It was Chen Bilan. She had a letter of introduction from Luo Yinong, asking Peng to look after her because she was young and green. We already knew Chen Bilan's name; in fact, she was quite famous, though she had gone to Moscow after we had returned to China. She was Huang Rikui's wife. She, Shi Jingyi (Liu Renjing's wife), Cai Chang, Guo Longzhen (who had both been in France), and others formed the first group of Chinese women students at KUTV. Li Heling (i.e., Li Helin), Huang Guozuo (i.e., Huang Ping), and Luo Jiao (i.e., Luo Yinong) immediately made advances to Chen Bilan, who was the prettiest of the women. Luo Jiao had the advantage, being secretary of the Chinese Communist Party's Moscow branch. Huang Guozuo beat a quick retreat; Li Heling cried his eyes out. Luo Jiao returned home before Chen Bilan. Although Chen Bilan had broken with Huang Rikui, she kept Luo Jiao at arm's length, for she was not really in love with him. After her return to China, she shunned him. He was in Beijing, she in Henan; when he hastened to Henan, she rushed off somewhere else. Luo Jiao bit his finger until it bled and wrote Chen Bilan a letter in blood; her defenses weakened, and she promised to get back together with him. Later, in prison, He Zishen told me, "The blood was fake. Luo Jiao discussed his plans with me in Beijing. I told him that if you mix milk with red ink, the effect is the same." He Zishen also told me that afterward, he had met Chen Bilan in Shanghai and told her, but she had only laughed and tried to hit him.

Later, Chen Bilan often used to turn up at the Propaganda Department. Xiang Jingyu already knew Chen Bilan, having advised and lectured her in Shanghai in the old days about romance. But now Xiang had reason to dislike her. Every time Chen Bilan turned up, Xiang Jingyu urged her to leave early, saying that Fusheng Road was too far from Chen's home in Caojiadu, that she would miss the last tram, that she would get stranded and have to stay the night. After Xiang Jingyu and Cai Hesen left for Russia, Peng Shuzhi became melancholic and depressed. He started drinking and used to get hungover. Qu Qiubai advised him to stop drinking Chinese spirits and switch, instead, to foreign brandy to stop the hangovers, so Peng got himself a bottle of brandy and carried it around with him in his overcoat pocket. Zhang Guotao invited him out for a walk and tried to console him by telling him about his own romantic disappointments. It turned out that Zhang had fallen in love with Liu Qingyang, who did not return his feelings. But Chen Bilan's consolation proved more effective than Zhang Guotao's. This time, Peng initiated the courtship, to fill the hole left in his heart by Xiang Jingyu. And this time, the affair lasted.[248]

In 1925 or early 1926, Luo Yinong (Luo Jiao) came to Shanghai. He had been transferred from Beijing on the recommendation of Zhang Guotao to become secretary of the Jiangsu-Zhejiang Regional Committee. Peng Shuzhi did not oppose the appointment, but we were all worried that there would be a row, for Luo Yinong was unaware of what had happened. Wang Yifei, who was acting secretary, told me: "When Yinong gets here, bring him to my place first. I'll have a word with him about it." The day that Luo arrived, Peng was not at home, and I was out somewhere on business. Suddenly, Luo dashed in and went straight up to the first floor, looking for Peng. The only person at home was Chen Bilan. Luo noticed that there were two beds in the room, along with some women's things. "Has Shuzhi found a wife?" he asked Chen Bilan. Chen did not know what to say. Just at that moment, Wang Yifei turned up and took Luo off. I found out about this incident from Chen Bilan after I got back.

Qu Qiubai proposed trying to reconcile the two old friends. One evening, we all met together in Peng Shuzhi's room: Qu Qiubai, Luo Yinong, and me, along with Peng and Chen, who hosted the gathering. First, Qu Qiubai mouthed a few pious words, intermingled with criticism of the three concerned. All I remember is a Russian word he used while criticizing Chen Bilan. It was *legkomyslennaya*, which can be translated as "light-minded" or "fickle." After Qu Qiubai, it was Luo Yinong's turn. Luo said that the whole thing was unimportant, as if there were no problem. Peng Shuzhi disagreed. "He is being pompous," he protested. "Pompous" is the only other word I can remember from our attempt at conciliation.

So after that, "there was no problem." Luo Yinong frequently came to the Propaganda Department to pass the time of day, and Peng and Chen frequently visited him in his home, where they laughed and joked together. During Chen Duxiu's "disappearance," on several occasions, Luo turned up early in the morning at the Propaganda Department to ask for instructions concerning his work on the Shanghai Regional Committee from Peng Shuzhi, representing the Central Committee. Luo would sit there and talk to Peng while Peng lay in bed with Chen Bilan. At the Fifth Congress, both men were subjected to attack. After the Wuhan debacle, Luo gradually rose in status. At first, he became secretary of the Hubei Provincial Committee, then he joined the Standing Committee of the Politburo, then he became secretary of the Chang Jiang Bureau and directed the Autumn Harvest Uprising in Xiang'egan,[249] and finally, he became director of the Central Committee's Organization Bureau, like Stalin in the Soviet Union. When Peng came back from Beijing, he had to report to Luo and ask for instructions. Luo contributed to Cai Hesen's secret denunciation of Peng.

One day, while I was talking and joking with Wang Ruofei and Zhao Shiyan at Luo Yinong's place, the conversation naturally turned to Luo's love life. Later, Luo said to me: "Today at an activists' meeting there was a woman student who kept on staring at me. Do you know who she is?" He began to describe her, and I quickly realized who he meant. "That's Zhu Youlun," I told him. "She is He Chang's wife. Don't do anything silly." He replied that he had no intention of trying to steal a comrade's wife. Indirectly, he was criticizing Peng Shuzhi. At the time, He Chang was in Moscow. After a while, Zhu Youlun and Luo Yinong started living together. Zhu's mother brought her youngest son with her to Shanghai from Sichuan and moved into Luo's residence as his mother-in-law. Several of us used to spend much time there playing mahjong with her.

It was not He Chang himself but two professor comrades, Shi Cuntong and Li Ji from Shanghai University, who protested this love affair. Shi Cuntong's protest was entirely reasonable. He proposed a principle: If a female comrade wants to live with another male comrade, she should first formally break with her original lover. Li Ji's protest was harder to explain. He argued from the point of view of Party interest. He said: "Luo Yinong told us in one of his speeches: We should hate as deeply as if he had dug up the grave of one of our ancestors anyone who harms the Party. Luo Yinong's behavior today has harmed the Party." There was an imminent danger of revolt by the students and teachers of Shanghai University, which was averted only by the intervention of Peng Shuzhi, who went to speak with these people on behalf of the Propaganda Department.

He Chang himself suppressed his feelings right up to the time of the defeat of the revolution, when Luo Yinong took over as director of the Organization Bureau. Only then did He Chang join with Lin Yunan, Liu Changqun, and a few other Hubei comrades to denounce Luo to the Central Committee for various crimes committed in the course of his work in Hubei. So Luo was toppled from his special position on the Central Committee and was even removed from the Organization Bureau. Other members of the Central Committee—for example, Li Weihan—also had a hand in his downfall.

Zhu Youlun lived for more than a year in Luo's residence before going to Moscow to study. In Moscow, she fell in love with Shao Lizi's son, Shao Zhigang. In 1928, she drowned while out rowing on the Moscow River.

When Zhu Youlun went to Moscow to study, we all sweated for Luo Yinong. When people coming back from Moscow began to gossip about her, no one dared tell Luo—not until after he had become secretary of the Hubei Provincial Committee and joined the Politburo. At the time, Wuhan was already under the pall of reaction. Of the beautiful women comrades who had previously sought the limelight in Wuhan, some had gone to other places and others—especially the local ones—had withdrawn from the Party. But there was one exception. Li Zheshi, who had been in charge of the Hubei Women's Association during the high tide of the revolution, continued to work actively for the Party. Li Zheshi was a spinster by choice and an intellectual, no longer young. A few months before, during Wuhan's great storm of romance, she had stayed a spectator, but this time she was unable to withstand the determined advances of Luo Yinong and ended up abandoning her celibacy. I knew about this liaison even before I left Wuhan. Not long after I had gone back to Shanghai, Luo Yinong arrived there with his new lover. Less than a year later, Li Zheshi went to Longhua to collect Luo's corpse. After that, she went to Moscow to study.

Only now did the sequence of events set in motion by Xiang Jingyu on the night of the Mid-Autumn Festival in 1925 draw to a close. How much distress and hatred it had provoked, how many struggles it had unleashed within the Party! Cai Hesen against Peng Shuzhi, Li Lisan against Cai Hesen, He Chang against Luo Yinong, Luo Yinong against Peng Shuzhi! In the New Huizhong Hotel in Shanghai, I saw He Chang ask Zhou Enlai for an interview and then venomously denounce Luo to Zhou. I realized even then how intimately love and politics are intertwined. It struck me that various other struggles had also been caused by love. Generally speaking, if love is not involved in an internal struggle, both sides are cooler, more objective, more rational, and more restrained; whereas in every struggle that is excessively violent and heated, a love entanglement can generally be detected. Once, I half-jokingly, half-seriously developed this argument in the presence of some friends, but none of them could be persuaded. They said that it was "un-Marxist." I certainly did not base my case solely on facts, which may be incidental. What I meant was that if a comrade or a friend steals your lover, then even if you can reason it away and regard it as something separate from politics and revolution, subconsciously you will find it hard not to develop an *antipathie*[250] toward the thief. If a quarrel develops in which you might otherwise have stayed neutral, you will come out against him; if you would have come out against him anyway, you will do so all the more bitterly; and if you might otherwise have joined him, you will hesitate to do so. He Chang did not necessarily oppose Luo Yinong solely out of revenge, but since he already felt an antipathy toward Luo, he used the opportunity to vent it. And it was less because of the revolution in Hubei than because of Zhu Youlun.

But there were exceptions. I remember my friend Yan Changyi, who was so noble-minded that even when his lover was stolen away from him he harbored not the slightest rancor. He and Xia Zhixu had been together for many years, but at a certain point, one of them had to go to Shanghai for the Party while the other stayed in Beijing. One day, when Zhao Shiyan was passing through Shanghai, someone—I forget who—invited us out for a meal at the Xinya Cantonese Restaurant on North Sichuan Road, and Yan Changyi was among the guests. At the time, I had never met Xia Zhixu; all

I knew was that she was Yan's lover. During the meal, I asked Yan whether she had written recently. "She is Zhao Shiyan's lover now," he told me. He said it quite innocently, but Zhao Shiyan blushed violently. It was only then that I realized that I had said the wrong thing. Yan was not being insincere. I knew his character quite well; he was not that sort of person.

Chen Qiaonian lacked Zhao Shiyan's good fortune. His love affair with Shi Jingyi happened at more or less the same time as Zhao Shiyan's with Xia Zhixu, but it caused an almighty storm. Shi Jingyi had originally been Liu Renjing's wife, but after Liu brought her to the city, he fell out of love with her, so he sent her to Moscow to be a student. After she had become more cultured, she, in turn, fell out of love with Liu Renjing, who then gradually fell back in love with her. When she returned to China, she stayed in Beijing to work for the Party, having no wish to go to Shanghai to live with Liu Renjing. Liu Renjing was then editor of *China Youth*, and since I often used to go to Communist Youth headquarters to pass the time of day, I became his friend and wrote something for *China Youth* almost every week. One Sunday in the autumn of 1926, some young people at Communist Youth decided to organize an outing to Wusong. Liu Renjing and I went along with them. Liu seemed downcast throughout the entire trip. On the way back, while we were waiting for the train at the railway station, I suddenly noticed that Liu Renjing had a bandaged finger. I asked him what had happened. He did not answer, and someone else steered the conversation around to another subject. I thought that it was all very strange. Later on, someone else—perhaps it was Liu Changqun—quietly told me, "Liu Renjing cut his finger on purpose to write a letter to Shi Jingyi. We organized the excursion to drive away his cares." And it was true! His was real blood, not milk and ink.

Shortly afterward, Liu Renjing went to Moscow to become a student. It was not Liu Renjing himself but Liu's fellow provincials from Hubei who criticized Chen Qiaonian. They had always harbored an antipathy toward Chen. Later, when the Hubei comrades were accusing Luo Yinong, one item on the charge sheet was that when Chen Qiaonian had fallen ill with typhoid fever (at the time, he was in charge of the Hubei Committee's Organization Department), he had been given several thousand dollars for his medical expenses by Luo, who was secretary of the committee. Before the Fifth Congress, Chen Yannian went to Beijing for a meeting and found out about the attacks on Chen Qiaonian. Passing through Shanghai on his way back to Guangdong, he revealed to me his dissatisfaction with his younger brother. It was the first time I had heard him speak like that. Chen Yannian never had a single love affair, from the day he was born to the day he died.

Like Chen Qiaonian, Yin Kuan and Wang Ruofei also got into trouble over women. Yin Kuan was sent to Shandong to be secretary of the Provincial Committee. In that land of Confucian rites,[251] the boundary between men and women was extremely sharp. When Yin Kuan first arrived, the women comrades in the organization always used to sit with bowed heads whenever there was a meeting, so Yin Kuan worked hard to raise their self-esteem. In their eyes, his theories, his methods of work, and his ways of dealing with problems were quite new. Everyone believed in him, worshipped him. We in Shanghai heard nothing but good things about him. It would have been wonderful if only he had not become involved in a love affair. His lover, Wang Bian, was a girl of talent, a pearl in the palm of her aging father. Her father was a veteran Shandong Communist; the daughter, too, was a Party member. She and Yin Kuan had fallen secretly in love. Shortly after that, the Central Committee transferred Yin Kuan to Shanghai to be secretary of the Jiangsu-Zhejiang Regional Committee. I am talking about 1925, in the wake of the May Thirtieth Movement, when Party activity was on the rise. Zhuang Wengong was not up to his job, so the Central Committee, impressed by Yin Kuan's record in Shandong, decided to give him Zhuang's post. I went to say hello. In his room was a short, fat girl. "This is Comrade Wang Bian," he said, though I had already guessed who she was even before he told me. She bowed her head and smiled.

Soon after that, I heard that some of the comrades in Shandong had written to the Central Committee denouncing Yin Kuan for "abducting" Wang Bian to Shanghai. They were highly indignant and demanded that Yin Kuan be punished. Most indignant of all was Wang Bian's father, who was prepared to go to Shanghai with a dagger to fight Yin Kuan to the death. To my knowledge, this was the sole occasion of a comrade being denounced to the Central Committee for a love affair, and in such sharp terms. (It could happen only in the land of Confucius.) But the Central Committee did not handle the matter. Later, the Shandong comrades wrote a second letter, announcing that Wang Bian's father had set a condition that, if met, would settle the matter. He wanted Chen Duxiu, representing the Central Committee, and Yun Daiying, representing Communist Youth, to be chief witnesses at the couple's wedding. Again, the Central Committee ignored him. It so happened that at around this time, Yin Kuan was stricken again with tuberculosis, and was unable to work, so the Central Committee let him go on leave and sent Wang Yifei to replace him. The Comintern wanted the Chinese Party to send a batch of students to Moscow, so the Central Committee sent Wang Bian. As a result, the people in Shandong calmed down. But Wang and Yin stayed in love and kept in touch by letter.

Moscow, at the time, was a hive of "flag-switching,"[252] by which I mean that women with lovers back in China were dropping them for men in Moscow. The men whose lovers were away in Moscow—Yin Kuan included—considered themselves threatened. Comrades who came back to China after attending meetings in Moscow often used to tell stories about the Moscow love scene. Once, when Li Lisan came back from Moscow, I asked him on behalf of Yin Kuan whether any stories were circulating about Wang Bian. "How could anyone suspect Wang Bian?" he asked me. "She is completely loyal to Yin Kuan." That put Yin Kuan's mind at rest.

Wang Bian arrived back in China from Moscow shortly before the Guangzhou Insurrection. The Central Committee sent her and another woman comrade to Guangzhou to work for the Party. She knew that Yin Kuan was head of the Guangdong Committee's Propaganda Department. Her arrival in Guangzhou coincided with the Guangzhou Insurrection, so she and the other woman sought out the insurrectionary troops on the Guangzhou streets. Clutching her identity papers, she told the troops that she was looking for the Provincial Committee, but they paid her no attention. Actually, by then Yin Kuan had already returned to Shanghai, where he contacted the Central Committee on behalf of the Guangdong Provincial Committee. He was staying in a hostel. When he heard that Wang Bian had also returned to Shanghai and was unable to track down the Central Committee, he placed an advertisement in the missing persons column of a newspaper. After that, the Central Committee sent Yin Kuan to be secretary of the Anhui Provincial Committee. Wang Bian eventually went to Wuhu, where she and Yin Kuan were reunited.

But shortly after that, Wang Bian was arrested and sent to prison, and Yin Kuan escaped back to Shanghai to await another assignment. It was then that he joined the Left Opposition and was expelled from the official Party. Wang Bian served her sentence in Anhui and was released, and then she too went to Shanghai. The Central Committee told her that Yin Kuan had already been expelled, but she demanded to see him, so the Central Committee allowed her to pay him a visit. She stayed with him for two or three days. On one occasion, I met her there; she was already a fat woman and no longer a shy young girl.

In Moscow, Wang Bian had been an anti-Trotskyist, and during her brief reunion with Yin Kuan in Wuhu, he had not yet seen any Trotskyist documents, so there had been no differences in their thinking. But now, in Shanghai, they no longer had a common language, so eventually, she went back to the Central Committee.

Wang Ruofei's love affair caused just as great a storm as Yin Kuan's, but unlike his, it did not end badly. Li Peize was a woman student from Baoding who went to Henan to work for the Party. I never met her, but people told me that she had the classic feminine graces. She Liya and Wang Ruofei both pursued her, and Wang won, so She Liya kicked up a big fuss, and some other comrades joined him. The issue was raised at the Central Committee. The reason that Wang Ruofei was transferred from his job as secretary of the Henan-Shaanxi Regional Committee to Shanghai, where he led the Central Committee's secretariat, was obviously because he was needed there, but it was also a way of resolving this love entanglement. At the same time, Li Peize was sent to Moscow to be a student, like Wang Bian. You can split couples up and make them live in different places, but you can't make them stop loving each other. Whether they manage to stay together in the long run depends on who they are. In 1928, when the Chinese Communist Party convened its Sixth National Congress in Moscow, Wang Ruofei was sent as head of the Jiangsu delegation. After the congress, he stayed on in Moscow as Party representative to the Comintern and started living with Li Peize again.

Love affairs in Moscow must have been much livelier than those back in China. I heard any number of stories, but now I have forgotten them. In a word, Wang Bian and Li Peize in Moscow were considered "backward" because they were loyal to their old lovers. Sometimes women left their men, sometimes vice versa. But it's up to someone else to tell these stories.

In China in those years, I knew of only one case in which a male comrade left behind in China gave up his lover in Moscow. That case was Wang Yifei. When Wang Yifei first got back to China, he felt so deprived of female company that any woman would do for him, and he quickly ended up married to one called Zhang Liang. But they soon discovered that they were mismatched in character and found it hard to keep their relationship going. So Wang sent Zhang to Moscow to be a student, and he quickly found another lover whose character was more compatible with his own. Zhang Liang in Moscow bitterly denounced Wang Yifei. When she returned to China, she proved to be capable and efficient. She stayed behind in southern China after the start of the Long March in October 1934. Later, she and a group of people under Qu Qiubai tried to slip through the blockade thrown around the old Central Soviet and reach Shanghai, but they were caught in Fujian, and someone revealed who Qu Qiubai was.[253] I was in prison at the time, but I read a newspaper report about this episode. Some people say that by then, Zhang was the wife of Liang Botai; others say that she was the wife of Xiang Ying. I do not know which, if either, is right.

At the start of this chapter, I said that I intended to write only about other people's love affairs and not about my own. However, having gotten this far, it seems wrong not to say a few words about myself. But I will keep my remarks short.

Not long after I got back to Shanghai from Wuhan, I arranged to meet Jiang Guangchi in a room above the Creation Society publishing department on North Sichuan Road. After talking for a while about what each of us had been up to since we had last seen each other, Jiang took out from under his coat the latest edition of a Shanghai tabloid. It contained a news item the gist of which was as follows. "Zheng Chaolin and Jiang Guangchi have fallen out within the Chinese Communist Party over a woman. Zheng stole Jiang's wife, and the two men took their quarrel to the Central Committee; the outcome was that Chen Duxiu decided that the woman was Zheng Chaolin's wife. So Jiang buried his head in his hands and wept bitterly." I laughed, and so did Jiang. I forget which tabloid it was. Naturally, I knew that Jiang had been married, for he had always boasted about his Henan student wife. But I had never even seen her face, for she had died of tuberculosis at Lushan. So the report was completely without foundation. Even so, weakness lends wings to rumors, and the report can be seen as a distorted reflection of the numerous love affairs in which senior Party members became entangled in those years.

After getting back to China from the Soviet Union, for some inexplicable reason it seemed to me that I had already outgrown the age of love, so I had no interest in it and made no preparations for it. The disintegration of the "model couple" made me even warier of romance. But at more or less the same time as Cai Hesen was languishing in agony, downstairs I was laughing and joking with Yang Fulan. Yang Fulan was a student at Shanghai University who used to come to the Propaganda Department every day to do two or three hours' administrative work: clipping newspaper articles, sticking up posters, sorting out materials, that sort of thing. I was in charge of this work. One day, when I had just gotten back from a workers' branch meeting in east Shanghai and was still wearing my workers' clothes, Cai Hesen—who happened to be in the guest room at the time—said to me, "Chaolin, I've got some good news for you."

I asked him what the good news was.

"We'll speak about it later," he said. While this conversation was going on, Yang Fulan was sitting there with her head bowed. After a while she went out. Then Cai told me, "You should hurry up and propose. She has fallen in love with you." He explained, "I've just spoken to Fulan, I knew she wasn't married, so I said jokingly that I would introduce you to her. To judge from her expression, she agreed."

He seemed to me to be talking nonsense. But after that, I began to pay attention to this nineteen-year-old girl, and it gradually dawned on me that maybe Cai was right. So I became friends with Yang, and we often used to go out together. In those two months, I had numerous chances to "say what was necessary," but I did not, and later she left Shanghai and went to Guangzhou. She was Lin Boqu's adopted daughter. When Chen Yannian met her in the Propaganda Department on one of his visits to Shanghai, he recruited her to work for the South China Regional Committee. There, she got to know my friend Huang Guozuo (Huang Ping), and after a while, they became partners. After she left Shanghai, instead of waning, my feelings for her intensified, and I regretted never having "said what was necessary." I tasted the bitterness of love lost. Only after Zhao Shiyan got back from a meeting in Guangzhou and told me about Fulan and Huang Ping's marriage did I gradually forget her.

But the interlude was not without its uses, for I now realized that the age of love had not passed me by after all, and that I could still find a girl to love me, even though I had not vanquished my antipathy toward the love wrangles I had witnessed in the Party.

In mid-November 1927, more than a month after reading in the tabloid about my alleged theft of Jiang Guangchi's wife, Wang Ruofei came to my home to take me out for a meal at the Jufengyuan Restaurant to celebrate the marriage of two comrades. The bridegroom worked in the Organization Department of the Jiangsu Provincial Committee. It was the first time that I had ever met him, but I had known the bride for a long time. Her previous lover had worked in the Central Secretariat and had been seized and shot by Yang Hu half a year earlier. Another person I had never met before was a friend of the bride who also worked in the Jiangsu Organization Department. She had a plump face, white skin, and rosy cheeks, and she was wearing a padded jacket and a black skirt and a pair of thick spectacles. Wang Ruofei introduced her: Comrade Liu Jingzhen[254] from Yunnan. During the course of the meal, my attention was focused less on the bride than on Liu Jingzhen. After the meal, I sought out Wang Ruofei to make some inquiries about her. Wang told me that he had deliberately engineered the meeting because he knew that her views on love were more or less the same as those of his friend Chaolin.

Battle commenced between her and me. She was not averse to seeing or talking with me, but she acted as if she were ignorant of my intentions toward her, and whenever I visited her, she pretended to treat me just like any other comrade. Just when we started becoming amicable, she told me that she was preparing to go back to Yunnan. On several occasions, I actually lost hope, but then she would reawaken it with a few words or gestures. For several weeks, I was swayed violently this way and that, wanting to win her and at the same time fearing to do so. Every time we met it was at her home, never at mine.

On December 24, 1927, the Central Committee wanted to discuss something with Chen Duxiu, so it sent a car to take him to my home, which was in the editorial offices of *Bolshevik* on Yuyuan Road. He was going to stay for three days. I prepared a dinner to entertain them. "Do you want to meet the Old Man?" Wang Ruofei asked Liu Jingzhen. "We're eating together tonight, and I'll take you if you like." Naturally, she agreed. Only when she got there did she realize that the dinner was at my home, by which time, she had no choice but to stay. After the meal, I escorted her home. We walked together as far as the Bubbling Well Road Tramcar Station, and from there, we each took a separate rickshaw to her house at the intersection of Foch Avenue and Pére Robert Road. On the way, we arranged to meet the next day and go together to Castle Bay for an outing.

I was not involved in the discussions between the Central Committee and Chen Duxiu, so the next morning, I apologized to Chen and went to fetch Liu Jingzhen. We went together to the Northern Railway Station and took the train to Castle Bay. We went for a walk on the sandy beach fringing the Yangtze estuary. From then on, my mind was made up.

We began to live together in early April, at around the time of the Festival of Pure Brightness. Our love definitely "did not harm politics," for there were no complications.

FIGURE 1 The Second Congress of the (Chinese) Communist Youth Party, Paris, February 1923.
Back row, left to right: 1. Wang Linghan, 2. unknown, 3. Yu Lüzhong, 4. Ren Zuoxuan, 5. Fu Zhong, 6. Wu Qi, 7. Yin Kuan, 8. Zhou Weizhen, 9. Xue Shilun, 10. Zhou Enlai, 11. Wang Zewei, 12. Xiao Pusheng, 13. Lin Wei, 14. Wang Zekai, 15. unknown.
Middle row: 1. Zhao Guangchen, 2. Zhang Zengyi, 3. Liu Bojian, 4. Cai Zhihua, 5. unknown, 6. Mu Qing, 7. Wang Renda, 8. Qin Zhigu, 9. unknown, 10. unknown, 11. Wang Ziqing, 12. Yuan Zizhen.
Front row: 1. Gao Feng, 2. Zhao Shiyan, 3. unknown, 4. Zheng Chaolin, 5. She Liya, 6. Chen Qiaonian, 7. Yuan Qingyun, 8. Chen Yannian, 9. unkown, 10. Chen Jiuding, 11. Wang Ruofei, 12. unknown, 13. Liu Bozhuang, 14. Yang Jieren.

FIGURE 2 Leon Trotsky. (Photo courtesy of Alex Buchman.)

FIGURE 3 Zheng Chaolin, Shanghai, c. 1930

FIGURE 4   Chen Yannian

FIGURE 5   Chen Qiaonian

FIGURE 6   Ren Bishi

FIGURE 7   Mu Qing

FIGURE 8 Cai Hesen

FIGURE 9 Ge Jianhao (Cai Hesen's mother)

FIGURE 10 Wang Ruofei

FIGURE 11 Liu Bojian

FIGURE 12 He Chang

FIGURE 13 Zhang Bojian

FIGURE 14 Deng Yanda

FIGURE 15 Maring (Henk Sneevliet)

FIGURE 16   Li Lisan

FIGURE 17   Luo Yinong

FIGURE 18   Qu Qiubai

FIGURE 19   Xiang Jingyu

FIGURE 20 Liu Jingzhen, Shanghai, the 1930s

FIGURE 21 Peng Shuzhi just before his and Chen Duxiu's trial in Nanjing in 1932

FIGURE 22 The Provincial Central Committee of the (Trotskyist) Communist League of China, Shanghai, winter 1936, in Frank Glass's (Li Furen's) apartment in the French Concession. Clockwise from left: Wang Fanxi, Frank Glass, Hua Zhenbin (not a CC member, responsible for printing work), Han Jun, Chen Qichang, Jiang Zhendong. (Photo courtesy of Alex Buchman.)

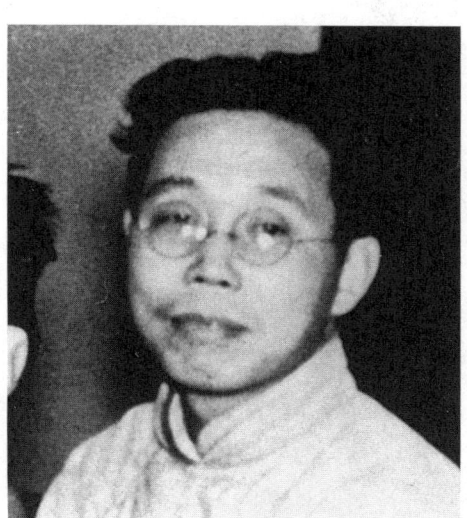

FIGURE 23 Chen Qichang, a Trotskyist leader tortured to death by the Japanese occupiers in 1943, seen here in Shanghai in 1936. (Photo courtesy of Alex Buchman.)

FIGURE 24 Chen Duxiu. Chen's own penned caption reads "Taken in the First Nanjing Prison in the spring of the 26th year of the Republic" (i.e., 1937)

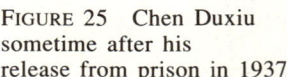

FIGURE 25 Chen Duxiu sometime after his release from prison in 1937

FIGURE 26 Zheng Chaolin, Liu Jingzhen, and their soon-to-die son, Frei, Shanghai, c. 1942

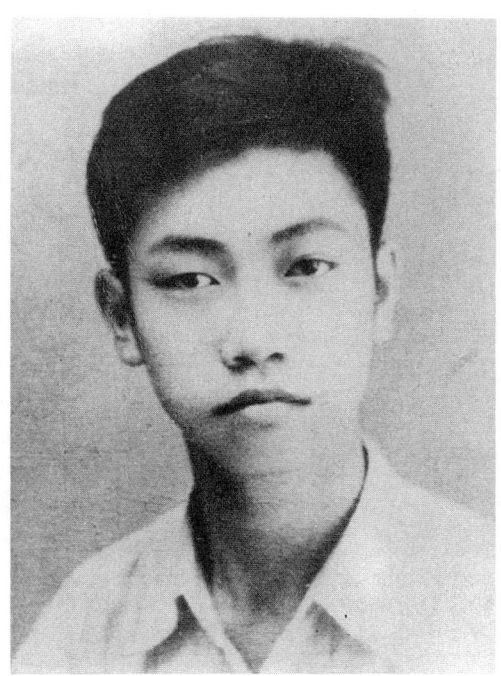

FIGURE 27 Lian Zhengyan (1928–1951), a young Trotskyist shot by the Maoists in Wenzhou Prison

FIGURE 28 Zheng Chaolin and Liu Jingzhen in detention in Shanghai in 1979, on the eve of their freedom

FIGURE 29 Zheng Chaolin in 1979 outside the building in Wuhan in which the August 7 (1927) Conference was held

FIGURE 31 Zheng Chaolin, Shanghai, 1984

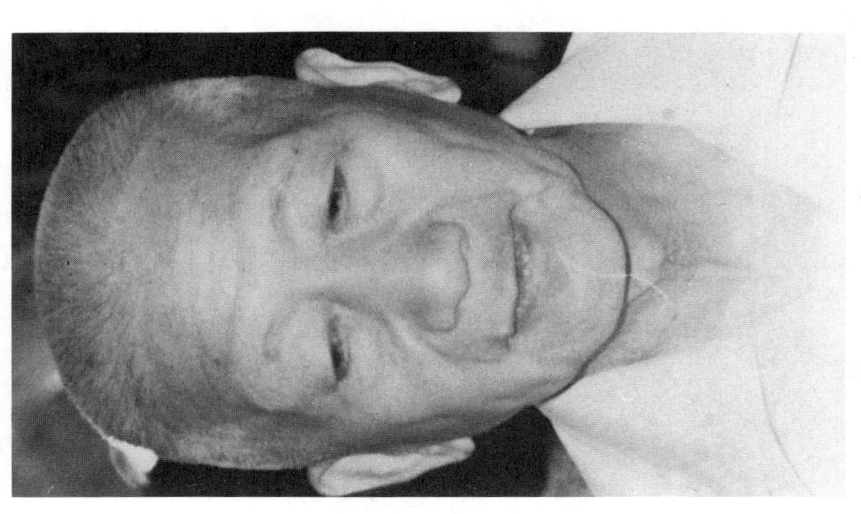

FIGURE 30 Lou Guohua, Hong Kong, 1980

FIGURE 33 Zheng Chaolin, Shanghai, 1989

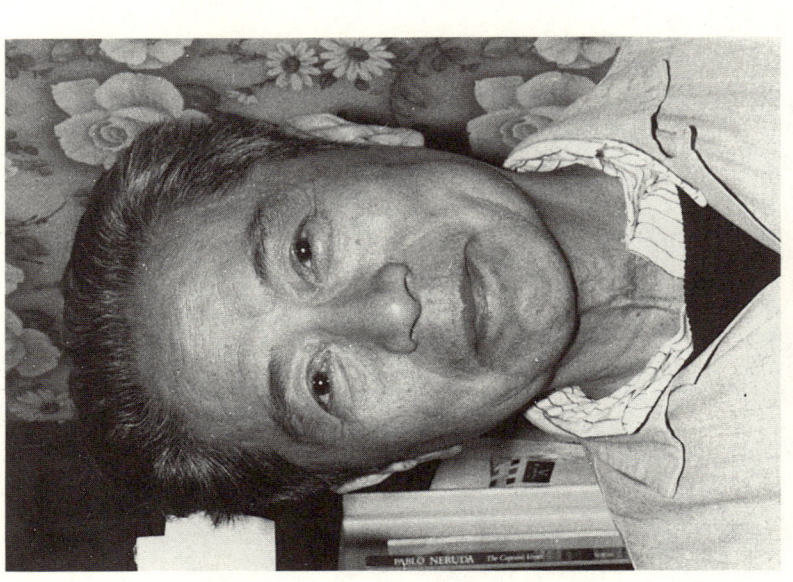

FIGURE 32 Wang Fanxi, Leeds, England, 1989

FIGURE 34 Zheng Chaolin, Shanghai, 1989

8

An Ebbing or a Flowing Tide?

I followed the Central Committee from Hankou back to Shanghai. Qu Qiubai told me to rent a small foreign-style house, for the Central Committee was preparing to move to Guangzhou[255] when Guangdong fell to the Ye-He army,[256] in which case I would be left behind in Shanghai to run the Central Committee office, as a permanent contact point between Shanghai and other places. I rented the first house—a foreign-style terrace house—in the last alley off Hengchang Road on the eastern side of Jessfield Park. I shared the place with Huang Wenrong. After we had been there for a few days, a woman comrade called Huang also came to live with us. Not long after that, she married Zhang Baoquan, who worked as liaison man for the Central Committee.

The plan to move the Central Committee to Guangdong came to nothing,[257] so our house became the editorial office of the Party journal and also headquarters of the Propaganda Department. But apart from the Party journal, very little was actually done by way of propaganda.

I proposed bringing out another publication rather than reviving *Guide Weekly*, and Qu Qiubai agreed. The two of us drew up a list of possible names and finally chose *Buersaiweike* (Bolshevik), which had been my suggestion. From the point of view of editing, *Bolshevik* was an improvement over *Guide Weekly*. In the old days, articles had been thrown together quite haphazardly, but now they were properly coordinated, at least in form. Every issue carried an unsigned editorial, signed articles, letters from all over China, and occasional obituaries. It was the same size as *Yusi* (Threads of talk);[258] that is, it was a big newspaper cut from one sheet of newsprint into twenty-four pieces. We held editorial conferences once a week to check one another's articles and assign next week's articles. Qu Qiubai represented the editorial board on the Standing Committee of the Central Committee and reported to the editorial board on behalf of that body. He wrote all the editorials except for one. Apart from him and me, the editorial board consisted of Cao Dianqi and Xue Juezai, who had both come over from Hunan, and Luo Qiyuan, who had come up from Guangdong.

In my capacity as editor in chief or secretary of the Propaganda Department, I also ran a printing press and a publishing company. The printing press had been in Shanghai all along; the publishing company had been moved to Shanghai from Hankou, where it had been known as the Chang Jiang Bookshop. The printing equipment that I had sent from Hankou had still not been retrieved from customs. Not until a long time later did several comrades pool their capital and open a printing house for money-making purposes.

The situation was quite chaotic when the Central Committee first moved back to Shanghai: Our theory was in chaos, our organization was in chaos, and relations between people were in chaos. Qu Qiubai liaised with the Russians on behalf of the three-person Standing Committee, so he knew sooner than anyone about important new developments and was the first to see documents of the International. People gradually came to look on him as the political and theoretical center of the Party, but he was not officially its general secretary, and he was never able to establish the authority that Chen Duxiu had enjoyed. He was on the same level as the other two members of the Standing Committee. Luo Yinong gave the post of secretary of the Hubei Provincial Committee to Chen Qiaonian, and Wang Zekai took over the Organization Department there. Luo himself came to Shanghai to join the Standing Committee. He not only represented real power in Hubei and Shanghai but also was viewed as a representative of the "Chen Duxiu group." Gradually, he increased his authority. He set up a Chang Jiang Bureau and an Organization Bureau in the Central Committee, both of which he personally controlled. His position had come to resemble that of Stalin in the Soviet Union. Li Weihan, the third member of the Standing Committee, had brought a crowd of people with him from Hunan and assigned them to various bodies under the Central Committee. None had ever worked outside Hunan before.

If Qu Qiubai or Luo Yinong came up with a resolution, they had to rely on the apparatus of the Central Committee to carry it out—that is, they had to rely on Li Weihan's Hunanese. These people were well-disposed toward Qu but violently prejudiced against Luo, so Luo's Chang Jiang Bureau and his Organization Bureau were of no avail to him.

The only way Luo could consolidate his position was by really becoming leader of the "Chen Duxiu-ites," which he was not prepared to do. After the Fifth Congress, he vacillated between the two factions. He had been moved from Jiangxi to become secretary of the Provincial Committee in Hubei partly because he was needed there. People felt that Zhang Tailei's Guangdong style would get nowhere, so they replaced Zhang with Luo, who had earlier served as secretary of the Shanghai Regional Committee. Another reason was that Luo had promised Zhang Guotao and Qu Qiubai never to stand against them on the side of Chen Duxiu. There was nothing that Luo would not tell me save this, about which he kept absolutely silent.

When I first got back to Shanghai, the two groups—for and against Chen Duxiu—were by no means clearly counterposed. The old conspiratorial organization that had existed in Wuhan had already been disbanded. Qu Qiubai, Zhang Guotao, and Tan Pingshan—the three main figures in it—had gone their separate ways. At first, Qu stayed in Hankou, where he controlled the Central Committee; Zhang and Tan both went off to join the Ye-He army. Tan was chairman of the Revolutionary Committee of the Guomindang during the August 1 Nanchang Uprising, and Zhang wielded the goose-feather fan behind the screen.[259] Had the Ye-He army succeeded in taking Guangzhou, Tan and Zhang would have set up a Central Committee there and excluded all those leaders who had not joined the army. But after Ye and He were routed in the Chaozhou-Shantou region, Tan and Zhang returned by a devious route to Shanghai, where they were blamed for the defeat. Tan was dismissed outright from the Party, and Zhang was kept under examination; I do not know for how long. They were made scapegoats for what had happened in Guangdong, just as Chen Duxiu had been made a scapegoat for the Wuhan defeat. But there was more to it than that. The people on the Central Committee in Shanghai used the occasion to oust their rivals. Other people close to Tan were attacked too. To stop Tan's friends from causing trouble in Guangdong, Zhang Tailei ordered Yang Bao'an and Luo Qiyuan to go to Shanghai, which is how Luo Qiyuan ended up in the Propaganda Department. Luo Qiyuan, who commanded a mass following in Guangdong, wrote well and had a good sense of humor. When he came to stay in the Propaganda Department, we told the neighbors that he was my cousin. Not long after that, my "cousin's wife" turned up with four or five of my "cousin's children." He knew why the Central Committee had assigned him to the Propaganda Department. On one occasion, he told me that he was not a member of Tan Pingshan's group and that he and Yang Bao'an had always despised Tan.

The anti–Chen Duxiu mood started to evaporate. Actually, there had never been any document clearly opposing Chen, just some vague pronouncements against "opportunism." The resolution passed by the August 7 Conference had not mentioned Chen Duxiu by name. Perhaps the rank and file were baffled, but people close to the Central Committee knew that responsibility for the defeat at Wuhan could not be pinned on Chen Duxiu alone and that the only reason Chen had withdrawn from the leadership was that the International had ordered it. After Qu Qiubai arrived in Shanghai, he also believed that theory, or at least he pretended to. After he had been back for two or three days, he visited Chen Duxiu and behaved respectfully toward him, just as in the old days in Shanghai. When Chen Duxiu sent back Huang Wenrong, his personal secretary, to the Central Committee, Qu accepted Huang and assigned him to help me out. When *Bolshevik* appeared, he asked

Chen to write for it, but Chen's only contributions were items along the lines of his old "Inch of Iron" column under the name Sa Weng, along with space fillers such as a highly appreciated song that began "The Three People's Principles are completely muddle-headed." He lived on Fusheng Road near the building that had formerly housed the old Propaganda Department and rarely went out. Once he went to Luo Yinong's place for a meal, and on another occasion he came to stay for three days at my house. I never heard anyone say anything disrespectful about him during the first six months after the Central Committee moved back to Shanghai, and I rarely saw any articles or proclamations attacking "opportunism." Every time something important happened, he wrote to the Standing Committee and gave his opinion, but it was never accepted.

All the same, he was frequently implicated in the inner-Party struggle during this period. In reality, there was no such thing as a "Chen Duxiu group." In the first place, the Old Man himself was opposed to having one. In Wuhan, he had shown not the slightest intention of gathering a coterie of supporters to enable him to fight back against his detractors. He made no distinction between his opponents and his supporters—he looked on each and every one as a comrade. In Wuhan, he had carried out the new line, the Comintern line, the line represented by Qu Qiubai, but he did not consider that doing so meant that he was submitting to other people's judgment. On the contrary, he thought that it was the right thing to do, for the Northern Expedition had been victorious and the revolution was deepening as a result of it. True, it had produced the reactionary force of Chiang Kai-shek, but it had also borne us into power. He had a wealth of political experience and acute political antennae, but he was short of skills in basic and systematic theoretical analysis.

After the Wuhan debacle and the move to Shanghai, he developed new ways of looking at things and often expounded on them in his letters to the Standing Committee. Unfortunately, these letters have not been preserved, and even though I read them at the time, I can no longer recall their contents. All I remember is that the views expressed in them were disjointed and achieved no system or formula, though they were completely out of sympathy with the views of the Standing Committee. At the time, he still had no intention of forming another group. He was confident that Qu Qiubai and Luo Yinong were as objective, as sincere, and as public spirited as he was, that they would gradually come around to his way of thinking and the old spirit would revive.

But imperceptibly, a "Chen Duxiu group" did exist, though it had no definite form. The Jiangsu Provincial Committee (i.e., the old Shanghai Regional Committee) was almost solidly in support of Chen. Deng Zhongxia was its secretary, but the main power was in the hands of Wang Ruofei, who had inherited Luo Yinong and Zhao Shiyan's old base. The rank-and-file cadres submitted to Wang, just as they had originally submitted to Zhao Shiyan. Deng Zhongxia used to joke self-deprecatingly that he was "only the deputy secretary" of the committee. Actually, he was not even that. He tried hard to build himself a base to counter Wang, but he failed. On the Hubei Provincial Committee, Chen Qiaonian, Wang Zekai, and Ren Xu all supported Chen Duxiu, as did Peng Shuzhi in Beijing. On the Standing Committee, Luo Yinong was considered to belong to the Chen group. Had Chen really lived up to people's expectations, the Chinese Communist Party could have restored the old pre-Wuhan style without difficulty. This was what Wang Ruofei was working for, and after Chen Qiaonian arrived in Shanghai, Wang and Chen approached Luo Yinong for talks and tried to win him over to their position. Luo not only resisted but also told Qu Qiubai about the approach, so the new Central Committee went on the alert and prepared for battle.

After the defeats suffered in various parts of the country, many leaders congregated in Shanghai. Some were punished, and some lost their jobs, after which, most of them went to live in a big house near the Chongqing Road, where they killed time playing mahjong. This group included several confirmed opponents of Chen Duxiu, such as Zhang Guotao and Li Lisan. They made it known that they supported the Central Committee line and that they wanted to help the Central Committee attack the "Chen Duxiu group," starting with Luo Yinong. Zhou Enlai came to Shanghai and immediately became a member of the Standing Committee. Everyone complained to him about Luo Yinong. The forces under Wang Ruofei and Chen Qiaonian were not prepared to back Luo, who became completely isolated. The Organization Bureau was dissolved, and the Chang Jiang Bureau was split between Luo and Li Weihan; in short, Luo was relegated to the role of an ordinary member of the Standing Committee and gradually dropped lower still.

Peng Shuzhi in Beijing also came under attack and brought his wife and daughter back to Shanghai; he too had time to kill. Luo Yinong and Peng were enemies. Wang Ruofei and Chen Qiaonian despised Peng, and there was no way that he could play any role in this struggle. All he could do was "clasp the feet" of Chen Duxiu.[260] If there was a "Chen Duxiu group," its leader was Wang Ruofei. As for the Old Man himself, he not only was not a member of it but even opposed its activities.

I was not the slightest bit interested in this sort of organizational struggle. Wang Ruofei often dropped by for a drink and started complaining about this and that once he was in his cups; he told me a great deal. He knew that even though I was not inclined to help him actively, I would never give away his plans. It seemed to me that there was little difference between the political proposals of these various leaders—at least not insofar as they had revealed them—and that they were simply jockeying for position in the Party.

I got a headache just thinking about the situation. The Old Man came up with some uncommon ideas, but they lacked a system, so I paid no special attention to them. Thinking back on it, after the defeat of the revolution, he was the only person who ever did any thinking—none of the rest did. Certainly Qu Qiubai did not; he simply spun Comintern directives into resolutions or essays of the Chinese Communist Party. Cai Hesen was lecturing on the history of Chinese opportunism at the Party school in Beijing and later published his lectures in mimeograph form. His aim was not to do any original thinking about problems of the revolution but to attack Chen Duxiu and Peng Shuzhi. I leafed through Cai's pamphlet but put it aside, unread. Qu Qiubai, however, read it carefully from start to finish.

"Cai's book is against me too," he told me. "Cai has always opposed me."

I have no idea what part of Cai's book was directed against Qu. There were so many things in those days that required thought, but only Chen Duxiu was prepared to make the effort.

Our thinking was in such a shambles that even I, the editor of the Party journal, was unclear about what to write. I wrote an article for the inaugural issue of *Bolshevik* roughly titled "What Should We Do Now That the National Revolution Has Been Defeated?" The article's contents are clearly stated in the title. I argued that since the revolution had already been defeated, we would have to start again from scratch. After the article appeared, a circular arrived from the Central Committee that seemed to say that the revolution had not been defeated; on the contrary, it had advanced to a new stage, and we were now even closer to victory. I waited for a letter from the Central Committee or some other comrade opposing my article, but none came. The issue was never broached, and no one even drew attention to the fact that there was a contradiction between an article in the Party journal and a circular of the Central Committee. Everyone was so caught up in the organizational struggle that they slighted thought and theory. No one even noticed the contradiction!

But I had learned my lesson. "From now on, I will be more careful when I write articles," I told myself. I was so careful that, for the next few weeks, I wrote nothing. That is to say, I wrote only odds and ends, or general articles, or inconsequential articles on themes that would not get me into trouble. It was not that I suddenly believed that the revolution had not been defeated after all. The opposite was true: I still thought that the revolution had been defeated. But I also thought that the International and the Central Committee (for the Central Committee had no views of its own—it got all its ideas on theory from Moscow or from the Russians in Shanghai) must have some reason for saying that the victory of the revolution was even closer; perhaps the reason was that, in our position, we could not proclaim the defeat of the revolution. But later, when I noticed that the Central

Committee's plans were premised on the imminence of the victory of the revolution, I started to have doubts. Did it really think that? How come I thought so differently? Not only the Central Committee was saying that the tide of revolution was rising; even opponents of the Central Committee, such as Wang Ruofei and Chen Qiaonian of the Party's Jiangsu Provincial Committee, thought so. One day, Wang brought some wine over to my place, and we sat there drinking it and chatting about Party matters. The conversation got around to Chen Duxiu's letters to the Central Committee. I told him that I thought that the letters were simply a collection of odds and ends, that I understood some bits of them but not others. He said that he by no means approved of what Chen had written in his letters.

"But sometimes Chen sees deeper than other people," he continued. "For example, a few days ago, at his place, he told me that the revolution was on the decline. I said no, it's rising. We got into an argument. He asked me: 'Over the past few days, most of the foreign troops in Shanghai have been sent home. Do you believe that the imperialists would withdraw most of their armies if the Chinese Revolution was still ascending?' I suddenly saw the light: The revolution was on the decline."

I simply replied that the observation was perceptive and did not mention my article in *Bolshevik*. But after that, I took Chen's letters more seriously. Chen himself certainly had not committed this view to paper, nor did Wang Ruofei formally publicize his conviction. I do not know when the struggle between the Jiangsu Provincial Committee and the Central Committee first began to take on political and theoretical dimensions. Perhaps it was after Wang Ruofei acquired that conviction.

For quite a few issues, I contributed nothing of any substance to the journal, yet I had no need to explain myself to anyone, for no one ever asked me why I had stopped writing. But when news arrived of the Guangzhou insurrection, I had no choice but to put pen to paper. Qu Qiubai was busy holding meetings and had no time to write the editorial, so I had to write it; in any case, I felt that there could be no doubt about the fate of the revolution. Previous editorials had analyzed current Chinese or world affairs. I could not write an article of that sort, so I wrote about what was uppermost in my mind at the time. I cannot remember what I called the editorial, but I do remember that it used the insurrection to prove that China had only two possible futures: either the Great Dragon Empire that Zhang Zuolin was preparing to set up, or the "dictatorship of the proletariat." There could be no third way. I published it without having Qu Qiubai check it. At the next editorial conference, Qu—who presided—said nothing. At the conference after that, he delivered a report: "On such-and-such a day at the Standing Committee, Comrade Luo Mai [i.e., Li Weihan] raised the question of Comrade Chaolin's editorial in the last issue of *Bolshevik* opposing the line of the International. The International considers that the revolution in China is a bourgeois-democratic revolution that will lead in the future to a workers' and peasants' democratic dictatorship, but Comrade Chaolin's article talks about a proletarian dictatorship. The Standing Committee resolved that I should take the responsibility for making a correction. In this issue, I intend to write an editorial containing such a correction. But Comrade Chaolin's editorial was a very useful revelation to me. In the past, I could never find a suitable subject to write about in editorials. But from now on, we can use this column to discuss theoretical questions." I raised a few doubts, and Qu replied that Lenin had issued the call for a workers' and peasants' democratic dictatorship in 1905. If, in those days, all that Russia could manage was a workers' and peasants' democratic dictatorship, surely the same applied all the more to a country like China. Qu said in his editorial that the editorial in such-and-such an issue of the journal had not been vetted by the editorial committee and that although most of it was right, one section of it required correction, etc., etc. I planned to write an article for the following issue in the discussion column rebutting Qu, so I started searching for relevant passages from Lenin's *Selected Works* in Russian that we had in the bookcase. I found several articles on the workers' and peasants' democratic dictatorship and read them carefully. Then I lost heart and gave up, because Lenin argued that Russia could implement only a workers' and peasants' democratic dictatorship, just as Qu had said. After that, I became even more timorous about writing articles and stayed that way until I quit as editor of *Bolshevik*.[261]

Seen from the point of view of past developments and the present Guangzhou insurrection, the Chinese revolutionary state could be only a dictatorship of the proletariat. But going by what Lenin had written before the Russian Revolution, the Chinese revolutionary state could be only a workers' and peasants' democratic dictatorship. Could it be that Lenin was wrong? Or was the mistake mine? This question continued to haunt me until 1929, when I read some of Trotsky's writings and resolved the problem.

But the polemic in *Bolshevik*—a polemic waged between two unsigned articles—attracted next to no attention. No one wrote a letter or an article in response to it; no one talked to me about it. Today, Qu Qiubai is dead, and although Li Weihan is still alive, it is likely that he has forgotten the whole business. But I still remember it quite clearly, for it obsessed me for many months.

* * *

This Chinese Revolution started on May 30, 1925, with the Shanghai massacre, and ended on December 11, 1927, with the defeat of the Guangzhou insurrection. The result was that the Guomindang replaced the Beiyang warlords as China's rulers, and Nanjing took over from Beijing as its capital. Apart from that, almost nothing changed, though it is true that the Guomindang political system was more consonant with the interests of the Chinese bourgeoisie than was the political system of the Beiyang warlords.

What was the place of this Chinese Revolution in the general history of world revolution? On my way from Shanghai to Hankou, I bumped into Pan Jiachen, just back from Russia. He explained to me as we paced the deck of the steamship how people in Moscow viewed the Chinese Revolution as it was then happening.

"The comrades in the International think that of all the revolutions that have happened in the world, only the French Revolution of 1789, the Russian Revolution of 1917, and the present Chinese Revolution can be called 'Great Revolutions,'" he explained to me. This was the first time I realized that the revolution I had personally experienced was deemed so important by other people. I had my doubts about their estimation, but I did not tell Pan so. Four or five months earlier, I had given a lecture course called "The History of World Revolution" at the Party school run by the Shanghai Regional Committee; that lecture had given me the chance to make a general review of the subject, so the French and Russian Revolutions were still fresh in my mind. How could I compare our revolution with them? Moreover, for most comrades in those days—at least for those of the Shanghai style—revolution meant the proletarian socialist revolution that we ourselves would carry out after the conclusion of the Northern Expedition. However much effort the workers and peasants put into speeding the expedition's victory, we still did not consider that it constituted the revolution as we understood it. At most, it was a "national revolution," a transitional stage in the process leading from outright reaction to our own revolution, to the revolution without attributive. If calling this middle stage a "revolution" was already stretching the term, how on earth could one justify including it among the "Great Revolutions"?

After arriving in Wuhan and seeing so many causes for concern, I became all the more convinced that I was right. Later, after the defeat in Wuhan and then in Guangzhou, the question of whether it was right to call the Chinese Revolution "great" was resolved for me. But others continued to talk of the "Great Revolution," not only after the defeat at Guangzhou but even today, nearly twenty years later. The only Chinese author to write about the revolution was Hua Gang. He called his book, which appeared in 1931, *Zhongguo da geming shi* (History of the Great Chinese Revolution)! In my opinion, the view propagated by the International was excusable up to the defeat of the revolution, but to keep on calling it a "Great Revolution" so many years later must have been due to either ignorance about the history of the revolution or a wrong view of what revolution is.

From a positive point of view, although this Chinese Revolution was not a major event in the history of world revolution, it was important in a negative sense—that is, the mistakes committed by its leaders could be lessons for the future Chinese revolution and for revolutions in other countries. The contest within the world Communist movement between Stalinism and Trotskyism started around three issues, one of which was the Chinese Revolution. I will have more to say in the chapter on the Left Opposition about the debate on the Chinese Revolution, but I start here with a general observation.

Errors committed by the leadership must bear a great deal of the responsibility for this defeat, for the revolution broke out not as a spontaneous explosion provoked by objective factors but as a result of conscious preparation by revolutionaries. The relationship between the subjective input by the revolutionary party and the objective facts of the revolution was even more clearly visible in this revolution than in those of 1789 and 1917. The storming of the Bastille in Paris and the five-day strike, the demonstrations, and the insurrection in Petrograd were far more "spontaneous" than the speeches in Shanghai's International Settlement on May 30 and the general strike triggered by the massacre. The speeches and strikes were consciously prepared and led by the Chinese Communist Party, whereas the insurrections in Paris and Petrograd were not prepared or led by a political party, even though they were the result of the efforts of revolutionaries. The "planned" and "conscious" nature of the Chinese Revolution was preserved even after the revolution's outbreak and for a comparatively long time, right through until the revolution's second stage—the new wave set in motion by the Northern Expedition. That it was "planned" and "conscious" should by rights have guaranteed its victory, but actually, it brought about its downfall. Why so? It is easy at this point to answer, because the leadership made mistakes. But different people have different views of what the mistakes were and who the leaders were.

The "original sin" was the lack of a proper understanding of the relationship between bourgeois and proletarian revolution. The Third Congress of the Chinese Communist Party decided to join in the "national revolution" and used as its two main slogans "Down with imperialism" and "Down with the warlords." This decision represented an epoch-making change. The Chinese Communist Party was a product of the October Revolution. Revolutionaries in China and abroad, discerning no future whatsoever in bourgeois thought or politics, became Communists after succumbing to the influence of the October Revolution and the Soviet system. So they founded or joined the Communist Party. At first, they nurtured the ideal of proletarian socialist revolution, but later, they stowed this ideal away and no longer talked about it, reverting, instead, to the struggle for China's independence and democracy. Save for a tiny minority, everyone agreed to the new line, although there was still no unanimity about when to fetch the old ideal from storage or how to make the transition from national revolution to proletarian revolution.

Of the two main slogans, "Down with the warlords" was subordinate to "Down with imperialism." People viewed the warlords as no more than tools through which the imperialists controlled China. What's more, every disaster, every potential cause of disquiet, was blamed on imperialism. The compradors were the tools of imperialism, the right-wingers of the Guomindang were running dogs of imperialism, agricultural bankruptcy was the result of imperialist aggression, and so on. In a nutshell, people diverted the workers' and peasants' hatred for their Chinese oppressors onto the imperialists and the foreign oppressors. Perhaps it's true that, in the final analysis, everything that is wrong with China is a result of imperialist aggression, but to fight back against Chinese oppressors only when they are tools of imperialism can lead to wrong conclusions. For example, since peasant misery is a result of agricultural bankruptcy, and agricultural bankruptcy is a result of imperialist aggression, the natural target for the peasants is imperialism and not their most intimate enemy, the landlords. If peasants join in the revolution, it will be to fight against imperialism, not to raise the land question. It was no accident that the Chinese Communist Party raised the land question only after the Hunan peasants had spontaneously expropriated the landlords' fields and divided them among the peasants; on the contrary, this delay was intimately related to the Party's exclusive stress on anti-imperialism at the expense of class struggle. When the Communists raised the land question in the peasants' wake, it was not, according to them, for the sake of land revolution in itself but because expropriating the land would weaken the power of the landlord class, which represented imperialism in the villages; so it would strengthen the fight against imperialism.

The national bourgeoisie was not generally considered to be a tool of imperialism. On the contrary, it was considered to be rather anti-imperialist, raising the hope that this bourgeoisie would join hands with the proletariat to complete the national revolution.

In and around 1925, the Chinese Communist Party prepared, launched, and led the Chinese Revolution according to this theory of "national revolution." The workers, the petit bourgeois, and part of the peasantry responded to the call. They vigorously fought back against the imperialists, who were shaken by the wave of strikes in Shanghai and Hong Kong. In this period, most people followed behind the Communist Party, and hardly anyone went ahead of it. So as yet, there was no talk of "excesses."[262]

But there was no future for a revolution that concentrated only on imperialism. The strikes in Shanghai and Hong Kong got nowhere; the tide of revolution slowly ebbed, and normality returned. By the early spring of 1926, the movement was like an arrow at the end of its flight.[263] When news of the Beijing massacre of March 18 reached Shanghai, Qu Qiubai sighed and said, "Now that the tide has ebbed, not even a massacre can rouse the broad masses." He was right. Only twenty or so people had died in Shanghai's May 30 massacre, but a great movement had started; on March 18, 1926, in Beijing, even more people died, but there were no more than a few vague protests in other parts of the country.

The Northern Expedition was a watershed in the revolution. In a certain sense, we can say that the revolution that had broken out on May 30 was already over; not until after the Northern Expedition did a new revolution burst forth. This new revolution was spontaneous. What I mean is, the masses raised even more radical demands than the Communist Party leaders had—demands that these leaders never even contemplated—and surged ahead of them. Strictly speaking, only this new revolution merits the name; the old one was simply a movement against imperialism.

The new revolution burst forth in the Hunan countryside. Hunan was a fountainhead of the Chinese Communist movement. At its epicenter in Changsha, from May 4 through the birth of socialism, the growth of the revolution was no less tardy than that of its better-known counterpart represented in Beijing by *New Youth*. Hunanese predominate among the Chinese Communist Party's leaders. Geographically speaking, the Anyuan collieries are in Jiangxi, but most of the colliers are Hunanese, and Anyuan is linked by the Zhuzhou-Pingxiang Railway to Zhuzhou in Hunan. So from the very beginning, Communists from Hunan were active in Anyuan. Li Lisan is from Liling;[264] after he was deported from France, he too was active in Anyuan, fomenting strikes and organizing workers' clubs and cooperatives. The Communist Party had one of its most important branches in Anyuan; one of its members, the worker Zhu Jintang, was elected an alternate member of the Central Committee at the Fourth Congress. When Li Lisan left, Liu Shaoqi took over; after that, Wang Zekai (who came back from Russia with me) was sent there by the Central Committee to be branch secretary; he too was from Liling. The Party launched a string of victorious struggles in the collieries, which became an influential force in the movement, but it was finally defeated in 1925 or 1926. The owner of the collieries, Sheng Xuanhuai's son, colluded with Jiangxi warlords to get the clubs disbanded, and their leader Comrade X was shot; a great many colliers returned to their villages. At Anyuan, they had received an education and training, so even though they had achieved nothing in the pits, these people—especially the activists among the colliers—became teachers and leaders back in the villages. That's why the peasant movement in Hunan was so much stronger than in other provinces. When the Northern Expedition reached Hunan, the students of the Peasant Training Institute that Mao Zedong had set up in Guangzhou followed on its heels. This, too, helped the peasant movement grow. The

Hunan peasants were roused to greet and act in concert with the expeditionaries, to join in the fighting, and to disarm straggling northerners. But to the surprise of the instigators, the peasants refused to stop short at military actions of this sort and, instead, went on to make their own demands. These demands rapidly escalated, and the peasants were soon demanding land and power; in parts of some counties, they even took land and power.

After the defeat of the revolution, historians delving into piles of old paper, from the Twenty-Four Histories[265] to the *Jiu tong*,[266] discovered that on several occasions in ancient times the peasants had staged land revolutions. We knew even before these revelations that there had been peasant insurrections on several occasions in Chinese history, but we always thought that they had been carried out by "roving bandits" like those at the end of the Ming dynasty. We had no idea that the peasants had demanded land. When we read in histories of the Russian revolutionary movement about the Russian peasants' thirst for land and about the prime place that the land question occupied in the organization of the Narodniki,[267] we wondered why Chinese peasants never demanded land and why Chinese revolutionaries never discussed the land question.

Most Chinese revolutionaries knew nothing about the land question until the second half of 1926, when the Hunan peasants' fight for land shook the whole of China—not just the landlords, but the leaders of the Communist Party as well. The role played by the Communist Party in the peasant war for land was to try to pull it back. Even so, the movement surged forward. Many of the Communist Party's minor officials and rank-and-file members approved of and led this spontaneous action, for they themselves lived cheek by jowl with the peasants. Peasant associations were organized in many parts of Hunan. They formed armed units; in some places, peasant associations took power. When the expeditionaries marched toward Jiangxi and Hubei, the land struggle spread quickly in their wake. At the same time, the peasant movement under Peng Pai in the Dong Jiang region of Guangdong developed apace and also reached the stage of a struggle for the land.

After the Northern Expedition reached Wuhan, that metropolis of central China, it triggered a series of mass movements. Artisans and shop assistants started settling accounts with their masters. They demanded not only higher wages but also back payment of higher wages—in some cases going back several decades. In some cases, the eventual settlement was many times bigger than the original wage. This movement, too, was spontaneous and even ran counter to what the Party's agitators had intended. There were similar movements in small towns all over Hubei.

Landlords and shop owners who opposed these demands and people who had committed flagrant crimes were punished. Minor offenders were paraded around the streets wearing dunce's hats; major ones were shot. Notably, Ye

Dehui,[268] a learned scholar of the old school, was shot; another such scholar, Wang Guowei, drowned himself in a lake in Beijing[269] as a result of this incident. If scholars like Wang Guowei were so demoralized by the tragic fate of one of their ilk, how much more so must the landlords and the bourgeoisie have been? So the Chinese Revolution began to slip into a "civil war" mode. I do not mean the civil war between the armies of the Guomindang and of the Beiyang warlords, but that between the workers and peasants and the landlords and capitalists. Shanghai, that great anti-imperialist city, was rocked by a wave of "economic" strikes by workers who were out to better their lives regardless of whether the boss was an imperialist or a member of the national bourgeoisie. Shanghai workers had already started down this path in the interlude between May Thirtieth and the launching of the Northern Expedition, when the Communist Party was still in a position to control the strikes.

The special feature of this new revolution was class struggle—that is, the struggle between Chinese workers and peasants and Chinese capitalists and landlords, even to the point of civil war. Compared with this, the revolution of the earlier period had been no more than a national struggle—a struggle between Chinese and imperialists. Anti-imperialism was barely featured in the revolution that broke out later, except for the recovery of the concessions in Hankou, Jiujiang, and elsewhere.[270] It was this class struggle, not the national struggle, that compelled Chiang Kai-shek, Wang Jingwei, Tang Shengzhi, and others to go over to the reactionaries and massacre people. If the revolution had not gone beyond its "national" stage, if it had kept to slogans like "Down with imperialism" and "Down with the warlords" and demanded only national independence and national reform, then perhaps Chiang really would have waited until after taking Beijing to settle accounts with us. But the Chinese workers and peasants were not ready to do as the Comintern and the Communist Party wished; they were not ready to stay within the bounds of "national revolution."

I know that some people say, "By opposing capitalists and landlords, the workers and peasants were opposing the Chinese representatives of imperialism, so they were opposing imperialism itself!" And that's true. But it is also true that during the revolution of the later period, when the concessions in Hankou and Jiujiang were recovered, the masses struggled against imperialism because it was helping their sworn enemies, the landlords and the capitalists. The masses were fighting against Chinese capitalists and landlords in the person of imperialism. Without waging class struggle to the end, without seizing the land and taking over the factories, China will never be in a position to realize national independence and democratic reform, so it will not be able to make an effective stand against imperialism either. In other words, unless we step beyond the bounds of "national revolution" to carry out proletarian socialist revolution, we will not be able to complete the bourgeois-democratic revolution. The leadership of the Communist Party did not understand this fact during the events that I am describing, but the workers and peasants did, as they showed in action. When I say the leadership, I mean not just the Chinese leaders but also the Moscow leaders, the Third International, and the CPSU—in a word, all those people who set bourgeois-democratic terms on the Chinese Revolution.

The second stage of the revolution that I have just described was triggered by the Northern Expedition. Some people may conclude that had there been no Northern Expedition to start with, this new revolution could not have happened. But they would be wrong. It may be true that as long as the Communist Party leaders stuck to their wrong position, this new revolution needed the trigger of a Northern Expedition or some other similar military action. But if they had taken a correct position, they could have prepared, launched, and led this new revolution without a Northern Expedition, for it could have burst forth just like May Thirtieth. The revolution that did take place bequeathed a pernicious legacy, for it left people with a wrong idea of revolution.

Before the Northern Expedition, most people—at least those Party cadres of the Shanghai style—thought (rightly) that revolution is, in essence, the product of mass insurrection. The Party allocates its main forces and its outstanding cadres to the basic levels of the mass movement and to its own internal organization. It then sends its less capable members to work in the government or the army. The aim of this deployment is to prepare sufficient forces to carry out our own revolution. At the time, there was no other view of revolution than the one I have just described. But the question arose whether a Northern Expedition should be undertaken. The Central Committee in Shanghai said no. Later, to everyone's surprise, the expedition was successful and provoked an even more progressive mass movement of workers and peasants, whereupon most people (including the Shanghai-based Central Committee) changed their minds about the revolution. Occupy a territory, set up a government, organize an army, and then launch an expedition to seize power at the national level—this was now seen as the main way to make a revolution. Mass armed insurrection was relegated to the role of ancillary action, in support of the revolutionary army. Thereafter, the Party deployed its best cadres in the government and the army[271] and delegated its less capable ones to working in the mass movement. This concept of revolution even spread to the comrades of the Comintern.

The Sixth Congress of the Chinese Communist Party, held in the countryside outside Moscow under Bukharin's tutelage, produced a theory that substantiated this view of revolution by appealing to China's special national circumstances. The theory went like this: The Chinese Revolution, unlike other revolutions, could "win initial victory in one or more provinces." In one sense, this idea was obviously a result of the influence of the Northern Expedition; in another sense, it was an imitation of Stalin's theory of "socialism in one country." The large-scale "Red Army"[272] movement that started after the Sixth Congress corresponded precisely to this concept of revolution. The Chinese Communist Party occupied one or more counties in Jiangxi and other provinces, set up soviet governments, organized Red Armies, and then set out on expeditions against Changsha, Nanchang, and even Nanjing. The workers' movement in big cities like Shanghai was relegated to an ancillary role, in support of the Red Army. Naturally, this "revolution" later failed, and the Red Army set out on the Long March to northern Shaanxi.[273]

Now that the Guomindang and the Communists are once again cooperating, people no longer talk about revolution. They talk in code, using phrases like occupy a "border area," set up a "border area government," organize an Eighth Route Army and a New Fourth Army, and when the time is ripe, go on expeditions to the southwest, the southeast, or the northeast.[274] Even today, the mass movement in Guangdong is still seen as ancillary to the Eighth Route Army and the New Fourth Army. Unfortunately, there are antecedents in China for this view of revolution. Apart from the Northern Expedition, there is the Revolution of 1911, which was also carried out by armies. The Chinese Revolution cannot hope for victory until Chinese revolutionaries relinquish this wrong idea of revolution.

But I am getting ahead of myself. In the period that I am now describing (late 1927 to early 1928), I could never have said what I just said about the process and concept of revolution. I arrived at these ideas after reading Trotsky's speeches and writings about the Chinese Revolution some time later. These ideas were the fruit of my contemplation of problems of the revolution during my second spell in prison. Up to that time, even though I thought a great deal about it and had my doubts, I arrived at no firm conclusions.

* * *

By the spring of 1928, the state of the inner-Party struggle had changed, to the disadvantage of the "Chen Duxiu-ites." The attacks came from the direction of the Shanghai garrison headquarters. The headquarters of the Jiangsu Provincial Committee were raided, and many important Party leaders were arrested, including Chen Qiaonian. Wang Ruofei escaped by a whisker. Rumors later circulated that if a ransom of twenty thousand dollars had been paid while those arrested were still in police custody, they would not have been extradited to the Chinese authorities,[275] but the Central Committee was not prepared to come up with the money. I believe that either it did not have the money or the Russians would not agree to pay it. But Wang Ruofei, who was incensed by the affair, accused the Central Committee of deliberately sacrificing these comrades to resolve the dispute in the Party. The result was that they were handed over. Chen Qiaonian, Xu Baihao, and Zheng Futa were shot at Longhua. The rest were sent to prison. Not long after the incident, Luo Yinong was also arrested and handed over to be shot.

During this period, the Chinese Communist Party was preparing for its Sixth Congress, to be held in the Soviet Union. Starting in the spring, delegates set out from every part of China. The Russians wanted Chen Duxiu to go, but Chen refused. Qu Qiubai entreated Wang Ruofei to change Chen's mind.

"I originally thought he should go," Wang replied, "but then I thought to myself that they're in the middle of a campaign against Trotsky in the Soviet Union. If Chen goes, he is bound to stick to his own opinions and oppose those of the International, so people will attack him in order to attack Trotsky."

"Not necessarily, not necessarily," said Qu.

What Wang meant was that if the situation had not been complicated by the issue of the Soviet opposition, Chen's views might have won out. Ren Bishi, too, arranged to meet me in Jessfield Park for a chat and tried to get me to persuade Chen to go to Moscow. I promised to pass on what he had said. Peng Shuzhi also refused an invitation to go to Moscow. The rest of the top leaders all went—of the Central Committee members, only Li Weihan was left behind. The people left in charge all over China had been newly promoted into the leadership and were either inexperienced or incompetent; we all sensed a tremendous vacuum. I stayed behind in my old job. When the Standing Committee met, I was sometimes summoned to attend. The second person on the Standing Committee besides Li was Luo Dengxian, a worker from Hong Kong who had recently come up to Shanghai from Guangdong. There must have been a third, but I cannot remember who it was. We spent most of our time discussing trivialities. The only issue of political import that reached the agenda was the massacre at Jinan on May 3; that was one of the meetings I attended.

Apart from attending the Standing Committee in my capacity as editor of the Party journal, I received a new assignment in my capacity as secretary of the Propaganda Department. I was ordered to direct the activity of the Creation Society.[276]

The Creation Society started out as a literary association. In the past, it confined its activity to publishing literary books and journals, hardly any of which I had read. And if I did read one by accident, I never liked it. I thought that even realism was obsolete, let alone romanticism. I especially disliked the poems of Guo Moruo, who adulterated the vernacular with classical verbosity. Besides, after returning to China, I was completely absorbed by revolution and had no interest in literature. Before the Northern Expedition,

Creation Society writers had no connection with the revolution and were even against it. But the people in the Society for Literary Studies[277] were close to us; they included Shen Yanbing[278] and his brother Shen Zemin, who were our comrades. Needless to say, they were not close to us in a literary sense. On one occasion, Shen Yanbing and Jiang Guangchi were discussing literature in the office of the Propaganda Department on Fusheng Road. Shen Yanbing voiced some criticisms of the Creation Society; Jiang Guangchi defended it. "What sort of a writer is he?" said Jiang after Shen had left. "All he has done is introduce a few foreign writers to the Chinese public!" And it was true. In those days, Shen was no more than an "introducer of foreign writers." But he was a Party veteran who had worked as secretary of the Shanghai Regional Committee long before my own return to China. After I got back, he was secretary of the Party's Commercial Press branch. He had also been active in the Guomindang in Shanghai; he was a loyal and hardworking comrade. I used to attend the Commercial Press branch as Regional Committee representative, and, on occasion, he attended to some business in the Propaganda Department. So we often met, though we never discussed literary questions.

After the Wuhan debacle, Shen Yanbing returned to Shanghai and became imperceptibly estranged from the Party. In November 1927, not long after I had returned to Shanghai, I bumped into Song Yunbin in a Shaoxing wine bar on Fuzhou Road. (Song appeared as the character "Yunlang" in one of Shen Yanbing's stories about Guling.) In the course of our conversation, Shen Yanbing's name came up, and Song gave me his address. A few days later, I went to visit Shen in his home on Jingxing (or Jingyun) Alley off Darroch Road. I took along a copy of the inaugural issue of *Bolshevik*. Shen lived in a two-story house. His study was on the top floor. He told me that he had been back in Shanghai for more than fifty days but had not once been outside his front door for fear of being recognized. I asked him how he spent his time. He told me that he spent it writing stories.

"One of my stories is in the most recent issue of *Xiaoshuo yuebao* [Novel monthly]," he told me. "Read it and see if you can guess which one it is."

I was too busy to act on his suggestion. Not until a long time afterward did I discover that he had published his trilogy *Huanmie* (Disillusion), *Dongyao* (Wavering), and *Zhuiqiu* (Pursuance) under the pseudonym Mao Dun, originally in serial form. I read the trilogy later when it came out in separate volumes. When I told Qu Qiubai about my visit to Shen Yanbing, Qu told me that someone writing under the pen name Ding Ling had published a story in *Novel Monthly* that accurately depicted the popular mood at the time of the May Fourth Movement. He wondered who this Ding Ling was. In those days, I had so little interest in literature that I could not summon the energy to read this story. Only a long time later did I discover that Ding

Ling was the woman Jiang Bingzhi, who had at one time run after Qu.

On the day of my visit, Shen also told me something about his political views. He complained about the positions the Party had adopted after the August 7 Conference and opposed the policy of organizing peasant insurrections everywhere. He said that if one insurrection failed, the peasants would no longer be prepared to participate in insurrections, even if the situation became revolutionary. That was the first time I had heard a comrade come out clearly against the new policies of the Central Committee. Later, he incorporated his view on insurrections into his essay *Cong Guling dao Dongjing* (From Guling to Tokyo). During the period of Li Lisan's ascendancy,[279] Party-controlled literary publications attacked Shen, and the Central Committee instructed the Japanese section of the Chinese Communist Party not to recognize him as a comrade. In 1929, I met Yang Xianjiang just after he got back from Japan. When I asked him about Shen, he talked about him as if he were an enemy.

But all that happened later. Let's return to the subject of the Creation Society. When the Northern Expedition first set out, Guo Moruo somehow became deputy director of the main Political Department under Army Headquarters, so these romantic writers—who had never shown any interest in politics—began to discuss revolution. In late 1927 or early 1928, a new monthly publication began to appear alongside *Chuangzao* (Creation). I forget what it was called.[280] It was a Marxist discussion journal. The people who wrote for it were all nonentities. Members of the Creation Society, such as Cheng Fangwu, contributed nothing more than the editorial notes. I found it hard to understand the articles in it; after I had struggled through a page or two, my head began to ache, for the articles were written in long, convoluted sentences with peculiar grammar and terminology. The other members of the Propaganda Department felt the same way as I did about the publication. We concluded that these people must just have got back to China after studying in Japan and that, although their Japanese may have been good, their Chinese was extremely awkward. It never occurred to us that in five years' time, this deliberately unreadable style would become fashionable in China among young people and that it would stay so until checked by the "popular language" movement.[281]

I could not help noticing some articles in this publication directed against Lu Xun and Jiang Guangchi that I thought were right. Lu Xun adopted an aloof and cynical attitude toward this revolution. Later, people defended him by arguing that well in advance of anyone else, he had openly satirized the reactionary tendencies of the Guomindang government in Guangzhou. Actually, he satirized not only the reactionary tendency in the Guomindang government but also the entire revolution. After Jiang Guangchi's return to China, Jiang rejected the idea of working in the Party and set himself up in business under the shop sign "revolutionary man of letters," much to the disgust of most Party members. He set up the Sun Society and a like-named bookshop, and he began publishing a magazine called *Taiyang* (Sun). He was protected by the authority of the Party. Yang Chunren and Qian Xingchun, who worked under him, knew even less about Marxism and world literature than he did. Undoubtedly, the Creation Society people were more knowledgeable than Yang and Qian in these two respects.

Two or three weeks before he left the country, Qu Qiubai told us at a meeting of the editorial board that the Creation Society had asked the Central Committee to appoint someone to lead it. He added that Guo Moruo had links to the Party and that while in Shanghai, he had often gone to see Zhou Enlai; Guo had advised the group of returned students from Japan to work with the Party and had told them that there was no need to run a separate magazine. Qu also told us that we now had two comrades in the Creation Society—Li Minzhi and Ouyang Jixiu. Li had originally worked as Guo's secretary, and Ouyang was a student at Shanghai University. These two men did bring out a separate small-format magazine. The board proposed me for the job, but I refused and proposed Qu instead. I was unused to dealing with outsiders, especially writers. Qu declined, on the grounds that he was about to go abroad, so I had no choice but to accept. However, I procrastinated until the end of April or the beginning of May. Not until after the Jiangsu Provincial Committee had urged me several times to get on with the job did I finally fix a time to meet the writers.

The morning before my appointment with them, I received a brief note addressed to "Comrade" Chaolin, asking me to go to the sender's home at 12 Scott Road before going to meet the Creation Society people. The letter was written casually, as if to a very old friend, and was signed Duqing, who I realized must be Wang Duqing. I had heard the name, though I had never met the person nor even dealt with him indirectly. In any event, I did not go to Wang's house first but, instead, went straight to Yongan Alley, either because I had already agreed on a time with Li Minzhi or for some other reason. There were a dozen or so people waiting for me. It was the first time I had met any of them, including Li Minzhi (i.e., Li Yimang) and Ouyang Jixiu (i.e., Hua Han). Among the members of the Creation Society present were Cheng Fangwu, Zheng Boqi, Zhang Ziping, Peng Kang, Li Chuli, Zhu Jingwo, Feng Naichao, and Li Tiesheng. Cheng Fangwu, who seemed to be acting as their spokesperson, said a few words of welcome and introduced me to the gathering. Then he said that they were intending to set up a research association or symposium to discuss various questions, and he hoped that I would be its leader. At first, I politely refused to make a speech, but I ended up analyzing Chinese social structure and the nature and future of the Chinese Revolution, as formulated in a number of Comintern circulars. My speech was along Comintern lines, so it was Stalinist. These people were not members of the Party, so I was constrained to stick to the official line. After I had finished, I asked for their opinions on what I had said. Li Chuli spoke up first. He said that he had never heard anyone say such things before; all he had heard in the past was abstract theory. He had never heard anyone explain the problems of the Chinese Revolution with such lucidity, and he was deeply grateful. Clearly, he was just being polite. Others also spoke, but they had nothing relevant to say.

During my several years in the Party, I had never attended such a polite gathering. Once, in 1926, I was asked to speak at a Guomindang meeting in Zhabei. Liu Yazi introduced me and was very polite, but after my speech was over, no one in the audience opened his mouth. About the Creation Society meeting, I felt that it made no difference whether I had gone or not, for they had assigned their own tasks in advance. Cheng Fangwu's and Li Chuli's little speeches were set pieces designed to please the Communist Party. They had welcomed me because, through me, they were welcoming the Party.

I continued to believe this until two years ago,[282] when I met a certain Mr. Gao from Suzhou, who had spent some time with Li Chuli in the Suzhou Reformatory. One day, the authorities in the reformatory called all the prisoners together to hear speeches by prisoners who were eligible for release, to decide who should go and who should not. Some groveled shamelessly, but Li Chuli spoke out boldly and eloquently. He said that after returning from Japan, he had made an abstract study of social science, but in Shanghai, he had met someone sent to talk to the Creation Society on behalf of the Central Committee of the Chinese Communist Party (he said that he could not remember the man's name), and this person had convinced him to become a Marxist. At this point, the man in charge of the rally told someone to help Li down from the platform, for he had become quite agitated. Mr. Gao was full of admiration for Li Chuli; his story moved me. Assuming that Li meant me, his little speech that day in Yongan Alley was sincerely meant, and not just spoken out of politeness. And that's quite possible, because outsiders never got to see Comintern circulars, nor did they necessarily become acquainted with the theoretical debate in the Party, even though it had been published in pamphlet form in Hankou.

Later, I sent copies of the booklets by Qu Qiubai and Peng Shuzhi to the Creation Society. We had brought the plates with us from Hankou and reused them. Qu's was the second edition, but Peng's was, in effect, the first edition, for it had been typeset in Wuhan but not published. I was not in favor of publishing Peng's book, but Qu Qiubai read the plates and discovered a host of "opportunist errors," so he was very keen to bring it out as a way of keeping up the offensive against Peng.

After the meeting in Yongan Alley, I went alone to 12 Scott Road and went inside. A fat man got up from a bed, pulled on a pair of slippers, and said hello, all the while shooting me suspicious glances. When I told him my name, he warmly shook my hand, and we immediately became friends. This Creation Society man was casually dressed in Chinese clothes, unlike the others I had already met, who wore neat Western-style suits. He talked volubly and unconstrainedly, whereas they had behaved with gentlemanly decorum and reserve. On later occasions, the same distinction held.

Wang Duqing had waited for me in his home, which was why he had not gone to Yongan Alley; he was a little disappointed when I told him that I had already been there. He said that there was much he wanted to talk to me about. First, we reminisced about France, Montargis, and common friends. We also talked about his wife, Wu Ruoying, the daughter of Wu Yu. But then, Cheng Fangwu and Zhang Ziping came in, doubtless to tell Wang what had happened at the meeting. I sat for a while and then took my leave.

From then on, I went to Yongan Alley once a fortnight. No one was ever absent, and Wang Duqing came too. Each time, we took up a new issue. Everyone said what they thought, there was some discussion, and finally, I summed up. My judgment was definitive and incontrovertible. I realized that we were doing no more than performing a sort of ritual to show that the Creation Society accepted Party leadership and that we were not really a debating society or research group, so I gradually lost interest. We continued meeting until the end of July, when the Standing Committee sent me to Fujian to inspect our work there. During my absence, the group stopped meeting—proof that my suspicions were fully grounded.

Once, when I went to see Wang Duqing, he asked me to go for a cup of coffee with him at the Xinya Restaurant, newly opened at the intersection of Sichuan Road North and Qiujiang Road. He told me the inside story of the Creation Society.

"You can divide the Creation Society into two groups," he started. "One group consists of 'established authors' like Guo Moruo, Cheng Fangwu, Zhang Ziping, Zheng Boqi, and me; then, there is a group of 'unknowns' like Peng Kang, Li Chuli, and the rest. Apart from them, there are a few 'young employees' like Cheng Fangwu's nephew, Cheng Shaozong, and like Qiu Yunduo and Gong Binglu. They, too, sometimes write. Some people in the Creation Society are ambitious and want the Creation Society to talk with the Communist Party on an equal footing. Zhang Ziping belongs to the Third Party. He is completely unreliable. Zheng Boqi is a petty politician. As for the 'unknowns,' most of them are newly graduated and quite pure. Only a few individuals are ambitious. We must take care to subdue Zheng."

When I first started dealing with the Creation Society, it had already stopped attacking Lu Xun, and after that, we no longer discussed him. Nor did we discuss the Sun Society, though Jiang Guangchi and Qian Xingchun continued to complain to me about the Creation Society and pointed out a number of mistakes in articles attacking the Sun Society. For example, the first person in China to mention "revolutionary literature" was Jiang Guangchi, but the Creation Society said that it was Guo Moruo; also, an article in *Sun* had said that "knowledge is born from experience," but the Creation Society publication called this "an idealist error." I cannot remember how I replied to these criticisms, but it required an even greater expenditure of energy to mediate the disputes within the Creation Society than to mediate those between it and the Sun Society. When Cheng Fangwu went abroad, Zhang Ziping imperceptibly drifted away from the society, and Wang Duqing and Zheng Boqi—the two remaining "established authors"—were constantly at loggerheads. What's more, the 'unknowns' formed a common front against them. The issues were invariably personalized and trivial. For some reason, Li Minzhi and Ouyang Jixiu thought that I should intervene. In my name and at the Propaganda Department's expense, Li Minzhi invited them to a Sichuanese meal at his place. During the meal, we discussed their internal altercations and asked them to bring their differences out into the open and explain to each other what the problems were. But Wang Duqing did not want to.

"We're like a married couple," he said. "Before midnight we fight, after midnight we make love. There is no need to discuss anything."

The rest of them aired their points of view, we smoothed out the misunderstandings, and everyone parted amicably, though I do not know whether this reconciliation dinner was really effective. After each of the meetings I attended, Wang Duqing would drag me off to his place or to a coffee parlor, or sometimes to a bar or a dance hall. It was obvious that I was closer to him than to the rest. Zheng Boqi was very unhappy about this, and the others said that I had been "cordoned off." Through me, Wang Duqing got back in touch with Wang Zekai, whom he had known in France. Wang Zekai introduced him to Peng Shuzhi and Li Ji, and at Peng's place, he met Chen Duxiu. So that was the beginning of his friendship with us and of the association between this "established author" of the Creation Society and Trotskyism. The tie survived attacks and blandishments, right up to his death.

Wang Duqing's famous long poem about the Guangzhou insurrection was written after I got to know him. He showed me the draft and asked me what he should call it. I suggested "11 Déc."[283]

All along, I saw these writers as fellow travelers and never planned to draw them into the Party. After the Sixth Congress, when Cai Hesen took over as head of the Propaganda Department, the Communist Party caucus in the Creation Society asked him to attend its meeting. He adopted the same position I had and called the writers "Democracy." But sometime after Li

Lisan had taken over from Cai and I had quit the Propaganda Department, one after another, these 'unknowns' were admitted to the Party. On the whole, it must be said that they did not fail their duty. I have already described Li Chuli's steadfastness in prison. While I was in the Central Military Prison in Nanjing, Zhu Jingwo happened to occupy the cell next to mine. We saw each other every day, and though we could agree on nothing, we were never divided by bad feelings. He joined the New Fourth Army after his release; it is said that he shot himself with his own revolver to avoid capture during the Southern Anhui Incident.[284] (According to another version, he committed suicide by pitching himself off a stretcher and rolling down a cliff.) Peng Kang was jailed for terrorism and was at first held in a prison in the Shanghai settlement. While I was in prison in Nanjing, I read an article by him on Laozi in the Suzhou Reformatory magazine, in which he claimed that Laozi's theories were consonant with Chen Lifu's "vitalism."[285] If the Chinese Communist Party does not take the things comrades write while in the reformatory too seriously, then Peng Kang can be regarded as a good comrade following his release from prison.

* * *

After the defeat of the Guangzhou insurrection, confidence in the "revolutionary high tide" seemed to ebb a little. In February 1928, Stalin, Bukharin, Xiang Zhongfa, and Li Zhenying put their names to a brief manifesto in Moscow that was already less optimistic in tone than earlier pronouncements. After the delegates to the Sixth Congress had left China for Moscow, Li Zhenying, who was not a delegate and was already back in China, looked me up in Shanghai for a talk and to give me a French-language *European Almanac*. He said that, according to Stalin, although the Chinese Revolution was not yet back at high tide, it had already passed its trough and was once again rising. While Li was saying this, he formed a V with the thumb and index finger of his left hand and used the index finger of his right hand as a pointer.

"Comrade Stalin says that the revolution is no longer here," he said, tapping the bottom of the *V*. "He says it's on its way up, somewhere around here," he continued, tapping a point halfway up his index finger.

I do not recall Stalin or any other Comintern comrade ever saying that the Chinese Revolution was in the trough of a *V*. I do remember seeing circulars saying that the revolution was nearing a new high tide. Surely it was not forbidden in these circulars to say that the revolution had ebbed? And could it really be that, even if you had no choice but to admit that it had ebbed, you still had to add that it was "now beginning to rise again"? I had had some illusions at the time of the Guangzhou insurrection, but afterward,

I no longer believed that nonsense about a "high tide," and I used to hate hearing people use the term. Yet I was unable to draw any systematic conclusions from all this theorizing. After the delegates had returned to China, not only was the struggle on the outer front absolutely quiet, but even the Party's internal life seemed to have ebbed away to nothing. In July, Li Weihan sent me to Fujian to sort things out there, for a Provincial Committee member had defected to Zhang Zhen, a minor warlord in Zhangzhou. As a result, the Party was in chaos.

I went by boat from Shanghai to Xiamen.[286] Nine years earlier, I had set out from Xiamen for the continent of Europe; on my way back, I had taken the Trans-Siberian Railway to Vladivostok and then gone by boat to Shanghai. The only stretch I had not yet completed on my round-trip across Europe and Asia was between Shanghai and Xiamen; now I was about to fill the gap. In those days, various counties in western Fujian were in insurrection.[287] The Xiamen press was constantly reporting on these insurrections, but the Provincial Committee had lost touch with the insurrectionary areas, so the Party in Xiamen and Zhangzhou (not to mention Fuzhou[288]) was powerless to intervene. I called a conference of delegates from all over Fujian (but no one came from the insurrectionary areas), spurred on a few inactive comrades, had a new Provincial Committee elected, and went on an inspection tour of the villages outside Xiamen and Zhangzhou. I did not return to Shanghai until September. On my second day back, the newspapers reported that Communist Party offices in Xiamen had been raided. Several overseas Chinese students living in the Party's liaison center had been arrested, and a Party office outside Xiamen had been raided. But the main target had escaped: An official of the Central Committee on an inspection tour of the region had already left Xiamen. No one on the Central Committee knew that I was back, so they were thrown into a panic by the news.

At around this time, things began to liven up on the Central Committee. The Sixth Congress held in the Soviet Union had already elected a new Central Committee, and the Standing Committee members had already come back to Shanghai.

I returned amid a great storm to my house on Yuyuan Road. I went upstairs, clasped Jing[289] in my arms, and wept for joy. This was the first time we had been apart since getting married, and it had been more than forty days since I had left Shanghai. Jing told me that Cai Hesen, the new head of the Propaganda Department, had already arrived. The new general secretary was Xiang Zhongfa. Li Weihan had failed to be elected, even as an alternate member of the Central Committee, and was in the process of handing power over to his successor. Qu Qiubai, Zhang Guotao, and Wang Ruofei had been kept in Moscow and were not allowed to return. Li Lisan returned as an alternate member;[290] in the absence of one of the full members, he filled the vacancy. The new Central Committee had already decided at one of its first meetings to keep me on as editor of the Party journal and secretary of the Propaganda Department.

I was dismayed by what Jing told me, for I had no wish to continue working under Cai Hesen. His behavior in Wuhan and his *Jihuizhuyi shi* (History of opportunism) had led me to despise him. Surely they could find someone else to be secretary. After I had reported to Xiang Zhongfa on my inspection tour of Fujian, I asked to be allowed to resign, but they would not let me.

Wang Zekai also got back to China and looked me up. He told me all sorts of stories about what had happened at the Sixth Congress. The "Chen Duxiu-ites" had united around Wang Ruofei and had become the core opposition at the congress. They had joined with other opposition groups to attack the Central Committee. Qu Qiubai had been attacked so badly that he had not been allowed to leave Russia; Li Weihan had not been elected because of the criticism, and Li Lisan had just scraped by. Li Weihan had been completely smashed by He Zishen.

The Yunnan delegate Wang Maoting, Jing's fellow provincial, came to see me. It was the first time I had ever met him. He handed me a letter written in invisible ink and told me the formula. I bought the necessary chemicals and washed the paper with them; it turned out to be a long letter from Wang Ruofei to Chen Duxiu about developments at the Sixth Congress. It had originally been written as an open letter and given to the new Central Committee to be passed on to Chen, but because it contained some uncomplimentary comments about certain leaders or for some other reason, the Central Committee would probably have held on to it, so Wang Ruofei copied it in invisible ink and asked Wang Maoting to pass it on to me.

Wang Maoting had not had any previous dealings with the Chen Duxiu-ites; he had come out against the Central Committee as a result of his own experiences in the Party. In his theoretical thinking, he was even more progressive than the so-called Chen Duxiu-ites. According to reports, at one of the Moscow meetings—either at the Sixth Congress of the Chinese Communist Party or at a meeting of the Chinese delegation to the Congress of the Third International—he had publicly demanded a discussion of Trotsky's views on the Chinese Revolution. Many delegates—members of both the Central Committee group and the opposition—mentioned this incident in private conversation as evidence of Trotskyist activity in the Soviet Union. "Even a Chinese delegate has been influenced by it!" But because Wang Maoting had nothing to do with the Chen Duxiu-ites, he was not detained in Moscow like Wang Ruofei, Liu Bojian, and others; nor was he punished after getting back to China like Wang Zekai, Ren Xu, He Zishen, and others. He even returned to Yunnan and resumed his old job as secretary of the Yunnan Provincial Committee. Perhaps the only reason he dared to speak out publicly in Moscow was precisely because he had nothing to do with the Chen Duxiu-ites, who were at that time suffering repression. Less than a year after returning to Yunnan, Wang Maoting was arrested by Long Yun and shot.

The new Central Committee refused to let me resign, but actually, I had nothing to do anyway. After I got back to Shanghai from Fujian, the Party journal and the Propaganda Department came to a standstill. I had no idea how to break the deadlock. But to everyone's surprise, shortly—probably less than a month—after I got back from Fujian, Cai Hesen was toppled. Not until after the Sixth Congress did the northern comrades[291] accuse Cai, in a statement to the new Central Committee, of various misdeeds committed before the congress was held. I cannot remember what the accusations were, for during the hubbub created by the inner-Party struggle, I had no interest in the various charges brought against comrades. The new Central Committee dealt with Cai and removed him from the Standing Committee; naturally, he could no longer lead the Propaganda Department.

The newly appointed head of the Propaganda Department was Li Lisan, who had played an important part in Cai Hesen's overthrow. The Sixth Congress had elected Li as an alternate member of the Central Committee; as far as I remember, he had been chosen last,[292] but many of those elected to full membership had already died, defected, become inactive, or been punished, so he was gradually promoted to full membership. By now, he was on the Standing Committee as well as head of the Propaganda Department. The first time he attended a department meeting, he made a speech in which he said, "Our Party lacks a theoretical and political center." In the rest of his speech, he more or less proposed himself as that center. I laughed to myself, but it later turned out that I had laughed too soon. From then on, sure enough, Li Lisan became the Chinese Communist Party's "theoretical and political center." Luo Qiyuan asked him about the inner-Party struggle at the Sixth Congress. He made a short report, the gist of which was that some oppositionists had come together on an unprincipled basis and that factions formed on an unprincipled basis would not last. At the end of the meeting, I once again tried to resign, but he laughed away my request and started talking about some other subject. *Bolshevik* appeared for a few more issues at Li Lisan's insistence.

The inner-Party struggle that had begun in Moscow spread to China and continued to develop. Chen Duxiu, as ever, stood outside it, though Wang Zekai had reported to him on the Sixth Congress and asked him to become active.

"I won't," said Chen Duxiu. "If I do, it will be to create a new party."

Wang Zekai reported this exchange to me, shaking his head as he did so. At that time, we still thought that we should fight for the leadership of the old party. The idea of setting up a new party was treason and heresy. Ever since withdrawing from the leadership in Wuhan, Chen Duxiu had done nothing to fight for the restoration of his old position or to collect supporters. He had even opposed Wang Ruofei and Chen Qiaonian's efforts to form a group. After his return to Shanghai, he devoted himself to a study of the alphabetization of Chinese; he was the only member of the Communist Party to show any interest in this subject.[293] If someone visited him, he would almost immediately raise this question. If he met someone from Hubei, he would ask how this or that character was pronounced in Hubei dialect; if he met someone from Guangdong, he would ask how it was pronounced in Cantonese. He even asked me to take him to Shen Yanbing's place so that he could make a study of Jiangsu and Zhejiang pronunciation.[294] We had various theories about why he started this research. Yin Kuan thought that the best analogy was with Cao Can, whose story is told in the *Han shu*.[295] Whenever anyone went to visit Cao with a suggestion, he got them drunk to shut them up. In short, no one really believed that Chen Duxiu was serious about his phonological research. But I happen to know that he was quite accomplished in this field. More than a year later, he presented his research in a book in which he proposed a new Chinese alphabet that he had invented. The alphabet had thirty-odd letters—most of them Roman, a few Greek, and one or two new inventions. The rules for spelling were rather complicated. The Chinese language was divided, for the purposes of this study, into four dialects: Beijing, Wu, Yue, and Min.[296] After he had finished this manuscript, Chen sent copies of it to some of his old friends at Beijing University; I seem to remember that they included the linguist Zhao Yuanren. If it was not destroyed during the Japanese invasion of January 28, 1932, this manuscript must still be extant. It should be clear from Chen's earlier work *Ziyi leili* (A philological study of Chinese characters), and from studies he wrote later in prison, that his interest in linguistics was deeply rooted. His work on alphabetizing Chinese was actually an extension of his promotion of the vernacular in the May Fourth era.

But although Chen's research was like Cao Can's wine, his decision to stand outside the factional struggle still requires an explanation. His enemies said that he was arrogant, that he looked down on them, that he would not stoop to enter the fray with them. Wang Ruofei told Chen about this prejudice in the long letter he wrote to him from Moscow. According to Peng Shuzhi, Chen had the "political morality of an Oriental," which was out of place in the modern political arena. Let me try to offer a third view. In my opinion, Chen knew that Moscow was opposing him and not Chinese leaders in general; he believed that Moscow was sincere about revolution, even though it was wrong about China, and that future developments would convince Moscow that he was right. On no account did he see Wang Ruofei and the others as "his" base; for Chen, every Party member was his base, including Qu Qiubai. He therefore devoted himself to studying script and confined himself to offering his opinion on specific questions; he was not prepared to organize an opposition.

So the Chen Duxiu-ites were bound to fail. But Li Lisan was also wrong when he said that the people Wang Ruofei gathered around him were united merely by personal ties and that Wang's coalition had no basis in principle. A careful examination of the facts shows that Wang's group was different from other factions of the period. It was bound not simply by personal ties but also by a principle drawn from practical experience, or from pronouncements on various issues by Chen Duxiu (mainly his insistence that the revolution was in a trough rather than on the rise). True, the principle lacked clarity and no one overtly raised it as such, nor did anyone have the courage to think it through to the end. Even so, the group was grounded in principle, as evidenced not just by the fact that its members later joined the Trotskyists almost to a man and woman but also by the famous "resolution of the Jiangsu Provincial Committee." Wang Ruofei drafted this resolution before going to Russia for the congress, but another group in the Jiangsu Committee headed by Xiang Ying refused to pass it. For some reason, Sun Yat-sen University in Moscow translated it into Russian and made it available as material on the Chinese question. Trotsky was delighted and wrote an article about it.[297] He thought that it was unwittingly in concert with the ideas of the Left Opposition. But Wang's group committed one fundamental error—it kept within the bounds of Comintern *légalité*[298] and took as its target certain Chinese leaders rather than Stalin and Bukharin. It even borrowed Stalin's and Bukharin's ideas to attack the Chinese leaders. Its attack was rather successful, and Qu Qiubai and Li Weihan fell as a result. But what came after Qu and Li was even worse: Li Lisan.

Wang Ruofei was not allowed to go back to China, and Xiang Ying—Li Lisan's competitor and rival—used the Jiangsu Provincial Committee's past opposition to the Central Committee for his own purposes. In 1924, when I returned from Russia, the tiny Shanghai labor movement was under the leadership of Xiang and Li. One was in charge of east Shanghai, the other of west Shanghai; each tried to outdo the other, and Li Lisan won. Now that Li Lisan had become the Party's "theoretical and political center," Xiang Ying at first refused to submit. I do not know what job he had in the Party—probably it was in the All-China General Labor Union—but his base was in the Jiangsu Provincial Committee, of which he had been secretary before the congress, if my memory serves me correctly.[299] The new secretary of the Provincial Committee was Li Fuchun. On the committee, Li Fuchun was supported by He Mengxiong, but Cai Zhende and Ma Yufu continued to uphold the old Wang Ruofei tradition. Xiang Ying, Li Fuchun, and He Mengxiong united with Cai and Ma against the new Li Lisan Central Committee and declared their "independence." They had their own financial sources, so they were not reliant on the Central Committee; they could communicate on their own account with other provinces, and they expected responses from several of them. They made a lot of noise, but after a few days, their revolt fizzled out. Zhou Enlai called a meeting in Shanghai of the other provinces and ensured their loyalty. Xiang Zhongfa, Li Lisan, and the others threatened Xiang Ying and accused him of manipulating people from behind the screens, whereupon Xiang knuckled under.

The one who had tied the bell to the tiger took it off,[300] and as a result, the Jiangsu Provincial Committee was restored to its original condition, save for Cai Zhende and Ma Yufu, who resigned. While the storm was brewing, He Mengxiong constantly asked Cai Zhende, "Why hasn't Zheng Chaolin come yet?" I don't know how Cai told He that I was with them. Li Fuchun came to my place to look me up, by which time I had already resigned from agitprop work on the Central Committee, sold the lease on the house on Yuyuan Road, and moved to Li Minzhi's place. Li Fuchun asked me to go and help out and promised to make me head of the Jiangsu Committee's Propaganda Department. I was not surprised by his request, for it was an open secret that I felt wronged, but I was surprised by the offer of a quid pro quo. Perhaps it was a trick that Li had picked up while working as political director of the Guomindang's Second Army. All the same, I agreed to "help." Together with Peng Shuzhi, Liu Bozhuang, and Wang Zekai, I helped the Jiangsu Provincial Committee write some manifestos and resolutions in Cai Zhende's house, but none was accepted, for they exceeded the political bounds set by Xiang Ying, Li Fuchun, and He Mengxiong.

All this happened in January or February 1929. That was a long time after I had quit the Propaganda Department. My first attempt to resign, after Li Lisan took power, was turned down. The second time, Li said that there was no one to take over for me, so we should let the matter rest until someone suitable turned up. The third time, he still would not agree, but a few days later, he sent Pan Wenyu, who had just got back from studying in Moscow, with a request that I assign work to him. It was obvious to me that Li had already found his "suitable" person, so now I insisted on resigning, and he agreed. They assigned me no new work but promised to send Jing and me to Moscow to study. First, we went to live at Li Minzhi's place; from there, we moved to Cai Zhende's place. Cai Zhende insisted that we come, and Li Minzhi and Pan Hannian insisted that we stay. Originally, we had lived in the room belonging to Pan Hannian and his wife, for they had gone back to Yixing for the time being. When they returned from Yixing, they would not let us move out and went, instead, to live in a big room under Li Minzhi's. I felt bad about this, but it was mainly for political rather than personal reasons that we moved into the second story of the house next door to where Chen Qiaonian was arrested, in Hengfeng Alley off Scott Road. On the first floor lived Cai Zhende and his wife. He Zishen's wife, Zhang Yisen, and her daughter—a newborn baby who had not even been named—lived in the small room above the kitchen.

On March 18, we were arrested there.

9

My First Spell in Prison

In the summer of 1922, in the woods at Montargis, when Xue Shilun invited me to join the Communist Youth organization, I dragged my feet for a while before agreeing. The delay had nothing to do with ideas or beliefs, for by then, my Communist convictions had already ripened. But it required resolution to move from ideas to action: It required the determination to brave prison, torture, and the firing squad.

In China, Chen Duxiu was the first person to go to prison for communism. Shortly after the founding of the Chinese Communist Party, when he was made general secretary, he was arrested and held for quite a few days in a police station in the French Concession before finally being released and banished forever from the concession. That was actually the second or third time he had gone to prison, but it was the first time as a Communist.

I do not know whether any other Party members were arrested or killed in the period between the founding of the Party and the February 7 massacre.[301] February 7 was a tidal wave. Apart from those Party members and supporters shot on the spot and people like Lin Xiangqian and Shi Yang shot later, Party members who went to prison included Liu Fen and Xu Baihao in Hankou, Shi Wenbin and Wu Yuming in Changxingdian, and Li Qihan and Han Baihua in Shanghai. The arrests in Hankou and Changxingdian were directly connected with the railway strike; those in Shanghai were only indirectly connected: Li Qihan was a leader of the labor movement, and Han Baihua was publisher of *Guide Weekly*. In the spring of 1924, Zhang Guotao and his wife, Yang Zilie, were arrested in Beijing. When the news reached Moscow, we realized even more keenly what repression meant, for just a few months earlier, Zhang had delivered a speech to us at KUTV. There were rumors that Zhang and Yang had been severely tortured and that Zhang's arm had been broken. After Feng Yuxiang switched flags, they were released, and the following spring they came to Shanghai; I asked Zhang about the torture, but he said that there had been none.

After Feng's "switch of flags," the repression apparently came to an end all over China, until after the May Thirtieth Incident. I do not know whether Gu Zhenghong[302] was a Communist, but the four Shanghai University students (including Han Buxian and Zhu Yiquan) arrested at his memorial meeting on Gordon Road were. Their appearance before magistrates of the International Settlement on May 30 was one of the reasons for the street speeches and the ensuing bloodbath. Among the students arrested for making speeches, Qu Jingbai, Qu Qiubai's younger brother, was a Communist. So was He Bingyi, one of those who died in the massacre. Both were students at Shanghai University.

During the high tide of May Thirtieth, a Chinese section of the International Association to Aid the Fighters of the Revolution (MOPR)[303] was set up simultaneously with the Shanghai General Labor Union. Chen Duxiu chose a more popular name for it in Chinese: the Association to Relieve Distress. It was a public and rather affluent body, run by comrades disguised as members of the gentry to facilitate fund-raising and social intercourse with the upper classes. The association also functioned as a propaganda body. When it was first formed, there were no dead or imprisoned revolutionaries to assist, for the Chinese government and the authorities in the International Settlement either dared not or did not know how to intervene. After the return to work and the ebbing of the tide, ruffians smashed up the General Labor Union, and Chang Yuqing's thugs kidnapped Li Lisan and took him to Chang's place, where he was forced to accept a number of conditions. Finally, the Beijing government ordered the General Labor Union closed down and put out a warrant for the arrest of its leader, Li Lisan, but Li escaped.

The first revolutionary to come to the attention of the Association to Relieve Distress was Liu Hua, an outstanding young Sichuanese who studied at either Shanghai University or the middle school attached to it and was active in the labor movement at Xiaoshadu under Li Lisan's direction. At around the time of May Thirtieth, he was involved in every one of the innumerable strikes that took place in Xiaoshadu and became a well-known workers' leader, deeply hated by the Chinese and foreign capitalists alike. After Sun Chuanfang arrived in Shanghai, Liu fell seriously ill and was inactive for more than a month. One day after his recovery, he was riding a tram in the International Settlement when a plainclothes detective recognized him and arrested him on the spot. While he was crossing Fuzhou Road, some workers saw him and briefly spoke to him. Not long after that, he was handed over to Longhua. I heard, later, that Sun Chuanfang had had him shot in prison. Rumor had it that at banquets given by the General Chamber of Commerce, some capitalists had told Sun how "detestable" Liu was and had asked that Liu be shot. I commemorated him in an obituary in *Guide Weekly*. After the victory of the Shanghai insurrection, the General Labor Union advertised, asking if anyone knew where Liu's remains were, but apparently without success. The second case taken up by the relief association was that of Zhou Shuiping. Zhou was not a Communist but an anarchist, who individually instigated the peasants against the landlords in Jiangyin and was seized and shot by local despots acting in collusion with warlords. The relief association intervened on his behalf to show that it was not controlled by the Communist Party.

Jiangyin is, of course, outside Shanghai. As far as I know, no other Communist in Shanghai besides Liu Hua was persecuted in the period between the May Thirtieth massacre and the insurrection. But the same cannot be said of other places. At more or less the same time as the May Thirtieth massacre, there was another massacre in Qingdao that was, unfortunately, submerged by the great Shanghai wave, so few people know about it. The movement that preceded it was also led by Communists, in particular Li Weinong, with whom I had once worked in the factory in Montargis. In July, Li was seized and shot by Zhang Zongchang.

During the protests in China against the May Thirtieth massacre, work-study students in France also launched a protest movement. They resorted to traditional means of struggle, surrounding the legation and forcing Chen Lu, the minister, to sign a document. The French police scattered them, and their leader, Ren Zhuoxuan, secretary of the Chinese Communist Party branch in France, was arrested and sentenced to a year in prison; he spent several months behind bars in the famous Santé Prison.

Even more people died on March 18, 1926, in Beijing than on May 30. There were many Communists among the dead, but none that I knew personally. During the chaos, Chen Qiaonian was bayoneted in the chest. After the massacre, Duan Qirui put out a wanted list that included members of both the Communist Party and the Guomindang, the chief name being Li Dazhao. Large numbers of people in Beijing fled south.

Two days after the Beijing massacre, uproar broke out in Guangzhou too. Chiang Kai-shek sent troops to surround the Russian advisers and arrest the captain—a Communist called Li Zhilong—of the Zhongshan Gunboat; Communists in the Huangpu Academy and the First Army were detained or put under house arrest. Although no one was killed and all the Chinese and Russian revolutionaries except Li Zhilong were released (even Li was freed before long), March 20 was even more important than March 18 from the point of view of repression, for the main agent of the subsequent White Terror was not Duan Qirui but Chiang Kai-shek.

Between May Thirtieth and the Northern Expedition, there were two massacres in Hunan: one at Shuikoushan, and one at Anyuan. I do not know if any Communists died at Shuikoushan, but the chairman of the Anyuan Workers' Club was a Communist, and he was shot.

During this period, the Party organization in Baoding in the north was raided, and a great many comrades—both men and women—were arrested, most of them students. Their leader, Gao Feng, took the entire blame on himself in order to save his comrades, so he was the sole sacrifice.

After the launching of the Northern Expedition, there were undoubtedly many casualties, but again, none that I knew personally. Yuan Qingyun, who set out on the expedition, died at Chenzhou of cholera. In Wuchang, a memorial that had been set up at a busy street intersection was still new when I arrived there. Someone on the Hubei Provincial Committee told me that it was to commemorate a comrade who had been killed by the Northern Army during the siege of the city.

After that, the number of Communist martyrs gradually began to rise. Let us return to Shanghai. While the Communist Party was preparing the Shanghai insurrection, Luo Yinong, Zhao Shiyan, and He Jinliang said in idle conversation: If the insurrection succeeds, we will not all survive it, so which of us will die? In the first insurrection, Xi Zuorao, Tao Jingxuan, and others died. Their arrest, sentencing, and execution were reported in detail in the newspapers. All declared that they were members of the Guomindang. After reading the reports, Qu Qiubai gave vent to his feelings.

"When the Russian comrades were interrogated in their own days they could openly and boldly declare themselves to be Bolsheviks," he said to me. "The Chinese comrades don't even enjoy that right!"

I do not know if Qu drew any conclusion from his anguish. Anyone capable of consistent thinking would have concluded that the Chinese Communist Party should break with the Guomindang and become independent, that it should face the workers and peasants under its own colors.

During the second insurrection, Li Baozhang, commander of the Shanghai garrison, had the streets patrolled by teams of soldiers carrying broadswords. If they came across people giving out leaflets or shouting slogans, they beheaded them on the spot. Many people died; I do not know how many Communists were among them. Apart from the sword patrols, police and detectives arrested large numbers of suspects and people who had often appeared at demonstrations in the past, including many students from Shanghai University. Most of those arrested were sent to Caohejing Prison. After the victory of the third insurrection, the General Labor Union sent a group of people to greet them as they left the prison.

I knew none of the comrades who died on the barricades in this third insurrection. At the end of it, the pickets arrested the worst of the police officers and detectives; I do not know how they were punished. But by then, we perceived a new threat. Shanghai and the Jiangsu-Zhejiang area were occupied by Chiang Kai-shek's First Army; we had already heard about Chiang's reactionary activities on his way north from Guangzhou. The leader of the Ganzhou General Labor Union had been seized and shot, and the Jiujiang General Labor Union had been smashed up by Chiang's hired thugs.

Was our ally Chiang Kai-shek going to suppress us on behalf of Sun Chuanfang and Zhang Zongchang?

Yes, he was, starting on April 12, 1927. The preceding evening, He Jinliang went to visit Du Yuesheng. According to reports, Du phoned He to tell him not to come, but He went anyway. During the insurrection, Du's faction of the Green Gang had cooperated with us through Niu Yongjian.[304] When we set up our command post in the French Concession during the second insurrection, it was thanks to Du's protection. He Jinliang was one of the comrades who liaised with Du, under the false name of Wang Shaohua and in his capacity as leader of the Shanghai General Labor Union. On the evening of April 11, He Jinliang went by motorcar to Du's place but did not return. The next day, the chauffeur reported that He had been detained and killed. I do not know how. Recently, I sent this memoir[305] to my friend Xie Danru to read. He told me through an intermediary what he knew of He Jinliang's murder. According to him, Wang Shouhua was detained and handed over to the Public Security Police, but the police were afraid to take responsibility and dared not detain him, so the same night, they let him go. But while doing so, they dimmed the street lights and shot him from an ambush near Penglai Road Market. They dragged his dying body into the back entrance of the house of a relative of Xie Danru. Xie's story has the ring of truth, for other people were killed elsewhere by the same method.

I shall leave aside the number of people killed in the battle that took place during the disarming of the pickets and at demonstrations and confine myself to the subsequent White Terror. The organization responsible for the terror was the Longhua Garrison Command; the people responsible were Yang Hu, head of the detective force, and Chen Qun, the garrison's political director. In those days, their names were linked in a phrase that epitomized the terror: "Rearing a great throng of tigers."[306] But the troops who did most of the disarming belonged to Zhou Fengqi's Twenty-sixth Army. They wanted the demonstrators' weapons and did not necessarily kill everyone who was arrested. Wang Yifei, commander of the Nantao picket, was arrested after being disarmed. An officer asked him a few questions and then let him go. He pretended to be a Shanghai University student. Had he fallen into Yang Hu's hands, he would have died.

The people initially arrested by the Longhua garrison were comrades working openly for the Party—not just those from Shanghai, but also others who had fled to Shanghai from elsewhere. Many died, but I knew only a few of them. He Luo, a student from Shanghai University, and his wife, Liu Zunyi, were arrested. He Luo was an elected member of Shanghai's local government and the head of some bureau; Liu Zunyi, from Sichuan, was a leader of the Shanghai Women's Federation and a student at one of the Beijing universities. She had sworn sisterhood with Zhao Shiyan's two younger sisters and seven other women; these "Ten Sisters" had pledged not to marry. Half of them had already broken their vow, as had Liu, who was the prettiest of the "Ten Sisters." Now, she and her husband were awaiting execution. But Pan Yizhi, director of Commander Bai Chongxi's Political Department, fell in love with her, killed He Luo, and took her for his wife.

> In the past thousand years the only hard thing to decide upon was whether or not to kill oneself;
> "Marchioness Xi was not the only one whose heart was broken."[307]

Ouyang Jixiu, a fellow provincial of Liu Zunyi, often used to recite that couplet. He wrote about the incident in a novel, but I have never read it.

Of those killed, I also knew Xuan Zhonghua and An Ticheng, who were arrested after escaping to Shanghai from Hangzhou. Xuan Zhonghua was a member of the committee of the Guomindang's Zhejiang branch; An Ticheng was a professor at Hangzhou Law School. Both were well-known Hangzhou Communists. Many others were seized and killed in Hangzhou, but I did not know them personally.

At the same time as the massacre in Shanghai, there was one in Nanjing. The overwhelming majority of members of the Guomindang's Jiangsu branch consisted of Communists, and most of them were seized. The Public Security Police did not have the courage to detain them, so they were set free, but thugs ambushed them on the streets and shot them dead. Among those who died, I was personally acquainted with Hou Shaoqiu, the number-one member of the Jiangsu branch committee and former director of the middle school attached to Shanghai University, who had lived with Qu Qiubai on Rue du Marché; Xie Wenjin, who had studied at KUTV in Moscow; and Zhang Yingchun, head of the Women's Department and Liu Yazi's friend. (Liu wrote many articles in her memory.) Zhang had been in Shanghai in 1926 and had often come to the Propaganda Department to talk to Chen Bilan about the women's movement, so I had got to know her quite well.

Many people died during the April 12 reign of terror. We lost comrades everywhere in areas controlled by Chiang's armies. In 1928, when I went to Fujian on my inspection tour, the comrades in Xiamen praised a student from Xiamen University who had been among the dead. In 1940, on my way back through Ningbo to Shanghai, I noticed a memorial stone at the entrance to Zhongshan Park commemorating the "achievement" of the Guomindang in murdering Communists in Ningbo during the April 12 massacre. I know too little about the April 12 terror to give a thorough account of it; for that, we must await the future findings of historians.

In Guangzhou, the terror started on April 15, three days later than in Shanghai, but I know even less about what happened there. Li Qihan of the All-China General Labor Union lost his life. Among the victims at the Huangpu

Academy, I knew Xiong Xiong and Xiao Chunü. But I especially cherish the memory of a young man called Chen who was from the same part of Fujian as I. When I went to France, he was in his first year at Zhangzhou Normal School. While I was lecturing at Shanghai University, he wrote a letter to me from Zhangping in which he talked about the revolution. Later, when he went to Guangzhou, I introduced him to Chen Yannian, as a result of which he became a cadet at Huangpu. He too died in the terror. People told me that he was arrested on April 15, held in a concentration camp, and shot later.

At around this time, Zhang Zuolin, in Beijing, was competing with the Guomindang to see who could commit the most atrocities. Of those arrested at the Soviet embassy, I knew Li Dazhao, Fan Hongjie, Li Jida,[308] and Xie Chenchang. Li Jida had studied with me in Moscow; after getting back to China, he had worked in Tianjin for a long time. Xie Chenchang had worked with me in Montargis. Zhang Guotao announced their deaths at the Fifth Congress, and the delegates observed a few minutes' silence. Their case was reported in detail in the press.

After my arrival in Hankou, the terror in Shanghai reached new heights. Chen Yannian was arrested! The Shanghai press carried reports of the telegram of congratulations that the old dog Wu Zhihui had sent to Yang Hu. The telegram said that the arrest of Chen junior was even more significant than the arrest of Chen senior would have been, for the son was even more important in the Communist Party than the father. There was a reason for Wu's hatred. In the past, both he and Chen Yannian had been anarchists, but when the "Communist Youth Party" was set up, Chen abandoned anarchism and became a Communist. The Chinese Communists in France were Wu's sworn enemies—it was we who had torn off his false mask. The news of Chen's arrest shook the entire Party, for Chen had been one of its main leaders in Guangdong. When he first arrived in Guangdong, the Party had had no more than a few dozen members, but in less than three years, it had recruited more than ten thousand new ones and had become active in many fields. Everyone had great expectations of Chen Yannian, and some said that the Comintern wanted him to take over from his father as Party leader. Another reason for our shock was that until then, only those people who worked in the Guomindang or played some other open role had become victims of the terror. Now it was clear that comrades who played leading roles in the Party's own organizations were also to be victimized. I don't know the circumstances of Chen's death. On January 1, 1928, Luo Yinong invited some of us for a meal at his residence in Shanghai. After the meal, Su Zhaozheng, Wang Ruofei, and I sat together competing to see who could drink the most. Su was already drunk. Somehow, the conversation got around to Chen Yannian, and Su started weeping loudly. He said that up to then, he had been forced to shed his tears inwardly and silently.

One day—I cannot remember exactly when, but it was after the Guomindang in Wuhan came out against the Communist Party and Luo Yinong took over from Zhang Tailei as secretary of the Hubei Provincial Committee—Luo and I went to a bathhouse and started talking about Zhao Shiyan's skin disease. Suddenly, Luo said to me in Russian: *"Radin arestovan!"* (Radin has been arrested!) I was startled by the news. Radin was Zhao Shiyan's Russian name. At the time, the Party kept the news of Zhao's arrest a secret. If any of us accidentally heard about it and mentioned it to one of the Party leaders, they either denied it or said, "Yes, a group of comrades in Shanghai was arrested, and a worker comrade pretended he was Zhao Shiyan to fool Yang Hu and give Zhao time to get away." It was kept secret because the Party in Shanghai was trying to secure Zhao's release, by bribery or some other method. After the death of Chen Yannian, we could hardly stand another such loss. Many people in the Party were familiar with Chen Yannian, but outside Beijing and Shanghai, hardly anyone knew Zhao, and even in Beijing and Shanghai, few people knew how important he was. Chen and Zhao each had their own special talents; had they swapped jobs, I don't know whether their achievements would have been the same. Chen was not a mass leader in Guangdong; his special skill lay in masterminding comrades' work from behind the scenes. Zhao was a mass leader and, in my opinion, every bit as good at masterminding as Chen. Unlike Luo Yinong and Peng Shuzhi, both were utterly pure, honest, frugal, and untainted by the slightest trace of personal ambition. They easily won the faith and confidence of comrades. I never heard anyone say anything bad about either of them. After their deaths, the Chinese Communist Party entered a period of factional strife that eventually led to a split. If Chen and Zhao had lived, I do not know how things would have turned out. True, the split was unavoidable, but had they not died, it would have happened differently.

Although I knew that Zhao was dead, I did my utmost to keep the news from spreading. Zhao's elder sister Shilan lived with Li Hui, one of the "Ten Sisters," in Luo Yinong's residence in Lanling Gardens in Hankou. We met daily, but no one dared mention Zhao Shiyan. One day, just as we were about to leave Hankou, I went to Luo Yinong's place and found Shilan in tears. She reproached us for hiding the truth from her. She had found out that Shiyan was dead when her elder brother wrote to her from Qingdao or Tianjin.

Before I left Hankou, people were already being arrested in the Wuhan tri-city. After the so-called peaceful split on July 15,[309] Tang Shengzhi did not immediately carry out a great number of arrests, let alone killings. Only after the uprisings in a number of counties of southern Hubei did he gradually embark on a policy of terror. Zhou Weizhen of the Party's Military Committee in Wuchang was arrested. He was the Party's first important member to be seized after the start of the reaction. He had originally been responsible for military affairs on the Hubei Provincial Committee. He smuggled a letter out of prison asking us to rescue him, but we could think of no way to do so. I don't know what his eventual fate was. Before I resigned from the Hubei Provincial Committee, there was a raid on the office responsible for arranging meetings and contacts, but luckily, it happened at around dusk, so none of us was present except for two women comrades, both Henanese, who used to sleep there. Afterward, I heard that the office had been discovered when troops searched one of the Party's district secretaries crossing a railroad track and found a notice on his person about a meeting; I also heard that the two women comrades got ten years each. That was the only time that disaster struck the Central or Provincial Committee during my stay in Hankou.

The real terror in Wuhan started after I had returned to Shanghai. A string of raids on the Provincial Committee led to the deaths of many people, including Ma Junshan, Yu Zhongdi, a man called Wei, Fu Xiangyi, and Ren Kaiguo, all of whom I knew. Mu Qing was arrested but bailed out by a fellow townsman; he escaped with his life, for there was insufficient evidence to convict him. However, he died less than a year later, in Sichuan. Luo Yinong was almost arrested when he left Shanghai to inspect Party activity along the Yangtze. After this event, it proved impossible to maintain Party activity in Wuhan. Liu Shaoyou, Liu Bozhuang, and others succeeded one another as secretary of the Provincial Committee in Hubei. Each escaped back to Shanghai soon after arriving in Wuhan. When the Chinese authorities tried to extradite Xiang Jingyu from the French Concession in Hankou, they at first encountered difficulties, but eventually, she was handed over and died before a firing squad in Wuhan.

Our base in Hunan was much stronger than that in Hubei, but under the terror, we could not keep up Party activity in Changsha[310] either. Even more of our cadres were sacrificed in Changsha than in Wuhan. I don't know how many died in the Horse Night Incident, but most of those who did had been working in the trade unions, the peasant associations, or the Guomindang; very few had been active inside the Party. Xue Shilun was head of the Hunan Provincial Committee's Propaganda Department and was in Changsha during the incident. The gunfire scared him out of his wits, so the following day, he fled to another county and quit the Party. About Xia Xi's whereabouts I knew nothing. Peng Gongda, who like me had attended the August 7 Conference though not a member of the Central Committee, went back to Hunan after the conference to join the Provincial Committee; not long after that, he was killed.

People who had led the Party in Hunan in the past could no longer be active in Changsha. The Central Committee sent Wang Yifei from Zhejiang to Hunan, where he had never worked before. He was secretary of the Provincial Committee for a while, but eventually, he was arrested and shot. A strange lot befell the Sichuanese Ren Zhuoxuan. He was arrested and shot along with Wang Yifei. The same night or the following morning, a peasant passing by the execution ground noticed that one of the bodies lying there was showing signs of life. It turned out to be Ren Zhuoxuan. The peasant rescued Ren and took him where he said he wanted to go, and Party officials took him to a hospital to recover from his wounds. Just as he was about to be discharged, he was discovered and found himself back behind bars. But this time, to save his skin, he not only capitulated but actively helped the enemy catch his comrades. He did everything within his power to serve the White Terror. I do not know how many people died as a result of him. Fu Fengjun, the wife of Yan Changyi, was among them. She hid "Wu Tong" (He Zishen) for a long time, and in those days, no raid ever happened without Wu Tong being its main target. Later, Yuan Dushi (alias Yuan Dashi) was also arrested. He gave his captors the names and addresses of the entire organization under the Provincial Committee in Hunan, so the enemy could net everyone. After that, the Party organization in Hunan was completely extinguished. He Chang, the newly appointed secretary of the Hunan Provincial Committee, was obliged to set up his office in Shanghai! Ren Zuoxuan, Yuan Dushi, and a handful of other renegades in Changsha published manifestos urging other comrades to capitulate.

All these things happened after I had returned to Shanghai. One day, I began to talk to Zhou Enlai about comrades who had betrayed the Party. He sighed and said, "Who would have thought that Yuan Dushi could turn traitor!" Yuan had been among the first group of Chinese students at KUTV in Moscow. He was from a poor peasant family and, as a child, had been a cowherd. He had been one of the main actors in the factional strife among the Chinese students at KUTV. When he got back to China, he became active in the lower levels of the labor movement, where he worked loyally and hard. At the end of 1927, he became head of the Jiangsu Provincial Committee's Organization Department. He lived in the same house as Wang Ruofei. It was there that I actually met him, though I had known about him for a long time. Later, he was transferred to Hunan. I was not well acquainted with him, so his defection made less impression on me than did Ren Zhuoxuan's. Zhou Enlai had closer relations with Ren than with Yuan; I don't know why he mentioned only Yuan. Maybe it was because back in China, Ren played a less brilliant role in the Party than Yuan had. Ren, too, was from a poor peasant family. He belonged to a type often encountered in old Chinese novels. He was a typical Zhu Maichen:[311] the son of a poor family, endowed with natural talent, not afraid of hard work, who gradually came to the attention of his superiors and rose through the hierarchy of officialdom, after which he forgot and even came to despise his own class. In the 1920s, many Zhu Maichens joined the revolution, which they saw as a shortcut to high office. I often came across such people, most of them unreliable. But Ren was an old comrade, a founder of the Communist Youth Party who had taken over from Zhao Shiyan and Zhou Enlai as secretary of the European Branch of the Chinese Communist Party and had been sentenced in France to a year in prison for leading a movement. He appeared to be so loyal and hardworking that I even considered him on a par with people like Zhao Shiyan, Chen Yannian, and Wang Ruofei.

It was true that others had betrayed the Party in earlier years: On several occasions, hidden agents—some planted by the enemy, some turning traitor of their own accord—had acted against it from within. We looked upon these people as "political speculators," members of a different species. Ren Zhuoxuan was the first Party traitor among those that I considered to be our own people. At first, we did not believe the reports from Hunan. Chen Duxiu said indignantly, "Zhuoxuan would never do such a thing, people should stop slandering him." The Old Man had met Ren only once or twice and was going on Ren's past correspondence, speeches, and other activities; he had no reason to believe that Ren was any different from the rest of us. The Old Man never suspected for one moment that we could harbor among us someone capable of treason. Unfortunately, the report from Hunan was confirmed. From then on, we had one more piece of knowledge about how to assess people.

After he had done his foul work in Hunan, Yuan Dushi moved to Shaanxi, where he became a county magistrate. Ren Zhuoxuan went back to Sichuan, where he continued to study and propagate his "Marxism." In 1930, he came to Shanghai, where he ran the Xinken Book Company, publishing books and magazines and writing about theory under the pen name Ye Qing. The Stalinist Chinese Communist Party had no idea how to deal with him; they simply denounced him as a "Trotskyist." The Stalinists slandered the Chinese Trotskyist Opposition on countless occasions, but in my view, the most shameful of all their slanders was when they called Ren Zhuoxuan a "Trotskyist."

After my return to Shanghai, the White Terror increased daily in intensity, depth, and scope all over China. Countless people died after the defeat of the Guangzhou Insurrection. The Chinese proletariat has still not called in that blood debt. Among those who died in Guangzhou, the only one I knew personally was Zhang Tailei, who was commander in chief of the insurrection. After taking part in the Guangzhou mass rally, he returned to the Public Security Bureau building in a motorcar, unaware that this command post of the revolution had been retaken by Guomindang troops just a few minutes earlier. White soldiers fired on his motorcar and shot him through the chest, killing him instantly. The Comintern delegate Neumann, a German, who was riding in the same car as Zhang, had a lucky escape.

There was also a wave of terror in Beijing under Zhang Zuolin. Those who lost their lives included Wang Hebo, Fujian's first Communist, who had been elected onto the Central Committee at the Party's Third Congress and participated in several congresses of the Comintern.

It is strange but true that there was virtually no terror in Shanghai during that period. When Zhang Baoquan of the Central Committee's Communications Center and Huang Wanqing of the Propaganda Department got married, they invited a crowd of people to a banquet at the Laobanzhai Restaurant. Apart from Luo Yinong, people from every one of the Central Committee's various departments attended; it seemed just like the old days in Wuhan. Peng Shuzhi and his wife, Chen Bilan, who had just arrived in Shanghai from Beijing, both attended the festive occasion and were amazed by what they saw. "In Beijing there is not this freedom," they commented. Nor was there in other parts of China. The wedding banquet given at the Jufengyuan Restaurant by Deng Xixian of the Central Committee's secretariat and Zhang Xiwan, newly returned from Russia, was similarly profligate. For the banquet of Zhang Baoquan and his bride, the Party bookkeeper docked a few dollars from our living expenses—that is, we pooled part of our income in honor of the couple. But we did not pay for the banquet thrown by Deng and his bride, which someone told me was financed by Deng's relatives. I also got married then, but I did not throw a party and treat my comrades.

By then, Yang Hu had already gone. His terror was particularly cruel, and he used it as a way of extorting money from people, so even the big capitalists hated him. In the big cities, the Guomindang's rule had already stabilized, and the economy was reviving. The labor movement had already been rendered harmless. Communists sentenced to prison under Yang Hu began to make accusations against the judiciary, so the Justice Yuan[312] set up a special court to review their cases. Many were freed on bail. The Guomindang government in the big cities relaxed the terror, for it realized—just like the imperialists, who had withdrawn troops from China—that the revolution was on the ebb. But there were still political prisoners awaiting sentencing in the detention center at Longhua. These people were probably the victims of personal vendettas or their own careless behavior. Some were refugees who had fled to Shanghai from other provinces and been denounced to the authorities. The office under the Central Committee responsible for making contact with people from outside Shanghai was raided; Wang Jingdong, the younger brother of Wang Hebo and head of this office, was arrested and sent to Nanjing. That raid was an extension to Shanghai of the arrests and raids in the provinces. We kept calm, and the incident did not develop any further. The Central Committee sent someone to Nanjing to try to buy Wang

Jingdong's freedom, but the plan failed, and Wang was sentenced to life imprisonment. Later, I came across him in the Central Military Prison in Nanjing. His assumed name was Wang Kai, and his prison number was "1." When I left prison, he had still not been released.

In early 1928, Chen Qiaonian and a group of other people were arrested. That raid was the first time that terror struck the Party after my return to Shanghai. After Chen Qiaonian, Xu Baihao, and Zheng Futa had been shot, the others were sent to prison. I met them while I was in Suzhou Military Prison, but I know little about the circumstances of their cases.

I do not remember whether Zhang Baoquan was arrested at the same time as Chen Qiaonian or Luo Yinong; all I know is that it was during the same general period of terror. Zhang had been ordered to inform all Party bodies about the terror. After visiting the Propaganda Department to tell us about it, he was supposed to go to some other places too. His pockets were stuffed full of letters. I advised him to adopt a disguise, but he was in too much of a hurry. We were both wearing Western clothes, so we decided to swap overcoats. I swapped my relatively old and shabby one for his new and rather smart one. He left, never to reappear. It turned out that he was arrested, and the letters were discovered on his person. It was obvious to his captors that he was important, and all sorts of tortures were employed during his interrogation. But this loyal comrade from beyond the Hangu Pass[313] said nothing, and his secrets died with him. I continued to wear his overcoat in commemoration of him: throughout my first period of imprisonment, throughout my membership in the Opposition, and throughout my second period of imprisonment. I wore it from Shanghai to Hangzhou, from Hangzhou to Suzhou, and from Suzhou to Nanjing. Finally, one winter I lent it to a prison mate from Suzhou, a young political offender, but he never returned it to me. To my great regret, I was unable to wear it through the prison gate at the time of my release.

Perhaps one reason for Zhang Baoquan's visit was to inform me of the arrest of Luo Yinong. Luo's luxury residence had already been given up. He had just gotten back from an inspection tour of Party work in the Yangtze region and had nowhere to live, so for a while he stayed at the Propaganda Department, which was also my home. During the day, he went to work in a Party office at the intersection of Gordon Road and Avenue Road. One night, he failed to return. His absence was unusual, but I was not greatly worried by it. I learned the following day that he had been arrested. When the office of the Jiangsu Provincial Committee was raided, the Central Committee had not panicked, for the two systems were independent of each other. This time, however, there was a panic. My wife, Jing, and I moved to a hostel alongside the Great World Amusement Center. We left the maidservant in charge of the house and told her that we were going to Hangzhou on a pilgrimage. We returned to our old house only after the newspapers published reports and photos of Luo's execution. Zhou Enlai came to the hostel to see us. I learned from him that Luo had been betrayed by Huo Jiaxin and his wife, He Zihua. These two people—both Sichuanese—lived on the floor beneath the raided office. He Zihua had originally been Zhu De's[314] wife and had accompanied Zhu to Germany to study. She was pretty, intelligent, and spoke some German. After she and Zhu split up, she returned to China via Moscow and fell in love with Huo Jiaxin, who had studied in France. Immediately after Luo Yinong's arrest, the Party's intelligence service discovered through sources in the police station that the betrayal had been the work of this couple. Not long after Zhou Enlai had left, at around dusk, Deng Xixian called on me to ask for the evening newspaper. I was rather surprised by his mysterious manner. I immediately went out to buy one and found a report in it about an assassination that had taken place in the French Concession. The victims were a couple who had recently moved into the area. The man was dead, and the woman had been found hiding under the bed, wounded but not fatally. I realized at once why Deng was acting so mysteriously, and without a word, I handed him the paper.

For the next twelve months and more, there was not a single raid on an important Party body in Shanghai and not a single arrest of an important Party leader. In July 1928, I went to Fujian to inspect Party work and was almost arrested. I was the intended target, but I left Xiamen a day too early. Several comrades were arrested, including Li Liansheng, a newly elected member of the Provincial Committee, who was eventually shot in Zhangzhou. In prison, he met Chen Shaowei, former secretary of the Provincial Committee. Not long after that, Chen escaped by digging a hole through the wall.

What I have written cannot be taken as a history of the White Terror, for it is incomplete. I have simply noted what I heard and saw. Some of my comments are detailed, others are brief. Their length is not necessarily in proportion to the importance of the events they refer to—when I know more, I say more. The Association to Relieve Distress published a number of pamphlets containing brief biographies of comrades who died in the terror, including some photos. Perhaps future historians will unearth some of these publications. I hope that someone writes a comprehensive history of the terror.

I could continue, but first I want to write about my first spell in prison.

* * *

When I withdrew from the Central Committee's Propaganda Department, we—Jing and I—were originally planning to go to Moscow to study. According to reports, you had to walk several dozen *li*[315] to cross the frontier into the Soviet Union. Jing found walking difficult,[316] so I urged her to practice every day. Before we sold the lease on the house on Yuyuan Road, we often used to walk to the Bubbling Well Road tramway station or walk home from there. We took neither a rickshaw nor one of the newly operating trams or omnibuses. After we moved to Li Minzhi's house, we still continued to go for long walks, but we stopped doing so after we started living with Cai Zhende. The reason was that more and more people were beginning to advise us against going to Moscow. Chen Bilan told me that she had heard the Old Man say to Peng Shuzhi: "If Chaolin goes, we'll have even fewer writers if we decide to run a magazine." That was how I learned that the Old Man was planning to set up a magazine. In any case, the departure date was pushed further and further into the future, and in the end, no definite news of it ever came. Nor did we ask for any.

Whether or not we went to Moscow, we still needed to meet our daily living expenses. While waiting to leave the country, we comrades without jobs continued to receive half our original salary: twenty Mexican silver dollars a month for food, board, clothes, and sundry needs. Naturally, we could not live on that sum. Peng Shuzhi, Wang Zekai, Liu Bozhuang, and Ren Xu no longer lived off Party income but off writing, translating, or some other form of literary activity. When Cai Zhende withdrew from the Jiangsu Provincial Committee, Li Fuchun and He Mengxiong behaved reasonably well toward him and gave him sufficient funds to keep him for the next two to three months. Ma Yufu continued to work in the labor movement, so he was entitled to draw living expenses from the Party. I used to translate a few pages of *Religion, Philosophy, and Socialism*[317] each day, in the hope of earning enough to repay debts and stay alive.

Publishers were gradually becoming interested in Marxist literature at this time, and later it became even more popular. Small companies competing to publish Marxist books sprang up everywhere. The revolution had been defeated, but the Marxist theory that underlay it was now buoyant. It is not easy to explain this paradox, which is without precedent in history. In the past, revolutionary theory had always been extinguished following the defeat of a revolution. One example is Western Europe after 1848; another is Russia after 1905. Why was China different? I shall try to advance an explanation, though it is not wholly satisfactory: In my opinion, the reason lies in China's great size, huge population, and poor communications. The labor movement in the cities and the peasant movement in the Hunan countryside could suddenly display their formidable prowess and propel the Communist Party into state power, on a par with the Guomindang, but they were unable to rally all the peasants of China or all the middle classes, so they were just as suddenly crushed by counterrevolution. Only after the vanguard had fallen did the rear guard gradually begin to mobilize, but this rear guard was in no position to reverse the fate of the revolution. It was precisely this special circumstance that led Stalin's Third International to mistake an ebbing tide for a flowing one; it was also this special circumstance that facilitated the emergence of armed struggle in Chinese villages waged by a "Red Army." This struggle became the Communist Party's principal focus, and "Nationalist-Communist relations" evolved to their present state.[318] Finally, it was this special circumstance that made Marxist books and newspapers so popular in the world of Chinese publishing in the four to five years after 1929. Some middle-class people, mainly students, had been roused by the proletarian revolution of 1927, and even though they had not managed to join it, they showed sympathy with it and sought to grasp its theoretical premises.

I arrived at this opinion later, after reading Trotsky's analysis of the Chinese Red Army. In early 1929, while I was translating a book by Engels, I was still unaware of the new Marxist trend in Chinese publishing. I translated the book to broaden my understanding and to while away the time; it never occurred to me that my translation might appear in print.

Cai Zhende and his wife and child, Zhang Yisen and her daughter, and Jing and I cooked and ate together. We were often too poor to buy food. In the early days, Cai Zhende still had the money that the Jiangsu Provincial Committee had given him, but after that, he too was broke. It was March 18. We had barely enough money among us to buy rice and vegetables. Zhang Yisen went to Xia Zhixu's place to play mahjong; there, she could also get her dinner. Cai Zhende and his wife went to visit a fellow townsman or a friend to cadge a meal. Jing and I still had one silver dollar, which we were considering how best to spend in order to fill our stomachs for the evening. It was four or five o'clock in the afternoon. I was just preparing to leave the premises when a crowd of men rushed in brandishing pistols. They were policemen and detectives sent by the Public Security Bureau to arrest Zhang Yisen, who lived in the small room at the back of the house. But Zhang was not in. We said that we had no idea where she had gone or when she would be back. The detectives, satisfied with our explanation, settled down to wait for her in the downstairs guest room, where they stayed until long after nightfall, leaving us alone in our flat on the second floor. Panic stricken, we bundled up some documents and hid them in a hole in the tiled floor of the sun terrace. Just after we had finished doing this, Ma Yufu came in, probably in search of a free meal. The detectives let him enter but would not let him out again. He told them that he had come to visit us. We hurriedly and secretly arranged with him how to answer any potential questions. Just before night fell, a detective came up and stood at the door of our room to watch us, but he spoke politely.

"Just now," he said, "the fellow guarding the back of the house saw someone hide something on the sun terrace. We went and fetched it. It turned out to be Communist Party documents. We asked the maid. She said that you all ate as one family and that Zhang Yisen is your auntie." (We had a maid-servant from Jiangbei at that time.)

At around nine o'clock in the evening, Cai Zhende and his wife returned. The detectives escorted the couple to their room on the first floor, searched it, and found a pile of documents in the cupboard. Cai and his wife were immediately put under guard. Zhang Yisen and her daughter did not return until eleven. In her room, the detectives found a photograph of He Zishen, some written messages, and some documents stuffed in two leather suitcases. These items were confiscated, and we were all taken to a police substation in Chinese territory behind Dixwell Road, where we were asked to give our names and ages. We were then taken by truck to the Public Security Bureau in Nantao. The maid from Jiangbei was forced to accompany us.

We sat waiting in the interrogation room until dawn. Two robbers who had arrived earlier were treated like criminals, but we were treated like guests. The detectives approached us with great civility and called us "comrade."[319] An official with the ravaged face of an opium addict led Zhang Yisen into another room and interrogated her at length. When she returned, she told us that the Hunan Fellow Provincials' Association in Nanjing had written officially to the Public Security Bureau in Shanghai saying that she should be arrested. The official had showed her the document in question, which said that she was the wife of the notorious Hunan Communist leader Wu Tong[320] and that Wu Tong was now under arrest in Shandong. We had known for a long time that He Zishen had been arrested in Shandong, but we had no idea who could have given the Hunan Fellow Provincials' Association Zhang Yisen's Shanghai address. Later, He Zishen told me that the person who had done this was a cousin of his ex-wife. He Zishen had had an affair with this man's wife, so the man had gotten revenge by denouncing Zhang Yisen. This man, a student at a university in Wusong, had visited our house in Hengfeng Alley.

When the public security people heard that we were Communists, they were unhappy.[321] "They're fighting among themselves again," said one. They told us that yesterday, Chiang Kai-shek and Li Zongren had gone to war against each other, and Nanjing had sent a large body of troops against Hankou. When the detective sergeant, a short fellow, came into the office, things immediately livened up. He asked the two robbers to make a statement. They kept quiet, so he had them dragged off to an adjoining room, from which screams soon issued. I wanted to go over and have a look, but a detective stopped me. "You wouldn't be able to bear the sight," he said. He was trying to be kind to me. After that, the robbers came back in; both had confessed. The detective sergeant did no more than ask a few questions of Zhang Yisen and then retired to his office. Not long after that, an official emerged with a congratulatory look on his face.

"Your case isn't serious," he said. "You're 'for the country's sake.'"

Later, the director of the Public Security Bureau, a man called Huang, stepped in together with the detective sergeant.

"This woman is Zhang Yisen," explained the sergeant. "She lives in one of the Communist Party's offices. All these people were arrested there."

"We've been wrongfully arrested," we told the bureau head.

"Do not worry," he replied. "All those people who've been wrongfully arrested will be freed."

After he had gone, a man wearing Western clothes came in. I knew him. Damn it, I thought to myself. He looked at me.

"What's your name?" he asked.

"Wang Shengzu," I replied.

"Your face is familiar."

After he had gone, Cai Zhende asked me if I knew him.

"Yes," I replied. "He is a double agent. Before the Northern Expedition reached Shanghai, he used to live alongside Shanghai University. He knows Li Ji. He helped him publish *A Life of Marx*. On one occasion, he asked Li Ji to invite me to his house for a talk. At the time, I didn't know what sort of person he was."

"What's his name?"

"All I know is he's called Bao."

"Isn't he Bao Junfu? In that case, I know him too. He's very unreliable."

We bought one hundred steamed stuffed buns with my silver dollar and had them for breakfast. Director Huang ordered some food and invited us to lunch. At three o'clock in the afternoon, we heard someone in the detective sergeant's office shouting "*Fa ke, fa ke, fa ke*!" (Take them to the judicial department), whereupon a number of detectives came in and politely requested "the comrades" to follow them to another place, which turned out to be the lockup for prisoners awaiting trial. The men and women were now segregated. The lockup was crammed with people. It was dirty and smelly and far less comfortable than the interrogation room. The warder gripped a bamboo cane. He treated us like prisoners. We hankered after the interrogation room, but our cell mates told us that if you stayed in the interrogation room, you ran the risk of a "foreign meal,"[322] so they were always happy when they heard the words *fa ke*. "Going to the judicial department" meant that the arrest procedure was over and the prisoner was to be handed over to the Third Department (the judicial one) to be dealt with.

During our three to four days in the lockup, we were taken off on two occasions to appear in court. Zhang Yisen said boldly in court that she had nothing to fear or hide. Yes, she was the person that the Hunan Fellow

Provincials' Association wanted. Yes, her husband was a Communist and was now under arrest in Shandong. She had already told the detective sergeant so while under interrogation, and according to Zhang Yisen, there was an exchange along the following lines between her and the interrogator.

"'Under arrest'?" the detective sergeant had replied. "Does a young girl like you know what that means? Where did the documents come from?" he continued.

"A friend of my husband stored them there."

"Where is the friend?"

"He was shot in Hankou."

We denied that the documents had been found in our room. Li Xiusheng (Ma Yufu) and Mrs. Ju-Zhang, the maidservant, knew even less about the business. One day, Bao Junfu came over to the lockup and asked each of us which room we lived in.

"They've got into a real mess," he said angrily. "They've got all the documents mixed up, so they don't know which bundle was found in which room."

That made it even easier for us to deny that the documents had been found in our room. The second time we went to court, the judge took out several letters addressed to "Mr. Wang Shengzu." They were from me to Jing, written in Fujian, and contained many incomprehensible passages. The judge pointed out these passages and said that they were secret communications about a Communist conspiracy.

"What does little pussy mean? And little doggy? What does that refer to?"

I flatly denied that the letters belonged to me.

"We've treated you quite civilly," he shouted angrily. "Let's see if a spell of corporal punishment won't loosen your tongues! No more questions."

My fellow accused and I were taken back to the lockup. None of us was interrogated any further. The next day, we were handed over to the Longhua garrison headquarters. While we were being put aboard the vehicle, the head warder, a man from Pingjiang in Hunan, shouted out: "Be careful with those things! Don't break those two bottles of toxicants. And be careful with that bust of Marx." Clearly, they had been back to Hengfeng Alley a second time and found the cast-iron bust of Marx and the two bottles of chemicals that we used to wash down letters written in invisible ink. It was obvious that they had done their work well. This augured badly for our stay in Longhua.

The cells at Longhua were quite different from those we had just left. They were larger, there were more of them, and there were far fewer people in each cell. Once the main gate to the cell block had been locked, the prisoners in the ten cells that made up one block were free to come and go. There was as much rice as you wanted, and though the vegetables were inedible, the warders were prepared to go out and buy some for you if you wanted. The chief warder (or secretary) held a roll call every day at dusk; otherwise, he did not bother you. The guards would make friends with you, chat with you, and joke with you as long as you had money or were skilled enough to deal with them. In the spring of 1929, a dozen or so Communists were being held at Longhua. The only relatively important one was Wang Kequan, secretary or member of the Pudong District Committee, who had been arrested by accident. All the other political prisoners had been denounced by people with grudges against them. Some actually were Communists; others were being held on false charges. The political prisoners, who were solidly united, gave us a warm welcome. Seeing that they welcomed us, none of the nonpolitical prisoners dared to try to blackmail us new arrivals. Some of the suspected robbers at Longhua were, in fact, Communists. All knew Ma Yufu.

The four women—Zhang Yisen, Wang Shaohua, Liu Jingzhen, and Mrs. Ju-Zhang—were held separately in the women's block, which at that time was opposite the entrance to the third block. There were no political prisoners in this women's block. We three men (Wang Shengzu, Liu Shiqi, and Li Xiusheng[323]) were held in the first block, a concentration point for political prisoners. The block also held a kidnapper whose wife was in the women's block. Their five-year-old son, Xiaomao, used to move back and forth between his father and his mother, so we used his pockets as our postbox. The political prisoners, led by Wang Kequan, joined with the other prisoners to sing songs, indulge in various sorts of merriment and uproar, play chess, and gamble. It was as if we had forgotten where we were. In such an atmosphere, we soon cast off our worries and anxieties. The other prisoners told us that if no one pressed charges, we could easily bribe our way out. And even if someone did press charges and provide the necessary evidence, we would get only a few months behind bars. As for the death sentence or long sentences, even the political prisoners who had been there longest knew of such things only by hearsay and had never actually seen them applied to anyone.

The Association to Relieve Distress bribed one of the warders to smuggle messages in and out and sent in money and other necessities to help the political prisoners. A leader of the association, a Shanghai University student called Wu Yu (who later became a reporter on *Shishi xinbao* [New current affairs] and changed his name to Wu Suzhong), knew immediately that we had been arrested and managed to get help through to us, so we lacked for nothing. Wang Kequan suggested that we organize a Party branch in prison and hold regular meetings, but I thought the idea inappropriate, so nothing came of it. Wang Kequan was already familiar with Cai Zhende and Ma Yufu even before we arrived at Longhua, but not with me. Wang was a capable young worker who had been arrested by Yang Hu together with Zhao Shiyan; he had been tortured but had remained firm and staunch. After Zhao was shot, Wang had been kept in Caohejing Prison for several months until the Party managed to bail him out. Now that he was again under arrest, he was scared that the authorities would relate his present case to his old one; but fortunately, nothing came of his fear. Later, after we had been released from prison, he too was released and rose steadily in the Party and even became secretary of the Jiangsu Provincial Committee. He then became a leader of the so-called Conciliationist faction. In the end, he turned traitor and actively helped arrest Communist Party members, but that was not until after my second spell in prison.

I blended into this atmosphere and soon forgot that I was a prisoner. On the day of the arrest, our finances had barely stretched to an evening meal. Now, everything was suddenly assured. We paid no rent, electric light was free, the garrison headquarters sent up the rice, and the Association to Relieve Distress provided the subsidiary food. Whenever we felt hungry in the mornings or the afternoons, we could order flatbread or deep-fried doughsticks, though at a rather higher price than if we had been free. One afternoon, the warder came to tell us that the judge was coming down to inspect our cells. The long-term prisoners were astonished, for that rarely if ever happened. We all went back to our own cells. Soon, the main gate clanged open and the chief warder came in, accompanied by the judge, who entered each of the cells in turn. When he came through the door of mine, I gave a start and abruptly turned my face toward the window. This judge was Su Fushou, my old pal from middle school. I had shared the same study with him for half a year. I had not seen him for some ten years, but there was no mistaking him.

He addressed the prisoners in my cell: "Outside, some people are usurping the name of the court to extort money from your families. Next time you write home, make sure they don't fall for this trick. The court is an impartial body. It does not engage in corrupt practices."

He spoke Mandarin with a Longyan accent—the same sort of Mandarin I had been used to hearing at middle school in southern Fujian. After he had gone out through the iron gate, I rushed up to watch him walk toward the women's block, presumably to deliver the same message to the women prisoners. There was no doubt about it: This man was Su Fushou. I asked one of the other prisoners about him. This prisoner was an old hand who happened to have appeared before this judge. He took out his judgment for me to see. Sure enough, it was authenticated with the seal of Su Fushou. I was not sure if this was to my advantage or my disadvantage. Although I was calling myself Wang Shengzu, I had not bothered to change my place of birth or the name of my school. How could I have guessed at the Public

Security Bureau that one of the judges would turn out to be a graduate of Fujian's Ninth Provincial Middle School and, what's more, an old classmate of mine? To this day, I still do not know what sort of role Judge Su played in my case. I would not go so far as to say that he was instrumental in releasing me, but I know for sure that he did not harm me. All it needed was for someone to point out that "Wang Shengzu" was actually Zheng Chaolin and I would have been done for. Later, Bao Junfu told me that while I was being held by Public Security, Wu Kaixian had visited Director Huang regarding the warrant for the arrest of Gu Zhenggang. While there, he saw a letter on Huang's desk addressed to "Zheng Chaolin."

"If this case involves Zheng Chaolin, then it's a very important one," he told Huang.

"Do you know anyone who could identify him?" asked Huang.

Wu Kaixian said that he would fetch someone, but for some reason, this did not happen. Huang Zheng'an, one of Wu Kaixian's secretaries, was an ex-member of the Communist Party who had worked with me in the headquarters in Guanhua Alley off Route Lafayette during the second insurrection, so he knew me.

He sought out Mei Dianlong[324] and asked him, "Has Zheng Chaolin been arrested?"

"Don't talk nonsense," Mei replied.

I do not know whether this conversation took place later or while I was still in custody at the Public Security Bureau.

The judge in charge of our case was not Su Fushou but a man from Jiangxi whose name I forget. I also forget whether our first appearance in court took place before or after Su's visit to our cells. The judge from Jiangxi allowed me to talk rubbish and made virtually no attempt to rebut me. My testimony was recorded, and I was asked to sign it. Only then did this judge take out the letters addressed to "Wang Shengzu" and ask me what they meant. Again, I flatly denied that they belonged to me. He got angry and told me not to talk nonsense.

"Do you mean to imply that the detectives are out to frame you?" he asked. "All you need to say is that what is said in these letters is a joke, and then we can let the matter rest. At first, I didn't suspect you. Now, I'm really beginning to do so."

Then he told his secretary to add to my testimony that I denied owning these letters.

The second time I was taken from my cell was to go to the offices of the military court. This time, it was not to investigate my case but to meet Bao Junfu, who had come to visit me. He said that he had been asked by Mr. Li to come and find out if I needed anything. I thanked him, and returned to prison.

The third time was to be told about my bail. One or two days before this, Li Xiusheng (Ma Yufu) and Mrs. Ju-Zhang had been unconditionally released. Ma Yufu bundled up his clothes and said good-bye. Our Jiangbei maidservant (Mrs. Ju-Zhang) had innocently become involved in this disaster as a result of her connection to us; we never saw her again. Later, Zhang Yisen was sentenced to eight months in prison. She appeared several times in court and said that all the documents had been found in her room. After she had been sentenced, she petitioned to have her sentence commuted to a fine, but her petition was refused.

After I had been granted bail, I wrote and sent out a letter, but it was several days before the person who bailed me out arrived. Jing's elder brother, who had just arrived in Shanghai from Yunnan, learned from a fellow Yunnanese that we had been imprisoned and came to Longhua to visit us. We told him that we had already been granted bail. He was unable to find a *pubao*, that is, a shopkeeper who would stand as guarantor for us. I was more worried than the other prisoners, for Jing had fallen ill in the women's block, and the chief warder had told me that she had pneumonia. He gave me special permission to visit her.

On April 28 or 29, 1929, we were finally freed. Wu Yu came to meet us at the prison gate, and we hired a car to take us to the New Hotel on Jiujiang Road in Shanghai's International Settlement. The next day, I took Jing to the Red Cross Hospital, where she spent more than a month recovering. If our *pubao* had arrived a few days later, she would have died.

Gu Shunzhang came to the New Hotel that same day to visit us. He told me that Bao Junfu had done everything in his power to help us. The Central Committee had given Bao five hundred dollars to spend on our case. Gu then gave me thirty dollars and told me to ask Bao out for a meal and to see a film. I did as he said, and Bao told me frankly that he had done some things for us while we were still being held in the Public Security Bureau. For example, he had urged the Third Department to hand us over to Longhua, for by processing us through two offices, the circumstances of our case were likely to become muddled. As for Longhua, he said, we did not owe our release to him; even if he had not gone to speak with the judge, we would still have been freed. He did not know why the judge had behaved so leniently.

I did not tell him about the connection between Judge Su and me. In any case, since coming out, I had learned something else that Bao did not know. Here I must introduce a friend I had gotten to know ten years earlier.

In 1919, while our packet steamer was docked in Port Said at the entrance to the Suez Canal, a Chinese had climbed on board from the quayside and asked us to help him get to France. It turned out that, two weeks earlier, he had been aboard another ship carrying Chinese work-study students to France and had gone ashore to spend the night in a hotel, probably with a woman. The next day, when he went down to the docks, the ship had left. He was without friends or relatives, with no language but Chinese, and penniless. Luckily, he met up with some Cantonese sailors. Although they spoke a different language,[325] they were still Chinese, so they got him various odd jobs; in this way, he managed to stay alive. He was an unadulterated northerner and no longer young. We work-study students took him to the first-class salon to meet Zhang Ji, who recognized him as the famous revolutionary Li Zhongshan from Shaanxi. From then on, all his problems were solved. We considered the whole affair a joke. We also hit the town, but the playboys among us who might have spent the night ashore in hotels were careful not to do so in Port Said. Later, we forgot about this incident concerning Li Zhongshan.

When the thirty-odd students from Fujian arrived at the middle school in Saint-Germain to which they had been assigned, they noticed a stranger in their midst—the northerner from Port Said. The headmaster asked him how old he was. "Thirty-eight," he replied. The students from Fujian sniggered to themselves. So old, and so straightforward that he did not think to try to hide the fact! The students from Fujian had the habit of discriminating against outsiders, especially a gullible northerner like that. They often used to cheat him. As for me, I was at least an "interprovincialist" and did not share their prejudice. I used to talk with him about Chang'an,[326] Mount Hua,[327] and the ancient sites of the Han and Tang dynasties;[328] the more he talked, the more excited he became. In his luggage, he had a copy of Zhang Huiyan's *Cixuan* (Selection of *ci*) and another of Ke Zhai's *Ji gulu*. After a few months, he ran out of money for his studies and had to take a factory job, so he asked me to keep the Ke Zhai book for him. It was a collection by Wu Dacheng[329] of plates of ancient Chinese characters taken from bronze bells, tripods, and other vessels made in ancient times. The book ran to several volumes, which Li kept in a small wooden case; it was worth quite a lot of money. He was a work-study student in the real sense of the word and never engaged in self-advertisement like Xu Teli and others. He was strong but not skilled, so he did heavy manual work. A year later, he took his Ke Zhai back, saying that he had found a buyer for it. After that, he wrote to tell me that he was planning to return to China. When he arrived back in Xi'an, he wrote me another letter, but I did not reply.

I forgot all about him until after Feng Yuxiang's "switch of flags," when I came across his name among a list of generals. After that, I often saw his name in the newspapers. As representative in Beijing of the Second National Army, he went with two bodyguards to arrest Yao Zhen, then the incumbent prime minister of the Beijing government, and let him go only after Yao had fallen to his knees and other people had pleaded on his behalf for mercy. The Shanghai English-language press cited this incident as proof of China's "anarchy." The person responsible was, I believe, the same northerner plagued in France by the students from Fujian.

The first time I met Zheng Boqi at one of the Creation Society meetings, he told me that "Zhongsan is in Shanghai, and he often mentions you." I was surprised that he still remembered my name. Later, Cai Zhende told me the same thing. Zheng Boqi and Cai Zhende are both from Shaanxi, as was Li Zhongsan.

After our arrest, another friend of Cai's from Shaanxi sought out Li Zhongsan and told him about our arrest. Li went to Nanjing and looked up his friend Hu Yimin, who wrote to Xiong Shihui, commander of the Shanghai garrison, asking him to rescue the prisoners Wang Shengzu and Liu Shiqi. While we were living in a hostel in the French Concession, Li Zhongsan came to visit us. He brought with him Xiong Shihui's reply to Hu Yimin, which said that the military court would free the two prisoners.

After that, Li Zhongsan frequently came to visit us and broke with his former circles. Finally, he stopped being an old-style military man and became a member of the Trotskyist Opposition. He was the first person in China to become a Trotskyist without first passing through the school of Stalinism.

10

The Left Opposition

We were only forty days in prison, but coming out was like entering a new world. While driving along the Longhua Road, we saw that there were no longer any plum blossoms on the trees. The grass was high, and the air was full of orioles; it was a typical late spring in Jiangnan.[330] I remember that before we were arrested, there had been no air of spring in Shanghai, and the trees along the pavements had not yet put forth leaves. In Longhua Prison, no trees were to be seen, and the grass that grew in the prison courtyard was pitifully scant. At Qingming,[331] one of the guards had brought in a twig of plum blossom, so in my heart I knew that it was spring, but I had not imagined that it was so advanced. When we got to Shanghai, the noisy, bustling streets gave us a feeling we had never before experienced.

But something else, too, had changed—a change more abrupt than that between the seasons. Yin Kuan came to the New Hotel to visit us. He had originally planned to come to our house on March 18 to play mahjong; I don't know whether it was because he forgot or because something else happened, but by failing to show up, he had escaped the fate of Ma Yufu. We praised his good fortune. After some social talk, he took out a roll of mimeographed paper. It was an essay by Trotsky on the Chinese Revolution, later included in the first volume of *Zhongguo geming wenti* (On the problem of the Chinese Revolution), which we published.[332] The essay was very poorly mimeographed, but even so, it made a much deeper impression on us than Qu Qiubai's well-printed and well-translated Comintern circulars put out by the secretariat of the Central Committee. It was as if an electric beam had been shone into our skulls. For a while I was confused, unable to say whether the document was right or wrong. Later, when I met Peng Shuzhi and Wang Zekai, I discovered that they had already read some of these mimeographs and that Chen Duxiu had also read them. They had got them from Yin Kuan, who had obtained them from the Shandong comrade Wang Pingyi, just back from Moscow. Yin Kuan had once taken me to see him, but we had not talked much.

After that, I read a whole series of such documents, together with one or two issues of *Womende hua* (Our word).³³³ Since Yin Kuan had not sworn me to secrecy, after reading them I passed them on to Cai Zhende and Ma Yufu. Being newly out of prison, I had no idea that an opposition had already formed in the Chinese Communist Party, or what the Central Committee's attitude toward it was. I thought that it was an open secret that comrades were passing around Trotsky's articles. On one occasion, Huang Wenrong came to visit me.

"Has there been any reply from the Central Committee to Trotsky's ideas?" I asked him.

"Who told you about Trotsky's ideas?"

I thought for a while and then said, "Yin Kuan gave me an article of his to read."

A few days later, Yin Kuan came to remonstrate with me. After Huang had gone back and reported on our conversation, the Central Committee had interrogated Yin Kuan about the source of those articles. I apologized and said, "I didn't know it was so serious." Now the Central Committee knew that we were already acquainted with Oppositionist documents.

We by no means accepted Trotsky's analysis overnight. I accepted it only after much deliberation and repeated discussion. There were so many issues involved, and the issues were so complicated! The last to give in was Chen Duxiu. Every time he talked with Yin Kuan, he raised a different objection and held to it even after listening to Yin's reply; the next time they met, he would raise a new objection on the basis of what Yin (following Trotsky) had said the previous time. And so the discussion proceeded, layer by layer. By the time the rest of us were one hundred percent convinced, Chen still had doubts. Finally, he wrote an article saying that China could carry out a workers' and peasants' dictatorship, but not a proletarian dictatorship. The article was never published, but later, after he had come over completely to the Opposition, Liu Renjing attacked him on the basis of it. Apparently, Liu had not read it himself but had only heard about it from Yin Kuan.

* * *

So what were Trotsky's views on the Chinese Revolution? A memoir is not the place for a detailed political analysis of such questions, but it is not easy to describe them generally, for they touch on such a broad range of issues. Later, we published the articles Trotsky wrote in those years in two volumes, titled *On the Problem of the Chinese Revolution*; we eventually brought out a third volume. His views on China are set out in those three volumes. Besides that, three years ago I wrote a pamphlet titled *Buduan geming lun ABC* (An ABC of the theory of permanent revolution), one chapter of which is devoted to this theory's relevance to the Chinese Revolution and briefly reiterates Trotsky's views on this question.

But it's important to discuss these issues, at least briefly. Young people in the 1930s who were interested in politics and revolution were more or less acquainted with Trotsky's views on China, but young people today, in the 1940s, are not so fortunate, and some have never even heard his name. Since this memoir is written mainly with the young people of today in mind, I must devote at least a little space to explaining the differences between the Trotskyist and Stalinist views on the Chinese Revolution.

Three practical issues caused the Soviet Communist Party to split; they concerned the Soviet Union itself, the Anglo-Soviet Trade Union Committee, and the Chinese Revolution. In 1923, when the Left Opposition first took shape, Soviet issues dominated the inner-Party struggle; in 1927, when the new Opposition formed, the latter issue became central. Trotsky and Zinoviev, who together led this new Opposition, were by no means wholly in agreement about the Chinese Revolution. The Zinoviev group was unwilling to accept the theory of permanent revolution, so the views of the united opposition on questions of basic theory were often halfhearted and wrong. Only after the decisive split between Trotsky and Zinoviev was Trotsky able to present a thorough-going and systematic analysis of the Chinese Revolution. What I am about to say is based on what Trotsky said after going into exile.

In contrast to the schema that people had previously observed, Trotsky now said that the Chinese Revolution was proletarian-socialist. It did not need to complete the bourgeois-democratic stage before entering the proletarian-socialist one, contrary to what Stalin said. The bourgeois-democratic tasks of the Chinese Revolution—that is, the tasks of the so-called national revolution—could be fulfilled only under proletarian dictatorship; in order to set up and maintain a proletarian dictatorship, the revolution would have to go beyond bourgeois-democratic tasks and realize a number of tasks that belong properly to proletarian socialism.

Trotsky derived these conclusions from an analysis of Chinese class relations. China's semicolonial status and imperialism's pressure on China made it impossible to unite "all" of China's classes, which the Stalinists claimed as their goal. Quite the contrary, the more the revolution developed, the more the capitalists would tend to ally with the imperialists against the toiling classes, and the harder it would be to achieve China's liberation. This statement applied not only to the national question but also to the land question. China had no independent landed aristocracy. The big and middle landlords in China were inextricably connected to the urban bourgeoisie. So land revolution in China was intrinsically anticapitalist in nature; the capitalists would not only disapprove of it but also actively try to stop it.

So the bourgeoisie cannot achieve national independence or resolve the land question. But that fact alone does not prove that the Chinese Revolution must be proletarian-socialist. Ever since Lenin, one view has been that bourgeois-democratic revolutions are not necessarily led by the bourgeois themselves and are often achieved despite them. This was certainly how Lenin described the Russian Revolution before April 1917. His call was for a "workers' and peasants' democratic dictatorship." Since China and Russia are in many ways similar, can we not conclude, as Lenin did for Russia, that the Chinese Revolution is bourgeois-democratic in nature, and that it must aim for a workers' and peasants' democratic dictatorship?

But the Russian Revolution did not result in a workers' and peasants' democratic dictatorship. Lenin dropped this slogan immediately after returning to Russia in April 1917 and called for "proletarian dictatorship." The result was that the bourgeois-democratic tasks were achieved as a by-product of proletarian socialist revolution. Before April 1917, the only reason Lenin had proposed and insisted on a workers' and peasants' democratic dictatorship was the tradition in Russia of petit bourgeois peasant movements. Russia had a landed aristocracy. Serfdom in Russia had only recently been abolished, and relations between landowners and the urban bourgeoisie were less intimate than those in China. That is why Russia, unlike China, produced a Narodnik movement and a revolutionary party with a long history of struggle, namely, the Social-Revolutionary Party, which claimed to represent the peasants and harbored the illusion that Russia could achieve socialism without first going through a stage of capitalism. Before the revolution, Russian Marxists knew that Russia could not achieve socialism without first going through a capitalist stage, but they could not afford to overlook this petit bourgeois revolutionary organization and continued to come up with different formulas to express the nature of the relationship between the workers and the peasants—one of them being "the proletariat leads the peasantry." This was the source of Lenin's famous formula "democratic dictatorship of the workers and peasants." The Revolution of 1917 proved that despite all these formulas and slogans, the Russian peasants were still subordinate to the leadership of the proletariat and its political party, and that in the face of a real revolution, the petit bourgeois Social-Revolutionary Party, with its revolutionary traditions, would be revealed as impotent and disintegrate. So when the revolution finally broke out, Lenin said: "He who *now* speaks of 'revolutionary-democratic dictatorship of the proletariat and peasantry' only, is behind the times, is therefore in practice on the side of the petit bourgeoisie and against the proletarian class struggle; such a one should be placed in the archive of 'Bolshevik' pre-revolutionary antiques (it may be called the archive of 'old Bolsheviks')."[334]

If this is true of Russia, how much truer must it be of China! The Chinese agrarian economy has even fewer feudal relics than the Russian economy and no petit bourgeois revolutionary party claiming to represent the interests of the peasantry. Events have proved that the Chinese peasants can submit to proletarian leadership. There is no future in China for a workers' and peasants' democratic dictatorship. The only revolutionary state possible is one grounded in the dictatorship of the proletariat. But to set up and maintain a dictatorship of the proletariat, the revolution must exceed the limits of bourgeois democracy.

The Guangzhou Insurrection is living proof of this. The Guangzhou Soviet proclaimed as law, among other things, that factory committees should control production; big industry, communications, and the banks should come under state control; and the mansions of the big bourgeoisie should be confiscated to house the workers. Trotsky asked, if that's a bourgeois revolution, what will proletarian revolution in China look like?

Trotsky's views on the nature of the Chinese Revolution, though derived from an analysis of Chinese class relations and verified by the Guangzhou Insurrection, were fully in accord with his unique theory of "permanent revolution." There is no room here to elaborate on the development of this theory or its various implications. I shall simply say that it first took shape in Russia's 1905 Revolution, led by Trotsky. On the basis of an analysis of Russian class relations, Trotsky arrived at his conclusion that in a backward country like Russia, the bourgeois-democratic revolution, having been excessively delayed, cannot—unlike in the advanced countries of Western Europe—be led and completed by the bourgeoisie. Although the immediate tasks of the Russian Revolution in its initial stages were bourgeois-democratic, they could be achieved only by a further unfolding of the revolution in the direction of proletarian dictatorship and the realization of certain socialist goals. Proletarian dictatorship was a powerful guarantee that Russia's bourgeois revolution would cross over into proletarian revolution. Whether or not socialism, being the final goal of proletarian revolution, could be achieved in Russia, and to what extent it could be achieved, would depend partly on conditions within the country and partly on the revolution's international environment. The Russian Revolution can be seen only as a constituent of world revolution. On the basis of this theory formed in 1905, Trotsky insisted that the revolution in Russia should carry out proletarian dictatorship and would not need to go through the stage of workers' and peasants' democratic dictatorship. The October Revolution of 1917 showed that he was right.

Trotsky was always opposed to the Chinese Communist Party entering the Guomindang.[335] In 1923, when the Third International debated this question, he alone resolutely opposed such a step; in 1925, he again formally proposed that the Chinese Communist Party quit the Guomindang forthwith, but his proposal was not accepted. He saw clearly that the Guomindang represented China's bourgeoisie and that if the Chinese Revolution was to succeed, the proletariat should not only not support the bourgeoisie but also resolutely oppose it. Even before the massacre of April 12, 1927, Trotsky had pointed out that the Guomindang leaders would betray the revolution. He demanded the immediate establishment of soviet organizations and said that the revolution should first be deepened and then spread. His views were rejected; not long after that, the Guomindang's left wing in Wuhan went over to the reaction. After the defeat of the Guangzhou Insurrection, Trotsky concluded that the revolution was already finished and raised the question of what tactics to pursue "between two revolutions," in order to prepare for the third revolution.[336] But instead, people now adopted his earlier proposals and set about staging insurrections and organizing soviets. They mistook the ebb for the flow; they met the ebb with tactics appropriate for the flow.

According to Lenin, "An elementary truth of Marxism says that the tactics of the socialist proletariat cannot be the same in [the] face of a revolutionary situation as when this situation does not exist."[337]

Trotsky proposed the tactic of a "national assembly"[338] for this period between two revolutions. Seeing that the Chinese workers' and peasants' revolution had been defeated, he thought that the ruling class would be able to achieve a measure of political stability, which would in turn provide the basis for a revival of the economy. Industry and commerce, which had declined during the period of revolution and civil war, would gradually recover, the pool of unemployed would shrink, the workers' ranks would swell, and the proletariat's specific weight in Chinese social life would correspondingly increase and its self-confidence return. But barring unexpected developments, there could be no question, for the time being, of revolution, insurrection, and soviets. The Communist Party's immediate task was to lead the proletariat back onto the political stage. The best way to do so was by campaigning for a national assembly. Under conditions of political stability and economic revival, the ruling class itself also needed such an assembly, to help it clip the army's wings and lessen expenditures on unproductive ends; it would also help in bargaining with the imperialists. The petit bourgeois, too, were now likely to spring back into action and raise even more democratic demands. To that end, they would probably try to ally with upper layers of the urban workers and the peasants. The Communist Party should not stand by with folded arms but should actively take part in such a movement, in order to combat the influence of the bourgeoisie and the petit bourgeoisie on it and to lead the workers and peasants back into political life. The Communist Party should be in the forefront of the various classes and should call for a national assembly on its own account.

* * *

Trotsky spoke up about the nature of the Chinese Revolution before it was defeated; he proposed a national assembly after it was defeated and, moreover, after the Sixth Congress of the Third International—that is, after the autumn of 1928. The import of his earlier analysis was strategic, whereas his later proposal was tactical. But both the strategic and the tactical proposals reached China simultaneously, and we embraced them simultaneously. In the meantime, this created no end of confusion, especially among the broader public, which knew little about the debates in the world Communist movement. On one occasion, Deng Yanda, leader of the Third Party,[339] arranged to meet Gao Yuhan for a discussion.

"You Trotskyists claim that the revolution in China is proletarian," he said, "but you call for a national assembly; the Stalinists say that it is bourgeois but call for soviets. Aren't the positions of both sides self-contradictory?"

What Deng meant was that if the Chinese Revolution was proletarian, soviets should be set up; and if bourgeois, a national assembly should be convened. I can't remember how Gao answered him.

Even though by then we had all accepted Trotsky's analysis and proposals, not everyone understood and weighted them identically. In 1940, when I returned to Shanghai,[340] one of the first things that Peng Shuzhi said to me was, "In the early days, we understood the ideas of the Fourth International from a right-wing point of view." Actually, that's wrong. Although it is true that Peng himself stopped being a Stalinist and became a Trotskyist "from a right-wing point of view," the same is not true of other people. Peng Shuzhi not only accepted the national assembly proposal but also elevated it from the tactical to the strategic level. He saw it as the means by which the proletariat would take power in China's coming third revolution. But Trotsky was quite clear on this question. He systematically set out his views on the national assembly in "The Chinese Question After the Sixth Congress,"[341] under the subheading "The Inter-Revolutionary Period and the Tasks That Present Themselves in the Course of It." At the end of this essay, he returned to the theme with an explicit warning against potential misinterpretations of the slogan: "The party must have in mind and must explain that in comparison with its principal aim, the conquest of power with arms in hand, the democratic slogans have only an auxiliary, a provisional, an episodic character. Their fundamental importance consists of the fact that they permit us to debouch on the revolutionary road."[342]

Peng Shuzhi agreed that the revolution was "proletarian in nature," but he specifically attacked two points of view: that "China's third revolution will be proletarian from the very start," and that "in China, bourgeois-democratic tasks will be achieved as a by-product of proletarian revolution." He vigorously attacked these ideas in the unification talks; in Nanjing Prison, he wrote articles attacking them; and in the 1941 debate, he attacked them for a third time. He failed to see that once these two ideas were dropped, there was nothing to distinguish Trotsky's analysis of this particular issue from Stalin's. The Stalinists never denied that once China's third revolution reached its final stage, it would be proletarian-socialist in character; what distinguished them from Trotskyism on this point was their belief that only after solemnly completing the "bourgeois-democratic tasks" could proletarian revolution be carried out. So it's true: Peng did interpret Trotsky's ideas "from a right-wing point of view."

Chen Duxiu agreed with Trotsky from a different angle. I mentioned earlier that the Chinese Communist Party followed a certain scheme in the revolution: Its leaders considered that China must first pass through "national revolution" before embarking on "socialist revolution." But there are two different ways of understanding this scheme. According to one, since China can carry out a national revolution, we should concentrate single-mindedly on doing so; for those who understand the scheme in this way, socialist revolution remains a vague idea that we need think about only after the achievement of national revolution. Others thought that since China must go through national revolution before it can carry out socialist revolution, we should go ahead and carry out national revolution but not forget that national revolution is merely a precondition for our revolution, that we're engaged in national revolution only for the sake of the future socialist revolution.

Actually, these two interpretations are not opposites but Stalinist twins, for both split the Chinese Revolution into two stages: Carry out first national revolution, then socialist revolution. But if we consider them more carefully, they differ in one regard: The latter can develop in the direction of the theory of permanent revolution if it jettisons the idea of two stages, whereas the former cannot. Chen Duxiu belonged to the latter tendency. For the sake of the future socialist revolution, he stressed the importance of the workers' and peasants' movement, even to the point of opposing the Northern Expedition and secretly proposing to the Comintern that the Chinese Communist Party withdraw from the Guomindang. But the Northern Expedition unexpectedly succeeded. Was not a revolution carried out by a trained standing army even more powerful than strikes and mass insurrections? So Chen Duxiu gradually switched from the latter to the former interpretation of national revolution. Only after the Wuhan debacle did he realize that revolution was impossible without the broad masses as its main force. Mercenaries, however steeled and trained, are in the long run unreliable. The ideas of the Left Opposition jibed with this new realization. As soon as Chen had accepted them, he wrote an essay opposing both the "Red Army" movement and the wholesale abandonment of the urban labor movement by Party organizations and members, who flocked to the villages to set up a "Red Army."

I know little about the Red Army's origins. Before the Fifth Congress, the only two leaders of the Chinese Communist Party who I knew merely by sight were Li Dazhao and Mao Zedong. Li Dazhao had always been based in Beijing. As for Mao, when I first got back to China, he was still in Shanghai, but he apparently held no office in the Party,[343] for I never saw him attend any of the Central Committee meetings. Not long after that, he returned to Hunan. He did not stay there long, and again, he apparently held no office in the Party. Later, I either read in a report from the Guangdong Regional Committee or heard from someone that Mao had become secretary of the Propaganda Department of the Central Committee of the Guomindang in Guangzhou and that his boss Wang Jingwei prized him highly; he also ran the Peasant Movement Training Institute in Guangzhou. In April 1927, I saw him at the Wuchang congress and gave him a letter from his younger brother, Mao Zemin. By coincidence, it was also at around the same time that I read his "Report on the Hunan Peasant Movement."[344] He was the first of the Party's main leaders to pay attention to the peasant movement.[345] He personally visited various counties in Hunan to investigate this movement firsthand. His booklet on the Hunan peasants was published without first going through the Central Committee's Propaganda Department, which in any case had not yet acquired the power of censorship. After the Fifth Congress, he was instructed to go to Hunan to take over from Li Weihan as provincial secretary, but he did not do so until after the Horse Night Incident, by which time the Party in Hunan had gone underground. When Tang Shengzhi returned to Hunan, the Provincial Committee assigned Party members to stick up posters "welcoming Commander in chief Tang, who has labored so hard and achieved so much!" The people sticking up the posters were seized and roundly beaten by Tang's troops. It was only after He Zishen protested to Mao about the slogan that he rescinded it. People were still hoping to rope in Tang against Xu Kexiang and He Jian![346]

After the Fifth Congress, I do not know what role Mao played in the Party's internal scheming. Needless to say, he was dissatisfied with Chen Duxiu, but he did not merge with Qu Qiubai, Zhang Guotao, or Tan Pingshan. He was independent: His views and proposals were different from those of the Party's other leaders. He once said that "power comes from the barrel of a gun." He scorned the Communist leaders of the labor movement and any movement unconnected to the gun. A founding member of the Party, he was unhappy and frustrated during the high tide of revolution and held merely a few unimportant posts. It was only when the revolution ebbed that he really came into his own, only when the means of struggle changed that he leaped to preeminence in the Party. This might appear odd at first sight, but actually, it is wholly in accordance with his character and views.

After July 15, when Zhang Tailei was about to hand over his job as Hubei provincial secretary, he reported to me on the intentions of various Party leaders, including Mao Zedong. "Runzhi[347] is planning to go to Sichuan to become a modern Shi Dakai,"[348] he told me. Mao attended the August 7 Conference and spoke, but I cannot remember what he said. As far as I remember, he did not say anything about going to Sichuan. That was the last time I saw him. He Zishen was close to him. The two of them worked together for a while in Hunan after the Horse Night Incident. They got on well together and were united by their common dislike for the former provincial secretary.[349] In late 1927 or early 1928, they were both in Shanghai. When Mao Zedong was about to go back to Hunan, He Zishen—who was aware of Mao's plans—gave him a copy of *Shuihu zhuan* (Water margin) punctuated by Wang Yuanfang[350] for the Oriental Book Company, together with post office maps of all the counties in Hunan. Mao treasured these gifts, especially the maps, which some comrades working for the post office had given to the Party. They were not available for sale and were hard to come by. They were much more detailed and reliable than other maps. They showed villages and small towns and the distances between places.

In Hunan, Mao unified the surviving armed forces of the peasant associations in the various counties and detached them from the villages, in order to keep them intact. This is one source of what later became the Red Army.

When Ye Ting and He Long staged their insurrection in Nanchang on August 1, a dispute was said to have arisen among the staff officers about what direction the insurrectionary army should take. Liu Bocheng proposed going to Hunan to "make land revolution," and the others wanted to go to Guangdong to seize Guangzhou, organize a government, swell their forces, and then launch a "second Northern Expedition." The latter view prevailed. Everyone knows the fate of the Ye-He army,[351] so there is no need to go into it here. But a small part of it, under Zhu De,[352] escaped destruction and roamed between the borders of Guangdong, Jiangxi, and Hunan. For a while, they joined up with Fan Shisheng's Guomindang troops,[353] but after that, they somehow merged with the troops that Mao had salvaged from Hunan's peasant forces.[354] This is how the nucleus of the Red Army was formed. It slowly grew in strength, and after numerous setbacks, it became what we now know as the Eighth Route Army and the New Fourth Army. But that's another story.

The Red Army was not a deliberate creation of the Central Committee or the Comintern. At first, the Central Committee had no interest in it, believing that it had no future. During the Li Lisan period, the Communist Party had not yet decided to abandon the big cities. But against all expectations, this tiny military nucleus managed to grow into an army, and Zhu and Mao assumed the mantle previously worn by Ye and He; at the same time, the Communist Party gradually found it impossible to keep up its work in the cities, so it switched its forces to the Red Army and pinned all its hopes on the Red Army. To the extent that it continued to work in the cities, it was simply to prepare the workers to respond to the Red Army, just as they had responded to the Northern Expedition in earlier years. By the time we accepted Trotsky's views, the whole Party had come around to this way of thinking. Whenever we discussed political questions with other comrades, we eventually came up against the same argument. Whatever the mistakes of the Central Committee and the Comintern, the one undeniable truth was that the Red Army was going from strength to strength. Since the Party was going to seize power through the Red Army, what was the point of a national assembly? In this way, Mao Zedong-ism came to dominate the whole Party. On one occasion, Xiang Zhongfa and Zhou Enlai went to talk to Chen Duxiu, just before the split. The conversation naturally got around to the Red Army.

"According to Marxism," said Chen, "should the cities control the villages, or the villages the cities?"

"It's obvious," Xiang blurted out, "the villages should control the cities!"

Zhou Enlai interrupted to correct him: "Theoretically, the cities should control the villages. However...."

We all thought that the idea of a Red Army was dangerous. We were afraid that as a result of it, the Party would abandon the real revolution and concentrate exclusively on military adventures, that it would abandon the proletariat and start representing the peasants or even bandits. At the time, we never imagined that the Party would degenerate to the point that it has now reached.

Chen Duxiu wrote a long essay opposing the Red Army campaign. It had a big impact. Needless to say, the Stalinist Central Committee was furious. The so-called Conciliationists, under the leadership of Xiang Ying and Luo Zhanglong, also thought that the Old Man was "in his dotage." When the other Oppositionists[355] wrote to Trotsky criticizing the "opportunist" Chen Duxiu for his essay on the Red Army, Trotsky wrote back to say that we should not completely oppose the Red Army, for in some ways it was an important and positive movement. Under attack from several sides, those of us who had at first agreed with Chen's article now began to doubt it. Yin Kuan said that it was "badly worded." Later, Chiang Kai-shek had many copies of the article reprinted and distributed in Jiangxi province.[356] Perhaps he smuggled some changes into it, I don't know. I don't have Chen's essay at hand, and I forget on what grounds he opposed the Red Army. But there can be no doubt that he talked about the need to stress the urban workers, to base the revolution on the power of the broad masses, and to accord military might a secondary role in seizing power. These are the lessons that Chen drew from the Wuhan defeat, and they were the basis on which he embraced Trotskyism.

In my own case, Trotsky's ideas took me back to positions I had adopted ten years earlier in France, when I had come out against joining the Guomindang. For me, Trotsky's ideas meant putting the Chinese Revolution on the same footing as revolutions in other countries rather than seeking differences between it and them or discovering "special national characteristics" that restricted the application of Marxism to China. When I first retreated from "socialist revolution" to "national revolution," I had found it necessary to divide my Marxism into two parts: one part that could simultaneously be applied to China, and another part that could be applied only to the West. But now, everything I had learned in the past suddenly came to life and was of immediate practical relevance. Apart from this, the two main questions that had haunted me during my period as editor of *Bolshevik*—"a rising or an ebbing tide?" and "a proletarian dictatorship or a workers' and peasants' democratic dictatorship?"—had finally been answered.

In discussions with fellow members of the Opposition or with other comrades, I paid special attention to the question of the nature of the revolution: bourgeois-democratic or proletarian-socialist. Cai Zhende and Ma Yufu did too. But Yin Kuan disagreed. He said: "Trotsky never stressed that question, he only said incidentally that the Chinese Revolution is proletarian in nature. If you insist on arguing about it, you run the risk of turning a debate about politics into a debate about metaphysics." The question Yin Kuan liked to emphasize was what should we promote, soviets or a national assembly? In those days, there was not much written about the nature of the revolution, and Trotsky said different things at different times. It was not until after Liu Renjing got back to China that we became acquainted with the several long and systematic essays that Trotsky had written in Alma-Ata. It was clear from those essays that the question of the nature of the revolution was not unimportant in Trotsky's thinking.

* * *

When Liu Renjing got back to China, he lived in a hostel in the French Concession, where Yin Kuan and I went to visit him. He spoke with us, and with supporters of the Central Committee, from an openly Oppositionist standpoint. He told us that Yun Daiying had been to see him and that he had told Yun that, in his view, the Party had become bureaucratized. Yun had denied this and told Liu that he was free to express his criticisms and that he, Yun, could guarantee that the Central Committee would discuss them.

"And if the Central Committee isn't prepared to let my criticisms be known?" Liu had asked.

"Then I would fight alongside you."

Liu Renjing also told us that he had been to Constantinople to see Trotsky on his way back to China. I set a time for Liu to meet Chen Duxiu at my place.

On our release from prison, Cai Zhende and I gave up the house on Hengfeng Alley and moved out our furniture and effects. We had nothing of any value. The only thing that had disappeared during our absence was a fur coat that Jing had brought with her to Shanghai from her parents' home. At first, we rented the rear part of a wing room on Wuchang Road, but two months later, Cai Zhende invited us to live with him in his newly rented house in Yuqing Alley, off East Youheng Road. That was where Liu Renjing came to see us. It became the headquarters of our section of the Opposition. At first, we used to gather there informally; later, we held official meetings there. There can be no doubt that the Central Committee heard about it. It adopted a policy of trying to win us over. Pan Wenyu, secretary of the Propaganda Department, came to visit me and very politely invited me to go back to work in his department; I refused to accept a fixed job but agreed to do some translating. Every few days I would deliver what I had done and fetch new material. They gave me forty dollars a month to live on. He Mengxiong came to see Cai Zhende and told Cai about a job at a news agency. The work was for only a few hours a day, but the pay was good. I translated documents for the Party and used my spare time to carry on with my translation of *Religion, Philosophy, and Socialism*; I had already completed some two-thirds before being arrested. The Public Security Bureau had sent the manuscript to Longhua along with the documents seized in the raid, but I got it back from the judge the day I was set free.

I asked many people to sell the manuscript for me, but to no avail. Eventually, Yang Xianjiang managed to sell it to the newly established Hubin Book Company. This company was managed by Ma Renzhi, who came from the same county as Peng Shuzhi. Not long after that, he joined the Opposition. Yang Xianjiang was our branch secretary at the time. Wang Zekai and I, who were both in his branch, repeatedly argued about basic questions of the Chinese Revolution with people delegated by the Jiangsu Provincial Committee to discuss them with us. Yang Xianjiang wavered between the two sides, so the branch never made a decision on these issues. Not long after that, Chen Duxiu, Peng Shuzhi, and Wang Zekai were expelled by the Central Committee. I didn't see the circular, so I do not know on what grounds they were expelled. Five or six comrades protested to the Central Committee about these expulsions; my name was among the protesters, though I did not know so at the time, nor did I know who was responsible for putting it there. The first thing I knew of the protest was when I turned up at the Central Committee's Propaganda Department and Pan Wenyu asked me why I had put my name to it. But I was not going to deny it.

"I have the right to protest," I said.

"Of course, you have the right to protest at any irregularities surrounding the expulsion, but first you should say that you agree politically with the Central Committee."

Now I knew that the protest was about procedures, not politics. "I don't agree politically, either," I said. "I've already raised it in my branch."

There had been no conclusion in our branch to the discussion of the political problems that Wang Zekai and I had raised. Although Wang had been expelled, I was still a member of the branch, and I demanded an answer from the Party leaders. Eventually, Wang Kequan, secretary of the Provincial Committee, came to the branch with Li Chuli, who made a transcript of my comments. After I had systematically explained my political opinions, I once again protested the procedural irregularities surrounding the expulsion of Chen, Peng, and Wang Zekai. Wang Kequan simply said that he would answer me officially at a meeting to be held the following week, but Yang Xianjiang finally chose sides: He stood with the Central Committee and thought that the expulsions were right. I was surprised at his change in attitude, but not long afterward, I discovered that before the meeting, he had been put under pressure and even intimidated. The following week, when Jing and I turned up at his place for the meeting, Yang Xianjiang cordially welcomed us and explained that the others probably had some other business that temporarily prevented them from attending. We took our leave after fixing a time for the following week, but a few days later, I learned that I too had been expelled. I never received formal notification of my expulsion, nor did I see any notice of it in *Hongqi bao* (Red flag),[357] but I heard from others that I had been charged with inciting the newspaper workers' branch and the Yunnan delegate (sent to Shanghai to make a report) to oppose the Central Committee.

And it was true. Under the influence of Ma Yufu and Cai Zhende, several branches—together with individuals such as Luo Shifan and Xue Nongshan—went over to the Opposition, among them the newspaper branch. The branch secretary was Tu Yangzhi, a typesetter for *New Current Events*; Tu, along with a number of other workers' leaders, had followed Ma Yufu. Our people elected me to represent the Opposition point of view at branch meetings. We met several times. The entire branch supported the Opposition. No one spoke up for the Central Committee. But someone told the Central Committee about our activities, so the branch was disbanded and Tu Yangzhi was expelled. I forget the name of the Yunnan delegate. I spoke with him once at Liu Shaoyou's place. I do not know whether it was this person or Chen Jiru (the wife of Liu Shaoyou) who reported my activities to the Central

Committee or the Provincial Committee; whatever the case, I had been exposed. Those of us who had been expelled refused to recognize the validity of the decision and still considered ourselves members of the Chinese Communist Party; the new organization we set up was not a second Party but an internal faction—the Chinese Communist Party's Left Opposition. Chen Duxiu, father of the Chinese Communist Party, was with us. Trotsky, the second great leader of the October Revolution, was with us too. And if Lenin had still been alive, so would he have been. His widow, Krupskaya, told people: "If Lenin had not died, Stalin would have thrown him in prison!"

The struggle was worldwide. There was scarcely a section of the Third International that did not split. Left Oppositions were formed in almost all of them. These Oppositions elected leaderships, issued journals, and tried to promote international unity. The International Left Opposition, forerunner to the Fourth International, was also formed.

Had the struggle been confined to China, things would have been completely different. We would not have so readily abandoned the Comintern and the Party, and the Central Committee would not have dared to expel us without further ado. Our expulsion was ordered by the Comintern; it was not simply a decision of the Central Committee.

During the struggle, many honest revolutionaries were worried that the two sides would grow further and further apart. Even though they may not have agreed with us, they opposed our expulsion. But since the instruction to expel us had come from the International, there was nothing they could do about it. They did not even dare protest. I know of only three comrades who, under special circumstances, spoke out on this question. In the autumn of 1929, Peng Pai, Yang Yin, and Yan Changyi[358] were arrested. Peng and Yang I knew only by sight; Yan was a good friend of mine. These three fair-minded comrades hated all plots and schemes in the Party. On one occasion, when I had gone to the Propaganda Department to fetch or hand over some materials, Pan Wenyu showed me a message that those three had smuggled out from Longhua Prison. In it, they said that although they were doomed, they wanted to use what time remained to make propaganda for the revolution in prison; as for the Party itself, they hoped that the Central Committee would be able to resolve the present internal disputes by peaceful means. Such was the last testament of these three important leaders, but no one heeded their advice.

In those days, Zhou Enlai was the most influential figure in the Party. He was head of the Organization Department and director of the Military Commission, and organizationally responsible for our expulsion.

The Chinese Left Opposition had already been in existence in an organized way for quite some time; it was around even while we were still drowning in the Stalinist swamp. This organization had its origins in Sun Yat-sen

University in Moscow, where it already had a glorious history of struggle. I hope that at some future date, those qualified to tell the story will do so.[359] In late 1928 or early 1929, Left Oppositionist students returning from Moscow formally set up an organization in China and started publishing a journal called *Our Word*. Gradually, people who had never been abroad began to join. This organization was distributing the documents we had seen. Although we had accepted Trotsky's ideas, we were by no means satisfied with this Our Word Society. Perhaps Yin Kuan, Peng Shuzhi, and the rest had other reasons to be dissatisfied with it—for example, because it was led by people without experience and ability or by people who were not prepared to subordinate themselves to one another—but I had only one reason, namely, *Our Word* claimed that the revolution in China was still in spate or already on its way up after a period of ebb. After reading Trotsky and then reading the articles in *Our Word*, it seemed to me that these self-styled "Trotskyists" had completely failed to understand what Trotsky meant.

When Liu Renjing, on his way back to China via Western Europe, stopped off in Turkey to visit Trotsky, Trotsky asked him to be his China correspondent, so Liu went around claiming that he was "Old Trotsky's representative" and was unwilling to submit to the existing Opposition's discipline. He brought together a number of Oppositionists outside the existing Oppositionist organization and put out a journal called *Shiyue* (October). But Liu Renjing was unable to control the October Society. Chen Duxiu or Yin Kuan told me that Liu Renjing was nothing more than an isolated figurehead and that the guiding spirit behind the October Society was Wang Wenyuan,[360] a student who had returned from Moscow. This story reminded me of something Ma Renzhi had once said. The Hubin Book Company had published a Chinese edition of Plekhanov's *From Idealism to Materialism*. When I asked Ma who had translated it, he said that it was a "kid" just back from Moscow, who was very bright and very able. Not long afterward, Liu Renjing was kicked out of the October Society, but he still claimed to be "Old Trotsky's representative" and even issued his own journal called *Mingtian* (Tomorrow).

Apart from these two Oppositionist organizations, there were a few undecided people such as Liu Yin, Zhao Ji, and Wang Pingyi. They too decided to put out a journal. While discussing what to call it, they remembered that the magazine (regularly mailed to China) published by the American Left Opposition was called the *Militant*, so they decided to call their journal *Zhandou* (Combat), though *Zhanshi* would have been a better translation. The Combat Society had no distinctive and consistent political position that I need mention here.

Apart from these three organizations, there were still some people working in the official Party, including some in positions of responsibility. They had

had no organizational ties to the Opposition in Moscow, but now that they were back in China, they gradually began to declare themselves for the Opposition. They included Wu Jiyan and Tu Qingqi.

Although those of us who had been expelled from the official Party as "opportunists" agreed with Trotsky, in the eyes of the Oppositionists who had returned from Moscow, we still did not count as part of the Left Opposition; they too denounced us as "opportunists." They may have welcomed our rank-and-file supporters, but they opposed our leaders, especially Chen Duxiu. When Liu Renjing wrote to Trotsky, telling him about this attitude, Trotsky wrote back to correct it. He said that the line Chen Duxiu had followed in the past was not his own but the Comintern's, that Chen himself was a good revolutionary, and that young people should learn from him. Trotsky proposed that representatives of the four societies form a joint "Negotiating Committee" to unify the societies. So the other three societies had no choice but to consider us part of the Left Opposition.

By that time, we already had an official organization that had grouped together several branches and elected a Standing Committee. Chen Duxiu was naturally general secretary, and the other members of the Standing Committee were Peng Shuzhi, Yin Kuan, Ma Yufu, and Luo Shifan; the secretariat was headed first by Wu Jiyan and later by He Zishen. We issued a manifesto titled "Our Political Views" that was signed by more than eighty people, including some worker comrades using false names. We also published a journal. While we were discussing what to call it, I proposed the name *Wuchanjieji geming* (Proletarian revolution), and everyone agreed, but for some reason, it later got called *Wuchanzhe* (Proletarian). The first two issues were set in lead type; after that, it was mimeographed.

The process of negotiations was extremely protracted, complicated, muddled, and a waste of time. The different organizations looked upon one another not as comrades but as enemies and fought one another with diplomatic tricks. Meanwhile, struggles also broke out within the Proletarian Society and the Our Word Society, which were the two biggest organizations.[361] Wu Jiyan, one of the Proletarian Society delegates, told me jokingly, "These tricks will come in handy in any future parliament." I was not the slightest bit interested in such disputes; secretly, I despised them. Nor was I interested in the controversies about points of principle, for they were all tied up in one way or another with organizational squabbles and were artificially raised to serve organizational ends. I barely paid the slightest attention to the "negotiations"; I buried myself, instead, in translating salable Marxist texts. I finally decided to throw myself into the factional vortex only after the Proletarian Society split into two clearly differentiated wings.

The Proletarian Society's first representatives on the Negotiating Committee were Ma Yufu and Wu Jiyan. They reported that the members of the three other societies had no intention of uniting, and I believed them. I did not know a single person in any of the other three societies. Since they had not previously recognized us as Oppositionists and were negotiating only because Trotsky had told them to, I thought that it was only natural for them to be against unification; as for us, I thought that unification was necessary, and the others thought the same. What's more, He Zishen told me that the tiny base we had salvaged from the old Party was rapidly crumbling, and that if we did not unite soon, our organization would become an empty shell. Chen Duxiu, too, was very worried. I knew that he was most anxious to achieve a united organization. After Trotsky's letter, the October Society and the Our Word Society sent representatives to meet him. He bared his feelings to me.

"These young people are like the young people I came into contact with at the time of May Fourth and May Thirtieth," he told me. "They're full of youthful vigor and vitality."

In one sense, this was an admission of his disappointment with the old cadres. Having been through one revolution, they had lost heart and lapsed into apathy. I, too, was dissatisfied with them, and also with myself; I looked to the new comrades for salvation, and I hoped that they would shake me from my lethargy. But finally, I discovered that the main reason for the lack of progress toward unity lay in the bad faith not of the other three societies but of the representatives of our own Proletarian Society. Ma Yufu and Wu Jiyan were tightly controlled by Peng Shuzhi, who was the chief obstacle to unity.

Chen Duxiu all along despised organizational plots. You need only look at his attitude in the official Party from the Wuhan period through the time of the Sixth Congress to know that. But the same was not true of Peng Shuzhi. He craved to be a leader. I have already described how he climbed into the leadership not because large numbers of people supported him but through organizational maneuvers. He had created and maintained his leadership position among the twenty or thirty Chinese students in Moscow by those famous "Moscow branch" training methods. After getting back to China, he was looked upon as a representative sent to China by the Comintern. In that capacity, he joined its presidium and gained the confidence of Chen Duxiu. Later, he tightly latched onto Chen in order to make himself more important. "The Old Man's views are identical with mine," he would say. In one period, between his coming out of the hospital in 1925 and Qu Qiubai's attack on him in 1927, he was even crazy enough to believe that except for Chen Duxiu, he constituted the leadership of the Chinese Communist Party. Cai Hesen was then in Moscow, and there were only four people on the presidium.

"Qu Qiubai is a higher technician,[362] Zhang Guotao is a higher administrator," he used to say.

But to tell the truth, Cai, Qu, and Zhang (not to mention Chen Duxiu) were all far more able than Peng, who was the least distinguished of the five-member presidium. After going to Wuhan, he was easily toppled. Even Wang Ruofei and Chen Qiaonian, who were trying to build a nucleus in the Party and to resist the anti–Chen Duxiu campaign within it, had no good feelings toward Peng. After his downfall, Peng clung even more tightly to Chen Duxiu. When Yin Kuan wanted to talk with Chen after getting hold of the Oppositionist documents, he had to go through Peng,[363] who remained in attendance every time the two men met. Peng's only hope of getting back into the leadership was by relying on Chen Duxiu.

When the question of unifying the four societies came up, what concerned us most was whether or not our political views were identical in principle. What animated Peng and the people under his influence, however, was the question of how to unite. The Our Word Society considered itself to be the orthodox Opposition in China. Before the arrival of Trotsky's letter advocating negotiations, the Our Word Society permitted the "converted opportunists" to enter their organization only singly and reserved the right to accept or reject them. Apart from this procedure, there could be no other form of "unity" for them. Peng Shuzhi could not even bear to hear of this method of selection. After the arrival of Trotsky's letter, the Our Word Society's status fell to the same level as that of the other three societies; the aim now was to unite in a new organization—there could no longer be any talk of orthodoxy or unorthodoxy. But Peng Shuzhi opposed this approach as well. The real reason he slighted and mistrusted the other organizations was that he knew that most of the young people in them had no good feelings toward him and that he was unlikely to become a leader of the new organization. He dared not openly express his view that the Proletarian Society was the orthodox Opposition, so his only alternative was to sabotage the talks.

It was a long time before we realized this fact. Although Yin Kuan was not a delegate to the talks, he knew a large number of people in the other three societies and often got together with them. So he found out that what our delegates were telling us was not true, and that Peng Shuzhi was staunchly opposed to unity. On one occasion, Yin managed to meet Chen Duxiu independently of Peng (no easy matter) and arranged for Chen to go to his home for a discussion. He told Chen what he had found out. Chen was thoroughly awakened. At a meeting of the Standing Committee, he proposed recalling Ma Yufu and Wu Jiyan as delegates to the talks and replacing them with him and Yin Kuan as the Proletarian group's delegates. After that, the talks went smoothly.

As soon as Chen Duxiu awoke, he immediately split from Peng Shuzhi and even ceased being friends with him. Chen was a man of strong feelings. He easily trusted people and easily overestimated the value of those he trusted, but if he was ever disappointed, he quickly went to the opposite extreme. Now he hated Peng in the same way he had once trusted him: to excess. He Zishen once said of Peng that he was a paper tiger, all teeth and claws, but easy to punch holes in.

"He is not a paper tiger," replied Chen Duxiu, "he's a rotten watermelon. Paper tigers are full of air. Rotten melons are pretty on the outside but stink like hell if you burst them open." After that, every time the Standing Committee of the Proletarian Society met, there was inevitably a row, and a violent one at that. Chen Duxiu, Yin Kuan, and He Zishen were in favor of unity, and Peng Shuzhi and Ma Yufu were against it; I cannot say for certain what Luo Shifan thought. Things carried on like this until unity was realized and the Proletarian Society's existence as a separate organization came to a natural end.

The split between these two old friends was final. After I went to prison the second time, Peng Shuzhi rose once more to become a leader and once again cooperated with Chen Duxiu, but there was no longer any friendship between them. After they were arrested and sent to prison together, they quarreled senselessly and interminably until their release. Chen Duxiu had no interest in discussing his and Peng's wrangles. When I met him after my release from prison, he never once mentioned Peng. Wang Wenyuan in Hankou once mentioned him to Chen. "Don't use that man's name in my presence," said Chen. Peng Shuzhi, in contrast, loved to talk about his prison clashes with Chen. In 1940, when I met him in Shanghai, he raised the subject many times. He even went so far as to malign Chen in the ugliest terms and tried to pass off his petty wrangles as part of a battle between Peng's correct political position and Chen's wrong one. When news of Chen's death[364] reached Shanghai, Peng wrote an essay to blacken him and a couplet in which he cursed him with the words "He lost his integrity in his later years."

Although most people on the Standing Committee of the Proletarian Society favored unification, those in the branches did not. The branches were made up partly of people that Cai Zhende and Ma Yufu had brought with them from the official Party in Shanghai, and partly of cadres who in the past had worked for the Party in Shanghai or elsewhere in the country; the latter supported Chen Duxiu, but most had to do so through Peng Shuzhi. By this time, Cai Zhende had become apathetic, and Peng and Ma were opposed to unification. None of the old cadres trusted Yin Kuan. Yin was intelligent and quicker off the mark than Peng, both as a thinker and as an activist, but he was a cynic. Actually, he was a harmless cynic, and cynical not so much in dealing with other people as in selling himself as a person of great intelligence. But whatever the case, this cynicism caused people to dislike him. Peng could easily present the question of whether or not to unify as a dispute between him and Yin and thus win support for his position.

In the several months that elapsed between the arrival of Trotsky's letter and the establishment of the Negotiating Committee, I stayed aloof from the various disputes. The Standing Committee of the Proletarian Society sent me as a representative of the east Shanghai district organization to discuss our merging with the east Shanghai district organization of the Our Word Society. I met with Shi Tang in a primary school. There I learned that he had worked as a typesetter in the printing factory that I had been responsible for running. He knew me, but I did not know him. In 1927, he had gone to study in Moscow, where he had joined the Opposition. After returning to China, he had taken on a responsible position in the Opposition. "Why did I never hear your name during all these arguments over the last few months?" he asked me. I cannot remember how I answered him, but after that, my name did start to crop up in the discussions, for I became a firm supporter of unification. Supporters of unification gradually came to predominate in the branches of the Proletarian Society. Among the delegates they elected to the Unification Congress were Chen Duxiu and me. Chen's election was a matter of course, as was Peng Shuzhi's and Ma Yufu's nonelection; it might seem strange that such a firm supporter of unification as Yin Kuan was not elected, but it goes to show that although people favored unification, they still opposed Yin and thought that he was using the unification issue as part of his vendetta against Peng. As for me, no one suspected that I harbored any personal ambition.

In the course of the negotiations, the Our Word Society also split. The Liang Ganqiao faction had its base in Guangdong, and the Ou Fang faction in Shanghai, where many people joined the Opposition. At the time, Ou Fang was in Caohejing Prison. The person who represented the Ou Fang faction at the Unification Congress was Song Jingxiu, who had joined in Shanghai.[365]

* * *

The Unification Congress of the Left Opposition of the Chinese Communist Party was held in a newly rented lane house on Dalian Bay Road.

The Negotiating Committee gave the job of finding a venue to the Proletarian Society, which gave it to He Zishen. We funded the congress with the help of Li Zhongsan's lynx-fur gown, which I pawned for more than two hundred dollars. He Zishen sent Wang Zhihuai's whole family to live as tenants in the house we rented. Wang, a worker, was also a Proletarian Society delegate. The other delegates gathered in groups of three or four and were then conducted to the house. Once you entered it, you were not allowed out again until after the congress had finished, three or four days later. The only exception was Chen Duxiu, who was allowed to go home after every session.

I forget how many delegates attended, but I do know that they included Chen Duxiu, Jiang Changshi, Jiang Zhendong, Wang Zhihuai, and me for the Proletarian Society;[366] Liang Ganqiao, Chen Yimou, Song Jingxiu, and four Hong Kong workers for the Our Word Society; Wang Wenyuan, Pu Dezhi, Song Fengchun, and Luo Han for the October Society; and Lai Yantang for the Combat Society. I had never met any of the delegates of the other three societies before, nor had I met Jiang Zhendong representing our own group.

The resolutions had all been drafted by the Negotiating Committee and agreed to by the main leaders of the four societies, most of whom were delegates, so there was virtually no debate. All I remember is that while we were discussing the political resolution, I stood up to speak and got into an argument. It was about the relationship between political stability and the national assembly. It was now 1931. Two years had passed since 1929. In the months leading up to the congress, the various societies had argued violently, both verbally and in writing. Everybody had made progress during these confrontations. *Our Word* was no longer claiming that the revolution was back in spate, and no one denied that the Guomindang had already achieved political stability. But could it be maintained? Yes, and for quite a long time—that was what I believed. In my view, it was precisely because of this political stability that we must call for a national assembly. But others, including Liang Ganqiao and Song Fengchun, criticized my way of thinking, though I forget on what grounds.

The final session of the congress was given over to elections. Some people were especially interested in this procedure, since more often than not, it is the reason they attend congresses. I forget how many Central Committee members were chosen. Chen Duxiu and Wang Wenyuan got an equally high number of votes; every delegate voted for them. Of the other candidates, some got more votes, some less. Peng Shuzhi and Liang Ganqiao were last among the successful candidates, with the same number of votes, but in a runoff, Peng won. Liang's failure to get elected came as a surprise to many people. Later, Chen Yimou said that it was due to a misunderstanding. The Hong Kong workers had not realized that Liang Ganqiao and Liang Daci were one and the same person, so they had not voted for him.

Even after the Negotiating Committee had decided in favor of unification, Peng Shuzhi continued to oppose it. He said that "on behalf of the rank and file," he opposed "collusion by the high-ups."

"Others may represent the rank and file, but it's hardly seemly for Peng to claim to do so," was Chen Duxiu's comment.

Even so, people feared that he would stir up trouble.

"It's easy to settle," I told them. "Just guarantee him a seat on the Central Committee. Then he will be most unlikely to oppose anything."

Yin Kuan and He Zishen told me not to talk such nonsense. They accused me of having a simplistic view of politics and of Peng Shuzhi.

"Perhaps it's true that I don't understand politics," I said, "but I do understand Peng."

After the start of the congress on May 1, when Chen Duxiu was back at home, He Zishen handed him a long letter by Peng that criticized unification as "hypocritical" and "meaningless," to name just two of the adjectives Peng used. The letter also said, "I would rather die than recognize it." But Peng had not expected that he would be elected. At the first meeting of the new Central Committee, Chen Duxiu took out the letter, showed it around, and then asked Peng, "Do you still think unification is 'hypocritical,' 'meaningless,' and all the rest of it?" I can see Peng to this day, sitting on the side of the bed, blushing violently and completely speechless. Finally, I intervened to help him out of his embarrassment and save him the trouble of a reply. Later, He Zishen told me angrily that to tolerate evil is to abet it, and that I was politically irresolute. He thought that people like Peng should be completely crushed, and that the letter had been the best chance of doing so. "He has already suffered enough," I said. He Zishen now admitted that he had been wrong when he said that I had a simplistic view of Peng. But Yin Kuan never raised the matter again, so I do not know what he thought.

The first meeting of the Central Committee elected a Standing Committee made up of Chen Duxiu, Chen Yimou, Wang Wenyuan, Song Fengchun, and me. Chen Duxiu was general secretary, Chen Yimou was in charge of organization, I was in charge of propaganda, Wang took care of the Party journal, and Song was head of the secretariat.

Not long after that, just when we had begun our real work, our organization was uncovered, and the entire Standing Committee, apart from Chen Duxiu, was arrested. So I went to prison a second time. This time was less pleasant than the first, two years earlier. The first spell had lasted forty days; the second lasted six years and three months. I was freed only when the reactionary Guomindang government was preparing to abandon its capital at Nanjing under the bombardment of the Japanese imperialists.

A Self-Description at the Age of Ninety

My name is Zheng Chaolin. I was born in 1901, so according to the old Chinese way of counting, this year I am ninety.

I was born in Zhangping, a small mountainous county in the south of Fujian province. My family was an old, established landlord family already in decline, but it still maintained the ancient trappings of culture and education. When I was a child, a "foreign-style school" had already started up in my hometown, but I acquired my schooling at the old-style private academy until I entered the graduating class of the foreign-style school to get my certificate of primary education. I graduated under the old-style middle school system, that is, after a course in traditional Chinese culture lasting only four years.

I graduated from middle school in the same year that the May Fourth Movement broke out. In our small county high up in the mountains, we heard only about the student movement to boycott Japanese goods and knew nothing about the "new culture movement."

In the spring of that year, while I was preparing to take my graduation exams, some Guomindang troops under Chen Jiongming invaded Fujian from Guangdong and occupied the southern corner of the province, including my hometown. Chen Jiongming ordered each county under his control to select two students to go to France under the work-study scheme. Each student would get an annual subsidy of three hundred dollars from his local authority. That is how I ended up in France. Those who went from Fujian were work-study students like the rest of the Chinese in France; the only difference was that they received these local subsidies.

I experienced my "new culture movement" on the boat from China to France. The first time I saw *New Youth* and found out about the "new culture movement" was on board the boat. Only then did I go through the struggle between the old culture in which I had received my schooling and the new culture that I learned about at sea.

In France, I got close to the progressive students in the work-study program.

I studied with them, I struggled with them, and together with them, I organized the "Communist Youth Party" and embarked on the road of revolution.

In 1923, the Communist Youth Party chose its first group of members—twelve people in all, including me—to go to study at the Communist University for the Toilers of the East in Moscow. In the summer of 1924, the Moscow branch of the Chinese Communist Party chose its second group of students to send back to China. I was among them.

As soon as I got back to Shanghai, I was sent to work as secretary in the Party's newly formed Propaganda Department. My job was to write, translate, edit, and publish the Central Committee organ and its various publications and, at the same time, to teach "sociology" (i.e., historical materialism) at Shanghai University. I participated in the May Thirtieth Movement and in Shanghai's second and third workers' insurrections.

In the spring of 1927, when the Central Committee moved to Wuhan, I went too and took part in the Fifth Congress there. After the congress, I was assigned to the Hubei Provincial Committee to take charge of its Propaganda Department. I experienced the defeat of the revolution and attended the August 7 Conference. After that, I returned to do propaganda work in the Central Committee. In late September, the Central Committee moved back to Shanghai and so did I, to take charge of the Central Committee's Publishing Bureau and to edit *Bolshevik*. In the summer of 1928, I was sent to Xiamen to sort out organizational work in the Fujian Provincial Committee. In late September, I returned to Shanghai to continue editing *Bolshevik*.

At the end of 1928, I resigned from *Bolshevik* and from various other propaganda tasks because of differences of opinion with Li Lisan, who was then in charge of the Central Committee's propaganda work. After that, I had nothing to do but wait for the Central Committee to assign me new work.

This period marked the end of the first stage of my work in the Party. During it, my main activity was literary propaganda, though I also did some oral propaganda, teaching, and organizing. Everything I did was in line with the Central Committee's policy; that, in turn, was based on the line set for China by the Communist International, which one was not allowed to doubt. So during this stage, I scarcely needed to do any thinking of my own about basic questions of policy. After the August 7 Conference, I began to question the line of the Communist International and to disagree with some of the Central Committee's policies, but whenever I made propaganda outside the Party, I stuck to its line.

Factions had already started fighting one another inside the Party. The main struggle was between the Chen Duxiu supporters around Wang Ruofei and the Central Committee faction of Comintern loyalists around Qu Qiubai; the General Labor Union faction, previously under Zhang Guotao and now under Luo Zhanglong, vacillated between these two groups. I personally inclined, for ideological and historical reasons, toward the Chen Duxiu group.

While editing *Bolshevik*, I went through the motions of propagating the policies of the Central Committee, but gradually, I exposed my own thinking. Because the revolution had been defeated, I could not help but ponder certain fundamental questions of the Chinese Revolution, and in the course of this thinking, I gradually began to doubt the Comintern's position on the Chinese Revolution, both past and future. In the articles I wrote, I consciously or unconsciously betrayed my own ideas. The clearest instance of this was an unsigned editorial I wrote for the eleventh issue of *Bolshevik*, after the defeat of the Guangzhou insurrection, in which I clearly proposed that the Chinese Revolution had no choice but to institute a dictatorship of the proletariat, even though the Central Committee was proposing a democratic dictatorship of workers and peasants, in accordance with the Comintern line. The Central Committee then got Qu Qiubai to write another unsigned editorial for the fourteenth issue of *Bolshevik*, correcting my previous editorial. But I had only just begun to develop my own ideas, which had not yet grown into a systematic vision of the Chinese and world revolutions.

After I withdrew from the Central Committee's Propaganda Department in early 1929, I continued my independent reflections. It was then that I was first arrested. I had already married, and my wife, Liu Jingzhen—from Kunming and a member of the Communist Party—worked with me on *Bolshevik* and left the Central Propaganda Department with me. We lived with other comrades in a Party building. When one of our number was arrested, the others were implicated and seized. Through the intercession of the Central Committee, those of us who had been drawn into the incident were bailed out after spending forty-odd days at Longhua garrison headquarters.

Not long after that, we Chen Duxiu supporters set eyes for the first time on documents of the Soviet Trotskyist Opposition. We discussed them among ourselves and with Chen Duxiu; finally, we accepted Trotsky's proposals for the Chinese Revolution and for the world revolution. After that, we Chen Duxiu supporters and Chen Duxiu himself became Trotskyists and joined the international Trotskyist organization. This was a big event in my political life. It was of no less consequence than organizing the Communist Youth Party in 1922.

On May 1, 1931, I was a delegate at the Chinese Trotskyists' Unification Congress and was elected to its Central Committee and put in charge of its Propaganda Department. Before three weeks had passed, our leadership was uncovered by the Guomindang, after we had been betrayed from within. The majority of the Central Committee members were arrested. I was among them and was described as the ringleader. The death sentence was said to have been passed on me, but as a result of personnel changes in the Guomindang government, there was a new appointment to the Shanghai garrison, and my death sentence was commuted to fifteen years. The Central Committee members who had escaped arrest, among them Chen Duxiu, restored the leadership and carried on the struggle, but in October 1932, they too were unearthed and arrested. In prison, I continued to reflect independently on basic questions of the revolution and on other political questions.

Those of us arrested by the Guomindang during these two waves were not freed until late 1937, after the start of all-out war with Japan, the aerial bombing of Nanjing, and the Guomindang decision to move its capital east to Wuhan. After my release, I decided that because communications with Shanghai were broken, I would go for a while to southern Anhui to escape the turmoil, recover my health, and await the opportunity to return to Shanghai. I never guessed that I would spend three years in Anhui, that my son would be born there, and that my wife and I would earn our living as schoolteachers. Not until 1940 did we leave Anhui through Zhejiang and sail to Shanghai via Ningbo. Back in Shanghai, I joined the leadership of the Chinese Trotskyist organization. I also translated into Chinese Trotsky's *History of the Russian Revolution* (volumes 2 and 3).

There was a controversy in the Trotskyist leadership about what attitude to adopt toward the war against Japan. There were three different points of view: that the war itself had a progressive meaning, and we should support the Guomindang's resistance; that the war itself had a progressive meaning, and we should resist independently; and that the war was part of the Second World War, and we should prepare to carry out proletarian socialist revolution during it, like Lenin had during the First World War. I supported the third position. As a result of the dispute, the Chinese Trotskyists split.

During the dispute and the split, my group independently brought out a mimeographed journal that was at first nameless and was later officially published under the name *Guojizhuyizhe* (Internationalist). After the Japanese surrender, we started to bring out *Xin qi* (New banner), in lead type. I wrote numerous articles for the nameless publication, for *Internationalist*, and for *New Banner*. Apart from that, I also wrote some books: *Buduan geming lun ABC* (ABC of permanent revolution), *San ren xing* (Three travelers), and *Guojia zibenzhuyi lun* (On state capitalism). These articles and books are products of my second stage; that is, they represent conclusions I arrived at by using my own brain and reflecting independently. Unfortunately, today I am no longer in a position to gather together my writings of that period. I value them above the writings of my first period, which were written according to a set line and cost me no great effort. Since *New Youth* (later period), *Guide Weekly*, *Bolshevik*, and other publications are still available, my articles must have been preserved as well.

After "liberation," I had no wish to flee abroad. I had devoted my entire life to proletarian socialist revolution in the world and in China. I was fully aware that the Stalinist system could not tolerate the existence of the likes of me in this world—we had already learned that from the Moscow trials of the 1930s. But I still wanted to stay in China. Sure enough, three and a half years after the "liberation" of Shanghai, on December 22, 1952, "like a thunderclap the net fell," and all the Chinese Trotskyists were arrested. Again, I was singled out as the ringleader. Imagine—someone like me, who never sought the limelight, arrested three times and twice named as ringleader! This time, I (together with four others) was locked up for twenty-seven years (from December 22, 1952, to June 5, 1979). We were never sentenced and never even charged. Strange? People told us that there were not many prisoners like us, but there were a few.

Starting in 1964, I was allowed to express my opinions openly in prison, to write books, and to criticize current policies and theories. I was also allowed to form a study group with other prisoners arrested in connection with the same case. They were Trotskyists who, like me, had not yet been sentenced (at first there were three of us; then there were two). (In 1956, we had all been brought together to study, but at that time, there were as many as a dozen in a study group and the sessions never lasted long, so it was impossible to speak freely.) We studied so-called antirevisionist documents—the theoretical dispute between the Chinese and Soviet Communists. Afterward, we each had to write a "summary." Although no one told us "you may write whatever you like," I used the occasion to develop a comprehensive critique of the Stalinist system on the basis of the ideas that I had formed during my isolated prison reflections. I decided to disregard any possible consequences. Finally, I compiled my "study summaries" into a book of 85,000 characters, which I called *Ganbuzhuyi lun* (On cadreism).

In 1965, each of us got a set of Mao's *Selected Works* (volumes 1 to 4) and was told to study "Mao Zedong thought." Needless to say, after studying it, we were expected to write summaries. So I wrote another book, of 135,000 characters, called *Yuzhong du Mao Zedong xuanji* (Reading Mao Zedong's *Selected Works* in prison). Apart from this, after reading Stalin's *Problems of Leninism*, I wrote a book of criticism. I also wrote a great many articles on current affairs as reported in the press. During the Cultural Revolution, after the prison came under military administration, the army representative ordered all these political and nonpolitical writings to be confiscated and destroyed.

But the ideas that I developed in prison were indestructible. In 1972, the serious offenders in our case (including those not yet sentenced), having spent twenty years in prison, were no longer kept behind bars but released under strict supervision; in 1979, we were released from strict supervision and had our civil rights restored. At last, we were restored to freedom. I was co-opted onto the Shanghai Municipal People's Consultative Committee. But the Chinese Trotskyists arrested in December 1952 had still not been rehabilitated and were still categorized as "counterrevolutionaries." In 1988, the Soviet Union completely reversed the verdicts on the three great wrongs perpetrated by the Moscow show trials of the 1930s: the 1936 trial of the "Trotsky-Zinoviev anti-Soviet coalition," the 1937 Pyatkov-Radek trial, and the 1937 trial of Bukharin, Rykov, and others. In the same year, I wrote three letters to the Standing Committee of the Politburo of the Central Committee of the Chinese Communist Party demanding a reversal of the 1952 case against the Chinese Trotskyists, but like a stone dropping into the vast ocean, it disappeared without a ripple.

In the eleven years between the restoration of my civil rights in 1979 and now, I have written several articles and a number of books, and some of my letters are worth publishing and preserving. All in all, my output amounts to some 800,000 characters. These are the works of my third period. Like those of my second period, they are the product of independent reflection, but the conclusions are not wholly the same as those of my second period. Only a small proportion of them has been published; the overwhelming majority have been copied or photocopied and circulated among a small number of readers.

During this third period, three books of mine have been published in China, but none of them was written in this period. One is my book of memoirs, written in the second half of 1944, during my second period. The manuscript, taken as evidence of my "counterrevolutionary crimes," followed me into prison. After my civil rights were restored, it too became Party history material and was circulated internally, in an edition printed by the state publishers. The supplement, on Chen Duxiu and the Trotskyists, was newly written in 1980. The second book is *Yu Yin canji* (Surviving poems of Yu Yin), which contains the remnants of the poems I wrote in prison. The third is my translation of Merezhkovsky's *Resurrection of the Gods*, a novel that was published in the 1940s. As for what I have written in the last eleven years, I have no idea when it can be published.

It is a matter for rejoicing that now as I celebrate my ninetieth birthday, important events are taking place in the world that show who was right and who was wrong in the greatest debate of the century. I mean the great debate about whether socialism can be built in a single country.

In early 1924, Lenin died. In the autumn of that year, the contours of the internal struggle in the Soviet Communist Party gradually became visible. It was not a debate about styles of work but a difference of opinion about what basic line to follow. Stalin proposed the theory that socialism can be built in a single country. This theory was incompatible with the Marxist tradition and also with what Stalin himself had written in early 1924 in the

Foundations of Leninism. Old Bolsheviks like Zinoviev and Kamenev, who had previously sided with Stalin against Trotsky, gradually left Stalin and began to ally with Trotsky. The united Opposition upheld the old view that socialism is possible only within the framework of world revolution, and it opposed the Stalinists.

For sixty years now, Stalin and the Stalinists have used the reality of the Soviet Union, and later the reality of the "socialist states" of Eastern Europe and elsewhere, to prove that socialism can indeed be built in one or a few relatively backward countries. But what do the events of last year and this year in those countries show?

Seventy years ago, when I was around twenty, the Socialist or Social Democratic Parties in various countries changed their names and became Communist Parties (though, naturally, some did not change and continued to maintain their old positions). But this year and last year, we have seen the opposite happen: Communist Parties in various countries have changed their names to Socialist or Social Democratic Parties (though, naturally, some have not changed and continue to maintain their old positions).

Seventy years ago, one process took place; now the opposite process has taken place. What does this fact signify? Most say that it is an expression of the bankruptcy of socialism. But that is wrong. It is merely an expression of the bankruptcy of Stalinism, of the doctrine of socialism in one country. We Trotskyists are the only ones who have dared—and with justification—to reach this conclusion, for we alone have maintained that socialism cannot be built in one or a few countries. We have never conceded that the system realized in the Soviet Union or the other "socialist states" is socialist. Socialism cannot be built in a single country.

The greatest dispute in twentieth-century history, which has been going on now for almost seventy years, has finally been settled: Trotsky was right, Stalin was wrong.

It is good that I lived to the age of ninety to see the end of this dispute. Will I live long enough to see the outbreak of the second high tide of world revolution?

May 1, 1990

12

A Brief Account of My Third Spell in Prison

Question: Would you please tell me about the case against the Trotskyists in 1952?
Answer: In my *Memoirs*, I wrote a chapter titled "My First Spell in Prison"; I drafted another chapter titled "My Second Spell in Prison," but I never actually wrote it, and now it's unlikely that I ever will. If I had the chance and the opportunity to work further on my *Memoirs*, they would naturally include a chapter devoted to my third spell in prison, but I'm afraid that's impossible, for even if I had the chance and the opportunity, my great age and [lack of] energy would prevent me from doing so. However, since you are kind enough to ask, I will do my best to sum up in a few thousand words what happened in the course of those twenty-seven years.[367]

* * *

The case went down in history as the movement to "purge Trotskyism." The case was prepared over a long period of time, with great thoroughness, and was executed most successfully. Later, the official in charge of the case, who was extremely proud of himself, told me, "With the suddenness of a thunderbolt we netted you up in one fell swoop and invited you to this place." I still remember to this day his choice of words. Actually, I knew in advance about the raid, but there was no way I could escape; I had no choice but to let things take their course. I never imagined that they would take our case so seriously, "using so many human, financial, and material resources." (Again, I'm quoting the official in charge of our case.)

Just after ten o'clock at night on December 22, 1952, I was seized on my way home and taken directly to be locked up in No. 1 Detention Center. No one asked me any questions. I was simply placed in an empty cell on the second floor; a card bearing my name had already been attached to the cell door. The cell was some sixteen square meters large and could have housed a dozen or so people, but I was its only occupant. I asked myself whether only I had been arrested, or whether the entire group had been rounded up. Surely my wife had not been arrested too?

The next day, no one came to question me, nor the next day nor the next, right through until the new year. But in the meantime, my question had been answered. On the third or fourth day after my arrest, I suddenly heard many people on the floors above and below me singing the *Internationale*. At first, I thought it was the prison guards, but when the singing finished, people started shouting slogans. Then I heard cell doors opening and large numbers of people being taken away. Only then did it dawn on me that those who were singing and shouting were our people. It later came to light that a large group of comrades had been arrested.[368] But it was all over. I could no longer join in the singing and shouting, in solidarity with them.

I could understand them arresting just me, or arresting a few of us, but I was unprepared for arrests on such a scale. The entire organization was finished; our movement of twenty-odd years was at an end.[369] Nevertheless, the case would be easier to fight. I could tell the whole truth, and not just part of it. I would need to hide nothing.

So on January 31, 1953, twelve days after my arrest, when I was first fetched for interrogation, I promptly admitted to being "Zheng Chaolin" and expressed my willingness to submit to questioning, to provide answers, and to write to my fellow detainees urging them to abandon their boycott.

I was then interrogated for several days in succession. I gave them information that they already knew or could easily discover. But I kept one piece of knowledge back. It seemed to me that they were unlikely to know where the Trotskyist archives were being stored. We had sorted everything into two wooden boxes and hidden them in a place known to only a handful of people. The interrogation was exceedingly hostile. Normally, there would be two interrogators, but on this occasion, there was only one person present in the room, with another outside, listening through the hatch in the cell door. The interrogator wanted me to tell him about the entire structure of our organization, its entire membership, and all our archives. He particularly emphasized the word "archives"; I pricked up my ears. "I've already told you everything," I replied. He went on with his questions. One question in particular alarmed me. (I can no longer remember exactly what the question was.) If they had not yet found the two secret boxes containing our archives, he would have been unlikely to raise this question. It was clear to me that they had unearthed our two boxes, so I told him of their hiding place. The air of tension immediately dissipated, the man behind the desk smiled, and the other man at the cell door came in and offered me his congratulations. "If you had not told us this," he said, "we would have interrogated you no further." (That was a coded way of saying that I would have been executed immediately.)

One evening following this experience, I was again summoned for interrogation. However, I was taken not to the interrogation chamber but to one of the offices in the detention center. I sat down on a sofa. Three or four other people sat on chairs beside a table. The conversation was informal and relaxed. It was during this meeting that the official I quoted earlier made his comments. The official asked me, "What do you think of this case?" I replied, "It's simply a political difference between us and you." After I said that, they all burst out laughing—real laughter, not feigned laughter.

After many years of propaganda and education, they considered Trotskyists to be even greater "war criminals" than the "war criminals," and even more "counterrevolutionary" than the "counterrevolutionaries." It was just as Wang Ming and Kang Sheng had said: "We can cooperate with the special agents of the Guomindang, but not with the Trotskyists." So it was hardly surprising that my answer roused them to such hilarity. Later, in the course of interrogations or conversations, they often mocked me on account of that comment, but I stuck to the truth of it. Such was my conviction during my twenty-seven years in prison; such, too, is my conviction now that I have been restored to freedom.

Today, most people see the Trotskyists as "political dissidents." Even within the Chinese Communist Party, more and more people are of that opinion. In the new annotation to the second edition of Mao Zedong's *Xuanji* (Selected works) published a year ago, this point of view found formal expression.

According to note 33 on page 168 of volume 1, "The Chinese Trotskyists considered that the Chinese bourgeoisie had already vanquished imperialism and the feudal forces, that the Chinese bourgeois-democratic revolution had already been concluded, that the Chinese proletariat had no choice but to wait until some future date to carry out socialist revolution, and that for the time being, it could simply wage a legal struggle around the call for a 'national [i.e., constituent] assembly.'" Whether or not this note can be regarded as accurate, the reference in the original annotation to Stalin's description of the Trotskyists as "a gang without principles and without ideas, of wreckers and diversionists, intelligence service agents, spies, murderers, a gang of sworn enemies of the working class, working in the pay of the intelligence services of foreign states" had been completely excised. The new annotation simply made the point that the Trotskyists had different political ideas.

Note 9 on page 516 of volume 2 says: "During the Anti-Japanese War of Resistance, in their propaganda the Trotskyists proposed resisting Japan, but they attacked the Chinese Communist Party's policy of an Anti-Japanese National United Front. The equation of the Trotskyists with national traitors was a product of the mistaken conclusion commonplace at the time in publications of the Communist International that the Chinese Trotskyists had links to Japanese imperialist intelligence organizations." This passage states even more clearly that the Chinese Trotskyists were not "national traitors"! During the war against Japan, the Chinese Communist Party and the Chinese Trotskyists were separated by mere political differences.

If my old interrogators read these two notes to the second edition of Mao Zedong's *Selected Works*, they should realize in retrospect that the answer I gave them at the time was by no means so ridiculous.

* * *

In 1955, when the case against the Trotskyists was concluded, the result was not a death sentence but prison sentences of life, fifteen years, twelve years, ten years, five years, or three years. The sentences were to be served in Shanghai's Tilanqiao Prison. I had not yet been sentenced and remained locked up in No. 1 Detention Center, in my lonely cell (though I was by now in a new, smaller cell).[370] I was no longer interrogated, and I was allowed to read *Jiefang ribao* (Liberation daily), although the copies I received were always several days old.

In 1956, I read in my newspaper that the Communist Party of the Soviet Union had held its Twentieth Congress. I was puzzled: Why, during the opening ceremonies, had the delegates not stood in silent tribute to Stalin (who I knew from the wireless had died in 1953)? Also, Mikoyan's speech showed that he was dissatisfied with Stalin.[371] In June 1957, I received some pamphlets along with my newspapers. I remember only that they included the text of a speech on intellectuals by Zhou Enlai.

On June 29, 1956, I was suddenly summoned to collect some things. I went down from the third floor to the second, where I met Yin Kuan, who had also been summoned. We sat side by side in a jeep and were driven out through the prison gate. No one had informed us of our destination, and we dared not ask, but we knew that we were not headed for the execution place. We ended up at Tilanqiao Prison. That day and the next, we saw people from far and wide who had been convicted in connection with our case and transferred [to Tilanqiao]. There were some forty of us in all; it turned out that we had been brought together for the purpose of studying [documents or books supplied by the officials]. We were divided into three small groups, and after a few days of studying, we were taken out on a series of trips [to see the achievements of the government]. After that, we again studied for a while, and at the end of our study, we wrote "summary reports." These events were not wholly without value, but it would take too many pages to write about them, so I prefer not to.

Our "summary reports" were submitted to higher levels. On August 11, those of us who had not been sentenced were sent back to the detention center. I imagined that we would be sent to No. 1 Detention Center, but instead, we ended up in No. 2 Detention Center, where the atmosphere was considerably more relaxed.

In No. 1 Detention Center, the guards had fetched our food, brought up our night-soil buckets, and cut our hair; we had been segregated not only from prisoners involved in our case but also from people involved in other cases and prisoners in penal servitude. In No. 2 Detention Center, I still had a cell to myself and did not participate in study groups, but I could observe other prisoners studying outside my cell and converse with my neighbors; I was even less segregated from prisoners in penal servitude. I was even allowed to go downstairs with other prisoners to "take air" in the open space.

Even more important, I had my own subscription to *Liberation Daily*: I could read the news every day, as it was reported. I was even allowed to buy pen, paper, and ink with which to comment on my reading, and to purchase publications advertised in my newspaper. I could do research.

After the Mid-Autumn Festival[372] in 1959, I was able to have contact with my wife. She came each month to visit me and to bring me things. She had received a sentence of ten years in prison but had been released early in 1957 for health reasons.

I spent six years in No. 2 Detention Center, during which time I went several times to Tilanqiao Prison for joint outings [with other Trotskyist prisoners]. We watched the contingents of paraders on People's Square, but after returning, I did not take part in the subsequent study sessions. The director, political instructors, and guards at No. 2 Detention Center were all very good to me and treated me politely. Had I ever received a sentence, I would have asked to serve it in No. 2 Detention Center rather than go to Tilanqiao Prison.

In October 1962, however, I was escorted to Tilanqiao. This time, it was not to join up with the other Trotskyist prisoners. I had to take all my clothes and belongings with me. The people escorting me told me that even my census register was being transferred to Tilanqiao. It turned out that after the end of "three years of natural disasters," the government thought that I was malnourished and decided to transfer me to a certain floor of Prison No. 5 to enjoy a "nutritious diet." At the place to which I was sent, there were already a dozen or so malnourished prisoners, but not one of them was a Trotskyist. I was still kept in a single cell and did not take part in the study sessions attended by the other prisoners. Each day, I received my newspaper. The "nutritious food" consisted of a few slices of pork two or three times a week with the midday meal, along with the usual diet of rice and vegetables. Gradually, pork appeared daily on our menu, and the number of prisoners on the nutritious diet doubled.

In Prison No. 5 (I was later transferred to Prison No. 3), where I spent a year and a half on the nutritious diet, I continued to do what I had done in No. 2 Detention Center—study phonology and grammar, translate foreign texts, and write poetry. Every month, I received food or other things sent by my wife; sometimes I was allowed to see and talk with her. Generally speaking, I was left alone [i.e., without interference], but the authorities did not treat me with the same regard as those in No. 2 Detention Center had.

* * *

In May 1964, the government took new measures regarding the Trotskyists. It concentrated in Shanghai those Trotskyist prisoners throughout China who were still serving their sentences; the Trotskyist prisoners scattered across Shanghai's various reform-through-labor groups and prisons were concentrated on the third floor of Prison No. 1. I, too, was taken there from Prison No. 3. This time, the transfer was not temporary but permanent; the aim was to "reform" us more effectively.

Those of us who were brought together on the third floor of Prison No. 1 included four prisoners whose sentences had not yet been settled (Yin Kuan, Yu Shouyi,[373] Huang Jiantong, and me), eight who had been given life sentences, three who had been given fifteen years, and four who had been given ten years (those who had been sentenced to less than ten years had already left prison). Apart from these people, there was still a woman prisoner who had been sentenced to twelve years and had not yet participated in any study groups;[374] Du Weizhi[375] did not participate in study groups because he had been transferred to Beijing after his arrest.

Those whose sentences had not yet been settled were still kept apart from the rest. The fifteen prisoners who had already received their sentences were kept on the third floor of the west wing and were formed into a study group. They lived three to a cell, whereas I still had a cell to myself. We could see these people only during exercise periods. But they were at the front of the exercising column and we were at the rear, so we were not able to have any actual contact with them.

What did we study? We studied "antirevisionist documents." The contradiction between the Soviet and the Chinese Communist Parties had become public knowledge. The Central Committee of the Communist Party of the Soviet Union had published an "open letter" to all Party comrades, and the Chinese Communist Party had publicly criticized this open letter. The criticism had gradually escalated into open ideological warfare. (The extreme criticism had been made public when we were gathered together in one place for the purposes of joint study.)

I decided at this study session to explain without any attempt at concealment the systematic views that I had developed over my previous few years of reflection. All that was expected of us was that we "study"; no one ever explained to us that we were free to "speak our minds" (i.e., that even if we said the wrong things, we would not be found guilty). However, I demanded no such guarantee; I intended to speak out freely, just as we had done when we edited *Guojizhuyizhe* (Internationalist) and *Xinqi* (New banner).[376] I paid no attention whatsoever to any possible consequences of my action.

Those of us in the small group of prisoners who had not yet been sentenced paid a visit to Shanghai municipality after nine preparatory meetings. During that visit, the two small groups [those who had been sentenced and those who had not yet been sentenced] could not avoid contact with each other. As a result of this contact, I learned for the first time that we Trotskyist prisoners in Tilanqiao Prison were in a different position from that of other prisoners: Not only could we be locked up together and formed into one study group, but one of the guards inadvertently let slip that we were enjoying something of a "guest status." We were still under the control of the unit that had been dealing with our case, and the prison authorities had nothing to do with it—if we violated prison regulations, the violation would be dealt with by that unit.

Sometime after the visit but before the start of formal study, Yin Kuan shouted to me from the neighboring cell, "Chaolin, I'm dying." I said, "Don't talk nonsense!" But I reported the matter to the guards and got them to request a physician-prisoner[377] to take him to the hospital to be examined. I saw him pass by my cell door, after which I received no further news of him. Three days later, the hospital sent some people to disinfect his cell, so I concluded that he must have died. I wrote two poems in the classical style in memory of him. (I have long forgotten how they went.) I was very sad not to hear him voice his opinions at our study session, but I knew what his attitude was, for when the two of us had been transferred from No. 2 Detention Center on June 29, 1956, we had been put in the same cell and talked together until late at night. The next day, we were moved apart, but we had the chance to exchange a few comments during visits and study meetings. I realized that his admissions of guilt and expressions of contrition were feigned. He had been arrested in 1950 in his hometown of Tongcheng [in Anhui] and had been held in Hefei. At first, he had refused to admit his guilt, and as a result, he had suffered considerable hardship. His wrists had been handcuffed behind his back, someone else had had to feed him, someone else had had to wipe his backside when he went to the toilet, and so on. He had no choice but to admit his guilt. After his transfer to Shanghai, he was sometimes kept in a cell by himself and he sometimes shared a cell with another; the government did not take his admission of guilt at face value.

By the time we formally started studying the antirevisionist texts, our small group had only three members left. I spoke out freely, and was refuted by the other two. Every "criticism" took a long time to study. While studying, we had to take notes, and at the end of the period of study, I wrote up [my contribution to] the entire discussion in a systematic "summary report" of some 85,000 characters. I read out my "summary report" at a meeting of the small group and then handed it over to the head of the small group for forwarding to higher authorities (while keeping a copy for myself). This pamphlet was titled *Ganbuzhuyi lun* (On cadreism).

Either before or after I wrote my summary, the unit dealing with our case supplied each member of our small group with the four volumes of Mao Zedong's *Selected Works*. I believe that this was our next study task. After completing our study of these four volumes, we had to write a summary. I conscientiously read every article in them and took notes. But we no longer studied as we had, either because one of our number had fallen ill and had gone to the hospital and the remaining two could no longer meet, or because both groups stopped studying Mao's *Selected Works*. Nevertheless, I edited my notes into a book of 135,000 characters under the title *Yuzhong du Mao Zedong xuanji* (Reading Mao Zedong's *Selected Works* in prison). By the time I made a copy of the notes to keep for myself, the Cultural Revolution had already started; just as before, I handed the text to my guards.

During the same period, my wife sent me Stalin's *Problems of Leninism*, which a good friend had bought for me. I read this book from start to finish and took notes on it that I wrote up into a volume, but I failed to submit that volume to the authorities. I forget what I called it.

I kept the manuscripts of these three books by my side, but in 1968, when the prison came under military control, they were burned along with other manuscripts found when the army representative ordered that the cells be searched and all the property in them confiscated. I do not know whether any copies of the first two studies, which were submitted to the authorities, have been preserved.

In mid-1965, I was still alone in a cell and did not take part in study sessions. The only other member of my small group had been assigned to study with those whose sentences had already been passed. Two memorable things happened in that year.

In my *Yinyu canji* (Surviving poems by Yu Yin), there is a poem that goes as follows:

> You kindly advise me to follow others' suit.
> Though I would love to make concessions,
> there is a gulf that I can never cross.
> Though seemingly just inches wide,
> in fact, it reaches for a thousand miles.
> It is the gulf between a human and a beast.
> Should I drink the sweet and not the bitter cup,

> I would disgrace my father and my mother!
> And even if I crossed this gulf,
> my mind would be forever dissident.
> Do you not see some old acquaintances of mine
> bending their heads low
> and saying yes whenever yes is wanted,
> but all to no avail?
> Like me, they spent these thirteen years in gaol,
> hungrily looking upward at the goose
> that wings its way across the sky[378]—
> where is the leniency?

The line "Like me, they spent these thirteen years in gaol" shows that I wrote the poem in 1965.

On one occasion, when my wife came on a special prison visit, three stools were set out. A prison guard sat to one side to supervize our conversation. Before the start of such meetings, the guard would inform relatives of the prisoner that it was their duty to persuade the prisoner to admit his or her guilt and undergo reform. So at the start of such visits, relatives would deliver some such "exhortation." I replied to the "exhortation" in the presence of the guard. I said that I, too, wanted to compromise out of consideration for the general interest, but there were limits beyond which I would not go. And even if I did go beyond those limits, it would be to no avail. Others involved in our case had admitted their guilt but had still received no leniency and, like me, had spent the previous thirteen years in prison. That same evening, I wrote the above poem and posted it along with a letter to my relatives, but it was returned to me.

As if to rebut my supposition, not long after this incident, something else happened that seemed to say: If you admit your guilt and undergo reform, you definitely will receive lenient treatment. One afternoon in early autumn, Section Chief Li of the unit dealing with our case suddenly turned up at the prison and had all the Trotskyists assemble on the ground floor of Prison No. 1. It turned out that the government had decided to let Yin Kuan go home and wanted him to say a few words to us. For a long time, I had thought that Yin Kuan was dead, yet there he was in a wheelchair. Although he saw us, he no longer recognized us. He spoke a few sentences to us, the gist of which was that we should admit our guilt and undergo reform, in which case, we would be released before our time, as he had been. His daughter had come to visit him from Tongcheng, and the next day, he would return with her. After he had finished speaking, a prisoner undergoing penal servitude helped him back into his wheelchair and returned him to the hospital. Section Chief Li then asked each of us to say what we felt. I deliberately kept my remarks to the end.

A Brief Account of My Third Spell in Prison

I said: "Yin Kuan was ill in prison for a long time. Several years ago, I asked the government to let Yin Kuan and another prisoner who had been ill for a long time go home, since both of them had loving families to look after them, and, once home, their illness could be cured. My request was ignored for several years. It's wonderful that Yin Kuan is now to be released. We've seen the state that Yin Kuan is now in. Naturally, it's unlikely that Yin Kuan's release had anything to do with the request I made several years ago."

Section Chief Li stood to one side and listened while I spoke. He made no attempt to silence me, and after I had finished speaking, he did not upbraid me. But sighing loudly, he said: "Hum! You made the request! Hum! And you made it several years ago!"[379]

But there were no consequences.

* * *

The following year, 1966, was an "unprecedented year in history."[380] We knew from press reports and prison rumors that there was a "craze for struggle" in the outside world. Some people[381] were "encircled and suppressed" on the highways and were "struggled to death."[382] Rumor had it that there would be a "struggle" within the prison too.

The "struggle" had already started among the prison officials and guards. In the western wing of Prison No. 1, people could be heard shouting slogans in the offices. According to reports, the prison walls and the surrounding streets were plastered with newssheets. A "struggle" was evidently being prepared among the prisoners. One day, Section Chief Li of the unit in charge of our case turned up at the prison for a meeting with me and several other Trotskyists. It turned out that I was to be the target of a "struggle." On October 24, 1966, my "struggle meeting" started. On the first day, the guards told me to prepare a speech explaining the situation regarding my reform. Thirty-odd people turned up at the meeting; they had been mobilized by the prison authorities, who had secretly planted among these people a number of others charged with saving my life. There was no obvious hatred between me and the [common] prisoners, so why would they want to beat me to death? Because they were keen to show that they were activists who would stop at nothing, and hoped thereby to gain lenient treatment. But because of the measures taken by the authorities, although I was wounded at the struggle meeting, the wounding was not serious.

After the start of the struggle meeting, I read out my speech, the gist of which was as follows: The Trotskyists were not counterrevolutionaries, Trotsky was not a counterrevolutionary, Chen Duxiu was not a counterrevolutionary, I myself was not a counterrevolutionary, and none of the Trotskyists was a counterrevolutionary. Even before I had finished reading my speech, the meeting erupted into violence. I was dragged out and forced to my knees. I was cursed, I was beaten, my ears were pulled, my cheeks were pinched, and I was ordered to retract what I had said. On the day itself, the violence was without effect. Thereafter, however, I was subjected to new struggles lasting for two or three days, after which the number of participants diminished. Those seated at the long table no longer used violence but relied simply on verbal intimidation. After a week or so of this sort of treatment, I was forced to admit that I was a "counterrevolutionary." The struggle against me ceased only after a record of the proceedings had been made and I had been allowed to thumbprint and sign it.

From then on, my lifestyle changed. I no longer lived alone but shared a cell with two other prisoners. I no longer studied by myself but joined a small group with other Trotskyists. At first, I was instructed to listen to the views of others and not to utter my own opinions, but later, things gradually loosened up and I was expected to air my opinions; even so, I restricted myself to a few innocuous comments. I no longer wrote any books, did any translations, or wrote any articles. If I read any books or articles and was required to write notes on them, I did not dare express myself freely. I wrote hardly any poetry, and I was much more careful about what I said in the course of everyday conversations. One guard who had recently been promoted to the office sought me out for a chat after the struggle meeting. He told me, "This struggle meeting was aimed at curtailing your arrogance. Just think how arrogant you were when you were first transferred to Prison No. 1!" Some people said that the guard was representing the unit in charge of our case, and that he knew that struggle was incapable of achieving its aim of "reforming" me. But if the intention was to beat the arrogance out of me, it succeeded.

From the time of the struggle meeting until I left Tilanqiao Prison six years later, there is nothing worth noting, except for the military administration of the prison in 1968. At that time, the entire prison was put in the hands of the People's Liberation Army. Three representatives of the People's Liberation Army controlled the whole prison, including its director and administrators; each prison, each floor, was placed under the control of three representatives of the army, and the original guards had to obey the orders of these people. The main consequence of this development for me personally resulted from the order that the cells be searched and all publications save Mao Zedong's *Selected Works* and [the Communist Party journal] *Hongqi* (Red flag) be confiscated. The order applied even more surely to manuscripts; my books and my manuscripts of more than one million characters were taken from me. When I left the prison, my books were returned to me, but not a single page of manuscript was given back. Later, after repeatedly inquiring about the matter, I was informed that all the manuscripts had been burned on army orders. The army continued to administer the prison until the rebellion and subsequent flight [in September 1971] of [People's Liberation Army Commander] Lin Biao. Only then was the administration put back into the hands of the prison authorities.

* * *

We left the prison on September 28, 1972. The Public Security Bureau sent someone to tell us that we were to be released and to give us certificates of release. We affixed our thumbprints to the certificates, but the unit concerned with our case immediately took the certificates back. We were not allowed to return to our homes but could live only in a reform-through-labor factory (a glassworks) or on a reform-through-labor farm (Qingdong Farm), under administrative surveillance. I went to the glassworks, where I lived with five other people in one courtyard, one person to a room. The entrance to the courtyard was open, but we were not allowed to leave through it. Sometimes, when we did leave, we were required to go in pairs. If we left the factory gate, we had to be escorted by someone from the factory security force. This person, too, lived in the courtyard. He was responsible for our supervision. He took us shopping in Zhoupuzhen once a fortnight.

In December 1972, my wife moved in with me, so my monthly living allowance rose to eighty yuan. (The others received sixty yuan a month.) According to what I heard, eighty yuan was more than the salary of the factory director. Our three daily meals were brought to us from the canteen. We participated in manual labor, helping the factory clinic grow and harvest medicinal herbs. But our main activity was study. I continued to speak my mind freely at study meetings, even though I did not retract my admission that I was a "counterrevolutionary."[383]

We spent seven years under supervision in the glassworks, during which time Zhou Enlai, Zhu De, and Mao Zedong died; Hua Guofeng took over the succession; the Gang of Four was smashed; Deng Xiaoping rose to power; and, finally, the Third Plenum of the Eleventh Central Committee inaugurated reforms.

On June 5, 1979, we attended a sort of ceremony in a small assembly hall on Qingdong Farm, along with six other people being held there who were implicated in our case. On the platform was a representative of the courts and another of the Public Security Bureau, from whose hands we received certificates restoring our civil rights. Afterward, we were put up in the Oriental Hotel. We discussed our impressions, received information, attended a banquet given by Jing Renqiu, deputy head of the United Front Department, in the Hengshan Hotel, and went on a tour of Nanjing and Suzhou (which I didn't join). We then returned to the factory or farm to await allocation of housing. In late June, eight of us (not including four who had relatives outside Shanghai) were moved to new accommodations, where we started new lives.

APPENDIX

On December 30, 1993, Zheng Chaolin wrote a short reply to various questions put to him concerning this article. On the number of Trotskyists and their sympathizers arrested on December 22, 1952, he wrote as follows:

> It's impossible to put an exact figure on the number of alleged Trotskyists arrested in 1952. According to my estimate, the number of both those who were arrested and imprisoned and those who were merely put under surveillance (whose freedom was restricted)—like Wang Mengzou, Wang Yuanfang,[384] and so on—if not one thousand, must have been very close to that figure. Some of our young people were sent on courses for surveillance and training, where they were ordered to "disclose" one another's (and other people's) [crimes]. The courses lasted for six months. In Shanghai, there were two such courses. Of those [sent on such courses], only a few were finally sentenced on account of their bad "attitude," whereas most were freed after completing the course. (Deng Shuzhen[385] and Fang Xiong were among those freed. In fact, both had already surrendered [to the Chinese Communist authorities] before the national raid took place.)

In a subsequent letter, he said that seven of the twelve survivors released in 1979 were supporters of the group of Trotskyists led by Wang Fanxi and himself, and five of Peng Shuzhi's group. He was unable to estimate the ratio of Peng's followers to followers of the Zheng-Wang group among those arrested in 1952.[386]

Postscript to the English Edition

I remember that a famous Westerner once said that when someone writes a book, that book starts to live independently. That statement is certainly true of this book. In late 1944, the Japanese army of aggression was a spent force, like an arrow at the end of its flight, and the Shanghai economy was languishing in deep depression. Publishers were no longer accepting manuscripts for publication, so I devoted the time I normally spent each month writing for publishers to recording what I had seen and heard in past years. I wrote ten chapters and then was unable to continue. The war ended. I circulated the manuscript among friends and asked someone to make a copy of it. Then I bundled it up and put it on a shelf. In late 1952, after "liberation," during the "campaign to eliminate Trotskyism," when Trotskyists all over China were "rounded up at one fell swoop," this manuscript, along with the copy and the entire Trotskyist archives, was inventoried and confiscated as "criminal" evidence. No doubt the official in charge of the case scoured the manuscript for clues about the organization and its members. After the case was closed, the Shanghai Public Security Bureau cleared out duplicate documents—a dozen or so sackfuls according to reports—and sent them to the Ministry of Public Security in Beijing. As luck would have it, there were two copies of my memoir, so one was kept in Shanghai, and the other was stuffed into a Beijing-bound sack. My book, like my person, disappeared into captivity: I behind bars, it into the archives of the public security organs.

During the "Great Cultural Revolution" of 1966–1969, it was decided—either by the Red Guards who stormed the Ministry of Public Security or by the ministry itself, in the course of sorting out its archives—to consign these sacks to the paper factory for reprocessing, but someone with a conscience secretly carried away two of the sacks and hid them. He took the sacks at random and had no idea what documents they contained.

After the Third Plenum of the Eleventh Central Committee of the Communist Party in 1978, the situation changed, and some historians were instructed to carry out research on Chen Duxiu and the Trotskyists. Materials on Chen Duxiu before his expulsion and after his release from prison were easily available, but there were no materials on the Trotskyists or on the

Trotskyist Chen Duxiu. Just as they were about to admit defeat, the aforementioned man of conscience remembered the two sacks, and the problem was partly solved. The researchers discovered the manuscript of my book of memoirs. At first, they had no way of knowing who had written it, but when they reached the account of the May Thirtieth massacre, they found my name and knew that the memoir was by me.

They then began to think of publishing the book. I had already been completely restored to liberty, so they sent someone to Shanghai to ask me if I would agree to their plan. At the same time, they mimeographed several copies of the manuscript under the title *Zheng Chaolin's 1945 Memoirs* and distributed them as reference material to important organizations concerned with Party history. I have seen only references to this mimeographed edition in articles by experts on Party history, and not the publication itself. I don't know whether it is the complete text, excerpts from the text, or summaries of it.

The publication of the printed version went less smoothly than that of the mimeographed edition. Agreement to publish was reached in 1980, but only in 1986 did the book actually see the light of day. In the meantime, its fortunes fluctuated with the ever-changing political tide. Before 1983, the question was whether or not to send it to the compositor. In 1983, after the final proofs had been read and the text had been made into a plate, the question was whether or not to send it to the printer, and then whether or not to send it to the distributor. Only in 1986 did the book finally appear.

At that point, the book was finally delivered from the fate of "humble prisoner," but it was certainly not yet an "honored guest," it had merely regained its "civil rights." I, the author, received my payment at the going rate. The book, published as "internal reference material" by the Association to Edit and Publish Materials on Contemporary History,[387] was unobtainable in the shops. It was what Chinese readers call a "gray book." Fewer than ten such "gray books" have been published. What unites them is that their contents are valuable as reference sources for students of the history of the Communist Party, though their standpoints are quite dissimilar to that of the Party. Needless to say, the standpoints of the books themselves also differ from one another.

When, in 1980, the publishers asked me for permission to publish, they also asked me if I would agree to cut the chapter titled "Love and Politics." In my 1945 preface, I had already envisaged cutting this chapter, so I said yes. But I still think it's a pity. In those days, many of the conflicts and fights among Chinese Communist officials were explicable only in terms of quarrels about love. So without that chapter, they could no longer be explained. Quite apart from this consideration, to cut an entire chapter from a book inevitably creates discontinuities. Unfortunately, I had not set eyes on the manuscript since it "went to prison," so there was no way that I could control its fate. Luckily, both the original manuscript and the copy are still around, one in Beijing and the other in Shanghai, and one day, they will surface. When that day comes, not only the chapter "Love and Politics" but also words and sentences excised from other chapters can be restored.

I wrote the appendix "Chen Duxiu and the Trotskyists"[388] at the invitation of a certain research institute in 1980, shortly after I had regained my freedom. At the time, public opinion tended to distinguish between Chen Duxiu and the Trotskyists. People said that Chen Duxiu was a good man and that his good name should be restored, but they made no evaluation of the Trotskyists. So the aim of this long article is to show that Chen Duxiu and the Trotskyists cannot be dealt with separately. Today, however, public opinion no longer insists on this distinction, so the chapter may appear redundant.

When I learned that my book was to appear in English, I joyfully wrote these few lines to describe its independent life: how it grew from manuscript to printed page regardless of my intentions.

December 11, 1987

Select Biographical Reference List

The Chinese names in this list are given in Hanyu Pinyin transcription. After each main entry, the Wade-Giles transcription is given in parentheses, except where the two are identical. The list includes all the main characters in Zheng's book and others who occur only once or twice but whose identities are important for explaining the events in which they participated.

Blücher, General Vasilii K. (1889–1938)
A veteran revolutionary of peasant origin. Under the pseudonym Galen, headed the military advisers working with the Guomindang between 1924 and 1927. Alias: Bliukher.

Cai Hesen (Ts'ai Ho-sen) (1895–1931)
A leader and martyr of the Communist Party and author of *The History of Opportunism in the Chinese Communist Party*.

Cai Yuanpei (Ts'ai Yüan-p'ei) (1868–1940)
A veteran Guomindang leader and important liberal educationalist. Sponsored the New Culture Movement around 1919 in his capacity (between 1916 and 1926) as chancellor of Beijing University. Founded and became president of the Academia Sinica.

Chen Bilan (Ch'en Pi-lan) (1902–1987)
Joined the League of Socialist Youth in 1922 and the Communist Party in 1923. Sent to Moscow to study in 1924 and returned to China one year later. Active in the women's movement. Became a Trotskyist together with Chen Duxiu in 1929. Self-exiled at the end of 1948, first to Hong Kong, then to Vietnam, France, and the United States; finally went back to Hong Kong, where she died. Wife of Peng Shuzhi. Alias: Bi Yun.

Chen Duxiu (Ch'en Tu-hsiu) (1879–1942)
Editor of *New Youth*, leader of the New Culture Movement, founder of the Communist Party, and its general secretary until 1927. In 1931, became a Trotskyist and helped found the Chinese Left Opposition, which he then led. In 1932, went to prison on charges of seeking to overthrow the government and replace it with a proletarian dictatorship. Aliases: Shi An, Sa Weng, Xue Yi, Kong Jia, Zhong Fu, San Ai, Zhi Mian.

Chen Kunpei (Ch'en K'un-p'ei)

An ex-anarchist who joined Chen Duxiu's Communist organization before leaving China and worked in the Communist Youth League upon returning to China from France; left the Party shortly thereafter. Alias: Wu Ming ("without a name").

Chen Qiaonian (Ch'en Ch'iao-nien) (1902–1928)
Chen Duxiu's second son. Joined the Party in 1922 in France and studied in Moscow. Elected to the Central Committee in 1927. Arrested and executed by Chiang Kai-shek in the spring of 1928, by which time he had become head of the Organizational Department of the Jiangsu Provincial Committee.

Chen Qichang (Ch'en Ch'i-ch'ang) (1901–1943)
A Beijing student leader and a member of the middle-ranking cadre of the Communist Party after 1925. Turned to Trotskyism in 1929 and became a leader of the Chinese Trotskyist movement. Arrested and executed by the Japanese gendarmerie. Aliases: Chen Qingchen, Jiang Weiliang, Chen Zhongshan.

Chen Tanqiu (Ch'en T'an-ch'iu) (1896–1943)
One of the thirteen participants in the founding conference of the Communist Party in 1921 and a member of its Central Committee. Arrested and executed by Sheng Shicai, warlord of Xinjiang.

Chen Yannian (Ch'en Yen-nien) (1899–1927)
Eldest son of Chen Duxiu and a founder of the European branch of the Chinese Communist Party. Secretary of the South China Regional Committee of the Party until 1926, then became secretary of the Jiangsu Provincial Committee. Executed by Chiang Kai-shek in Shanghai in May 1927.

Chen Yimou (Ch'en I-mou) (1907–1932)
See under Ou Fang.

Dai Jitao (Tai Chi-t'ao) (1891–1949)
Leader and theoretician of the Guomindang right wing (organized in the Society for the Study of Sun Yat-sen-ism). Committed suicide when the Communists came to power.

Deng Yanda (Teng Yen-ta) (1895–1931)
Director of the General Political Department of the Northern Expedition, a leader of the left Guomindang, and an opponent of Chiang Kai-shek. Resigned from the Wuhan government in July 1927 in protest against its decision to expel the Communists. Arrested and executed by Chiang Kai-shek in 1931 because of his launching of the Third Party and his activities against Chiang's Nanjing government.

Dong Biwu (Tung Pi-wu) (1886–1975)
Veteran Communist and Central Committee member after 1945 and vice-head of state. Member of the Politburo after 1966.

Du Yuesheng (Tu Yüeh-sheng) (1888–1951)

Leader of the Green Gang in Shanghai's French Concession, to which Chiang Kai-shek had links.

Galen, General.
See Blücher.

Gao Yuhan (Kao Yü-han)
Veteran revolutionary and a political instructor at the Huangpu Military Academy. The first Communist to attack Chiang Kai-shek openly. Became a Trotskyist in 1929. Alias: Wang Linggao.

Glass, Frank (1901–1987)
Born Cecil Frank Glass in Britain. Arrived in China from South Africa in 1930 and worked in Shanghai as a journalist on various English-language newspapers and as a radio commentator; his last job there was as an assistant editor of the *China Weekly Review*. A leader of the Chinese Trotskyist movement from 1934 to 1938. Aliases: Li Furen (Li Fu-jen), Frank Graves, John Liang.

Gu Shunzhang (Ku Shun-chang) (1895–1935)
A worker and leader of the Shanghai insurrections in 1927. Chief of the Communist Party "special service" and member of the Politburo of the Central Committee. Arrested by the Guomindang and became one of its most vicious anti-Communist agents. Finally executed by Chiang Kai-shek, despite his defection to the Nationalists.

Gu Zhenggang (Ku Cheng-kang)
Younger brother of Gu Zhenglun, then commander of the Nanjing garrison and a henchman of Chiang Kai-shek. Zhenggang himself belonged to Wang Jingwei's "reformist" faction in the Guomindang, which at the time was in opposition to Chiang.

Guan Xiangying (Kuan Hsiang-ying) (1904–1946)
A printer who joined the Communist Party in 1925. A member of the Central Committee until 1928. He Long's political commissar in the anti-Japanese war.

He Long (Ho Lung) (1896–1969)
A legendary Communist military leader. At the time of the split between the Wuhan government and the Communist Party, He was commander of the pro-Communist 20th National Revolutionary Army.

He Mengxiong (Ho Meng-hsiung) (1898–1931)
A labor leader in northern China during the 1925–1927 Revolution. Head of the Organization Department of the Jiangsu Provincial Committee of the Chinese Communist Party after 1927. Leader of those Communists who opposed Wang Ming's Central Committee. Arrested and executed by the Guomindang.

He Zishen (Ho Tzu-shen) (1898–1961)

A Beijing student in the early 1920s. Participated in the Northern Expedition. Was active in Hunan and succeeded Mao as secretary of the Hunan Provincial Committee. Became a Trotskyist in 1929 and spent several years in prison under the Guomindang. Arrested by the Maoist secret police in 1952; died in prison.

Hu Shi (Hu Shih) (1891–1962)
Philosopher and writer. Advocate of the vernacular literature. Collaborator with Chen Duxiu on *New Youth*. After May Fourth, Hu split with Chen Duxiu and was strongly criticized by the Communists. A supporter of the Guomindang and pro-American.

Hu Zongnan (Hu Tsung-nan) (1895–1962)
A Guomindang military leader who became known as the "King of the Northwest."

Isaacs, Harold (1910–1986)
A U.S. journalist who published *China Forum* in Shanghai in the early 1930s. Influenced by Frank Glass, he became sympathetic to Trotskyism, and while in Beijing he wrote *The Tragedy of the Chinese Revolution*, with the help of Liu Renjing as his translator; he discussed the text with Trotsky, who wrote an introduction to it. The first (1938) edition was followed by several reprintings with Trotsky's introduction deleted. After Trotsky's assassination in 1940, Isaacs left the Trotskyist movement. He worked for the Columbia Broadcasting Company and *Newsweek* before entering academic life in 1950; in 1965, he became professor of political science at the Massachusetts Institute of Technology. Aliases: Yi Luosheng, Harold Roberts.

Jiang Zhendong (Chiang Chen-tung) (1906–1982)
A textile worker and veteran Communist and one of the leaders of the Shanghai insurrections of 1927. Became a Trotskyist in 1929. Arrested by the Maoist police in 1952 for his dissident activities. Released from prison in 1979.

Kang Sheng (K'ang Sheng) (1898–1975)
An intelligence and security specialist. Trained in Moscow as a henchman for Wang Ming by the NKVD, he became a Mao supporter after getting back to China. Was Mao's main inquisitor in the Cultural Revolution and is depicted as an "ultra-leftist" by the rehabilitated "moderate" Chinese Communist leaders who were his victims.

Kang Youwei (K'ang Yu-wei) (1858–1927)
Led the reform movement that culminated in the short-lived Hundred Days Reform of 1898 and was a prominent scholar of the New Text School of the Confucian classics.

Katayama Sen (1860–1933)
Founded the Japanese Socialist Party in 1906 and later became a Communist. Worked for the Comintern in Moscow from 1921 until his death.

Kautsky, Karl (1854–1938)
Leader of the German Social Democratic Party. Best known before 1914 as a Marxist theoretician. Opposed the Bolshevik Revolution in 1917 on the grounds that a genuine socialist proletarian revolution could be achieved only by democratic means—that is, by universal suffrage—and not by the insurrection of a minority of the nation. Opposed Lenin's theory and practice of the dictatorship of the proletariat.

Kawakami Hajime (1879–1946)
An economist who became a Marxist in 1919, though at first he was considered unorthodox. Joined the Japan Communist Party in 1932.

Kirov, Sergei Mironovich (1886–1934)
An Old Bolshevik, elected to the USSR Central Committee in 1923 and to the Politburo in 1930. A staunch supporter of Stalin. His assassination in 1934 was followed by the Moscow trials. It has now been revealed that Stalin masterminded the assassination when he discovered that Kirov was becoming estranged from him. Stalin then used the assassination as an excuse to persecute his opponents.

Li Dazhao (Li Ta-chao) (1889–1927)
One of the founders of the Communist Party, second only to Chen Duxiu. Executed in Beijing in 1927.

Li Ji (Li Chi)
Known as the first Marxist scholar in China. Author of *A Biography of Karl Marx*. Became a Trotskyist in 1929; recanted after 1949.

Li Liejun (Li Lieh-chün) (1882–1946)
A military leader of the 1911 Revolution; as military governor of Jiangxi, he led the Guomindang's so-called Second Revolution in 1913. Served between 1917 and 1923 as Sun Yat-sen's chief of staff.

Li Lisan (Li Li-san) (1899–1967)
A veteran Communist and labor organizer. Elected to the Politburo in 1927. The chief executor of Stalin's ultra-left line in China from 1929 to 1930; removed from the leadership in 1931 as a scapegoat for its failure and was detained in Russia until 1945. Attacked during the Cultural Revolution, and reportedly committed suicide.

Li Qihan (Li Ch'i-han) (1898–1927)
An early activist in the labor movement. After the defeat of the February 7, 1923, Hankou-Beijing rail strike, he was imprisoned in Shanghai and finally murdered during the April 15 Guangzhou massacre.

Li Qiushi (Li Ch'iu-shih) (1903–1931)
A writer and member of the Communist Youth League of China; active in the Party after the defeat of the revolution. Arrested and executed with the "Conciliationists."

Li Weihan (Li Wei-han) (1896–1984)
Joined the Communist Party in France in 1922. Head of the Orgburo in 1936. After 1949, mainly in charge of the Party's United Front work. Accused of "anti-Party" activity in December 1966 and purged in June 1967. Alias: Luo Mai.

Li Zhenying (Li Chen-ying)
An activist in the labor movement and member of the Communist Party. Joined the "Conciliationists" in 1931 and was arrested the same year. Left politics after his release from prison.

Li Zhongsan (Li Chung-san) (1882–?)
A veteran Guomindang revolutionary, active in northwest China. Was a work-study student in France and became a Trotskyist in 1929.

Liang Botai (Liang Po-t'ai) (1899–1935)
A veteran Communist who returned to China in the early 1930s and worked for a while in the Jiangxi soviet.

Liang Ganqiao (Liang Kan-ch'iao)
Studied in Moscow after graduating from the Huangpu Military Academy. Active in the Chinese Trotskyist movement for a few years, but became a leader of Chiang Kai-shek's "Blueshirt Clique."

Liang Qichao (Liang Ch'i-ch'ao) (1873–1929)
A journalist and historian and a constitutional monarchist who became leader of the so-called Study Clique after the downfall of the Qing dynasty.

Lin Boqu (Lin Po-ch'ü) (1886–1960)
A veteran Communist and member of the Communist Party's Politburo. After 1949, became a vice-chairman of the National People's Congress.

Lin Yunan (Lin Yü-nan) (1898–1931)
A Communist labor leader and secretary of the National Federation of Labor. Arrested and executed by the Guomindang along with He Mengxiong and other "Conciliationists."

Liu Bozhuang (Liu Po-chuang)
A "frugal study" student. Turned to Trotskyism in 1929 but became a professor soon afterward and left the movement.

Liu Jialiang (Liu Chia-liang) (?–1950)
Liu Jialiang, Si Chaosheng, and Wang Shuben were three leaders of the second generation of Chinese Trotskyists. Liu died in a Vietnamese prison sometime in 1950, Si left the movement long before that, and Wang was executed by the Guomindang in a concentration camp on the eve of their military debacle. Aliases: Yao Ru, Liu Haisheng, Liu Shaoyan.

Liu Jingzhen (Liu Ching-chen) (1902–1979)
Joined the Party and took part in the Revolution of 1925–1927. Married

Zheng Chaolin and became a Trotskyist together with Chen Duxiu. When Chen was in prison, she acted as a link between him and the surviving underground Trotskyist organization. Arrested by the Communists in 1952 and freed five years later. Rejoined her husband in a labor camp during the Cultural Revolution. Released in June 1979 and died in October of the same year. Alias: Wu Jingru.

Liu Renjing (Liu Jen-ching) (1902–1987)
A founding member of the Communist Party and general secretary of the Socialist League of Youth. Joined the Left Opposition in Moscow and visited Trotsky in Turkey in 1929. Played a part in organizing the Trotskyist organization in China and helped Harold Isaacs write *The Tragedy of the Chinese Revolution*. Arrested in 1934 and recanted in prison. Recanted again after 1949, this time to the Maoists. Died in a car accident in 1987. Aliases: Nelsi, Niel Sih, Liu Jingyuan, Lieershi, Xu Yong.

Liu Shaoqi (Liu Shao-ch'i) (1898–1969)
A veteran Communist and prominent Chinese labor leader from the mid-1940s on. Head of state of the People's Republic of China after 1959. Purged in the Cultural Revolution but rehabilitated in 1979.

Liu Yin
A leader of the Wuhan student movement during the 1925–1927 Revolution who studied in Moscow. Active for a while in the Chinese Trotskyist movement, then became a publicist for the Guomindang. Alias: Li Maimai.

Lominadze, Vissarion (1898–1934)
Known as "Stalin's prodigy," he was the Comintern representative in China from July to December 1927. Masterminded the August 7 (1927) Conference and, together with Heinz Neumann, directed the December 1927 Guangzhou Insurrection. Fell into disfavor after 1930 and committed suicide in 1934.

Long Yun (Lung Yün) (1884–1962)
Governor of Yunnan from 1928 to 1945.

Lou Guohua (Lou Kuo-hua) (1906–1995)
A Communist since 1925 and became a Trotskyist in 1928. Was one of the few survivors of the first generation of Chinese Trotskyists, and in Hong Kong was the chief publisher of Trotskyist literature in Chinese. Aliases: Zi Chun, Yi Ding, Shao Yuan, Ze Cheng.

Lou Shiyi (Lou Shih-i) (1905–)
A veteran Communist, left-wing writer, and translator into Chinese of several novels (including *Mother*) by Maxim Gorky. Cousin of the late Lou Guohua. Sentenced to life imprisonment under the Guomindang. Became a leading official in Beijing's People's Press after 1949.

Lu Xun (Lu Hsün) (1881–1936)

Modern China's best-known novelist, essayist, and critic, known as "China's Gorky." Original name: Zhou Shuren.

Luo Han (Lo Han) (1898–1941?)
Expelled from France in 1921 and joined the Communist Party in 1922. Active in the Guomindang army until the March 20 (1926) Incident. Became a Trotskyist in 1928 in Moscow and a leader of the Left Opposition of the Chinese Communist Party. Died in Chongqing during a Japanese air raid.

Luo Qiyuan (Lo Ch'i-yüan) (1893–1931)
A leader of the peasant movement in Guangdong. Arrested in Shanghai in 1931 and executed, despite recanting.

Luo Zhanglong (Lo Chang-lung) (1897–)
A student leader at Beijing University during the May Fourth Movement of 1919. Joined the Communist Party when it was formed and became very active in the workers' movement. A leader in 1929–1930 of the so-called Conciliators. Arrested by the Guomindang and released, probably on the condition that he retire from active politics.

Ma Yufu (Ma Yü-fu)
A Communist labor activist who became a Trotskyist in 1929 and defected to the Guomindang two years later.

Mif, Pavel (1901–1938)
Patron of the so-called Twenty-Eight Bolsheviks at Sun Yat-sen University in Moscow. Arrested in 1937 and disappeared during the purges.

Ou Fang (?–1931)
With Chen Yimou, Song Fengchun, and Shi Tang, one of the main founders of the first Trotskyist group in China. Returned from Moscow in early 1928. Active among workers in Hong Kong, he was arrested in 1930 in Shanghai and imprisoned by the Guomindang. Ou and Chen died in prison; Song and Shi left the movement after their release. In 1931, Chen was elected head of the Organizational Department of the unified Chinese Trotskyist organization.

Pan Wenyu (P'an Wen-yü)
Former student in Moscow and collaborator with Li Lisan. Later purged by the Wang Ming group.

Peng Pai (P'eng P'ai) (1896–1929)
Leader of the peasant associations in Hailufeng, Guangdong, after 1922. Organized a peasant insurrection in October 1927 and led the armed peasant struggle in that area. Fled to Shanghai after the defeat and was arrested and executed by the Guomindang.

Peng Shuzhi (P'eng Shu-chih, otherwise written as P'eng Shu-tse) (1896–1983)

Former student in Moscow and a member of the Central Committee of the Chinese Communist Party after 1925. Chief editor of the Party organ during the 1925–1927 Revolution. Expelled together with Chen Duxiu in November 1929 for supporting Trotskyism. Lived for several years in Los Angeles, California, before his death there in 1983. Aliases: Ivan Petrov, Xi Zhao, Nan Guan, Tao Bo, Ou Bo.

Pu Dezhi (P'u Teh-chih) (1905–)
Joined the Communist Party in 1926 and was active in literature and the theater. Became a Trotskyist in Moscow in 1928. Arrested for the second time together with Chen Duxiu in 1932. Released from prison in 1937. Aliases: Xi Liu, Pu Qingquan.

Qu Qiubai (Ch'ü Ch'iu-pai) (1899–1935)
A writer and translator. A veteran Communist and de facto general secretary of the Chinese Communist Party from August 1927 to July 1928. Executed by Chiang Kai-shek.

Radek, Karl (1885–1939)
Went over to Stalin in 1929 and was a defendant at the second Moscow trial. Died in prison.

Roy, M. N. (1887–1954)
An Indian nationalist and Communist. Went to China in May 1927 as a representative of the Comintern.

Shen Yanbing (Shen Yen-ping) (1896–1981)
The pen name of Mao Dun. A veteran Communist and a participant in the Revolution of 1925–1927. Became a famous writer, second only to Lu Xun. Was the first minister of culture in the post-1949 Communist government.

Shen Zemin (Shen Tse-min) (1900–1933)
Studied in the Soviet Union and was active in the Eyuwan Soviet area in the 1930s. A member of the Central Committee of the Chinese Communist Party.

Sheng Xuanhuai (Sheng Hsüan-huai) (1844–1916)
One of China's pioneer industrializers.

Shi Cuntong (Shih Ts'un-t'ung) (1889–1970)
Participated as a member of the Communist Party in the 1925–1927 Revolution but left the Party after its defeat. Remained an opponent of Chiang Kai-shek and a Communist Party sympathizer. Later changed his name to Shi Fuliang.

Shi Tang (Shih T'ang)
See under Ou Fang.

Si Chaosheng (Ssu Ch'ao-sheng)
See under Liu Jialiang.

Snow, Edgar (1905–1972)
Author of *Red Star Over China*, the classic study of the Chinese soviet movement.

Song Fengchun (Sung Feng-ch'un) (1907–?)
See under Ou Fang.

Song Yunbing (Sung Yün-ping) (1897–1979)
A journalist, essayist, and historian. Participated in the Revolution of 1925–1927 as a Communist. Became a member of the National People's Congress after the Communists came to power in 1949 and was purged in 1957 as a "Rightist."

Su Zhaozheng (Su Chao-cheng) (1885–1929)
A seaman, leader of the famous 1925–1926 Hong Kong–Guangzhou general strike, and chairman of the short-lived Guangzhou Soviet Government in December 1927.

Sun Ke (Sun K'o, usually known as Sun Fo) (1891–1973)
Minister of the Wuhan government and member of the State Council.

Tan Pingshan (T'an P'ing-shan) (1887–1956)
An early leader of the Communist Party, expelled in 1927. Joined the Guomindang in 1937 and later became a supporter of the Revolutionary Committee of the Guomindang, which backed the Beijing government after 1949.

Tang Shengzhi (T'ang Sheng-chih) (1889–1970)
Commander of the 8th Nationalist Army during the Northern Expedition. Became the military bulwark of the Wuhan government when the latter split with Chiang, and then turned with Wang Jingwei against the Communist Party.

Tao Xisheng (T'ao Hsi-sheng) (1899–)
The writer responsible for Chiang Kai-shek's *China's Destiny*. Became a member of the National Defense Council under Wang Jingwei in 1937 and briefly supported Wang's attempt to conclude a peaceful settlement of the war against Japan.

Wang Duqing (Wang Tu-ch'ing) (1898–1940)
A poet and one of the four founders of the Creation Society. A professor at Zhongshan University in Guangzhou, he went over to Trotskyism in 1929 together with Chen Duxiu. Died of typhoid.

Wang Fanxi (Wang Fan-hsi) (1907–)
Joined the Party in 1925 while a student at Beijing University and became a Trotskyist in Moscow in 1928. Returned to China in 1929 and worked for a while as an aide to Zhou Enlai. Worked as a Trotskyist with Chen Duxiu in 1930–1931, after being expelled from the Party. Arrested for the first

time in 1931 and again in 1937. Spent most of the intervening years in prison. Has lived in exile since 1949. Aliases: Vasilii Pavlovich Kletkin, Wang Wenyuan, Wang Mingyuan, Lian Gen, Shuang Shan, San Nan, Feng Gang, Shou Yi, Yi De, San Yuan, Hui Quan, Liu Shuxun.

Wang Hebo (Wang Ho-po) (1882–1927)
A well-known activist in the workers' movement in northern China, particularly among railway workers. Killed in Beijing in November 1927 by the warlord Zhang Zuolin.

Wang Jingwei (Wang Ching-wei) (1883–1944)
A veteran member of the Guomindang and at first a leader of its left wing. Later compromised with Chiang Kai-shek and ended up a Japanese puppet.

Wang Kequan (Wang K'o-ch'üan)
A Shanghai labor leader and member of the Central Committee of the Chinese Communist Party. Purged by the Wang Ming group in 1931 for belonging to the "Conciliationist" group. Became an agent of the Guomindang and was murdered by other agents.

Wang Mengzou (Wang Meng-tsou) (1877–1953)
A publisher friend of Chen Duxiu and supporter of all progressive movements in China since the beginning of the century.

Wang Ming (1904–1974)
The pseudonym of Chen Shaoyu, Stalin's main supporter in the Chinese Communist Party. His group dominated the Party after 1931 but was defeated during the Long March. His influence was finally eliminated at the Seventh Congress of the Chinese Communist Party in 1945.

Wang Ruofei (Wang Jo-fei) (1896–1946)
Joined the Communist Party in 1922 and was a member of its Central Committee until 1945. While in Moscow in 1928 as a member of the Chinese delegation to the Comintern, he secretly expressed sympathy for the Trotskyist Opposition.

Wang Shuben (Wang Shu-pen) (?–1949)
See under Liu Jialiang.

Wu Jiyan (Wu Chi-yen) (1898–1940)
Former student in Moscow and nephew of Chen Duxiu. Became a Trotskyist in 1929.

Wu Ming.
See Chen Kunpei.

Wu Yu (Wu Yü) (1872–1949)
A scholar and a poet whose essays attacking Confucianism were an important contribution to the May Fourth Movement.

Wu Zhihui (Wu Chih-hui) (1865–1953)

An ex-anarchist, a veteran member of the Guomindang, and one of the sponsors of the Society for Frugal Study by Means of Labor.

Xia Douyin (Hsia Tou-yin) (1884–1951)
Commander of a division of Guomindang troops stationed at Yichang, Hubei province, who, on May 6, 1927, rebelled against the Wuhan government in collusion with Chiang Kai-shek. His army was annihilated on the outskirts of Wuhan on May 18.

Xiang Jingyu (Hsiang Ching-yü) (1895–1928)
One of the Communist Party's earliest members and its first important female leader. She was the founding head of its Women's Department in 1922 and was very active in the movement until her execution in 1928.

Xiang Ying (Hsiang Ying) (1898–1941)
An early labor leader, a member of the Politburo after 1931, and leader of the remnant military forces in Jiangxi after the Long March. Became vice-commander of the New Fourth Army in 1938 and was killed by a traitor after the Wannan Incident of January 1941.

Xiang Zhongfa (Hsiang Chung-fa) (1880–1931)
General secretary of the Chinese Communist Party from 1928 to 1931. A workers' leader, he was promoted because of his record in the labor movement and his proletarian credentials at a time when the 1927 defeat was being blamed on the shortage of workers in the Party leadership. Lacked political ability and was largely ignorant of Marxist theory. Executed by Chiang Kai-shek in spite of capitulating after his arrest.

Xie Juezai (Hsieh Chüeh-tsai) (1884–1971)
Joined the Communist Party in 1925 and participated in the Long March. After 1949, became minister of the interior and then head of the Supreme Court.

Xu Kexiang (Hsü K'o-hsiang) (1889–1964)
The garrison commander at Changsha, where he carried out a coup against the workers' and peasants' organizations on the night of May 21, 1927.

Xu Qian (Hsü Ch'ien) (1871–1940)
A prominent Guomindang left-wing leader in the Wuhan regime.

Xu Teli (Hsü T'e-li) (1877–1968)
Mao's teacher and a participant in the Long March. A member of the Central Committee of the Chinese Communist Party after 1945.

Yamakawa Hitoshi (1880–1958)
At first an anarchist but became a leading Marxist theoretician around 1916 and joined the Japanese Communist Party in 1922. Opposed the idea of a vanguard party, and in 1928, severed all connections with it.

Yan Zhong (Yen Chung) (1892–1944)

A Guomindang general of the Leftist persuasion. Sacked by Chiang when his division reached Hangzhou, capital of Zhejiang, and reportedly left politics after that.

Ye Jianying (Yeh Chien-ying) (1897–1986)
A professional military man who participated in the Northern Expedition and the Guangzhou insurrection of December 1927. Chief of staff of the Chinese Communist Party's Eighth Route Army after 1937. Became defense minister in the Beijing government and was a member of the Politburo's Standing Committee.

Yin Kuan (Yin K'uan) (1897–1967)
A veteran Communist who joined the Communist Party in France. Was active on its Shandong Provincial Committee, its Anhui Provincial Committee, and its Jiangsu-Zhejiang Regional Committee in 1925–1927 and became a Trotskyist in 1929. Arrested twice by the Guomindang for his revolutionary activities and was arrested by the Maoists in 1952.

Yu Qiaqing (Yü Ch'ia-ch'ing) (1867–1945)
A famous Shanghai capitalist, chairman of the Chamber of Commerce, and a benefactor of Chiang Kai-shek.

Yu Xiusong (Yü Hsiu-sung) (1899–1938)
A veteran Communist and early leader of the Chinese students in Moscow before Wang Ming. Framed by Wang in Xinjiang in 1937 as a "Trotskyist." He was sent back to the USSR, where he was executed.

Yun Daiying (Yün Tai-ying) (1895–1931)
A political instructor at the Huangpu Military Academy and member of the Central Committee of the Chinese Communist Party. One of the most respected leaders of the Party among revolutionary youth during the Revolution of 1925–1927. Executed by the Guomindang in 1931.

Zhang Boling (Chang Po-lin) (1876–1951)
The liberal founder and president of Tianjin's Nankai University and a prominent Christian educator.

Zhang Guotao (Chang Kuo-t'ao) (1897–1979)
A founder of the Communist Party and one of the main leaders of the Communist-sponsored labor movement in the 1920s. Directed the secretariat of the Chinese Labor Unions set up in July 1921 and was leader of the Party's Fourth Front Army during the Long March, when he clashed with Mao. Left the Party in 1938 and ceased political activity thereafter.

Zhang Shizhao (Chang Shih-chao) (1882–1973)
A journalist, educator, government official, and lawyer. Opposed the New Culture Movement and was a bitter enemy of the writer Lu Xun, but died a supporter of Maoism.

Zhang Te (Chang T'e)
Joined the Trotskyist movement in Moscow in 1927, left it in 1931, and was thereafter a supporter of the Guangxi warlords.

Zhang Yisen (Chang I-sen) (1909–1980)
The wife of He Zishen. Participated in the Revolution of 1925–1927 and, after its defeat, remained in the Party. Arrested twice by the Guomindang and served short prison terms. Became a Trotskyist in 1929 and remained so until she was arrested and persecuted in 1952 by the Mao regime. Died in a fit of schizophrenia.

Zhang Zuolin (Chang Tso-lin) (1875–1928)
The fiercely anti-Communist warlord leader of Manchuria, known as the Old Marshal.

Zhao Ji (Chao Chi) (1902–)
A veteran Communist who participated in the Northern Expedition as a political commissar and became a Trotskyist in Moscow in 1928. Active in the early stages of the Trotskyist movement in China.

Zhao Yuanren (Chao Yüan-jen, known as Y. R. Chao or Chao Yuen-ren in the West) (1892–1982)
An internationally known Chinese linguist.

Zheng Chaolin (Cheng Ch'ao-lin) (1901–)
A writer and translator. Joined the Communist Party in Paris in 1922. Returned to China in 1924 to edit the Party organ *Xiangdao* (Guide weekly). A member of the Party's Hubei Provincial Committee during the Revolution of 1925–1927 and a participant in the Emergency Conference of August 7, 1927. Became a Trotskyist in 1929 and was a founder and leader of the Chinese Trotskyist organization. Served seven years in prison under Chiang Kai-shek. Arrested by the Maoist secret police in 1952 and kept in prison without trial until 1979. His memoirs were published in China in 1986. Aliases: Yvon, Marlotov, Lin Chaozhen, Yi Wen, Wang Jian, Shuyan, Lin Yiwen, Jue Min, Yi Yin, Lan Yin, Tang Yushi, Ze Lian.

Zhou Enlai (Chou En-lai) (1898–1976)
Joined the Communist Party in France in 1922 and became its most prominent organizer, negotiator, and administrator. Survived all the Communist Party's internal factional struggles and was premier of the People's Republic of China from 1949 until his death.

Zhou Zuoren (Chou Tso-jen) (1885–1968)
An essayist and a main contributor to *New Youth*. Introduced Japanese and Eastern European literature into China. The brother of Lu Xun.

Zhu Zhixin (Chu Chih-hsin) (1885–1920)
A leading figure in popularizing the political and social ideas of Sun Yat-sen.

Notes

1. An English translation of this special study can be found in an appendix to Gregor Benton, *China's Urban Revolutionaries: Explorations in the History of Chinese Trotskyism, 1921–1952* (Atlantic Highlands, NJ: Humanities Press, 1996), which introduces the main themes and personalities of early Chinese Trotskyism.
2. Hu Shi used this phrase in his preface to *Chen Duxiu zuihou lunwen he shuxin* (Chen Duxiu's last articles and letters), first published posthumously by Chen's friends and later republished on Taiwan with Hu Shi's preface. An edited translation of this work, by Gregor Benton, will be published by Amsterdam's International Institute for Social History.
3. This criticism is directed mainly at memoirs rather than at other forms of history writing, and in particular at memoirs published in China before the 1980s. In recent years, Chinese historians and archivists have produced a flood of valuable studies on and collections of documents from the 1920s, and since the mid-1980s, the quality of memoirs has greatly improved. The two best-known memoirs by early leaders of the Chinese Communist movement, based on their personal experiences and written without official constraints, are those of Zhang Guotao and Peng Shuzhi (see note 8, below), but each is unreliable when discussing its author's role in events.
4. Wang Fan-hsi, *Memoirs of a Chinese Revolutionary*, 2d rev. ed., translated and with an introduction by Gregor Benton (New York: Columbia University Press, 1991), 251.
5. The volume, called *Yu Yin canji* (Surviving poems by Yu Yin), was edited by Zhu Zheng and published by Hunan renmin chubanshe in 1989. Yu Yin is similar in pronunciation to two other Chinese characters meaning "prison" and "hermit"—a hermit in prison; it is also a Chinese rendering of Zheng Chaolin's French name, Yvon.
6. The parents of the famous pianist Fu Ts'ong. Fu Lei, who translated R. Rolland and H. Balzac into Chinese, committed suicide in the Cultural Revolution and was rehabilitated in 1979.
7. Actually, Liu Jingzhen died on October 14, 1979, four months and ten days after the release of her husband.
8. Claude Cadart and Cheng Yingxiang, eds., *Mémoires de Peng Shuzhi: L'Envol du communisme en Chine* (Paris: Gallimard, 1983), 321. Actually, Zheng learned Esperanto in France.
9. Wang Fan-hsi, *Memoirs*, 48.
10. Wang Fan-hsi, *Memoirs*, 105.
11. The reference is to this book.
12. Wang Fan-hsi, *Memoirs*, 238–39.
13. Zheng Chaolin, *Surviving Poems*, 8.
14. Cheng Yingxiang and Claude Cadart, "Remarks on a Review of Peng Shuzhi's

Memoirs," *China Quarterly*, no. 197 (September 1986), 534. Cheng and Cadart are the daughter and son-in-law of Peng Shuzhi, Zheng's old adversary in the Chinese Trotskyist movement.
15. This comment and the following poem are translated from Zheng Chaolin, *Surviving Poems*, 88–91. Zheng also wrote in 1988: "Not until after I was released from prison in 1979 did I learn that the memorial proposed by Khrushchev had not been built. So even if the disembodied soul in my poem really had taken flowers to Moscow, it would have had to lay them before a disembodied stone. Today, there is every chance that the memorial of my dreams will finally be built, whether or not Trotsky's name appears on it in gold. As for myself, I am still not yet a wandering ghost. Now, I do not need to write about my dreams in ways that will fool the censor, for it is no longer a crime to speak out against Stalin. But I have no wish to write a new poem to voice my feelings, so I shall let the poem I wrote twenty-odd years ago stand, under its original title 'Memorial to Ding,' as a record of the events of those days."
16. Zheng Chaolin imagines a new Moscow, different from the one he left in 1924.
17. Mao once said of his opponents who refused to give up their positions: "Let them go to see their God with their granite brains."
18. The philosopher Zhuangzi (c. 370–300 B.C.) told a story about Chang Hong, a high official wrongly killed by a prince in Shu (now Sichuan). Chang Hong's blood, after being stored for three years, changed color from red to emerald—the basis of the popular saying that the blood of those wrongly killed turns green, and even becomes green jade.
19. In China, a person traditionally counts as one year old at birth and becomes a year older when the new year starts. For example, a person born on the last day of the last month of the lunar year will become two years old the following day.
20. Zheng Chaolin, *Surviving Poems*, 9.
21. The first revolution was that of 1911, the second that of 1925–1927.
22. When Zheng Chaolin wrote this memoir in 1945, the Chinese Communist Party was still nominally in a united front with the Guomindang (or Nationalist Party) against the Japanese; it had abandoned land revolution for the duration of the war and had become the most active champion of the patriotic resistance to Japan. To the Chinese Trotskyists, it no longer seemed to be a party of class struggle.
23. Fuzhou is the capital of Fujian province.
24. The Japanese had occupied Taiwan, across the water from Fujian, in 1895, so their pressure on the province was greater and more direct than on other parts of the Chinese mainland. As a result of Japanese economic competition, the market for Fujian's traditional products shrank dramatically after 1895, so anti-Japanese feeling was strong there.
25. In 1914, Japan seized German-controlled territory in Shandong. In 1917, Britain, France, and Italy secretly agreed to support Japan's claim to this territory, and in 1918, the government in Beijing acquiesced in this; in 1919, the Paris Peace Conference agreed to transfer German rights in China to Japan. On May 4, 1919, three thousand students demonstrated in Beijing against this "national betrayal" and beat a pro-Japanese official. There followed a nationwide movement of strikes, lecture strikes, and anti-Japanese boycotts. On June 28, the Beijing government gave in to the protest movement and refused to sign the peace treaty with Germany. So the May Fourth Movement in its narrowest

sense had been brought to a successful end. In its broadest sense, May Fourth was a movement of cultural renewal and revolution.
26. In June 1922, troops under Chen Jiongming, who had previously supported Sun Yat-sen, surrounded Sun's residence. Sun then escaped to a gunboat anchored off Guangzhou and remained there for more than two months, after which he left for Hong Kong.
27. Beiyang is the Qing dynasty name for the northern coastal provinces of Liaoning, Hebei, and Shandong. The Beiyang warlords were a military clique split into the Zhili and Anhui factions.
28. In the last years of the Qing dynasty (1644–1911), China began to modernize its armies. New-style officers became a mainstay of the radical movement that toppled the Qing in 1911.
29. In June 1915, Li Shizeng, Cai Yuanpei, Wu Zhihui and others founded the Society for Frugal Study by Means of Labor (in French, the *Societé rationelle des etudiants-travailleurs en France*). The aim of the society was to help poor students study in France by working part time in factories.
30. A Fujianese term meaning "from other provinces."
31. By Xiang Kairan.
32. The article that Zheng here quotes, called "Xianfa yu Kongjiao" (The constitution and Confucianism), appeared in *Xin qingnian* (New youth), vol. 2, no. 2, on January 1, 1916.
33. Before May Fourth, most writing was in classical Chinese, a dead language "no longer spoken by the people." The new literature movement that started in 1916 argued that writing should approximate the spoken language. One of May Fourth's greatest victories was its "literary revolution": the creation of "a literature in the national language and a national language suitable for literature." This switch to the vernacular also spread to the Chinese students in France.
34. The *Great Learning*, the *Analects*, the *Doctrine of the Mean*, and *Mencius*, i.e., the basic texts of Confucian orthodoxy from the Song dynasty onward.
35. Zhu Xi (1130–1200) wrote a new philosophical commentary on the Four Books to replace the old Han dynasty explanation. Zhu's school, called neo-Confucianism in the West, became orthodox (and sterile) in the fourteenth and fifteenth centuries.
36. In civil examinations in imperial China, candidates were expected to write a literary composition in eight parts. The "eight-legged essay," rigid in form and devoid of intellectual content, became the symbol of stale, stereotyped writing in China.
37. The Daoist teachings of Laozi and Zhuangzi are generally considered to be more creative and libertarian than the teachings of Confucius. They promote independence, spontaneity, freedom, and happiness, as opposed to morality and rites.
38. The *shenshi* or gentry class in imperial China was the class of officials and degree holders in and out of office.
39. Zhang Zongxiang was the pro-Japanese official beaten to the ground by students during the May Fourth Movement in 1919.
40. In other words, Zheng means the May Fourth Movement in its broad rather than its narrow sense. (See note 25, above.)
41. Partly as a reaction to the First World War, which disillusioned many Chinese who had previously looked to the West as a model for their own country, some thinkers after 1919 began to stress the superiority of the Chinese tradition and "national essence" over the mechanical, mercantile civilization of the West.

42. In 1915, Li Shizeng, Wu Zhihui, Cai Yuanpei, and Wang Jingwei organized the Societé Franco-Chinois d'education in Paris. In 1920, Li, Cai, and Wu founded the Sino-French University near Beijing and the Institut Franco-Chinois de Lyon in France.
43. The linguistic map of southern and western Fujian is extremely complicated. A large number of mutually unintelligible dialects, including Hakka, flourish in its separate valleys.
44. Han Yu (768–824), an orthodox Confucianist, was a notorious scourge of non-Confucian thought in China.
45. Actually, it was compiled not by Bai Letian, the great Tang dynasty poet, but by Shu Menglan of the Qing dynasty.
46. Gong Ding'an, alias Gong Zizhen (1792–1841), was a Qing dynasty thinker, writer, and poet.
47. A poem of four regular lines, each consisting of seven characters arranged in a strict tonal pattern and rhyme scheme.
48. In 1919, Li Shizeng set up a soybean factory (the Usine Caseo Sojaine) at Colombes; its more than thirty workers used their wages to pursue their studies in France.
49. In 1901, China paid 450 million silver taels to the Western Allies at the time of their invasion of Hebei to crush the Boxers. With interest, the actual sum rose to 982 million. After protracted negotiations, Li Shizeng finally secured the return of the French portion of this fund, to be used for cultural and educational purposes, in 1925.
50. During the Warring States period (403–221 B.C.), a man called Lu Zhonglian in the State of Qi (now Shandong) achieved fame by his distinguished and selfless efforts to resolve disputes among warring states. He was admired throughout history as a peacemaker and a unique hero. Three names mentioned in this passage are related to his name. Ze*lian* means to take Lu Zhong*lian* as an example; Song*lu* means to praise Lu; and *Q*isheng means man of the State of Qi.
51. According to a friend of mine who is familiar with the early development of Cai's thinking, Cai was essentially a Modiist (a follower of the school of thought founded by Modi, a philosopher and a contemporary of Confucius who emphasized the concept of *boai*, or "universal love") when he was in China and remained so during the early days of his stay in France, though he had already studied Marxism at the time. He finally and definitively became a Marxist only in 1920, when the French Socialist Party decided to join the Comintern and renamed itself at its Tours Congress the Communist Party of France. [Note added by Zheng Chaolin in the early 1980s.]
52. The Chinese Communist Party's First Congress met in Shanghai, on July 23, 1921, though July 1 has been settled on as the official date of its founding.
53. In August 1920, Chen Jiongming, having decided to support Sun Yat-sen's plan to establish a national government at Guangzhou, advanced into Guangdong at Sun's behest and defeated Lu.
54. Chen was killed in February 1939 by the Iron and Blood Army, which had undertaken to assassinate various prominent Chinese who collaborated with the Japanese occupiers.
55. In July and August 1919, Hu Shi broke with the radicals of May Fourth when he wrote an article attacking the "slaves of Marx and Kropotkin" who tried to provide "fundamental solutions" for all society's problems by resort to totalistic "isms."

56. In 1924, the Russian Borodin drafted a new constitution for the Guomindang based on that of the Communist Party of the Soviet Union, after which the Guomindang became a mass organization with a centralist structure and a systematic ideology.
57. Baiyunguan, then used by the Shanghai secret police as an interrogation center.
58. I.e., Zhou Enlai.
59. I.e., Li Weihan.
60. By 1918, between 140,000 and 175,000 Chinese workers had been recruited to help the war effort in France and elsewhere. This large-scale labor migration had a big impact on the development of the Chinese radical movement. It gave Chinese students in France the chance to live with and to lead these workers, who, as a result, took Communist, anarchist, and nationalist ideas back to China. On the *Huagong*, see Nicholas John Griffin, "The Use of Chinese Labor by the British Army, 1916–1920: The 'Raw Importation,' Its Scope and Problems," Ph.D. dissertation, University of Oklahoma, Norman, 1973; and Michael Summerskill, *China on the Western Front: Britain's Chinese Work Force in the First World War* (London: Michael Summerskill, 1982).
61. See chapter 6 on Wuhan.
62. In fact, he first went to Moscow and later went on the Long March after going back to China.
63. At the time, to have students write articles on such a subject was considered old-fashioned and an echo of the old system of imperial examinations.
64. This policy was imposed on the Chinese Communist Party in 1922 by Henk (Hendricus) Sneevliet (alias Maring), a representative in China of the Moscow-based Communist International.
65. By 1920, the left wing of the New Youth group, especially those around Chen Duxiu in Shanghai, thought that their liberal partners around Hu Shi were too conservative, whereas the liberals thought that Chen was too political. By May 1922, the alliance between the two groups had collapsed altogether.
66. I.e., Dai Jitao, a sponsor of the infant Chinese Communist Party, who immediately retreated to the Guomindang.
67. Yao and Shun were the last two of the eight "culture heroes" of Chinese pseudohistory. Yu founded the Xia dynasty (2205–1766 B.C.); Tang founded the Shang dynasty (1600–1028 B.C.); Wu, the son of Wen, founded the Zhou dynasty in either 1122 or 1027 B.C.; and Zhou Gong was the consolidator of the Zhou.
68. Leon Trotsky, *Perspectives and Tasks in the East*, translated from the Russian by R. Chappell (London: New Park Publications, 1973), 4–5.
69. By "democratism," Zheng Chaolin means bourgeois democracy.
70. See Wang Fan-hsi, *Memoirs*, 60ff., for an explanation of this term.
71. See *Wu Zhihui baihua wenchao* (An anthology of writings by Wu Zhihui in the vernacular).
72. This is a parody on the old adage "Adultery is the worst of ten thousand vices."
73. Chen Duxiu's father died when Chen was only a few months old.
74. Yue Fei (1103–1141), one of China's most famous generals, was distinguished not only for his brilliant victories over the Jin invaders but also for his poems and calligraphy. *Manjianghong* is a beautifully composed *ci*, bursting with heroism and patriotism, that was said to have been written in Yue Fei's own hand and later engraved on a stone tablet.

75. The Northern Expedition was launched by Chiang Kai-shek in 1926 from Guangzhou, to overthrow the warlords and unify China.
76. The Huangpu (also transcribed as Whampoa) Military Academy was organized for the Guomindang in 1924 by the Russians, who also subsidized its subsequent running. Its mission was "the training for the army of junior officers, well educated in the political sense." The Huangpu clique, denoting former faculty and students of the academy, later became a main political support of Chiang Kai-shek, who was the academy's founding principal.
77. See chapter 6.
78. He died in an air crash in 1946.
79. According to recently uncovered literature, Chen had already been removed as dean of letters by Cai Yuanpei, president of the university, nearly a month before the May Fourth demonstrations. Cai was acting under pressure from the reactionaries. [Note added by Zheng Chaolin in 1989.]
80. The Red Beards of Manchuria were said to be remnants of the White Lotus rebellion; they now lived by robbery. In Chinese opera, a red beard signifies that a character is fierce and lawless, whence the name.
81. Alias Luo Yinong.
82. A famous late-nineteenth-century scholar, among the first Chinese to awaken to the need to learn from the West.
83. See Cadart and Cheng, *Mémoires de Peng Shuzhi*, for Peng's own account of his political conversion.
84. Trotsky sometimes used this name.
85. The Profintern was the Moscow-based Red Trade Union International.
86. "Chervonets" means "rubles in gold," though it was actually a sort of bank note issued in November 1922. One chervonets was equal to ten new rubles.
87. In Esperanto, Sennacieca Asocio Tutmonda. SAT's inaugural meeting in 1921 emphasized the use of Esperanto in the class struggle, urged all class-conscious proletarians to join SAT, and condemned the mainstream Universal Esperanto Association for its political neutrality.
88. Here I am wrong. In fact, these people were accepted into the Party immediately after arriving in Moscow, for they had already joined the Communist Party of either France or Germany. [Note added by Zheng Chaolin in 1989.]
89. *The Ass of Guizhou* is a famous fable written by Liu Zongyuan, one of the "Eight Great Essayists of the Tang and Song." *Ass of Guizhou* has since been used to denote someone who appears or pretends to be great or able yet actually is not so.
90. In July 1927, General Tang's commanders suppressed Communist organizations in Wuhan.
91. The Socialist Youth League, founded on July 22, 1920, was renamed the Communist Youth League in 1925.
92. Jiang in normal transcription.
93. October 10, commemorating the Revolution of 1911.
94. See Cadart and Cheng, *Mémoires de Peng Shuzhi*, 338-39, for another account of this party.
95. Later to become a traitor to the Trotskyists.
96. Here my memory deceived me. According to Peng Shuzhi's *Mémoires*, 345-46, there were two meetings at that time of cadres and activists in Moscow, and they were not held at KUTV. Luo Jiao and Peng attended these meetings

as representatives of the Chinese section of the KUTV Party organization. I heard of their proceedings later, during an informal chat with Peng. [Note added by Zheng Chaolin in 1989.]

97. Albert Mathiez, *La révolution française*, 3 vols. (Paris: Max Leclerc et Cie., 1922–1927).
98. In early 1931, Li and thirty-five other people were arrested in Shanghai by the British police and handed over to the Guomindang. Most were shot on February 7 in Longhua Prison. Those shot included Li and four other writers.
99. The Anyuan coal mines in Jiangxi were one of the Party's main proletarian strongholds in the 1920s.
100. Qi Xieyuan, a warlord of the Zhili faction, was military governor of Jiangsu. Lu Yongxiang, military governor of Zhejiang, controlled the Shanghai area. In September 1924, Qi attacked Lu and defeated him (though the victory was short-lived).
101. I.e., Li Lisan.
102. On page 68 is a sketch of a typical lane house of the sort built in Shanghai, Hankou, Tianjin, and other foreign settlements in China in the early twentieth century. These houses were generally owned by foreign estate companies (Shanghai's best-known landlords being Hadoon and Sassoon, both British Jews). But except for a few White Russians, they were occupied almost exclusively by Chinese of the middle and lower classes. (Most foreigners lived in apartments, European-style terraced houses, or detached cottages in the suburbs.) There is no space between these houses; each opens onto a common lane. Most lane houses have a small front courtyard and a passage (which may or may not be roofed and contains a water tap and a brick basin) leading to the back door. They have no toilets. All lane houses have two stories, with a big room on each. The downstairs room can be used as a parlor or dining room; the upstairs one, as a bedroom. The small room off the landing is known as the pavilion room; being cheapest, in the old days it was usually let to a single person (often a student or a jobless intellectual; hence the term "pavilion-room writer"). Generally, all these rooms (including the attic, if there was one) were partitioned (sometimes more than once), with more than one family inhabiting each floor. The lane house described at the beginning of chapter 5 is a duplex variant on this pattern, with an extension reaching across the alley from part of the upper floor.
103. Wuhan is on the middle reaches of the Yangtze. Hankou is part of the tri-city of Wuhan, which comprises Hankou, Hanyang, and Wuchang.
104. I.e., Xiang Ying.
105. A workers' district in west Shanghai.
106. Wang Anshi was a Northern Song dynasty reformer who, according to conservatives, never washed his face.
107. The holder of a low-level imperial degree under the dynasties.
108. On February 7, 1923, Zhili warlords bloodily suppressed a Communist-led strike of railmen. In Wuhan itself, the labor movement never really recovered from this blow until the arrival of the Guomindang's Northern Expedition in the city in September 1926.
109. In 1913, Yuan Shikai, first president of the Chinese Republic, suppressed the Guomindang and started a reign of terror.
110. The warlord Wu Peifu executed two leaders of the strike on that day.
111. I.e., Deng Zhongxia.

112. The Chinese Socialist Party was founded in 1911 by Jiang Kanghu, who had encountered anarchist and socialist ideas in Japan and Europe. In 1913, Jiang claimed that his party had 400,000 members, but he was almost certainly exaggerating. His party went into decline after 1913, when he retired to the United States. His attempt to revive it in the early 1920s came to grief after his relationship with Puyi, the deposed emperor, was exposed.
113. I.e., Henk Sneevliet.
114. Here I am wrong. It was at the West Lake (Hangzhou) Conference, held shortly after the Second Congress, that Maring insisted on this point. By the time of the Third Congress, Chen Duxiu had already been persuaded and no longer opposed joining the Guomindang. [Note added by Zheng Chaolin in 1989.]
115. I.e., Harold Isaacs.
116. I.e., the Chinese Communist Party.
117. October 10, the anniversary of the 1911 Revolution, China's National Day.
118. The implication is that otherwise, He Shizhen would have refused to go quietly.
119. I.e., those of the Guomindang.
120. The literary revolution of the late 1910s and early 1920s was aimed at replacing *wenyan* or "literary Chinese," based on the old classical language, with a new style based on the vernacular. Zhang Songnian's complaint was apparently that Peng Shuzhi's style was regressing in the direction of a vulgar variant of literary Chinese.
121. Here my memory betrayed me. The Fourth Congress opened on January 11 and closed on January 22. [Note added by Zheng Chaolin in 1980.]
122. This is probably a reference to the French edition of *International Press Correspondence*, a news publication put out by the Comintern.
123. The ninth was Xiang Ying.
124. Cao Kun and Wu Peifu headed the Zhili clique of warlords.
125. The actual membership at the time of the Fifth Congress was 57,900.
126. Under Zhang Zuolin.
127. Feng Yuxiang, the "Christian General," occupied Beijing on October 23, 1924, and forced Cao Kun to dismiss Wu Peifu from his posts and to resign as president.
128. The "unequal treaties" were imposed on China by foreign powers; these treaties gave foreigners special status and privileges in China.
129. A worker whose killing by the Japanese marked the start of the May Thirtieth Movement.
130. Alias Li Lisan, alias Li Longzhi.
131. Before the Fifth Congress of April–May 1927, the District Committee was bigger than the Provincial Committee. The Shanghai District Committee controlled the organization in Jiangsu, Zhejiang, and Anhui. Later, district committees became constituent parts of the municipal committees, for example, the east Shanghai district or the district covering the French Concession and south Shanghai. [Note added by Zheng Chaolin in 1980.]
132. Modern-day People's Park.
133. I.e., the New Magistracy.
134. I.e., that of 1925–1927.
135. A supplement rather like a gossip column, often consisting of reports on society scandals, literary wrangles, and the like, but sometimes serious.
136. *Hot Blood Daily* was the name of the strike journal edited by Qu Qiubai during the events of May Thirtieth. Twenty-four issues came out in June and July.

137. I.e., the younger brother of the writer Mao Dun.
138. I.e., Mao Dun.
139. I.e., not to speak Red, but to disguise his Communist convictions.
140. Popular songs of the period, one of them sexually explicit.
141. "Great Britain" brand.
142. "Red tin wrapped."
143. A leader of the Green Gang in the International Settlement.
144. To enroll in the Huangpu Military Academy.
145. Written sometimes with one set of characters, sometimes with another.
146. A veteran Guomindang supporter.
147. In Shanghai dialect, a "pheasant" was a lower-class prostitute. The implication is that Shanghai University was not institutional and was second class.
148. I.e., they came from the interior rather than from the relatively prosperous and open provinces of central eastern China.
149. Karl Marx, *Das Kapital: Kritik der politischen Ökonomie. Gemeinverständliche Ausgabe*, edited by Julian Borchardt (Berlin: E. Laub'sche, 1922).
150. I.e., October 10.
151. I.e., its conversion to "proletarian literature."
152. By N. I. Bukharin and E. A. Preobrazhensky.
153. Zhang Jingsheng was a professor of philosophy at Beijing University. After returning to China from France, he became one of the first people to campaign against traditional ideas about sex in China. He edited many sex stories, the first collection of which became a best-seller. He championed the exaltation of sex and wanted to create a utopian society founded on sex.
154. Here I am referring to malpractices already evident at the time among Communist Party members, namely, fame seeking and the demand for extra pay for overtime. I particularly disapproved of Shi Cuntong. He was in bad health and wanted to return to his hometown to recuperate, but he had no money. He asked Peng Shuzhi for a loan from the Central Committee, saying that he would repay the money after selling one of his translation manuscripts. Peng acceded to this request without consulting me. [Note added by Zheng Chaolin in 1989.]
155. In early 1926, Chen Duxiu fell ill with typhoid fever and was in the hospital for more than a month. Before going, he told Ren Zuomin that he was ill but did not say that he was entering the hospital. While there, he wrote no letters. We all thought that he had been assassinated. Everyone was extremely worried. We made inquiries everywhere, but there was no news of his whereabouts. When Chen Yannian left Guangdong for Beijing, he passed through Shanghai and helped in the search. Finally, after he had already boarded the steamship for Tianjin, a messenger rushed to the quayside to tell him that his father had "emerged." [Note added by Zheng Chaolin in 1980.]
156. I.e., the Guomindang.
157. These armies were occupying Shanghai.
158. I.e., the Chinese territory, south of the French Concession.
159. Longhua was the site of the garrison headquarters.
160. I.e., Wang Jingwei. The character Wang is written with the water radical, which consists of three dots representing three drops of water.
161. In Beijing opera, the character in the red mask is the good man; the character in the white mask, the bad man. Here, however, the reference simply means that Wu and Chiang played the same role—that of the Communist Party's deadly enemy—in different guises.

162. Chen means the "respectable" press.
163. Mao Zedong's younger brother.
164. Luo Yinong's (i.e., Luo Jiao's) nickname.
165. Li Lisan's nickname.
166. Xiaguan is on the southern bank of the Yangtze, outside Nanjing; Pukou is on its northern bank.
167. I.e., Wang Ming, chief representative of the Moscow-trained, Moscow-oriented faction in the Chinese Communist Party.
168. Before Chiang Kai-shek's coup on April 12, 1927, most Guomindang organizations were set up and controlled by Communists, who officially posed as left-wing Guomindang members.
169. Chiang Kai-shek's anti-Communist terror in Nanjing took place on April 10 and 11.
170. In 1927, Qu Qiubai had circulated a pamphlet attacking Peng Shuzhi as a Menshevik.
171. I.e., a low-grade secretary.
172. Peng Shuzhi's wife.
173. Cai Hesen's wife.
174. Referring in both cases to Chen Duxiu.
175. It was titled *Zhongguo gemingzhi zhenglun wenti* (Controversial issues in the Chinese Revolution).
176. The Zhou brothers were Lu Xun (i.e., Zhou Shuren) and Zhou Zuoren.
177. *Jiayin* was a magazine published in Tokyo by Zhang Shizhao in 1914 (the Jiayin year, according to the traditional Chinese calendar) to combat the tyrannical regime of Yuan Shikai. Chen Duxiu and Li Dazhao were among its contributors.
178. These words are in French in the original text.
179. Kemal Ataturk (1880–1938) is known as the founder of modern Turkey; during his rule, he carried out a program of modernization and Westernization. Outer Mongolia, called the Mongolian People's Republic after 1921, was defined by its Communist leaders as an "anti-imperialist, antifeudal people's power" carrying out a democratic revolution.
180. This was the reactionaries' nickname for Sun Yat-sen.
181. Chen Yannian's first visit to Guangzhou was probably before the death of Liao Zhongkai. He had come to Shanghai from Guangzhou on a number of occasions. Here I am conflating a series of such visits, which in my memory I can no longer distinguish. The exact date of his first visit to Shanghai can be determined by consulting the missing-persons advertisement in *Republic Daily*. [Note added by Zheng Chaolin in the early 1980s.] Liao Zhongkai represented the left wing of the Guomindang. He was assassinated on August 20, 1925, by Guomindang conservatives.
182. Zheng Chaolin's pen-name.
183. I.e., Chen Yannian.
184. According to materials that I came across only recently, Chiang Kai-shek first demanded the launching of the Northern Expedition. His demand was supported by Borodin but opposed by the Soviet government. There was, at the time, a special Politburo Commission, chaired by Trotsky, charged with preparing recommendations for Soviet policy in the Far East. It produced a report in which, among other things, all the commission's members (Chicherin, Dzerzhinsky, and Voroshilov) opposed the plans for a Northern Expedition.

When the report was submitted to the Politburo, discussed, and finally approved, Stalin not only supported the anti–Northern Expedition position but even added an amendment that read: "The Chinese government [i.e., the Guangzhou government; note by Zheng Chaolin] should in the present period emphatically reject any idea of an aggressive military campaign and, in general, any activity that would push the imperialists onto the path of military intervention." (See *Leon Trotsky on China*, edited by Les Evans and Russell Block [New York: Monad Press, 1976], 108.) Chiang Kai-shek ignored the Soviet position. Having staged an anti-Communist coup in Guangzhou on March 20, 1926, he launched the expedition in July of the same year. So it was a concession on the part of Moscow to Chiang Kai-shek when the Moscow leaders supported the military campaign. Borodin returned to Guangzhou from Moscow and reached a "gentlemen's agreement" with Chiang, the third condition of which was Soviet support for the Northern Expedition. None of these changes in the Soviet attitude toward the Northern Expedition had been discussed by the Central Committee of the Chinese Communist Party. [Note added by Zheng Chaolin in 1989.]

185. This incident got its name from a gunboat in the Guomindang's tiny navy. The captain of the boat was a Communist. Chiang Kai-shek seized the ship, apparently fearing a coup, and took measures against Russian advisers and Communists in Guangzhou.
186. Between May 15 and 25, 1926, the Guomindang Central Executive Committee under Chiang Kai-shek put severe restrictions on Communist activity within the Guomindang.
187. The Western Hills group, founded at a meeting before Sun Yat-sen's bier in the Western Hills near Beijing in November 1925, represented the right wing of the Guomindang; in December 1925, its members voted for the expulsion of Communists from the Guomindang's Central Executive Committee.
188. Later to become a Trotskyist.
189. Qu Qiubai was executed by the Guomindang in 1935. His papers went to the Oriental Book Company, with which the Trotskyists enjoyed close relations. So Zheng had access to Qu's papers.
190. General Tang Shengzhi, originally a Hunanese warlord, agreed early in 1926 to support Chiang Kai-shek's Northern Expedition.
191. I.e., the socialist one.
192. The sign of an officer; the lower ranks wore cloth leggings.
193. At the time, bureaucrats of the revolution were known as *wupizhuyizhe* or "five leatherists,"—i.e., owners of a pair of leather boots, a leather bandolier, a leather whip, a leather portfolio, and leather gloves.
194. Chen Yannian continued to direct Party work in Guangdong after the start of the Northern Expedition in mid-1926.
195. This was probably the draft of Qu's attack on Peng Shuzhi, later published under the title *Fandui Peng Shuzhizhuyi* (Against Peng Shuzhi-ism), but initially kept secret from other Party leaders.
196. An assemblage, or *ji*, is formed by taking one line from this poem, another line from that, and so on, until a new poem has been formed that expresses the assembler's own feelings. The lines can be from the work of one poet or several.
197. Qu Qiubai was a fan of Gong Ding'an (1792–1841), and so was I; he was far more familiar with Gong's poems than I was. On that occasion, he told me that China's classical poets, especially Gong Ding'an, wrote ambiguously, so

that we could use their poems to express our own ideas. I remember that he assembled a poem describing the peasant insurrection in which there appeared the line "suddenly on the earth a lion's roar is heard." Later, when Qu was arrested in Fujian (in 1935), a few days before he went before the firing squad, he assembled several poems from the work of Gong Ding'an and changed the line "Do not waste energy to buy fame" into "Do not waste energy trying to be a hero." [Note by Zheng Chaolin.]

198. Between January and July 1927, an "international workers' delegation," comprising the American Earl R. Browder, the Frenchman Jacques Doriot, and the Englishman Tom Mann, visited China under the auspices of the Red International of Labor Unions.
199. In the "left" Guomindang government at Wuhan under Wang Jingwei.
200. Sun Fuyuan was editor of a newspaper supplement. He was a close friend of Lu Xun and not a Communist.
201. Wuchang is across the Yangtze from Hankou, which is where the Comintern delegates were staying.
202. I.e., the European language that Zheng Chaolin spoke best.
203. Sun Fo was the son of Sun Yat-sen. Sun Fo is the Cantonese transcription of his name, transcribed as Sun Ke in standard Chinese.
204. Against Peng Shuzhi.
205. I.e., a Northern Expedition against the Fengtian Army in Henan or an Eastern Expedition against the government of Chiang Kai-shek in Nanjing.
206. Conservatively interpreted, Sun Yat-sen's Three People's Principles—nationalism, democracy, and people's livelihood—were the doctrine of the Guomindang. The Communist Party interpreted them in a more radical way.
207. The Anyuan coal mines are in Jiangxi but up near the border with Hunan. The miners of Anyuan played a crucial role in the early history of the Communist workers' movement.
208. Changsha is the capital of Hunan province.
209. A *liangjin*, or two-hall mansion, the second hall being in a courtyard at the rear of the first.
210. Being within high compound walls.
211. This is a reference to *Taohuayuan ji* (Report from Peach Blossom Village) by the Jin dynasty writer Tao Yuanming. According to this story, the people in Peach Blossom Village were so isolated from the world that a fisherman who turned up there found that they were unaware of events that had happened centuries before.
212. Commander Xia Douyin turned against the Wuhan government in May 1927, probably at the instigation of Chiang Kai-shek, and attacked Wuhan in the name of anti-Communism.
213. General Ye Ting was a Communist and commander of the Wuchang garrison in Wuhan.
214. I.e., the flag of the Chinese Republic in its early days, with red, yellow, blue, white, and black stripes—one for each of the five "nationalities" of China: Hans, Manchus, Mongols, Mohammedans, and Tibetans.
215. I.e., that of Chiang Kai-shek.
216. The warlord Feng Yuxiang was defeated in late 1925 by forces under the warlords Zhang Zuolin and Wu Peifu.
217. Feng and Chiang met on June 20 and 21, 1927; Chiang united with Feng against the Wuhan government.

218. On May 21, 1927, known as Horse Day, which was the telegraph code word for that day, hundreds of peasant leaders and Communists in Changsha were massacred by a Wuhan general who had gone over to Chiang Kai-shek; the massacre was tolerated by Wuhan.
219. Around June 1927, the Guomindang's Political Council in Wuhan decided to prepare for an eastern campaign, ostensibly to take military action against Chiang Kai-shek's regime in Nanjing.
220. In Jiangxi province.
221. The Nanchang Uprising of August 1, 1927, was later taken to mark the birth of the Chinese Red Army.
222. Actually, Lominadze was not shot but committed suicide before the secret police could arrest him. His draft of the August 7 conference document was titled "Letter to Comrades." [Note added by Zheng Chaolin in the early 1980s.]
223. They included Cai Hesen, Xiang Zhongfa, Li Weihan, Su Zhaozheng, Zhang Tailei, Ren Bishi, and Deng Zhongxia.
224. The conference issued four documents. One denounced the old leadership, in particular Tan Pingshan and Chen Duxiu, for opportunism. The others called for insurrections to overthrow both the Nanjing and the Wuhan regimes under the banner of the "revolutionary left Guomindang."
225. According to C. Martin Wilbur, *The Nationalist Revolution in China, 1923–1928* (Cambridge: Cambridge University Press, 1983), 150, Chen was named, along with Tan Pingshan.
226. After the August 7 Conference, Cai Hesen went first to Beijing and then to Tianjin, where he, Wang Hebo, and others restored the Party's Northern Bureau.
227. I.e., Qu Qiubai's wife.
228. Hailufeng, in Guangdong, was the site of the first Chinese soviet government, founded in 1927 by Peng Pai and suppressed in February 1928.
229. This chapter, deleted by Zheng Chaolin's official Chinese editors from the 1980 Chinese edition of this book and kept in the Party archives, was discovered by chance in Hong Kong in 1990, in a copy of the manuscript sent there by the author in 1950. It is included here without Zheng Chaolin's authorization. In this chapter, Zheng talks not of "husbands and wives" but of "lovers," or *airen* in Chinese. The use of this term by revolutionaries is a reflection of the revolt by Chinese young people, in particular students, in the early twentieth century against old-fashioned views of marriage, and of their advocacy of "free love" as opposed to marriages arranged by parents and through matchmakers, "commercial unions," sexual inequality, and wedding ceremonies in general. When young men and women fell in love, they simply began to live together. They might or might not have marked the occasion by inviting some of their relatives and friends for a meal, but they dispensed with all ceremonies, either civil or religious. Although they lived as husband and wife, they avoided using these terms. Before 1949, this practice was confined mainly to Communists and progressive intellectuals, but after the Chinese Communists assumed power, it became—with modifications—a national way of marriage. Now, however, China has undergone a revival of the old-fashioned style of marriage.
230. *Xiaolaopo*, literally "little wife," actually means "concubine."
231. *Yizhi* means "to know one thing." It is used in a phrase together with the word *banjie*, meaning "to understand half of it." Together, *yizhibanjie* means "to have scant knowledge."

232. Here, there is a play on Shi Cuntong's other name, Fuliang, which means to "restore the shine."
233. Shen Xuanlu's native place, near Hangzhou.
234. Shen Xuanlu's son.
235. Literally, "only she." Yang meant by this that, in the world, only this girl was truly hers.
236. Ding Ling is the Chinese Communist movement's best-known woman writer.
237. I have traced the advertisements. They were placed on November 17, 1924. [Note by Zheng Chaolin.]
238. Jianlong means "sword dragon"; Daohu means "knife tiger."
239. Qiubai means "autumn white"; Chunhong means "spring red."
240. Yang Zhihua means "poplar flower"; Liu Shiye means "willow leaf."
241. Both Xuanlu and Heidian mean "black shop."
242. Yang Zilie paints a completely different picture. She recalls Yang Zhihua telling her: "My former husband led a life of debauchery. He had the habits and characteristics of the pampered son of an influential family. After my parents had decided to marry me to him at the age of nineteen, I gave birth to a daughter I called Duyi. Naturally, I tried to persuade him to put some effort into his study. My father-in-law Shen Xuanlu, a modern-minded person, asked me to stick closely to his son. I even used to traipse around the brothels after him. There was no way I could reform him. Father-in-law wanted me to go to Shanghai University to study and to divorce his son. He approved my marriage to Qu Qiubai." (Yang Zilie, *Zhang Guotao furen huiyilu* [Memoirs of the wife of Zhang Guotao] [Hong Long: Zilian Chubanshe, 1970], 196.)
243. Confucian scholars of the Han dynasty (206 B.C. to A.D. 220) were famous for the diligent scrutiny of texts; those of the Song dynasty (960–1279) paid more attention to the essence of Confucian ethics and, in particular, emphasized the importance of suppressing human desire.
244. The fifteenth day of the eighth lunar month.
245. A popular song of the 1920s.
246. Last king of the Southern Tang dynasty, and a well-known poet.
247. Shuntian and Zhili, now Beijing and Hebei.
248. Peng Shuzhi and Chen Bilan stayed married to one another for the rest of their lives; Peng died in 1983, Chen in 1987.
249. Xiang'egan means Hunan, Hubei, and Jiangxi.
250. This word is in French in the original.
251. Qufu in Shandong is the birthplace of Confucius.
252. "Flag switching" was the term used at that time to denote General Feng Yuxiang's rebellion against his superiors Cao Kun and Wu Peifu during their war against the Fengtian warlord Zhang Zuolin. Communists applied it, by extension, to relations between men and women.
253. The first person to identify Qu was a cook-soldier, but according to a Guomindang newspaper, Zhang Liang, too, confessed. Zhang later joined the New Fourth Army and was reprimanded by Xiang Ying, its leader.
254. Later, Liu Jingzhen adopted the alias of Wu Jingru.
255. The capital of Guangdong province.
256. The Ye (Ting)-He (Long) army staged the Nanchang Uprising on August 1, 1927, and then marched south to Guangdong.
257. The Ye-He army was defeated.
258. *Threads of Talk* was a weekly edited in the 1920s by Lu Xun and Zhou Zuoren.

259. A reference to Zhuge Liang, a statesman and strategist in the period of the Three Kingdoms (220–265) who masterminded things from behind the scenes and is depicted in Chinese opera holding a fan made of goose feathers.
260. A play on "clasping the feet of Buddha," i.e., trying to seek protection from Chen Duxiu.
261. My editorial, published in issue no. 11, was called "Long Live Soviet State Power!" Qu's editorial, called "Chinese Soviet State Power and Socialism," appeared in no. 14. I wrote about the Great Dragon Empire and the Guomindang government on the one hand, and proletarian dictatorship on the other, and I stated that there could be no third way. [Note added by Zheng Chaolin in 1980.]
262. In 1927, Chen Duxiu said that peasants in Hunan had committed "excesses" during their land revolution.
263. According to a Chinese saying, at the end of its flight, an arrow shot from a crossbow cannot pierce even thin cloth.
264. In Hunan.
265. Dynastic histories from remote antiquity through the Ming dynasty.
266. Old encyclopedia-style compilations divided into three sections dealing with manners, customs, costumes, and the like; biography; and geography.
267. The Russian Narodniki or Populists, derided by Marxists as "utopian" and "petit bourgeois," had a predilection for the peasantry and terrorism.
268. Ye Dehui was shot during the revolutionary turmoil not because he was a "scholar of the old school" but because he had served as a high official under the Qing dynasty and was a big landowner and member of the so-called evil gentry.
269. I.e., Kunming Lake in the Yiheyuan or Summer Palace.
270. Chinese demonstrators seized control of these concessions in January 1927.
271. In the first instance, before the final split in July 1927, this meant the government and army of the left-wing Guomindang.
272. I.e., the Chinese Red Army.
273. The Long March, beginning in southern China in October 1935 and ending in northwestern China a year later, is portrayed by Chinese Communist historians as a victory march to open up a new front against the Japanese in northern China. Actually, it began as an evacuation of the old central soviet in southern China after the defeat of the Red Army by Chiang Kai-shek in the so-called Fifth Encirclement campaign. See Gregor Benton, *Mountains Fires: The Red Army's Three-Year War in South China, 1934–1938* (Berkeley: University of California Press, 1992), ch. 1.
274. After the formation of the second united front between the Guomindang and the Communists in 1937, the Communists temporarily moderated their policies and changed the name of the territory they occupied from soviet to "border area" and the name of their Red Army to Eighth Route Army (later joined by the smaller New Fourth Army). Between their arrival in the northwest and 1945, when Zheng finished this memoir, they expanded southward and eastward in a series of expeditions and campaigns.
275. They were arrested in the International Settlement.
276. The Creation Society was a literary group organized in 1921 by Guo Moruo, Yu Dafu, and other students returned from Japan and France. At first, it espoused "literature for art's sake" and romanticism, but later it moved to the left and ended up advocating "proletarian literature."
277. The Society for Literary Studies, founded in Beijing in January 1921, promoted

"literature for life's sake," in opposition to the Creation Society's "literature for art's sake."
278. I.e., Mao Dun.
279. The "ultra-left Li Lisan line," imposed on the Chinese Communist Party by Stalin, lasted from 1929 to 1930.
280. It was called *Wenhua pipan* (Cultural criticism). [Note by the Chinese editors of Zheng's book.]
281. In 1928, a group of young supporters of the Creation Society returned from Japan and launched the magazine *Wenhua pipan* (Cultural criticism). In it, they used a style of writing strongly influenced by Japanese, in both terms and structure. As a result, their articles were practically unreadable and unintelligible. Not even book-trained intellectuals could understand them, let alone the workers for whom they had supposedly been written. About five years later, a campaign was started up by other left-wing writers (including Qu Qiubai) to promote a *dazhongyu*, a language for and of the masses.
282. I.e., in 1942.
283. In French in the original. This is the day on which the Guangzhou Insurrection started in 1927.
284. An incident that took place in January 1941, when superior Guomindang forces attacked and destroyed the Communist New Fourth Army headquarters in southern Anhui, after which the united front was over in all but name.
285. Chen Lifu led the Guomindang's Investigation Division for some ten years after 1928. His book *Weisheng lun* (On vitalism, translated into English as *Philosophy of Life*) was intended to restore a conservative interpretation of China's cultural tradition and provide a philosophical basis for the ideas of Sun Yat-sen.
286. Xiamen is also known as Amoy in the West.
287. In 1929, the Red Army marched into western Fujian and founded a Soviet base there in conjunction with local Communist forces.
288. The capital of Fujian province.
289. I.e., Wu Jingru, Zheng's wife.
290. Here, my memory played a trick on me. Li was elected as an alternate member of the Politburo at the Sixth Congress. By the time he came to head the Propaganda Department, he had already been promoted to full membership of the Politburo after a certain other full member left. [Note added by Zheng Chaolin in 1989.]
291. Cai Hesen had been leader of the Party's Northern Region.
292. Actually, Li Lisan came second to last, before Zhang Guotao.
293. A few years later, Qu Qiubai also became interested in the question of the Latinization of Chinese.
294. Shen Yanbing was a native of Zhejiang.
295. Cao Can was a prime minister in the Han dynasty. The *Han shu* is a history in 120 chapters of the Former or Western Han dynasty (206 B.C to A.D. 23).
296. Beijing speech is used as the basis for modern standard spoken Chinese. The Wu languages (or dialects) of Chinese are spoken in eastern China; Suzhou (or ancient Wu) dialect is their best-known representative. The Yue languages, including Cantonese, are spoken in Guangdong and parts of Guangxi. The Min languages are spoken mainly in Fujian. Between them, these four language systems account for the majority of Chinese speakers.
297. This is a reference to the appendix, titled "A Remarkable Document on the

Notes to Pages 200–215   305

Policy and the Regime of the Communist International," to Trotsky's long article "The Chinese Question After the Sixth Congress." (See Leon Trotsky, *Problems of the Chinese Revolution* [London: New Park Publications, 1969], 171–84.)
298. This word is in French in the original.
299. In late 1927 or early 1928, Xiang Ying replaced Deng Zhongxia as secretary of the Jiangsu Committee.
300. I.e., the person who had begun the trouble ended it.
301. On February 7, 1923, the Beijing-Hankou railway workers called an organizational conference of their union in Zhengzhou, Henan province. The warlord Wu Peifu ordered his troops to break up the meeting, and sixty workers were killed.
302. Gu Zhenghong (1905–1925), a worker activist in the Japanese Neiwai Cotton Mill in Shanghai, joined the Chinese Communist Party after the February strike in 1925.
303. Short for Mezhdunarodnaia Organizatsiia Pomoshchi Bortsam Revolutsii, the association's Russian name.
304. Niu Yongjian (1870–1965) was a republican revolutionary, a military leader under the Guomindang, and governor of Jiangsu province between 1927 and 1929. The Green Gang, under Du Yuesheng, was an underworld society that operated from Shanghai.
305. I.e., the draft of it.
306. *Yang* written with a different character means "to rear"; *Hu* means "tiger." *Chen* written with another character and pronounced slightly differently (*cheng*) means "to become"; *Qun* means "crowd." So *yang hu cheng qun* means "to rear tigers in large numbers."
307. These two well-known lines are from a poem by Deng Hanqi, a little-known poet of the Qing dynasty. The poem is grounded in historical fact. In China's Spring and Autumn period (770–476 B.C.), the small State of Xi (in part of present-day Henan province) was conquered by the king of Chu (now Hubei and Hunan). The king of Chu killed Marquis Xi, head of Xi, but held Marchioness Xi (a beautiful woman) captive and then married her. She did not take her own life and bore the king of Chu three sons. But she refused to utter a single word during all those years. Finally, under pressure, she explained to the king of Chu why she had remained mute: "For a woman like me, who has served two husbands yet cannot die, there is no point in speaking."
308. Li Jida did not die at the same time as Li Dazhao. He was arrested and killed in Tianjin a year after Li Dazhao's execution. [Note added by Zheng Chaolin in the early 1980s.]
309. On July 16, 1927, the Guomindang Central Committee in Wuhan ordered restrictions on the Communists but also said that no harm should be done either to them or to the workers' and peasants' movements they controlled.
310. The capital of Hunan.
311. A poor man who was eventually elevated to the position of a high official in the Han dynasty. While still humble, he married a woman who despised him, and she wanted a divorce. After he became rich and powerful, his wife wanted to go back to him, but he refused, saying "Divorce is like water poured onto the ground." His wife then committed suicide.
312. The Nanjing government was organized into five *yuan*, or branches.
313. I.e., the Shaanxi-Gansu region of northwestern China.

314. Zhu De (1886–1976) was one of the Chinese Communist Party's greatest military leaders.
315. One *li* equals one-third of a mile.
316. She was somewhat lame.
317. A pamphlet compiled and translated into French by Paul and Laura Lafargues. It probably consisted of the following three works by Friedrich Engels: *Zur Geschichte des Urchristentums* (On primeval Christianity), *Die Entwicklung des Sozialismus von der Utopie zur Wissenschaft* (The development of socialism from utopia to science), and *Ludwig Feuerbach und der Ausgang der klassischen deutschen Philosophie* (Ludwig Feuerbach and the outcome of classical German philosophy).
318. This is a reference to the second united front between the two parties, which by 1945 was no more than nominal.
319. By using this term of address, they were implying that they knew that they were dealing with Communists.
320. I.e., He Zishen.
321. At that time, the public security officials of the Guomindang were not yet specially trained as agents of anticommunism and had no great interest in arresting Communists. [Note added by Zheng Chaolin in 1989.]
322. Slang for torture.
323. I.e., Zheng Chaolin, Cai Zhende, and Ma Yufu.
324. A Communist.
325. Cantonese is unintelligible to speakers of standard Chinese.
326. The capital of the Tang dynasty, now Xi'an.
327. One of China's five sacred mountains, in Shaanxi province.
328. Also mainly in the part of northern China whence Li Zhongsan came.
329. A famous connoisseur of antiquarian objects and an important official in the Qing dynasty.
330. Jiangnan is that part of eastern China directly south of the Yangtze.
331. Clear Brightness, i.e., the fifth solar term, roughly corresponding to Easter, around April 5.
332. Here I got the time and place wrong. Yin Kuan did not give us any Oppositionist documents when we first left prison. He did so only after we had moved home. [Note added by Zheng Chaolin in 1980.]
333. *Our Word*, founded in 1928, was published by the first group of Chinese Trotskyists to be deported back to China from the Soviet Union.
334. V. I. Lenin, *Collected Works* (London: Martin Lawrence, n.d.), vol. 20, bk. 1, 120.
335. In fact, Trotsky probably did not oppose Communist entry into the Guomindang until April 1926; see Alexander Pantsov and Gregor Benton, "Did Leon Trotsky Oppose the CCP Joining the Guomindang 'From the First'?," *Republican China* XIX (1994), 2: 52–66.
336. China's first revolution had been in 1911, so the revolution between 1925 and 1927 counted as the second, and the future revolution would be the third.
337. Quoted in Trotsky, *Problems of the Chinese Revolution*, 132.
338. Chinese Trotskyists preferred the term *guomin huiyi*, or "national assembly," to the term *lixian huiyi*, or "constituent assembly." In China, the word *lixian* had been discredited as a result of successive attempts first by the dying Qing dynasty and then by Yuan Shikai and the warlords after the Revolution of 1911 to draft a constitution and convoke a constituent assembly. In the 1920s

and the 1930s, the memory of these "constitutional tricks" was still very fresh in China. The word *lixian* was not only unpopular but sounded positively reactionary. Trotsky accepted the arguments of his Chinese comrades on this question, and after 1930, he used the term national assembly instead of constituent assembly, which he had originally proposed.

339. In November 1927, Deng Yanda called for the setting up of a "provisional action committee" of the Guomindang to act as the true heirs of Sun Yat-sen against the usurpers in Nanjing. This later became known as the Third Party, whose goal was a socialist state, though it opposed the idea of class struggle and proletarian dictatorship.

340. After he was freed from prison in 1937, Zheng and his wife, Jing, went to Anhui, where Zheng recovered his health.

341. Translated in Trotsky, *Problems of the Chinese Revolution*, 120–84.

342. Trotsky, *Problems of the Chinese Revolution*, 167.

343. Throughout this period, Mao held office not in the Communist Party but in the Guomindang.

344. For an expurgated version of this article, edited to make it seem more Marxist than it originally was, see vol. 1 of Beijing's English-language edition of Mao's *Selected Works*. For a translation of excerpts from the original article, see Stuart R. Schram, ed., *The Political Thought of Mao Tse-tung* (Harmondsworth: Penguin Books, 1963).

345. Actually, the first important Party leader to pay attention to organizing peasants was not Mao but Peng Pai. Peng was a leader of the Guomindang's Peasant Department; the first director, before Mao, of the Peasant Movement Training Institute set up in 1924; and founder, in 1927, of the earliest Chinese soviet government, in Hailufeng.

346. Xu Kexiang and He Jian were military leaders who suppressed the Communists and their mass organizations in Hunan in mid-1927.

347. I.e., Mao Zedong.

348. Shi Dakai was a leader of the Taiping Revolution (1851–1864) who split with its main leader Hong Xiuquan and went to Sichuan.

349. I.e., Li Weihan.

350. *Water Margin* (translated into English by Pearl Buck as *All Men Are Brothers*) is about a group of bandit heroes who set up a mountain base from which they fight against injustice in society. Traditionally, this and other classical novels in China were published without punctuation, which was added (in the form of commas and full stops) by the reader. Wang Yuanfang, of the Oriental Book Company, helped introduce Western punctuation to China. His contribution to the movement for a modern literature was to punctuate the classics.

351. The Ye-He army marched south after the Nanchang Uprising on August 1, 1927, and captured Shantou on the Guangdong coast on September 23, where it was defeated a week later.

352. Luo Yinong, who was secretary of the Jiangxi Provincial Committee, knew Zhu De. Zhu had been a general in the Yunnan (warlord) Army. He had gone to Germany to study, where he apparently joined the Chinese Communist Party. On one occasion after Luo Yinong had been transferred to Hubei, he invited me to accompany him to a certain hotel to meet a comrade who was an army officer. When I got there, I discovered that it was Zhu De. We hastily exchanged a few words, and then I left. I seem to recall that he was thin, but apart from that I cannot remember anything about him. [Note by Zheng Chaolin.]

353. Fan Shisheng was a Guomindang commander and an old acquaintance of Zhu De from Yunnan. Zhu briefly "allied" with Fan and got some supplies from him, but he soon broke the alliance when the Central Committee criticized it.
354. In early September 1927, Mao was sent to his native Hunan to lead peasant uprisings. The uprisings failed, but Mao took the survivors into the Jinggang Mountains and formed them into a guerrilla army.
355. I.e., other than the Chen Duxiu group.
356. Jiangxi was the site of several Red Army bases, including of the Chinese Communists' Central Soviet and its capital Ruijin, in the late 1920s and early 1930s.
357. In this period, *Red Flag*—the new Party organ published after Zheng Chaolin quit the Propaganda Department—regularly announced the names and offenses (real or invented) of people expelled from the Party.
358. Peng Pai and Yang Yin fled to Shanghai in 1928, after the suppression of the Hailufeng Soviet, which they had led. On August 24, 1929, they were arrested along with Yan Changyi; a week later, the three of them were executed.
359. See Wang Fan-hsi, *Memoirs* (1980), 44–104; and Yueh Sheng (Sheng Yue), *Sun Yat-sen University in Moscow and the Chinese Revolution: A Personal Account* (New York: Center for East Asian Studies, University of Kansas, 1971), 164ff.
360. I.e., Wang Fanxi (Wang Fan-hsi).
361. At the time, each of the four organizations claimed the title "Chinese Communist Left Opposition." None called itself a *she* (society), which was a term used by outsiders. But to distinguish between them, even their members all tacitly accepted the term. [Note added by Zheng Chaolin in 1982.]
362. I.e., a translator and interpreter from and into Russian.
363. At the time, Peng was the only person who knew Chen's address.
364. Chen Duxiu died on May 27, 1942, in Jiangjin, Sichuan province.
365. Wang Fanxi has written to me to say that there was no organizational split between the Guangdong faction (led by Liang Ganqiao) and the Shanghai faction (led by Ou Fang) in the Our Word group. The entire northern organization of the Our Word group had split away nearly one year before the Unification Congress and become part of the founding nucleus of the October group, in whose name they participated in the unity negotiations and the congress. This is the first I knew of this. [Note added by Zheng Chaolin in the early 1980s.]
366. After counting the membership of each group, the Negotiating Committee finally awarded the Proletarian and Our Word Societies one extra delegate each. The Proletarian Society then decided to send Peng Shuzhi, but he arrived either on the second or third day of the proceedings or not at all. [Note added by Zheng Chaolin in 1982.] As far as Wang Fanxi recalls, Peng did not attend this congress. He also recalls that there were seventeen delegates in all: seven representing Our Word, six representing the Proletarian group, four representing the October group, and two representing the Combat group. Since one delegate was allowed for every twenty members, this means that there were approximately 340 Trotskyists in China in 1931.
367. This article appeared in the Hong Kong Trotskyist journal *Xinmiao* (New sprouts), August 1993, 41–47, under the title "Disanci ruyu genggai" (A brief account of my third spell in prison). The same article appeared, but with many deletions, in Hong Kong's *Kaifang*.
368. For an estimate of the number of Trotskyists and their sympathizers arrested on December 22, 1952, see the letter from Zheng Chaolin appended to this article.

369. According to Wang Fanxi (personal communication), the raid was coordinated at the national level and carried out more or less simultaneously in Guangxi, Guangdong, Fujian, Anhui, Zhejiang, Yunnan, the northeast, Beijing, and Shanghai. Some of those arrested were removed to other places to serve their sentences. For example, those arrested in Guangdong were taken to Wuhan, those in north and northeast China to Beijing, and those in Wenzhou and Anhui to Shanghai; but those arrested in Yunnan were detained locally.
370. More important prisoners were usually kept alone.
371. Anastas Ivanovich Mikoyan, an Armenian revolutionary who was on the Politburo after 1939, supported Khrushchev's criticism of Stalin.
372. I.e., on the fifteenth day of the eighth lunar month.
373. Yu Shouyi, alias Mai (or Mei) Erduan, was a Trotskyist activist in Beijing who spent a short period in 1950 in Hong Kong.
374. This woman, surnamed Cao, was a leader of the Trotskyists' Wenzhou Youth League. Her younger brother, also Cao, escaped from prison in Wenzhou along with his warder, Wang Guoquan, whom he had converted to Trotskyism and who masterminded the escape; Wang later worked as a seaman from Hong Kong and was eventually blacklisted for leading strikes.
375. Du Weizhi was not a Trotskyist at the time of his arrest, having already left the Trotskyist organization. He translated Engels's *Dialectics of Nature* and Plekhanov's *Militant Materialism* into Chinese. He died in 1992, in Shanghai.
376. Two pre-1949 Trotskyist journals.
377. A medical doctor who, though a prisoner, served as a physician in the prison.
378. I.e., cherishing an illusion that cannot be realized.
379. The section chief probably meant to imply that Yin Kuan's release had had nothing to do with Zheng's request.
380. This was the year in which the Cultural Revolution started.
381. I.e., prisoners working outside the prison.
382. "Encircled and suppressed" is a term ironically borrowed from Chiang Kaishek's policy of surrounding and destroying the Communists in southern China in the early 1930s.
383. After the struggle meeting, I did not retract my statement that I was a "counterrevolutionary." Sometimes, government workers would ask me, "Does that amount to an admission of guilt?" I would answer, "I am a counterrevolutionary." If they then asked, "Why are you a counterrevolutionary?" I would reply, "Because I oppose the Communist Party." On one occasion, this answer proved insufficient, and my interlocutor said, "Opposing the Communist Party is not [the same as being a] counterrevolutionary." I was thrown aback, and retorted, "Isn't opposing the Communist Party counterrevolutionary?" He said no, it isn't. I suddenly hit on a way out of my predicament. "The Communist Party represents the people," I said. "By opposing the Communist Party, I oppose the people." Only then did he give up. After the Third Plenum of the Eleventh Central Committee of the Party, held in December 1978, when my citizenship was about to be restored, the authorities arranged for each of us to write a summary report, which we discussed and passed around at a meeting. I made sure that I was the last to read my report. In it, I said that "I had not been successfully reformed" as a way of pointing out that I had never been guilty of any crime. [Note by Zheng Chaolin.]
384. The Wangs, who were not Trotskyists themselves but were considered Trotskyist sympathizers, ran Shanghai's leftist Oriental Book Company.

385. Deng, a woman, had been a student leader at Shanghai's Jiaotong (or Communications) University.
386. Wang Fanxi, letter, February 9, 1994.
387. The Xiandai shiliao biankan she.
388. See note 1, above.

Index

Ai Mier, 30. *See also* Xiao Zizhang
All-China General Labor Union, 88, 90, 200
All-China Students' Federation: dominated by communists, 86; mentioned, 126
An Ticheng, 208
anarchism, 25
anti-Montargis group, 20–22
Asian Nations' Conference, 59
Association to Relieve Distress, 204, 216, 222
August 1 Nanchang Uprising, 131, 174
August 7 Conference, 132–33

Bai Chongxi: takes over as commander of Shanghai, 102; mentioned, 208
Baku Conference of the Peoples of the East, 46
Bao Junfu, 220, 224, 225
Bao Pu: short description, 50; interpreter at Moscow, 52; his friendship with Zheng Chaolin, 56–57; his knowledge of Esperanto, 56; mentioned, 54
Baoshan Road massacre, 104
Barbusse, Henri: editor of *Clarté*, 34; mentioned, 17
Beijing government: orders the closing down of the Shanghai General Labor Union, 90
Beijing massacre of 1926, 183
Beijing-Hankou rail strike, 73
Blanqui, Auguste, xiv
Bolshevik: production of, 172; and Zheng Chaolin's articles in, 177–79; ceases publication, 198; mentioned, 155, 174, 189, 239, 252–54
Borodin, Mikhail M.: his role as adviser to the Guomindang government, 72; and "national revolution", 110; and support for the Northern Expedition, 112; and the Fifth Congress, 120, 122; and the 1927 Moscow directive, 131; mentioned, 70, 116
Bu Shiqi, 48, 139
Buduan geming lun ABC (ABC of permanent revolution), 229–30, 254
Buersaiweike. See Bolshevik
Bukharin, Nikolai I.: at KUTV, 64; and the impact of *The ABC of Communism*, 94–95; and *Lenin as a Marxist* and *The Peasant Problem*, 95; and reversal of Moscow verdict, 255; mentioned, 92, 186, 195

Cai Chang: and Ouyang Ze, 138; at KUTV, 146
Cai Hesen: biographical sketch, 275; in Europe, 19, 21, 32; and the house on Moulmein Road, 69; a short description, 71; and the meetings at Moulmein Road, 71; at South Minhouli, 76; and his work on *Guide Weekly*, 77; and the Fourth Congress of the Chinese Communist Party, 78, 80; article in *Guide Weekly* on the overthrow of Cao and Wu, 83; in Hankou, 108; and "national revolution," 110; and conflict with Qu Qiubai, 112; in Wuhan, 116; and Central Committee Meetings in Hankou, 117; elected head of the congress secretariat, 118; and slogans at the Fifth Congress, 119, 122; and Tang Shengzhi, 127; with the Communist armed forces, 133; and Xiang Jingyu, 142–46; and Li Yichun, 145; and the publication of his lectures on Chinese opportunism, 177; head of the Propaganda Department, 196; and *Jihuizhuyi shi*

311

312 INDEX

(History of opportunism), 197; removed from the Standing Committee, 198; mentioned, 20–21, 41, 70, 86, 91, 93, 149, 154, 245
Cai Yichen, 124
Cai Yuanpei: biographical sketch, 275; mentioned, 14
Cai Zhende: and the Jiangsu Provincial Committee, 200–201; his accommodation, 201–2; imprisoned, 218–25; and the Trotsky essays, 229; and the significance of permanent revolution, 239; mentioned, 217, 227, 240
Cai Zhihua: and his return from Russia to China, 65; mentioned, 70
Cao Can, 199
Cao Dianqi, 172
Cao Kun, 83
Chang Jiang Bureau: and split between Luo Yinong and Li Weihan, 176; mentioned, 173
Chang Yuqing: and the kidnapping of Li Lisan, 204; mentioned, 90
Chen Bilan: biographical sketch, 275; in charge of the Women's Department, 81; and Peng Shuzhi, 145–47; and Huang Rikui, 146; at marriage of Zhang Baoquan and Huang Wanqing, 214; mentioned, 217
Chen De'en, 127
Chen Dezheng, 74
Chen Duxiu: biographical sketch, 275; and Confucius, 5; and his standing in the Communist Party after the August 7 Conference, 17; his article on Marx, 32–33; and May Fourth Movement, 34; and Fourth Congress of Third International, 36; and University of the East, 37; his relationship with Chen Yannian and Chen Qiaonian, 39–40; his move to communism, 40, 73; and the Socialist Youth League, 46; and the meetings at Moulmein Road, 71; his opposition to joining the Guomindang, 74; his articles for *Guide Weekly*, 77, 91; and the Fourth Congress of the Chinese Communist Party, 78, 80; as general secretary and head of the organization department, 81; his role in the 1925 strike wave in Shanghai, 84–85; and the General Labor Union, 90; and the third Shanghai insurrection, 99; and his joint statement with Wang Jingwei, 102; departs for Hankou, 104; and the formation of the Communist Party, 108–9; Trotsky's opinion of, 109; and the policy of "national revolution," 109; and conflict with Qu Qiubai, 112; and opposition to Northern Expedition, 112–14; and debates at the Soviet consulate concerning the nature of the revolution, 115; in Shanghai while Central Committee established in Hankou, 116; and Central Committee Meetings in Hankou, 117; and the Fifth Congress, 118, 120, 122; and his recalcitrant character, 120–21; relationship with Guomindang in Hankou, 130; and the August 7 Conference, 131–33; and Xiang Jingyu, 142; and affair between Peng Shuzhi and Xiang Jingyu, 143–45; supporters and opponents after August 7 Conference, 174; contributions to *Bolshevik*, 175; his opposition to the "Chen Duxiu group," 175; attacked in Cai Hesen's book, 177; his letters to the Central Committee, 178; refuses to attend Sixth Congress, 188; and the inner-Party struggle, 198–99; and phonological research, 199; critical pronouncements after the August 7 Conference, 200; first communist arrested in China, 203; and the Trotsky essays, 228–29; the development of his understanding of the nature of the Chinese revolution, 235; his views of the Red Army, 235–39; expulsion from the Communist Party, 240; visits Liu Renjing on his return from Alma-Ata, 240; and the Left Opposition, 242, 244–45; on Liu Renjing, 243;

becomes a delegate to the Standing Committee, 246; and the divisions within the Proletarian Society, 247; and split with Peng Shuzhi, 247; and the Unification Congress, 248–50; mentioned, x, xvi, 75, 76, 93, 94, 97, 111, 123, 147, 151, 154, 155–56, 173, 176, 213, 252, 253, 254, 271–72
"Chen Duxiu group": birth of, 175
"Chen Duxiu-ites" at the Sixth Congress, 197
Chen Hua, 2
Chen Jiongming: in Fujian during the May Fourth Movement, 3; and the work-study program, 3–4; mentioned, 22, 40, 251
Chen Jiru, 241
Chen Jiuding, 41, 45, 52
Chen Kunpei: biographical sketch, 275. *See also* Wu Ming
Chen Lu: and the Lyon Campaign, 24; attempted assassination of, 42; mentioned, 15, 205
Chen Qiaonian: biographical sketch, 276; in Europe, 29–31, 39–40, 45; secretary of the Central Committee's Organization Department after the Fifth Congress, 123; in Hubei, 126, 130, 173; and support for Chen Duxiu, 176; on the prospects for revolution after the August 7 Conference, 178; arrest and execution of, 187–88, 215; and attempt to form opposition group, 199; and Peng Shuzhi, 246; mentioned, xv, 111, 134, 139, 150, 202, 205
Chen Qixiu, 59–60
Chen Qun, 207
Chen Shaowei, 216
Chen Shaoyu, 106. *See also* Wang Ming
Chen Tanqiu: biographical sketch, 276; and the Fourth Congress of the Chinese Communist Party, 78; in Hubei, 123–24; in Wuchang, 125; mentioned, 128
Chen Wangdao, 75, 92
Chen Yannian: biographical sketch, 276; in Europe, 25, 27–31, 37, 40, 53, 55, 59, 65–67; and the house on Moulmein Road, 69; in charge of Guangdong, 82; replaces Luo Yinong, 104; and "national revolution," 110; and meeting with Chen Duxiu, 111; and the Northern Expedition, 112; critical of Chen Qiaonian, 150; death of, 209; mentioned, 32, 39, 45, 115, 123, 154, 209
Chen Yi, 125
Chen Yimou: biographical sketch, 276; and the Unification Congress, 249–50
Cheng Fangwu, 190, 191–92, 193–94
Cheng Shaozong, 193
Chi chao ji (Red tide), 70
Chiang Kai-shek: and Guomindang delegation to Moscow, 60–61; and the Huangpu Military Academy, 73; arrival in Shanghai, 102–3; sympathy for within Hubei, 131; effect of class struggle on, 185; and the Northern Expedition, 112–13, 205–6; his government at Nanjing, 119; and the blockade of the Yangtze, 130; and Chen Duxiu's article on the Red Army, 238; mentioned, 175, 205, 219
Chinese Communist Party: and policy in the 1920s, xv; European branch of, xv; and discussion in France over relationship with Guomindang, 33; and relationship with the Socialist Youth League, 46; Moscow branch of, 54; Third Congress of, 61; role of in the early 1920s, 72; First and Second Congresses, 73–74; and activities in Shanghai labor movement, 75–76; Fourth Congress, 78–82; and the development of the Party's work among factory workers, 83; and the May Thirtieth uprising, 86, 88; and the District Committee's preparations for insurrection in Shanghai, 97; Fifth Congress, 118–20; and membership in Hubei in 1927, 124; and the split with the Guomindang, 129–30, 133; and "Letter to All Comrades," 133; and

ignorance before 1926 of the history of peasant struggles, 184; Sixth Congress, 186, 188, 196
Chinese Socialist League, 61
Chizhi University, 75
Chu Fu, 29. *See also* Li Weinong
Chu Minyi, 23–24
Clarté: influence of on Chinese in France, 34; mentioned, 17
Combat Society: established, 243
Comintern: and its role in forcing the Chinese Communist Party to join the Guomindang, 73–74; the acceptance by the Fourth Congress of its instructions, 78
Communist University for the Toilers of the East. *See* KUTV
Communist Youth League: its founding congress, 22; and disagreement over the name of, 28; and the Montargis branch, 33; and Fourth Congress of Third International, 36
Communist Youth Party: formation of, 27–29; and 1923 conference in Paris, 37; mentioned, 252
Creation Society: 188–95
Cultural Revolution, 271

Dai Tianqiu: and Sun Yat-sen, 35; and the formation of the Communist Party, 108
Deng Xiaoping, 269
Deng Xixian, 214, 216
Deng Yanda: biographical sketch, 276; his resignation, 127; mentioned, 128, 234
Deng Zhongxia: and Shanghai University, 75; secretary of the Jiangsu Provincial Committee, 175–76; mentioned, 39
Deng Zhongxie, 73
Dewey, John, 49
Diderot, Denis, 35
Ding Ling: and a story in *Novel Monthly*, 189; mentioned, 141
Dong Biwu: biographical sketch, 27; mentioned, 123. *See also* Dong Yongwei
Dong Yongwei, 123
Doriot, J.: in Wuhan, 116; at the Fifth Congress, 118
Du Weizhi, 263
Du Yuesheng: biographical sketch, 27; protector of Niu Yongjian, 98; mentioned, 207
Duan Qirui, 205

Esperanto, 56

Fan Hongjie: and his move to communism, 73; death of, 209
Fan Shisheng, 237
Fang Erhao, 30
Fang Jiaobo, 88
Federation of Workers' Associations in Shanghai, 75
Feng Naichao, 191
Feng Yuxiang: and meeting with Chiang Kai-shek, 128; protects female returnees from Moscow, 135; mentioned, 83, 203, 226
Fu Daqing, 65
Fu Fengjun, 212
Fu Lei, xiii
Fu Xiangyi: and the peasant uprising in Hubei, 129–30; death of, 211

Galen, General, 50
Ganbuzhuyi lun (On cadreism), 255
Gao Feng, 41, 45, 82, 206
Gao Junyu, 142. *See also* Gao Shangde
Gao Shangde: and his move to communism, 73; and the Fourth Congress of the Chinese Communist Party, 78; editor of *Guide Weekly*, 142
Gao Yuhan: biographical sketch, 277; at Shanghai University, 92; on slogans of "national assembly" and "soviets," 234
General Labor Union: role in the Shanghai insurrection, 99–101; denies intention of attacking the garrison headquarters at Longhua, 102; mentioned, 206, 252
general strike of July 20, 1927, in Hankou, 129
Geng Jizhi, 70
Gong Binglu, 193
Gong Yang, 32

Gongyu (After work), 25
GPU, 64
Green Gang, 103
Gu Shunzhang: biographical sketch, 277; and the Shanghai District Committee, 91; and his work for the Military Committee, 97; role in organizing the insurrections at Hangzhou and Shanghai, 99; mentioned, 225
Gu Zhenghong, 84, 204, 224
Guangzhou: and 1927 insurrection, 178, 232–33, 253
Guide Weekly: its role in advocating the policy of national revolution, 74; move to South Minhouli, 76; and the May Thirtieth uprising, 87, 91; limitations of, 95; production transferred to Hankou, 107; and opposition to Northern Expedition, 112; and plans to revive it, 133–34; mentioned, 77, 85, 142, 172, 203, 204, 254,
Guo Longzhen, 146
Guo Moruo: on the ship from Shanghai to Hankou, 106; and the Northern Expedition, 190; and the Creation Society, 191, 193; mentioned, 188, 194
Guojia zibenzhuyi lun (On state capitalism), 254
Guojizhuyizhe (Internationalist), 254, 264
Guomindang: and discussion in France over relationship with Communist Party, 33; significance of in the early 1920s, 72, 73; reorganization of in 1924, 72, 112; and Maring's proposal to revive, 74; and the split with the Communist Party, 129–30; Trotsky's views on the policy of the Communist Party entering, 232; mentioned, 25, 235

Hai Baicheng, 120
Han Baihua: short description, 85; imprisoned, 203
Han Buxian, 204
Han Juemin: as dean of Shanghai University, 75, 92
Han Qi, 26, 28–29, 31
Han Qibo, 29
Han Yu, 11
He Bingyi, 87, 204
He Chang: secretary of the Communist Youth League, 82; and Zhu Youlun, 148; secretary of Hunan Province, 212; mentioned, 149
He Jinliang: in Vladivostok, 66–67; and the Fourth Congress of the Chinese Communist Party, 78; and his work in the General Labor Union, 90; and his work in Shanghai, 97; marriage of, 139; death of, 207; mentioned, 206. *See also* He Songlin and Wang Shaohua
He Long: biographical sketch, 277; and the authority of the Wuhan government, 130; army leaves Wuhan for Jiangxi, 131; and the Nanchang Insurrection, 237
He Luo, 207–8
He Mengxiong: biographical sketch, 277; on the Jiangsu Provincial Committee, 200; hoped for support from Zheng Chaolin, 201; and the attempt to win back the Left Opposition, 240; mentioned, 217
He Shizhen: and Shanghai University, 75; mentioned, 92
He Songlin, 90, 98, 114. *See also* He Jinliang and Wang Shaohua
He Weixin, 89–90
He Zihua, 216
He Zishen: biographical sketch, 277; on Luo Yinong and Chen Bilan, 146; and the Sixth Congress, 197; and Mao Zedong, 237; and the Left Opposition, 244–45; and the divisions within the Proletarian Society, 247; on Peng Shuzhi, 247; mentioned, 117, 212, 236, 248, 250
Hongqi bao (Red flag), 241, 268
Horse Day Incident, 131, 211, 236, 237
Hou Shaoqiu, 208
Hu Jingyi, 83
Hu Shi: biographical sketch, 278; and *New Youth*, 34; and *Outline History of Chinese Philosophy*, 35, 50; Chen Duxiu's break with, 108; mentioned, x, 17

Hu Yimin, 227
Hua Gang, 87, 180
Hua Han (see also Ouyang Jixiu), 191
Hua Jiaxin, 216
Hua Lin, 134
Huagong, 31
Huang Baoshu, 5
Huang Guozuo, 154–55. *See also* Huang Ping
Huang Jiantong, 263
Huang Ping: and the Fourth Congress of the Chinese Communist Party, 78; and Chen Bilan at KUTV, 146. *See also* Huang Guozuo
Huang Qisheng: and the Montargis movement, 32; mentioned, 17, 40
Huang Ren, 75, 76
Huang Rikui, 146
Huang Wanqing, 214
Huang Wenrong: secretary to Chen Duxiu, 107, 130, 133; and the Trotsky essays, 229; mentioned, 96, 108, 172, 174
Huang Zheng'an, 224
Huangpu Military Academy: role of students compared to that of Shanghai University students, 93; mentioned, 61
Hubei General Labor Union, 126
Hubei Provincial Committee: and support for Chen Duxiu, 176
Hubin Book Company, 240, 243
Hunan: central role of in the Chinese Revolution from May Fourth, 183–84
Hunan General Labor Union, 127

International Association of Non-Nationals (SAT), 56
International Association to Aid the Fighters of the Revolution (MOPR). *See* Association to Relieve Distress
International Settlement: and the May Thirtieth movement, 86–87
Internationalist, 254, 264
Internationalist Workers' Party, xvii

Jean Christophe, 34
Jiang Bingzhi, 141. *See also* Ding Ling
Jiang Changshi, 249
Jiang Guangchi: short description, 50; interpreter at Moscow, 52; and Shanghai University, 75, 92; work in the 1925 strike wave in Shanghai, 84; publication of his novel, 94; and Zheng Chaolin, 94, 153–55; on Shen Yanbing, 189; criticism of, 190; and complaints about the Creation Society, 194; mentioned, 30, 56, 139
Jiang Youliang, 103
Jiang Zhendong: biographical sketch, 278; delegate to the Unification Congress, 249
Jiangsu Provincial Committee: and support for Chen Duxiu, 175; raid on, 187; resolution of, 200; mentioned, 178
Jiangsu-Zhejiang war, 83
Jing Renqiu, 269
Jinri (Today) faction, 50
Juewu (Awakening), 57

KUTV: role of, 46–68; struggle between communists and anarchists at, 47; teaching at, 51–52; mentioned, xv, 46, 58, 62
Kamenev, Lev B., 62, 257
Kang Sheng: biographical sketch, 278; mentioned, 260
Kang Youwei: biographical sketch, 278; mentioned, 5, 32, 35
Katayama Sen: biographical sketch, 278; at KUTV, 64
Kawakami Hajime: biographical sketch, 279; and the formation of the Communist Party, 108
Khrushchev, Nikita S., xviii–xix
Krupskaya, Nadyezhda K., 242

l'Humanité: and Fourth Congress of Third International, 36; mentioned, 34, 62
labor movement: communists work in during the early 1920s, 73; activities of Communist Party in Shanghai, 75 development of in 1925, 84
Lai Yantang: delegate to the Unification Congress, 249
Lefèbre, Raimond, 34
Left Opposition: an internal faction of

the Communist Party, 242; and
  international splits, 242; divisions in,
  244; mentioned, 235
Lei Yin, 30. See also Wang Ruofei
Lenin, Vladimir I.: on the "democratic
  dictatorship of the workers and
  peasants," 231; and tactics, 233;
  death of, 63–64, 256; on the First
  World War, 254; mentioned, 109,
  179
Li Baozhang, 206
Li Binxiang, 116
Li Cheng, 89. See also Li Lisan
Li Chuli: and the Creation Society,
  191–93; in the Suzhou Reformatory,
  192, 195; and the expulsion of the
  Left Opposition from the Communist
  Party, 241
Li Da: and *New Youth*, 34; his move
  toward socialism with Chen Duxiu,
  108
Li Dazhao: biographical sketch, 279;
  flees to Moscow, 65; his move to
  communism, 73; elected to Central
  Committee at the Fourth Congress,
  80; and the formation of the
  Communist Party, 109; death of,
  209; mentioned, 59, 123, 205, 236
Li Fuchun: and the formation of the
  Communist youth organization, 27;
  and Cai Chang, 138; new secretary
  of the Jiangsu Provincial Committee,
  200; asks Zheng Chaolin for support,
  201; mentioned, 217
Li Hanjun: and *New Youth*, 34; his
  opposition to joining the
  Guomindang, 61, 74; his move
  toward socialism, 108; and the
  formation of the Communist Party,
  109
Li Heling: and assassination attempt on
  Chen Lu, 24, 42; in Moscow, 61;
  rejoins the Communist Party,
  136–37; shot by Peng Pai, 137; and
  Chen Bilan at KUTV, 146;
  mentioned, 39
Li Houji, 22
Li Hui, 210
Li Ji: biographical sketch, 279; on love
  affairs, 148; at Shanghai University,
  92, 93; and Wang Duqing, 194;
  mentioned, 142
Li Jida, 209
Li Liansheng, 216
Li Liejun: biographical sketch, 279;
  mentioned, 16
Li Lisan: biographical sketch, 279; in
  Shanghai, 89–91; on the ship from
  Shanghai to Hankou, 106; and
  Central Committee Meetings in
  Hankou, 117; and Li Yichun, 145;
  and opposition to Chen Duxiu, 176;
  his origins in Hunan, 183; at the
  Sixth Congress, 196–98; his
  criticism of the "Chen Duxiu-ites",
  200; threatens Xiang Ying, 201;
  kidnapping of, 204; mentioned, 104,
  149, 190, 194–95, 237, 252. See also
  Li Longzhi
Li Longzhi: and the anti-Montargis
  group, 20–21; and Marxism, 22; and
  the house on Moulmein Road, 69;
  short description of, 69–70; his
  activities in the Shanghai labor
  movement, 75; active in Anyuan, 82;
  and the development of the Party's
  work in the factories, 83; mentioned,
  84. See also Li Lisan
Li Minzhi: and the Creation Society,
  191; mentioned, 194, 201
Li Peize: and She Liya, 152; and Wang
  Ruofei, 152–53
Li Qihan: biographical sketch, 279; and
  the Fourth Congress of the Chinese
  Communist Party, 78; imprisoned,
  203; death of, 208
Li Qiushi: biographical sketch, 279;
  mentioned, 125
Li Shizeng: and his influence upon
  Chen Jiongming, 3; in France, 13;
  mentioned, 17, 19
Li Sihao, 90
Li Tiesheng, 191
Li Weihan: biographical sketch, 280; in
  Europe, 26–28, 30–31, 33; and the
  Fourth Congress of the Chinese
  Communist Party, 78; and his
  conflict with Zhang Tailei, 80;
  elected to Central Committee at the
  Fourth Congress, 80; in charge of

Hunan, 82; at the Fifth Congress, 120–21; in Hankou, 133–34; and fears concerning reliability of Li Heling, 136; and Luo Yinong, 148; on the Standing Committee, 173; and the controversy surrounding Zheng Chaolin's article on the dictatorship of the proletariat, 178, 179; and the Sixth Congress, 188, 196–97; affected by the Jiangsu Provincial Committee's criticism, 200; mentioned, xvii, 41, 196, 236. *See also* Luo Mai and Luo Man
Li Weinong: in France, 26–27, 33; in Moscow, 61; in charge of Qingdao, 82; death of, 205; mentioned, 139
Li Yichun: and the house on Moulmein Road, 69; and Cai Hesen, 145; and Li Lisan, 145
Li Yimang, 191. *See also* Li Minzhi
Li Zhenying: biographical sketch, 280; trained by Zhang Guotao, 82; and the August 7 Conference, 132; in charge of the Workers' and Peasants' Department in Hankou, 136
Li Zheshi, 148–49
Li Zhilong, 205
Li Zhongsan: biographical sketch, 280; and the beginning of his association with Zheng Chaolin, 226; and the funding of the Unification Congress, 248; mentioned, 227
Li Zhongwu: short description, 49–50; in Moscow, 52, 59, 65; mentioned, 51, 53
Li Zhuo, 25
Li Zongren, 219
Liang Botai: biographical sketch, 280; in Vladivostok, 66; and Zhang Liang, 153
Liang Daci, 249. *See also* Liang Ganqiao
Liang Ganqiao: biographical sketch, 280; and the split in the Our Word Society, 248; and the Unification Congress, 249
Liang Qichao: biographical sketch, 280; and *Ou you xinjing lu*, 35; mentioned, 49
Liang Shuming, 35

Liao Zhongkai, 110
Lin Biao, 269
Lin Keyi: at KUTV, 58–59; his return to China, 59, 65
Lin Mu, 29; mentioned, 110. *See also* Chen Yannian
Lin Wei, 27
Lin Xiangqian, 203
Lin Yunan: biographical sketch, 280; and the meetings at Moulmein Road, 71
Lin Zuhan, 70
Liu Bocheng, 237
Liu Bochui, 123. *See also* Liu Fen
Liu Bojian: in Europe, 27, 42, 61; in Hubei, 128; and criticisms against Chen Duxiu, 133; replaced as head of the Organization Department, 134; and the Sixth Congress, 197; mentioned, 23
Liu Bozhuang: biographical sketch, 280; and 1923 conference of the Communist Youth Party in Paris, 37; gives support to Jiangsu Provincial Committee, 201; mentioned, 211; earns money from literary activity, 217
Liu Cenzhong, 7
Liu Changqun, 82
Liu Fen: imprisoned, 123, 203
Liu Fu: and *New Youth*, 34; Chen Duxiu's break with, 108
Liu Guozhang, 106
Liu Hou: in France, 13; and Lyon University, 23
Liu Hua: death of, 204; mentioned, 205
Liu Jiao: short description, 48–49; in Moscow, 52, 55; mentioned, 50, 53
Liu Jingzhen: biographical sketch, 280; and her support for Zheng Chaolin, xiii, xiv; and her arrest, xvi; as teacher, xvii; arrest of during Cultural Revolution, xviii; and Zheng Chaolin, 155–56; and Cai Hesen, 196–97; arrest of, 218–25; mentioned, 240, 253, 266
Liu Qingyang: and Zhang Guotao, 146; mentioned, 22
Liu Qiushi, 67

Liu Renjing: biographical sketch, 281; and Fourth Congress of Third International, 36; editor of *Chinese Youth*, 82; and Shi Jingyi, 150; and criticism of Chen Duxiu, 229, 244; returns from Alma-Ata with several of Trotsky's essays, 239; Trotsky's correspondent, 243

Liu Shaoqi: biographical sketch, 281; active in Anyuan, 82; and his work in the General Labor Union, 90; from Hunan, 183

Liu Shaoyou, 211

Liu Yazi, 192, 208

Liu Yin: biographical sketch, 281; mentioned, 243

Liu Zhi, 103

Liu Zongyuan, 59

Liu Zunyi, 207–8

Lominadze, Vissarion: biographical sketch, 281; and the August 7 Conference, 132

Long Dadao, 102

Long Yun: biographical sketch, 281; arrest and execution of Wang Maoting, 198

Longhua Garrison Command, 207

Lou Shiyi: biographical sketch, 281; and his tribute to Zheng Chaolin, x; mentioned, xviii

Lu Chen, 82

Lu Dingyi: secretary of the Communist Youth League, 82; departs for Hankou, 104; head of the Propaganda Department of the Central Committee of Communist Youth, 105–6; mentioned, 116

Lu Rongting, 22

Lü Xianji, 67

Lu Xun: biographical sketch, 281; and *New Youth*, 34; criticism of, 190; mentioned, xviii, 193

Lu Yin, 142

Lu Yongxiang: and war with Qi Xieyuan, 69; and the Jiangsu-Zhejiang war, 83

Lunacharsky, A. V., 64

Luo Dengxian, 188

Luo Han: biographical sketch, 282; and the anti-Montargis group, 20–21; and the Unification Congress, 249

Luo Jiao: and Guomindang delegation to Moscow, 61; in charge of Shanghai, 82; and the reorganization of the Shanghai District Committee, 92; mentioned, 59, 146. See also Luo Yinong

Luo Mai, 29, 30, 178. See also Li Weihan

Luo Qiyuan: biographical sketch, 282; member of the Propaganda Department, 174; mentioned, 198

Luo Re, 30. See also Chen Qiaonian

Luo Shifan: won over to the Left Opposition, 241; member of the Standing Committee of the Left Opposition, 244

Luo Ti, 30. See also Wang Zekai

Luo Xuezan, 21

Luo Yan, 104

Luo Yinong: correspondence with Zheng Chaolin, 94; secretary of the District Committee, 97; short description, 97–98; and the first Shanghai insurrection, 98; replaced by Chen Yannian, 104; on the ship from Shanghai to Hankou, 106; and rumor of Moscow's replacement of Chen Duxiu, 120; sent to Jiangxi after the Fifth Congress, 123; in Hubei, 128–30; and the August 7 Conference, 131–32; and criticisms of Chen Duxiu, 133; in Hankou, 133–34; and Chen Bilan at KUTV, 146–47; and his rise up the ranks of the Communist Party, 147; and Zhu Youlun, 148; and Li Zheshi, 149; considered to be representative of the "Chen Duxiu group," 173; sets up the Chang Jiang Bureau, 173; and support for Chen Duxiu, 176; and isolation within the Communist Party, 176; death of, 188, 215–16; mentioned, 121, 135, 136, 150, 175, 206, 209, 210, 211, 214. See also Luo Jiao

Luo Zhanglong: biographical sketch, 282; and his move to communism, 73; trained by Zhang Guotao, 82; at the Fifth Congress of the Communist

Party, 118; secretary of the Hankou Municipal Committee, 124; on the Red Army, 238; mentioned, 92, 253
Lyon Campaign, 21–25
Lyon University, 23, 110–11

Ma Daofu, 77, 110–11. *See also* Zheng Chaolin
Ma Junshan: secretary of the Wuchang County Committee, 128; death of, 211
Ma Renzhi: and the Hubin Book Company, 240; mentioned, 243
Ma Yufu: biographical sketch, 282; and the Jiangsu Provincial Committee, 200–201; arrest of, 218–25; and the Trotsky essays, 229; and the significance of permanent revolution, 239; member of the Standing Committee of the Left Opposition, 244; and his opposition to uniting the Left Opposition, 244–46; and the divisions within the Proletarian Society, 247; and the Unification Congress, 248; mentioned, 217, 218
Manifesto of Independence of Spirit, 17
Mann, Tom: at the Fifth Congress, 118; in Wuhan, 116
Mao Dun, 131, 189. *See also* Shen Yanbing
Mao Zedong: death of, xv, 269; and the School of the Common People, 47; and the house on Moulmein Road, 69; at South Minhouli, 76; and the August 7 Conference, 132; his work in Hunan, 183; his role in the birth of the Red Army, 236–38; and "Report on the Hunan Peasant Movement," 236; and *Selected Works*, 255, 260–61, 265
Mao Zemin, 103, 236
Maring: and the policy of national revolution, 73–74, 109; and his role in forcing the CCP to join the Guomindang, 74
Marxism: development of 34; development of among Chinese in France, 34–36
May Fourth Movement: and anti-capitalism, 34; and the development of radical thought, 35; nature of, 36; many students in Russia radicalized by, 46; and the Chinese Communist Party, 73; mentioned, 1–2, 9, 17
Mei Dianlong, 224
Mei Zhonglin, 127
Merezhkovsky, D. S., 256
Miao Boying: and Bu Shiqi, 139; mentioned, 48
Military Committee of the Communist Party, 96–97
Mingtian (Tomorrow): established, 243
Montargis students: and manifesto, 19; anti-Montargis group, 20–22
Montesquieu, 35
"Moscow group," xv, 82
Mu Qing, 211

Nanchang Insurrection, 237
National Assembly: discussion of at the Unification Congress, 249; tactic of, 233–34
"National revolution": introduction of concept of, 73; controversy over, 109–10; Zheng Chaolin's views on 181–82, 185–86
New Youth: and anti-capitalism, 34; under editorship of Qu Qiubai, 64; and controversy over Peng Shuzhi's editorship, 77; and the formation of the Communist Party, 109; mentioned, 5–6, 17, 70, 79, 183, 251, 254
Nie Rongzhen: studied at the Russian Military Academy, 97; mentioned, 104
Niu Yongjian: sent to Shanghai to take command, 98; mentioned, 20
Northern Expedition: progress of, 98; Chen Duxiu's evaluation of, 175; Zheng Chaolin's views on, 183, 186–87; mentioned, 235

October, established, 243
October Society: established, 243; representatives meet Chen Duxiu, 245
Ou Fang: biographical sketch, 282; and the split in the Our Word Society, 248

"Our Political Views," 244
Our Word, 194, 249, 243
Our Word Society: establishment of, 243; divisions within, 244; representatives meet Chen Duxiu, 245; and their view of the other Left Opposition groups, 246; split of, 248
Ouyang Jixiu: and the Creation Society, 191; mentioned, 93, 208
Ouyang Qin, 136
Ouyang Ze, 138

Pan Hannian: Political Department representative in Hubei, 127; mentioned, 201
Pan Jiachen: on the ship from Shanghai to Hankou, 106; work in the Propaganda Department in Hubei, 126; work as an interpreter, 135; on the 1925–1927 Revolution, 180
Pan Wenyu: biographical sketch, 282; takes over from Zheng Chaolin in the Propaganda Department, 201; and the attempt to win back the Left Opposition, 240; mentioned, 241, 242
Pan Yizhi, 208
Pan Zinian, xii
Peng Gongda: and the August 7 Conference, 132; death of, 211
Peng Kang: and the Creation Society, 191, 193; jailed for terrorism, 195
Peng Pai: biographical sketch, 282; shoots Li Heling, 137; and opposition to the expulsion of the Left Opposition members, 242; mentioned, 184
Peng Shuzhi: biographical sketch, 282; and his description of Zheng Chaolin, xiv, xv; short description, 49; in Moscow, 55; and criticism of Bao Pu, 57; and Lin Keyi, 58–59; and Guomindang delegation to Moscow, 61; and his return from Russia to China, 65–67; and the house on Moulmein Road, 69, 71; at Shanghai University, 75, 92–93; at South Minhouli, 76; and his work as editor of *New Youth*, 77; and the Fourth Congress of the Chinese Communist Party, 78–81; in charge of Propaganda Department, 81, 82; work at Fusheng Road, 93; and the move to Hengbin Bridge, 96; and his reply to Qu Qiubai, 107; in Hankou, 108; as Chen Duxiu's right-hand man, 109; and "national revolution," 110; and Central Committee Meetings in Hankou, 117; his speech at the Fifth Congress, 119; sent to Beijing after the Fifth Congress, 123; and Xiang Jingyu, 142–46; and Chen Bilan, 145–47; attacked in Cai Hesen's book, 177; criticizes Chen Duxiu, 199; gives support to Jiangsu Provincial Committee, 201; and the Trotsky essays, 228; expulsion from the Communist Party, 240–41; and dissatisfaction with the Our Word Society, 243; member of the Standing Committee of the Left Opposition, 244; and the negotiations to unify the Left Opposition, 245–47; and the Unification Congress, 248–50; mentioned, 48, 50, 52, 53, 64, 91, 115, 121, 149, 176, 192, 194, 214, 217, 234–35, 270
Peng Zexiang: short description, 50; mentioned, 53
Petrograd Conference of the Peoples of the Far East, 46
Petrov, 49. *See also* Peng Shuzhi
Plekhanov, Geórgy V., 243
Proletarian Society: divisions within, 244, 247; Peng Shuzhi's view of, 246; and the negotiations to unify the Left Opposition, 245
Pu Dezhi: biographical sketch, 283; delegate to the Unification Congress, 249

Qi Guang, 30. *See also* Xiong Xiong
Qi Xieyuan, 69
Qian Xingchun: and complaints about the Creation Society, 194; mentioned, 191
Qian Xuantong, 34, 108
Qin Diqing, 57. *See also* Bao Pu

Qin Zhigu: and research society in France, 33; mentioned, 16, 25, 29, 117
Qiu Yunduo, 193
Qu Jingbai, 204
Qu Qiubai: biographical sketch, 283; and criticism of Bao Pu, 57; as editor of *New Youth*, 64; and the house on Moulmein Road, 69; short description, 70; and Shanghai University, 75; leaves *New Youth*, 77; and his pamphlet *Against Peng Shuzhi-ism*, 77; and the Fourth Congress of the Chinese Communist Party, 78–81; editor of *Hot Blood Daily*, 89–90; writing articles for *Guide Weekly*, 91; and relationship to Jiang Guangchi, 94; discussions with Zheng Chaolin, 94; as Chen Duxiu's right-hand man, 109; supports Borodin, 111–12; and support for the Northern Expedition, 113; ridicules Peng Shuzhi, 115; and his document against Peng Shuzhi, 115–16, 122; transfers to Hankou, 116; and Central Committee Meetings in Hankou, 117; and the Fifth Congress, 119–23; and the "August First" Insurrection, 131; leaves Wuhan for Lushan, 131; and the August 7 Conference, 132–33; and instructions from Moscow to leave the Guomindang, 133; assumes leadership of the Communist Party, 133–34; moves to Shanghai, 137; and Yang Zhihua, 140–41; and the affair between Peng Shuzhi and Xiang Jingyu, 144–45; and the blockade of the Central Soviet, 153; editor of *Bolshevik*, 172; unofficial general secretary of the Communist Party, 173; implements line of Comintern, 175–76; and Zheng Chaolin's article in *Bolshevik* on the dictatorship of the proletariat, 178–79; and the Sixth Congress, 188, 196–97; affected by the Jiangsu Provincial Committee's criticism, 200; mentioned, xi, 49, 71, 85, 92, 93, 96, 107, 126, 135, 136, 142, 146, 147, 177, 183, 189, 191, 192, 206, 208, 228, 236, 245, 252, 253

Radek, Karl B.: biographical sketch, 283; mentioned, 62
Red Army, 187, 235–38
Ren Bishi: in the Soviet Union, 44, 52, 67; secretary of the Communist League, 82; marriage of 139; attempts to persuade Chen Duxiu to attend the Sixth Congress, 188; mentioned, 49, 51, 139
Ren Kaiguo: in Hubei, 123; death of, 211
Ren Xu: and support for Chen Duxiu, 176; and the Sixth Congress, 197; earns money from literary activity, 217
Ren Zhuoxuan: in Europe, 27–28, 31; arrested and later betrayed his comrades, 205, 212, 213; mentioned, 106
Ren Zuomin: the secretary and treasurer of the Communist Party, 76; marriage of, 139; mentioned, 81
Republic Daily: Zheng Chaolin's articles for, 77–78; mentioned, 74, 131
Rexue ribao (Hot blood daily), 89
Rolland, Romain: and controversy within the research society, 33–34; mentioned, 17
Rousseau, Jean-Jacques, 35
Roy, Manabendra N.: biographical sketch, 283; in Wuhan, 116; and the Fifth Congress, 118, 120–21; and the 1927 Moscow directive, 131; and the August 7 Conference, 132
Russell, Bertrand, 17, 49
Rykov, Aleksei I., 255

Sa Weng, 175. *See also* Chen Duxiu
SAT. *See* International Association of Non-Nationals
Self-Enlightenment Society, 17, 18
Serge, Victor L., 34
Shakee Road Bridge massacre of June 23, 91
Shanghai: first insurrection, 98; second insurrection, 98; third insurrection,

99–104; strikes of 1925–1927, 185
Shanghai General Labor Union: its role in the May Thirtieth events, 88–89
Shanghai University: political confrontation at, 74–75; staff at, 92
Shao Ji'ang, 105
Shao Lizi: and the *Republic Daily*, 74; assaulted, 75; on the betrayal of Cao and Wu, 83; denounces Party members' discrimination against Guomindang members, 85; and the formation of the Communist Party, 108; mentioned, 92, 140. *See also* Shao Zhonghui
Shao Zhigang, 148
Shao Zhonghui, 92. *See also* Shao Lizi
She Cuntong, 34
She Liya: short description, 41; after studying at the University of the East, 45; becomes a full member of the Chinese Communist Party, 57; and Li Peize, 152
Shen Bingquan, xii
Shen Jianlong, 141
Shen Xuanlu: and Guomindang delegation to Moscow, 60–61; and the Fourth Congress of the Chinese Communist Party, 78; and the formation of the Communist Party, 108; mentioned, 140–41
Shen Yanbing: biographical sketch, 283; at Fusheng Road, 93; in Hankou, 117; leaves Wuhan for Lushan, 131; as possible editor of *Guide Weekly*, 134; and the Society for Literary Studies, 189; and his criticism of the Communist Party after the August 7 Conference, 190; mentioned, 96, 199
Shen Yinmo: and *New Youth*, 34; and the *Republic Daily*, 74; work in the 1925 strike wave in Shanghai, 84; and articles for *Hot Blood Daily*, 90; and the Society for Literary Studies, 189; mentioned, 143
Sheng Xuanhuai: biographical sketch, 283; mentioned, 183
Shi Cuntong: biographical sketch, 283; and controversy over name of Communist Youth League, 28; at Shanghai University, 75, 92; and his move toward socialism with Chen Duxiu, 108; on love affairs, 148; mentioned, 140
Shi Fuliang, xvii
Shi Jingyi: at KUTV, 146; and Chen Qiaonian, 150; and Liu Renjing, 150
Shi Qiong, 94
Shi Tang: biographical sketch, 283; mentioned, 248
Shi Wenbin, 203
Shi Yang, 123, 203
Shi Ying, 32
Shishi xinbao (New current affairs daily), 57, 222
Shiyue (October), established, 243
Si Lian, 29. *See also* Zheng Chaolin
Sino-French Association, 19
Sino-French Education Committee, 23
Socialist Youth League: and Peng Zexiang, 50; members of in Russia, 54; changes its name to Communist Youth League, 81–82; at the Fifth Congress, 118; mentioned, 46, 49
Song Fengchun: and the Unification Congress, 249–250. *See also* Ou Fang
Song Jingxiu: delegate to the Unification Congress, 249; mentioned, 248
Song Yunbin: head of the National Press Agency, 105; mentioned, 189
Stalin, Joseph V.: and *Problems of Leninism*, 95, 255, 265; and "socialism in one country," 187; on the trough in the revolution, 195–96; and theory of socialism in one country, 256; and *Foundations of Leninism*, 257; death of, 261; mentioned, 64, 79
Standing Committee of the Left Opposition, 244
Su Fushou, 223
Su Zhaozheng: biographical sketch, 284; mentioned, 114, 209
Sun Chuanfang: and the "autumn exercises," 96; mentioned, 204, 207
Sun Fo, 118
Sun Fuyuan, 118
Sun Society, 191, 194

Sun Yat-sen: and the Guomindang delegation to Moscow, 60; and the reorganization of the Guomindang, 64; tries to hold back the development of radical thought in the May Fourth Movement, 72; and the Jiangsu-Zhejiang war, 83; calls for the convention of a national assembly, 83; death of, 83; and *Sanminzhuyi* (Three people's principles), 95; mentioned, 27, 35
Sun Yat-sen University: and the Left Opposition, 242–43
Sun Yue, 83

Tan Pingshan: biographical sketch, 284; elected to Central Committee at the Fourth Congress, 80; and "national revolution," 110; and the controversy over the policy toward the Northern Expedition, 112; in Wuhan, 116; and Central Committee Meetings in Hankou, 117; and the Fifth Congress, 120–21; leaves Wuhan for Lushan, 131; together with Chen Duxiu criticized by the Comintern, 133; with the Communist armed forces, 133; dismissal of, 174; mentioned, 114, 236
Tan Yankai, 118
Tang Ruxian, 62
Tang Shengzhi: biographical sketch, 284; and his massacre of the communists, 59; question of his reliability as an ally, 120; and military situation in Hubei, 127; and the authority of the Wuhan government, 130–31; effect of class struggle on, 185; mentioned, 108, 114, 119, 210, 236
Tao Jingxuan, 206
Third International: Fourth Congress of 36; anomolous status of Chinese communists while in Russia, 54; Fifth Congress, 65; and the Guomindang, 232–33
Today faction. *See* Jinri
Tong Lizhang, 75
Trotsky, Leon D.: Zheng Chaolin's support for, xv; on human consciousness, 35–36; international stature compared to Stalin's and Kamenev's, 62–63; attacked at Fourth Congress, 79; and his opinion of Chen Duxiu, 109; on the Chinese Revolution, 187; Stalin's campaign against, 188; controversy over at the Sixth Congress, 197; and the Jiangsu Provincial Committee resolution, 200; on the Chinese Red Army, 218, 238; and *Zhongguo geming wenti* (On the problem of the Chinese Revolution), 228–29; views on the Chinese Revolution, 229–32; and his policies after the defeat of the Guangzhou Insurrection, 233; and "The Chinese Question After the Sixth Congress," 234; and his views on Chen Duxiu, 244; on uniting the Chinese Left Opposition, 245; on the Chinese Revolution, 253; and the *History of the Russian Revolution*, 254; mentioned, 179, 240, 257
Trotskyists: and arrest of in 1952, ix, xvii; arrest of in Moscow, xvi, 255, 258–59; viewed as "counterrevolutionaries," 260
Tu Qingqi, 244
Tu Yangzhi, 241

Unification Congress of the Left Opposition, 248–50, 253
University of the East, 37, 38, 44

Vaillant-Couturier, 34
Voitinsky, Grigori: and the Fourth Congress of the Chinese Communist Party, 78; on the betrayal of Cao and Wu, 83; on the ship from Shanghai to Hankou, 106; and "national revolution," 114
Voltaire, François-Marie A., 35

Wang Anshi, 71
Wang Bian, 151–52
Wang Duqing: biographical sketch, 284; and the Creation Society, 191, 193–94
Wang Fanxi: biographical sketch, 284; his description of Zheng Chaolin,

x–xi; mentioned, 270. *See also* Wang Wenyuan
Wang Gui: in Europe, 38, 43; mentioned, 45
Wang Guowei, 185
Wang Hebo: biographical sketch, 285; and the meetings at Moulmein Road, 71; elected to Central Committee at the Fourth Congress, 80; on the ship from Shanghai to Hankou, 106; his arrest, 145; death of, 214
Wang Jingdong, 214–15
Wang Jingwei: biographical sketch, 285; meets Zhou Enlai in Shanghai, 102; question of his reliability, 120; his address to the Fifth Congress, 122; and the authority of the Wuhan government, 130; and the 1927 Moscow directive, 131; effect of class struggle on, 185; mentioned, 236
Wang Juexin, 118
Wang Kai, 215. *See also* Wang Jingdong
Wang Kequan: imprisoned, 222; and the expulsion of the Left Opposition from the Communist Party, 241
Wang Linghan: short description, 41; after studying at the University of the East, 45; and the formation of the Communist youth organization, 27
Wang Maoting: and the letter from Wang Ruofei to Chen Duxiu, 197; arrested by Long Yun and shot, 198
Wang Ming: biographical sketch, 285; mentioned, 260. *See also* Chen Shaoyu
Wang Pingyi: and the Trotsky essays, 228; mentioned, 243
Wang Renda, 139
Wang Ruofei: biographical sketch, 285; in Europe, 20, 22, 26–27, 30–32, 43, 55, 57; short description, 40; in charge of Henan, 82; his friendship with Zheng Chaolin, 94; his visit to Qu Qiubai, 115–16; in Hankou, 117; and the Fifth Congress, 120, 123; and Li Peize, 152–53; his influence in the Jiangsu Provincial Committee, 175; and support for Chen Duxiu, 176; and Chen Duxiu's letters to the Central Committee, 178; on the prospects for revolution after the August 7 Conference, 178; on the execution of leaders of the Jiangsu Provincial Committee, 187–88; and the Sixth Congress, 188, 196–97; and attempt to form opposition group, 199; and the resolution of the Jiangsu Provincial Committee, 200; and Peng Shuzhi, 246; mentioned, xv, 17, 41, 39, 44, 81, 84, 98, 121, 123, 147, 150, 155, 209, 252
Wang Shaohua, 207: arrest of, 222. *See also* He Jinliang and He Songlin
Wang Shengzu, 223. *See also* Zheng Chaolin
Wang Songlu: and Lyon University, 23; mentioned, 16–17, 18, 20
Wang Wenyuan: leader of the October Society, 243; and Unification Congress, 249–50; mentioned, 247. *See also* Wang Fanxi
Wang Yifei: short description, 49; interpreter at Moscow, 52; at Shanghai University, 92; head of the Military Committee, 97; and concern about Luo Yinong and Peng Shuzhi, 147; and Zhang Liang, 153; arrest of, 207; death of, 211–12; mentioned, 44, 51, 92, 139, 151
Wang Yizhi, 140
Wang Zekai: in Europe, 19, 28, 30–31, 55, 61–62, 65–67; in charge of Anyuan, 82; in charge of the Organization Department, 173; and support for Chen Duxiu, 176; from Hunan, 183; and Wang Duqing, 194; and the Sixth Congress, 197; encourages Chen Duxiu, 198; gives support to Jiangsu Provincial Committee, 201 earns money from literary activity, 217; and the Trotsky essays, 228; expulsion from the Communist Party, 240–41; mentioned, 26, 41
Wang Zewei: and the formation of the Communist youth organization, 28; mentioned, 26

Wang Zhendong, 106
Wang Zhihuai: delegate to the Unification Congress, 249; mentioned, 248
Wang Ziqing, 37
Wei Moshen, 49
Womende hua (Our word), 229
Work-study students, 3–4, 19–20, 31–32
Wu Fang, 66
Wu Hao, 29, 30. *See also* Zhou Enlai
Wu Jiyan: biographical sketch, 285; joins the Left Opposition, 244; on the divisions within the Left Opposition, 244–45; member of the Standing Committee of the Left Opposition, 244; replaced as delegate to the Standing Committee, 246
Wu Kaixian, 224
Wu Ming: biographical sketch (as Chen Kunpei), 275; and the anti-Montargis group, 20–21; and Yang Zhihua, 141. *See also* Chen Kunpei
Wu Peifu: and massacre on Beijing-Hankou line, 43; overthrown, 83; mentioned, 127
Wu Qi, 106
Wu Ruoying, 193
Wu Suzhong, 222. *See also* Wu Yu
Wu Tong, 212, 219. *See also* He Zishen
Wu Yu: biographical sketch, 285; mentioned, 222
Wu Yuming: trained by Zhang Guotao, 82; imprisoned, 203
Wu Zhihui: biographical sketch, 285; and his influence upon Chen Jiongming, 3; in Europe, 13, 15, 23–24, 32; on Chen Yannian and Chen Qiaonian, 39; curses the Communist Party, 102; mentioned 209
Wuchanzhe (Proletarian): established, 244

Xi Zuoyao, 98, 206
Xia Douyin: biographical sketch, 286; mentioned, 127
Xia Xi, 211
Xia Zhixu: and Yan Changyi, 149–50; and Zhao Shiyan, 149–50; mentioned, 103
Xiang Delong: his activities in the Shanghai labor movement, 75; and the development of the Party's work among factory workers, 83; mentioned, 70, 118. *See also* Xiang Ying
Xiang Jingyu: biographical sketch, 286; and the house on Moulmein Road, 69; at South Minhouli, 76; in charge of women's work for the Shanghai District Committee, 91; at Fusheng Road, 93; representative of Hankou, 126–27; and Cai Hesen, 142–46; and Peng Shuzhi, 143–45; and Chen Bilan, 146; death of, 211; mentioned, 19, 21, 70, 85, 145, 149
Xiang Ying: biographical sketch, 286; at the Fifth Congress, 118; and Zhang Liang, 153; refuses to pass the Jiangsu Provincial Committee resolution, 200; develops opposition to Li Lisan, 200–201; on the Red Army, 238
Xiang Zhongfa: biographical sketch, 286; in Hubei, 123; new general secretary, 196–97; threatens Xiang Ying, 201; mentioned, 195, 238
Xiao Chunü, 209
Xiao Jingguang, 97
Xiao Pusheng: and the formation of the Communist youth organization, 27, 29; at Shanghai University, 92
Xiao Zizhang: in Moscow, 44, 55; mentioned, 30, 43, 101
Xie Chenchang, 209
Xie Danru, 207
Xie Wenjin: in charge of the Organization Department of the Shanghai District Committee, 91; death of, 208
Xiong Rui: and the formation of the Communist youth organization, 27; mentioned, 30
Xiong Shihui, 227
Xiong Weigeng: and the formation of the Communist youth organization, 27; in Belgium, 42
Xiong Xiong: in Europe, 38, 42–44;

Index 327

after studying at the University of the East, 45; becomes a full member of the Chinese Communist Party, 57; mentioned, 16, 30, 52, 60, 209
Xiong Zhinan: and the anti-Montargis group, 20–21
Xu Baihao: in Hubei, 123; imprisoned, 123, 203; death of, 188, 215
Xu Deheng, 39
Xu Kexiang: biographical sketch, 286; and rebellion in Changsha, 127, 131; mentioned, 236
Xu Qian: biographical sketch, 286; at the Fifth Congress of the Communist Party, 118; mentioned, 120
Xu Teli: biographical sketch, 286; and work-study students, 32
Xuan Zhonghua, 208
Xue Juezai, 172
Xue Nongshan, 241
Xue Shilun: in Europe, 26–27, 61–62, 65–67; marriage of, 139; secretary of the Communist Party, 76; recruited Zheng Chaolin to the Communist Party, 203; mentioned, 211
Xue Yue, General, 100

Yamakawa Hitoshi: biographical sketch, 286; and the formation of the Communist Party, 108
Yan Changyi: his friendship with Zheng Chaolin, 94; head of the Military Committee, 97; and Xia Zhixu, 149–50; death of, 212; and opposition to the expulsion of the Left Opposition members, 242; mentioned, 117
Yang Bao'an, 174
Yang Chunren, 191
Yang Fulan: at Fusheng Road, 93; and Zheng Chaolin, 154; and Huang Guozuo, 154–55
Yang Hu: head of the detective force, 207; and the arrest of Wang Kequan, 223; mentioned, 155, 209, 214
Yang Muzhi, 96, 107
Yang Pusheng, 106
Yang Xianjiang: at Fusheng Road, 93; and Shen Yanbing, 190; and the Left Opposition, 240–41; mentioned, 24

Yang Yin: injured at Fourth Congress, 80; and opposition to the expulsion of the Left Opposition members, 242; and the Fourth Congress of the Chinese Communist Party, 78;
Yang Zhihua: in charge of the Women's Department, 81; instructed to go from Shanghai to Hankou, 104; moves to Shanghai, 137; and Qu Qiubai, 140–41; and Shen Jianlong, 141; and affair between Peng Shuzhi and Xiang Jingyu, 144; mentioned, 135
Yang Zilie, 203
Yao Zhen, 226
Ye Chucang: and the *Republic Daily*, 74–75; mentioned, 140
Ye Dehui, 184–85
Ye Ju, 3
Ye Qing, 213. *See also* Yuan Dushi
Ye Ting, and attack on Xia Douyin, 127; and the authority of the Wuhan government, 130; army leaves Wuhan for Jiangxi, 131; and the Nanchang Insurrection, 237
Yin Chang, 30. *See also* Xiong Rui
Yin Kuan: biographical sketch, 287; in Europe, 18–20, 26–27, 33–34, 37, 41, 55, 61–62; and the Fourth Congress of the Chinese Communist Party, 78; in charge of Shandong, 82; transferred from Shandong, 91; and the reorganization of the Shanghai District Committee, 92; correspondence with Zheng Chaolin, 94; and his views on Chiang Kai-shek, 103; in Hankou, 117; sent to Guangdong after the Fifth Congress, 123; and Wang Bian, 150–52; joins the Left Opposition, 152; and the Trotsky essays, 228–29; on Chen Duxiu's article on the Red Army, 238; and the significance of permanent revolution, 239; visits Liu Renjing on his return from Alma-Ata, 239; and dissatisfaction with the Our Word Society, 243; member of the Standing Committee of the Left Opposition, 244; becomes a delegate to the Standing Committee, 246; and

lack of support within the Proletarian Society, 247; and the Unification Congress, 248; mentioned, xv, 17, 98, 120, 199, 229, 250, 261, 263, 264, 266–67,
Youth (Shaonian), 29–31
Yu Lüzhong: in Moscow, 61; and his return from Russia to China, 65
Yu Qiaqing: biographical sketch, 287; and the General Labor Union, 90
Yu Xiusong: biographical sketch, 287; and the May Thirtieth uprising, 86–87
Yu Xuezhong, 127
Yu Yin canji (Surviving poems of Yu Yin), 256
Yu Youren, principal of Shanghai University, 75, 92; mentioned, 128
Yu Yuzhi, 75
Yu Zhongdi, 211
Yuan Dashi, 22. *See also* Yuan Dushi
Yuan Dushi, 212
Yuan Qingyun: in Europe, 27, 37–38, 43, 45, 57, 64; short description, 40; in Berlin, 43; after studying at the University of the East, 45; and the portrait of Chen Duxiu, 71; death of, 206; mentioned, 39, 106
Yuan Shikai, 27, 72
Yuan Zizhen: and 1923 conference of the Communist Youth Party in Paris, 37; in Moscow, 61
Yue Fei, 43
Yun Daixian, secretary of the Propaganda Department in Hubei, 125; mentioned, 114
Yun Daiying: biographical sketch, 287; professor at Shanghai University, 75; visits Liu Renjing on his return from Alma-Ata, 239; mentioned, xi, 114, 125, 151

Zelian, 17, 77. *See also* Zheng Chaolin
Zeng Qi: and the Young China Association, 13, 15; on religion, 18; editor of *Xing shi* (Awakening lion), 76
Zeng Zhongming: and Lyon University, 24
Zhandou (Combat): established, 243

Zhang Baoquan: marriage of to Huang Wanqing, 172, 214; death of, 215
Zhang Bojian: in Europe, 28, 30, 36, 55; and the meeting with Lin Zuhan, 70; and his work in printing and distribution, 71; and his relationship with Zheng Chaolin, 71; at South Minhouli, 76; his pay as full-time worker of the Communist Party, 76; and the Fourth Congress of the Chinese Communist Party, 78; in charge of distribution of *Hot Blood Daily*, 89; mentioned, 43, 86, 111, 143
Zhang Danfu, 141
Zhang Fakui: and the authority of the Wuhan government, 130–31; army leaves Wuhan for Jiangxi, 131
Zhang Guotao: biographical sketch, 287; his arrest in Beijing, 65; his move to communism, 73; his opposition to joining the Guomindang, 74; and the Fourth Congress, 78, 80–81; in charge of the Workers and Peasants Department, 81; source of cadres before the return of the Moscow students, 82; and his work in the General Labor Union, 90; at Fusheng Road, 93; proposes that the Communist Party prepares for insurrection in Shanghai, 96; and the formation of the Communist Party, 108; clashes with Chen Duxiu over the Northern Expedition, 113; in Wuhan, 116; and Central Committee Meetings in Hankou, 117; and the Fifth Congress, 120–21; secretary of the Hubei Provincial Committee, 123–24; urges attack on Xia Douyin, 127; leaves Wuhan for Lushan, 131; with the Communist armed forces, 133; in charge of *Guide Weekly*, 134; and Liu Qingyang, 146; and opposition to Chen Duxiu, 176; and the Sixth Congress, 196; imprisoned, 203; mentioned, 144, 173, 209, 236, 245, 252
Zhang Ji, 226
Zhang Jingshing, 95

Zhang Jueyu, 66
Zhang Kaiyun, 64
Zhang Kundi, 82
Zhang Liang: and Liang Botai, 153; and Wang Yifei, 153; and Xiang Ying, 153
Zhang Qinqiu, 143
Zhang Shizhao: biographical sketch, 287; mentioned, 37
Zhang Shushi, 106
Zhang Songnian: and his expulsion at the 1923 conference of the Communist Youth Party in Paris, 37; and the Fourth Congress, 37, 78–79; and his soured relationship with Zhou Enlai, 43; and his qualities as a leader, 48; and his protest about Peng Shuzhi's editorship of *New Youth*, 77; expelled from the Party, 79; mentioned, 17, 22, 30, 55
Zhang Tailei: and Guomindang delegation to Moscow, 60–61; and the house on Moulmein Road, 69; and the *Republic Daily*, 74; at Shanghai University, 75; and the Fourth Congress of the Chinese Communist Party, 78, 79–80; secretary of the Communist League, 82; secretary of the Hubei Provincial Committee, 124, 126; in Wuchang, 125; on the Communist Party's policy in Hubei, 127–28; and Wang Yizhi, 139–40; death of, 213; mentioned, 116, 140, 173, 210, 237
Zhang Taiyan, 32
Zhang Xiwan, 214
Zhang Yingchun, 208
Zhang Yisen: biographical sketch, 288; imprisoned, 218–25; mentioned, 202
Zhang Zhen, 196
Zhang Ziping: and the Creation Society, 191, 193–94
Zhang Zongchang, 205, 207
Zhang Zuochen, 91
Zhang Zuolin: biographical sketch, 288; mentioned, 178, 209, 214
Zhao Ji: biographical sketch, 288; mentioned, 243
Zhao Shiyan: in Europe, 20–22, 27–31, 36–38, 43–44, 48, 55, 57, 67; after studying at the University of the East, 45; in charge of Party work in northern China, 82; and the reorganization of the Shanghai District Committee, 92; correspondence with Zheng Chaolin, 94; and his work on the internal organization of the District Committee, 97; at the siege of the Oriental Library, 99; and Xia Zhixu, 149–50; death of, 210; arrest of, 223; mentioned, xi, 32, 40, 41, 98, 104, 123, 129, 147, 176, 206, 213
Zhao Yuanren: biographical sketch, 288; mentioned, 199
Zheng Boqi: and the Creation Society, 191, 193; mentioned, 194, 227
Zheng Chaolin: biographical sketch, 288; this book, ix; other people's views of, xi; and his early years in the CCP, xv; and the Moscow faction, xv; and the writings of, xvii; and his arrest in 1952, xvii; and Trotskyism, xvii; in Europe, 4–5, 9–15, 22, 25–27, 34, 37, 55–59, 65–67; his contribution to *New Youth*, 64–65; his attitude to national revolution, 74; at South Minhouli, 76; and *Guide Weekly*, 77, 81, 91, 133–134; and the Fourth Congress, 78; work in the 1925 strike wave in Shanghai, 84; and the May Thirtieth uprising, 86–87; on the editorial board of *Hot Blood Daily*, 89–90; in charge of Propaganda for the Shanghai District Committee, 91; and work on the Party journal, 92; at Shanghai University, 92, 93; and his work for the Military Committee, 97; instructed to go from Shanghai to Hankou, 104; in Hubei, 123; and the Hankou general strike, 129; and the August 7 Conference, 132–33; and criticisms against Chen Duxiu, 133; moves to Shanghai, 137; on personal relationships and politics, 140, 149; and Jiang Guangchi, 153–55; and Yang Fulan, 154–55; and Liu Jingzhen, 155–56; editorial board of *Bolshevik*, 172; secretary of

Propaganda Department in Shanghai, 173; and his attitude to the divisions after the August 7 Conference, 176; on Cai Hesen's book, 177; on the defeat of the 1925–1927 revolution, 177–78; on the dictatorship of the proletariat, 178; on the characterization of the 1925–1927 Revolution, 179–181; on "national revolution," 181–82, 185–86; on the Northern Expedition, 183, 186–87; and the Creation Society, 188–95; experiences in Xiamen, 196; gives support to Jiangsu Provincial Committee, 201; on comrades who were imprisoned or killed, 203–12; on those who betrayed their comrades, 212–13; arrest of, 218–25; release from jail, 228; on Trotsky's theory of permanent revolution, 230–32; on the Red Army, 236–39; and his opposition to the view that the Chinese revolution had special characteristics, 239; visits Liu Renjing on his return from Alma-Ata, 239; expulsion from the Communist Party, 241; on the negotiations within the Left Opposition to form a single organization, 244, 248; and the Unification Congress, 248–249; on the Central Committee of the Left Opposition, 250; early years, 251–52; and *Ganbuzhuyi lun* (On cadreism), 265; and *Yinyu canji* (Surviving poems by Yu Yin), 265; on the arrest of the Trotskyists, 270. *See also* Ma Daofu

Zheng Futa, execution of, 188; death of, 215

Zheng Yuxiu, 24

Zheng Zhenduo, 70

Zhong Fuguang, 140

Zhongshan Gunboat Incident, 112

Zhou Enlai: biographical sketch, 288; in Europe, 27–31, 37–38, 41–43; and his soured relationship with Zhang Songnian, 43; and the Huangpu Military Academy, 73; and the Fourth Congress, 78; in charge of organizational affairs, 81; and his work for the Military Committee, 97; at the siege of the Oriental Library, 99; his attitude toward Chiang Kai-shek and Wang Jingwei, 102; informed of Chiang Kai-shek's conspiracy, 103; and the controversy over the policy toward the Northern Expedition, 112; and "national revolution," 110; and the 1927 Moscow directive, 131; and criticisms of Chen Duxiu, 133; member of the Standing Committee, 176; contains revolt of Jiangsu Provincial Committee, 201; on those who betrayed their comrades, 212–13; and the expulsion of the Left Opposition members, 242; mentioned, 149, 191, 216, 238, 261, 269

Zhou Fengqi, General, 103, 207

Zhou Fohai, 34, 108

Zhou Shuiping, 205

Zhou Taixuan, 13

Zhou Weizhen: chief of the Military Department, 125; arrest of, 210

Zhou Yaoqiu, 65

Zhou Yueran, 75, 92

Zhou Zuoren: biographical sketch, 288; and *New Youth*, 34

Zhu De: and the formation of the Red Army, 238; death of, 269; mentioned, 216

Zhu Jingwo: and the Creation Society, 191; death during the Southern Anhui Incident, 195

Zhu Jintang: and the Fourth Congress, 78, 80; from Hunan, 183

Zhu Peide, 127, 131

Zhu Xi, 5

Zhu Yiquan, 204

Zhu Youlun: and He Chang, 148; and Luo Yinong, 148; and, Shao Zhigang, 148

Zhuang Dongxiao, 106, 135

Zhuang Wengong: secretary of the Shanghai District Committee, 91; mentioned, 85, 120, 151. *See also* Han Baihua

Zinoviev, Grigori Y., 64, 79, 230, 257